Terry,

Our many coffees and lunches are woven in the fabric of these later chapters. I always appreciate your kind nudges!

Best
Karen

THE EUROPEAN COURT'S POLITICAL POWER

The European Court's Political Power

Selected Essays

KAREN J. ALTER
Northwestern University

OXFORD
UNIVERSITY PRESS

OXFORD
UNIVERSITY PRESS

Great Clarendon Street, Oxford OX2 6DP

Oxford University Press is a department of the University of Oxford.
It furthers the University's objective of excellence in research, scholarship,
and education by publishing worldwide in

Oxford New York

Auckland Cape Town Dar es Salaam Hong Kong Karachi
Kuala Lumpur Madrid Melbourne Mexico City Nairobi
New Delhi Shanghai Taipei Toronto

With offices in

Argentina Austria Brazil Chile Czech Republic France Greece
Guatemala Hungary Italy Japan Poland Portugal Singapore
South Korea Switzerland Thailand Turkey Ukraine Vietnam

Oxford is a registered trade mark of Oxford University Press
in the UK and in certain other countries

Published in the United States
by Oxford University Press Inc., New York

© Karen J. Alter, 2009

British Library Cataloguing in Publication Data

Data available

Library of Congress Cataloging in Publication Data

Alter, Karen J.
    The European Court's political power: selected essays / Karen J. Alter.
    p. cm.
    Includes bibliographical references and index.
    ISBN 978–0–19–955835–3
    1. Court of Justice of the European Communities   2. Judicial power—
European Union countries.   3. Political questions and judicial power—
European Union countries.   I. Title.
    KJE5461.A957 2009
    347.24'012—dc22   2009002657

Typeset by Newgen Imaging Systems (P) Ltd., Chennai, India
Printed in Great Britain
on acid-free paper by
the MPG Books Group

ISBN 978–0–19–955835–3

1 3 5 7 9 10 8 6 4 2

For my parents, Tony and Judy Alter
For gratitude for all you have given me.
I am who I am because of your encouragement and constant support.

Preface: Seventeen Years of Studying the ECJ

I started studying the European Court of Justice (ECJ) in 1992, inspired by two talks—one by Federico Mancini and the other by Joseph Weiler—who told parallel stories of how the European Court of Justice transformed the European Union's legal system. I was fascinated by the ECJ's agency—that the ECJ issued maverick legal rulings expanding its authority, and over time managed to invent for itself a political role that was far beyond what its founders anticipated. I was far from alone in finding the ECJ's success to be tantalizing. I, like others, expected that the ECJ provided a model that other international judges could follow.

I was one of the first political scientists to seriously study the ECJ. While my qualitative methods of comparative political analysis are fairly conventional for American political science, my approach was unusual for European law scholars. In Europe the study of law and legal institutions had been largely ceded to legal scholars, leaving legal scholarship in what Martin Shapiro suggested was a stone-age of 'constitutional law without politics' (see Chapter 2). I felt this legacy. I shall never forget the European Community official who spent twenty minutes haranguing on me in a plenary session of a hundred and fifty scholars and officials for 'seeing conflict everywhere'. 'Why' he asked 'can't it be that everyone agrees? Why can't it be that there is a legal solution that people all see as beneficial and correct?' There was also the German law professor who strongly objected to my suggestion that EU law scholars acted as a sort of lobby for the ECJ (I have finally written up the analysis: see Chapter 4). As the professor berated my characterization, he explained how German legal scholars merely help to educate the larger legal community about European law. His was a far more persuasive analysis of the Euro-law lobby than I had presented.

What kept me going when far more senior and experienced people told me I was wrong? I think it was ECJ judge Federico Mancini who said 'Good question! Why have national judges accepted our doctrines?' My spirit was also kept alive by Joseph Weiler who assured me that my question was real and hadn't been adequately answered by him or others. A German Constitutional Court judge also unwittingly helped. After a journalist for Der Spiegel had argued over lunch that the newly minted German *Maastricht* decision did not reverse German legal doctrine, the author of the ruling told me—'absolutely we are reversing the *Solange* approach and challenging the ECJ'. He made an analogy of a soccer game and insisted that the German Constitutional Court, not the ECJ, was the 'referee of the match'.

I was also helped by being part of a trend. Hjalte Rasmusson had been largely alone when he published his 1986 book identifying and criticizing the activism behind the ECJ's rulings. I was writing in the 1990s, at the same time as a number of others who were seeking to learn from the political elements of the ECJ's experience. I may have also been unwittingly helped by Geoffrey Garrett. In Europe, Garrett's analysis represented the face of American political science. While Europeans might have found my approach unsettling and problematic in some respects, my efforts to be faithful to both legal and political factors, and to the empirics on the ground, were surely a far lesser evil than what one might get from an American political scientist studying the ECJ!

Being a lesser evil did not stop Oxford University Press from first rejecting what became my 2001 book *Establishing the Supremacy of European Law: The Making of an International Rule of Law in Europe* (Oxford University Press, 2001). My book was the first volume of their new Oxford Studies on European Law. While the editors of the series intended to be interdisciplinary, they did not have the infrastructure in place to be interdisciplinary. The book was first reviewed by lawyers only who told me that my argument was not nuanced enough, relied on outdated understandings of the law (all of those old sources!), and it was not adequately referenced. I did not contest this rejection, but I pointed out that I had submitted the book to the politics division, and that the critiques were from the perspective of law. A lawyer's 'nuance' can appear to a political scientist as an undifferentiated laundry list of factors. Moreover, the whole point of the analysis was to embed legal developments in legal understandings of the time, to explain how they had been rendered outdated by the events I was chronicling. Much to my surprise, I got a response the next day where the editors agreed to submit the manuscript to a different set of reviewers. The book was then quickly accepted, but before publication it had to be first signed off on by a lawyer who could attest to its legal correctness. Between my nervousness of being rejected, and the lawyer's own predilections, the book ended up looking a lot like a law book—with a list of cases in the front, and far more citations than most political science analyses. It was as much comparative law as it was political science.

As I summarize in Chapter 2, at this point comparative political analysis of the ECJ is the mainstream approach. Publishing this second book with Oxford has been a pure delight. Either I am old enough or established enough to no longer be subjected to the types of dismissive critiques of my early career, or the field itself has fundamentally changed. My guess is that both factors are at play—indeed I sometimes miss the deep challenges to my work that forced me to step back and redouble my efforts.

This book is a personal retrospective of my work on the ECJ. I see my scholarship as having a few hallmarks. My work includes a deep contextualization of the ECJ's legal developments. I analyze legal issues from the perspective of the moment and the context in which it was being considered, and I repeatedly ask the counterfactual—what roads were not taken? What would have been the outcome if not for the ECJ's intervention? The historical institutional method of analysis was one of my contributions to the developing literature—though I am now joined by many others in this endeavor.

For years now I have thought I was largely done studying the ECJ. Instead, I find myself continually drawn to the ECJ as a theoretical touchstone. While there is no end of new challenges for the ECJ, I remain most fascinated by the ECJ's past. I continue to mine the ECJ's history for insights about the politics of European law, examining how context shifts both law and politics, and how law and politics shift the larger European context. Historical cases also allow one to tell a more complete story—protagonists are more willing to share their experience and we can figure out what became of the issue under investigation.

My larger theoretical interest has always been to understand the ECJ in light of larger international political trends. I know my insistence on seeing the ECJ as an international court has frustrated many—and I continue to seek their patience. The ECJ remains a fantastic laboratory to study international institutions. The literature on the ECJ and European integration is probably the most theoretically sophisticated scholarship on any international legal institution, and the ECJ itself presents a far from straightforward case to understand the interrelationship between law and politics, international and domestic forces. The more I study other international courts, the more I can see exactly *why* the ECJ is so exceptional. Both the introduction and conclusion discuss where I am in my thinking about the ECJ in comparison to other international courts, and in comparison to other theories and approaches to understanding the political influence of the ECJ and of ICs more generally. For this volume, I included a selection of my articles that focus primarily or significantly on the ECJ. I have included at the end of the book a list of previous publication outlets for this volume, as well as a list of articles I chose not to include.

I want to thank my many friends who have been part of my journey. I have been part of a great cohort of European integration and international law scholars whose friendship, encouragement, and support I cherish. Many lunches and coffees with Jonas Tallberg, Milada Vachudova, Judith Kelley, Lisa Conant, Rachel Cichowski, Alberta Sbragia, Larry Helfer, Damian Chalmers, Richard Steinberg, Oona Hathaway, Andy Moravcscik, Anne-Marie Slaughter, Michael Zürn, Greg Shaffer, and Kal Raustiala make conferences worth going to. The intrepid MIT alumni continue to stick together and make life in the academy especially enjoyable, including Sophie Meunier, Brian Burgoon, Clifford Bob, Wade Jacoby, Inger Weibust, Dan Lindley, and Jerry McDermott. My colleagues at Northwestern have challenged me in many good ways, especially Kathy Thelen, Jim Mahoney, Risa Brooks, Hendrik Spruyt, Michael Loriaux, Ian Hurd, Bonnie Honig, Will Reno, John Hagan, Terry Halliday, Jide Nzelibe, and Bruce Carruthers. A number of very busy senior scholars took the time to help me early on in my career, when my thoughts and writing were quite muddled. Special thanks go to Peter Katzenstein, my senior honors thesis advisor at Cornell, Suzanne Berger and Anne-Marie Slaughter. Your feedback along the way has left an indelible mark on my thinking. I have enjoyed working with Alex Flach at Oxford. Special thanks to Jonas Tallberg, Rachel Cicowski, Antoine Vauchez, and Kathy Thelen for their comments on the introduction and conclusion of this volume. My deepest thanks go to my partner in life—Brian Hanson. While he repeatedly questions why I have agreed to write another article on the ECJ, his questioning in substance and in life improves the choices I make. Since I dedicated my first book to Brian, I dedicate this second book to my parents—Judy and Tony Alter—who are always happy to be bored with detailed discussions of international courts. My father even tries to read the things I write—though I try not to send him too many. Thanks for your constant encouragement, love, and enthusiasm as I seek to balance work, life, family, and ever-reoccurring problems with my right knee.

Karen Alter
Evanston, Illinois
December 2008

Acknowledgments

Thanks to Alex Flach, Lucy Page, Chris Champion, and Caroline Quinnell for making this book look so lovely.

Chapters 1 and 13: European Legal Integration Across Time and Space
Thanks to Antoine Vauchez, Kathy Thelen, Rachel Cichowski, and Jonas Tallberg for comments on these chapters.

Chapter 3: The Theory and Reality of the European Coal and Steel Community
Thanks to Kim Scheppelle for her insights on the chapter. Thanks to John Gillingham and Andrew Moravcsik for their very helpful comments, and to Sophie Meunier and Kate McNamara for their overall guidance.

Chapter 4: Jurist Advocacy Movements in Europe: The Role of Euro-Law Associations in European Integration
Thanks to Morten Rasmussen for the opportunity to rethink this material in another light. Thanks to Irene Berkey, Elena Herrero-Beaumont for their research support for this article, and to Laurence Helfer, Mikael Rask Madsen, Antoine Vauchez, Maria Florencia Guerzovich, Bill Davies, Antonin Cohen, Sid Tarrow, and participants of the Historical Roots of European Legal Integration conference for comments on earlier drafts. Thanks also to John Hagan for the Bourdieu tutorial! I am grateful for the financial support provided by the Center for the Americas at Vanderbilt and the Northwestern Dispute Resolution Research Center, which funded field research in Quito, Lima, and Bogota.

Chapter 5: The European Court's Political Power: The Emergence of an Authoritative International Court in the European Union
Research for this article was supported by the German Academic Exchange Service (DAAD), the Chateaubriand Fellowship from the French Government, the MacArthur Foundation, and the European Community Studies Association. Additional research and writing support has been provided by the Program for the Study of Germany and Europe at the Center for European Studies, Harvard University. I would like to thank Suzanne Berger, Erik Bleich, Cliff Bob, Brian Hanson, Wade Jacoby, Sophie Meunier-Aitsahalia, Anne-Marie Slaughter, Beth Simon, and Andy Tauber for their helpful comments on this paper.

Chapter 6: Who are the 'Masters of the Treaty'?: European Governments and the European Court of Justice

Research for this article was funded by the Program for the Study of Germany and Europe at the Center for European Studies, Harvard University. I would like to thank the anonymous reviewers of this article, and Suzanne Berger, Brian Hanson, Ken Oye, Paul Pierson, Mark Pollack, and Anne-Marie Slaughter for their helpful comments on earlier drafts.

Chapter 7: Judicial Politics in the European Community: European Integration and the Pathbreaking *Cassis de Dijon* Decision

An earlier version of this article was presented at the European Community Studies Association (ECSA) conference, 27–29 May 1993, Washington, DC and at the Center for European Studies, Harvard University. We would like to thank Suzanne Berger, Anne-Marie Burley, Maria Green, Brian Hanson, Lisa Martin, Andrew Moravcsik, Kalypso Nicolaïdis, Martin Shapiro, and Alec Stone, as well as the participants of the Study Group on European Integration and Domestic Policy Making, for their comments on an earlier version of this article. We would also like to thank the many people who kindly shared with us their experience regarding *Cassis*, and especially the protagonists of the case, Dr Gert Meier, Dr Alfonso Mattera, Judge Pierre Pescatore, and Professor Dr Martin Seidel.

Chapter 8: Explaining Variation in the Use of European Litigation Strategies: European Community Law and British Gender Equality Policy

We would like to thank Jim Caporaso, Damian Chalmers, Shivashish Chatterjee, Lisa Conant, Brian Hanson, Collin Hay, Alberta Sbragia, Jo Shaw, Tim Snyder, the participants of the discussion on transformations of domestic politics through European integration at the Tenth International Conference of Europeanists, and our anonymous reviewers for their helpful comments on this article. We also thank Alice Leoard at the Equal Opportunities Commission for her help in this research. Research on the British case was funded through a grant from Radcliffe College.

Chapter 9: The European Union's Legal System and Domestic Policy: Spillover or Backlash?

I would like to thank Benjamin Cohen, Lisa Conant, Peter Gourevitch, Brian Hanson, Robert Keohane, David Lake, Harm Schepel, Anne-Marie Slaughter, Martin Shapiro, Steve Weatherhill, the anonymous reviewers, the editors of IO, and participants of the Domestic Politics and International Law project for their helpful comments on earlier versions of this paper. Special thanks to Jeannette Vargas, who helped develop the framework this paper uses, and to Smith College which provided funds and time to write this paper.

Chapter 10: Banana Splits: Nested and Overlapping Regimes in the Transatlantic Banana Trade Dispute

An earlier version of this paper was presented at the Conference of Europeanists, 11–13 March 2004, Chicago, and at the American Political Science Association Conference, 2–5 September 2004, Chicago. We wish to thank Christina Davis, Brian Hanson, Robert Keohane, Andrew Moravcsik, Kenneth Oye, Mark Pollack, Elliot Posner, Mark Rhinard, Alberta Sbragia, Gregory Shaffer, and Daniel Tarullo, as well as two anonymous reviewers, for comments. We also wish to thank Cyrus Friedheim of Chiquita, and Jean-Francois Brakeland, Aldo Longo and Alberto Volpato at the European Union Commission. We deeply appreciate their help in sorting through the politics of the banana dispute, and freely acknowledge that the interpretation of the motives of actors involved is our own.

Chapter 11: Agents or Trustees? International Courts in their Political Context

This paper has generated interest and comments from so many people, I am sure to forget some. I would like to thank Judy Goldstein, Brian Hanson, Laurence Helfer, Ian Hurd, Ian Johnstone, Mona Lyne, Jide Nzelibe, Helen Milner, Jon Pevehouse, Eric Posner, Paul Stephans, David Steinberg, Erik Voeten, and the participants in PIPEs at University of Chicago for comments on earlier versions of this paper. Special thanks to Robert Keohane who defended me against a highly critical onslaught, encouraging me to pursue the idea of courts as Trustees, to Jonas Tallberg, Darren Hawkins, Dan Nelson, David Lake, and Mike Tierney, who while enthusiasts of P-A theory engaged my work constructively in numerous reads, and to Richard Steinberg who worked with me to strengthen the argument. This paper has benefited tremendously from the sustained challenges from participants in the project on Delegation to International Institutions and the later sharp critiques at the 'Transformations of the State' Sonderforschungsberich 597 at the University of Bremen and the Northwestern University International Law Colloquium.

Chapter 12: Private Litigants and the New International Courts

The author would like to thank Rachel Cichowski, Larry Helfer, Sally Kenny, Jonas Tallberg, and Erik Voeten for their helpful comments on an earlier draft of this paper, Elena Herrero-Beaumont and Kate Fugina for their research help, and Northwestern University, Northwestern Law School and the Dispute Resolution Research Center for its financial support for the research.

Summary Contents

Table of Contents

List of Tables and Figures

List of Abbreviations

AB	Appellate Body (of the World Trade Organization)
ACP	African-Caribbean Pacific
AJE	Association Française des Juristes Européens
AMU	African Magreb Union
ASEAN	Association of South East Asian Nations
ATJ	Andean Tribunal of Justice
BCJ	Benelux Court
CACJ	Central American Court of Justice
CCJ	Carribbean Court of Justice
CFI	Court of First Instance
COMESA	Court of Justice for the Common Market of Eastern and Southern Africa
EAT	Employment Appeals Tribunal
EC	European Community (formerly the EEC; since 1993 the name for the common market pillar of the European Union)
ECCIS	Economic Court of the Commonwealth of Independent States
ECHR	European Court of Human Rights
ECJ	European Court of Justice
ECSC	European Coal and Steel Community
ECU	European Currency Unit (used before euro existed)
EEC	European Economic Community (name for the European Community from 1958–1993)
EFTAC	European Free Trade Area Court
EOC	Equal Opportunities Commission
EPA	Equal Pay Act
EPD	Equal Pay Directive
ETD	Equal Treatment Directive
EU	European Union
FIDE	Fédération Internationale de Droit Européen
GATT	General Agreement on Tariffs and Trade (precursor to the WTO)
HA	High Authority (pre-cursor of the European Commission)
IACHR	Inter-American Court of Human Rights
IC	International Courts
ICC	International Criminal Court
ICJ	International Court of Justice
ICTR	International Criminal Tribunal for Rwanda
ICTSL	International Criminal Tribunal for Sierre Leone
ICTY	International Criminal Tribunal for the Former Yugoslavia
IGC	Inter-Governmental Conference
ILO	International Labor Organization
ITLOS	International Tribunal for the Law of the Seas

MS	Member State
MRP	Mouvement Républicain Populaire
NAFTA	North American Free Trade Agreement
NATO	Northern Atlantic Treaty Organization
OAPEC	Organization of Arab Petroleum-Exporting Countries
OECD	Organization for Economic Co-operation and Development
OHADA	Organization for the Harmonization of Corporate Law in Africa Court
P–A	principal–agent (theory)
PICT	Project on International Courts and Tribunals
SDA	Sex Discrimination Act
TUC	Trade Union Council
UN	United Nations
US	United States
USTR	United States Trade Representative
WGE	Wissentschaftliche Gesellschaft für Europarecht
WHO	World Health Organization
WTO	World Trade Organization

Table of Legal Citations

ANDEAN LEGAL DECISIONS

BELGIAN COURT DECISIONS

ECJ DECISIONS

FRENCH COURT DECISIONS

GERMAN COURT DECISIONS

ICJ DECISIONS

ITALIAN COURT RULINGS

UNITED KINGDOM DECISIONS

UNITED STATES COURT DECISIONS

WTO DECISIONS

Previous Publication Venues

The Introduction, Conclusion and Chapter 4 appear for the first time in this volume. Chapters underwent light revisions for cross-referencing, to update some citations, and to minimize repetition. Chapter 11 adds a case on the ECJ that had been cut out of the original publication for space reasons.

Chapter 2: The European Court and Legal Integration: An Exceptional Story or Harbinger of the Future? In Keith Whittington, Daniel Keleman, and Greg Caldiera (eds), *Oxford Handbook of Law and Politics* (Oxford: Oxford University Press, 2008).

Chapter 3: The Theory and Reality of the European Coal and Steel Community. With David Steinberg. In S. Meunier and K. McNamara (eds), *Making History: European Integration and Institutional Change at the 50th Anniversary of the Treaty of Rome* (Oxford: University Press, 2007) 89–107.

Chapter 5: The European Court's Political Power: The Emergence of an Authoritative International Court in the European Union. (1996) 19 *West European Politics* 458–87.

Chapter 6: Who are the 'Masters of the Treaty'?: European Governments and the European Court of Justice. (1998) 52(1) *International Organization* 125–52.

Chapter 7: Judicial Politics in the European Community: European Integration and the Pathbreaking *Cassis de Dijon* Decision. With Sophie Meunier. (1994) 24(4) *Comparative Political Studies* 535–61.

Chapter 8: Explaining Variation in the Use of European Litigation Strategies: European Community Law and British Gender Equality Policy. With Jeannette Vargas. (2000) 33(4) *Comparative Political Studies* 316–46.

Chapter 9: The European Union's Legal System and Domestic Policy: Spillover or Backlash? (2000) 54(3) *International Organization* 489–518.

Chapter 10: Banana Splits: Nested and Overlapping Regimes in the Transatlantic Banana Trade Dispute. With Sophie Meunier. (2006) 13(3) *Journal of European Public Policy* 362–82.

Chapter 11: Agents or Trustees? International Courts in their Political Context. (2008) 14(1) *European Journal of International Relations* 33–63.

Chapter 12: Private Litigants and the New International Courts. (2006) 35(1) *Comparative Political Studies* 22–49.

PART I

STUDYING THE EUROPEAN
COURT OF JUSTICE

1

The European Court's Political Power Across Time and Space (2009)

My work on the European Court of Justice (ECJ) builds on two seminal studies that document how the ECJ helped transform the European legal system. In 1981, Eric Stein published an article called 'Lawyers, Judges and the Making of a Transnational Constitution' that documented how a number of key ECJ decisions established important constitutional legal doctrines to transform an international treaty into a constitution for Europe. Joseph Weiler expanded Stein's analysis in his 1991 classic *The Transformation of Europe,* showing how the ECJ's constitutional doctrines stretched existing legal practices and 'closed exit' by making it harder for member states to escape their legal obligations through their own creative interpretations or via non-compliance. Stein's and Weiler's accounts remain classics, providing politically sophisticated legal explications of how the ECJ used creative legal interpretations to establish for itself a broader role in European politics. Both accounts, however, assume that the ECJ has an intrinsic power by virtue of being the Supreme Court for the European Economic Community.

My scholarship begins where Stein and Weiler end. I accept entirely their legal analysis, providing only scant summaries of the legal transformations they have so eloquently explicated. I investigate the political and social context that shaped the ECJ's legal intepretations, and the process through which the ECJ's legal doctrines became politically transformative. Where Stein and Weiler assume that courts have an inherent authority, I seek to explain when and how international legal authority is constructed, how legal rulings get translated into political change, and thus how the ECJ became a political actor that was capable of transforming European and international politics.

This book brings together 15 years of articles and book chapters regarding the European Court of Justice's political role in European politics and in the world. As a collection, the articles span the history of the ECJ, from the 1950s up to the latest enlargement, allowing one to see how the ECJ's role has changed as the political context within Europe and the European Union has shifted. While each chapter is self-contained—with its own set of questions, cases, and theories under consideration—the common story told across analyses is that the ECJ gains influence by allying with societal actors to encourage greater respect for European rules. Societal actors do not always choose to draw the ECJ into their campaigns. Also, the ECJ's agency matters—the ECJ can choose to play a minimalist role, interpreting law narrowly and even illogically when there is little social support for the law it is asked to apply. This general narrative means that factors exogenous to the ECJ, activation by others and the presence of societal actors who share the ECJ's substantive objectives, are the largest factors shaping the role the ECJ plays.

The different chapters embed this narrative across issues and cases so that we can see what makes societal actors want to work with the ECJ, and vice versa. This introduction brings out the commonalities across analyses, identifying the factors shaping variation in the law and politics of the European Court of Justice. In some respects the analyses show that there is no set of unidirectional hypotheses that predicts when, why, and how the ECJ will be activist or influential. The ECJ is often assertive vis-à-vis national governments, but this has not been uniformly true in the history of the European Court. So we cannot say that the ECJ simply follows the desire of powerful state actors, but nor can we say it is immune to their interests and concerns. The ECJ is often politically influential, but it is also sometimes sidelined, rendered politically irrelevant despite the presence of actors who might gain from seizing the ECJ to support their cause. Thus we cannot assume that the ECJ will be brought into contested political issues just because there are gains from European integration to be reaped. The ECJ is quite often expansionist, filling in legal lacunae and interpreting ambiguous rules in ways that extend the reach and scope of EC law, and thus its own authority. But the ECJ also eschews opportunities to expand European law, closing off for political reasons legal avenues that may well have made legal sense and that may have increased the Court's own jurisdictional authority and influence. The essays seek insight from this variation.

Individually, the articles address a variety of questions—In what ways are courts affected by the interests of governments? When do litigants turn to legal strategies of policy change? What factors shape the influence of courts over policy outcomes? The articles also address questions specific to the European experience—Why would national courts take on a role enforcing European law supremacy when doing so can compromise national sovereignty and their own independence? Why did European governments not stop a legal transformation that they neither intended nor desired? I address these questions mostly through analyses of specific cases or issues, animating the analysis over time so as to see how law and politics interact to shape political outcomes. Thus in addition to asking different theoretical questions, the articles focus on a variety of specific substantive issues (equality policy, coal and steel policy, the policy of mutual recognition, the European Banana regime, women in combat-related roles) and the influence of the ECJ across national (especially German, French, and British) and supranational (Commission, Council, and World Trade Organization) institutions.

I am interested in the ECJ's experience in order to understand the possibilities for international courts (ICs) and international law more generally. The ECJ was from inception an unusual international court. The ECJ had a unique design: member states could not opt out of the ECJ's authority, and non-state actors (the High Authority/Commission and private actors) were authorized to initiate suits and even to seize the ECJ to challenge member state policy. European integration also arguably had broader aspirations, compared to the United Nations for example. The concept 'supra-national' was created to capture these usual qualities. But what were once unique attributes of the ECJ are no longer so. Chapter 2 shows that the ECJ's institutional design—its compulsory jurisdiction, commission enforcer, and the fact that private actors can initiate suits—are increasingly common features found in international courts. My comparisons of the ECJ to other ICs show that the ECJ is far from alone in being independent, bold, and influential, and that increasingly there are international treaties and international courts that have broad aspirations. But the comparisons also reveal that the ECJ remains exceptional. Other international courts have developed important legal doctrines, but none have been as legally audacious or politically successful in altering so completely the terrain in which they operate.

Where others see the ECJ's success as *sui generis,* for me these exceptional qualities simply call for explanation. I see the ECJ as representing the far end of the continuum of influence for an international court—the ECJ is about the most powerful and influential international court that is realistically possible. I tend to view limits to the ECJ's power and influence as 'normal'—general limitations that even the most powerful courts face. This does not mean that I expect all international courts to follow the ECJ's trajectory. Rather I believe that if we can understand the limits of the ECJ, we can adjust our expectations—we can figure out what limits are inherent to even the most independent and powerful courts (after all, every actor faces limits), and what limits are specific for a particular court or particular political system. If we can unlock why the ECJ is so successful, I believe we can then understand better the challenges that limit the influence and political power of other international courts.

This introduction emphasizes aspects of the articles that are revealing of the larger factors shaping European Community legal politics across time and space. I also explain how the ideas fit into my own developing understanding of the emergence of the ECJ as a political actor in Europe, drawing out the implications of the analysis for contending theories of legal integration and IC autonomy. The reader must look to the individual chapters to see the fuller story, and in so doing they will find additional arguments about the forces shaping European integration and driving law and politics. The end of each section's discussion pulls out what the chapters collectively posit. The conclusion of this volume speculates on why the ECJ is exceptional while identifying a number of historical and institutional questions that are left unaddressed by myself and others.

The introduction and volume are organized in terms of the historical period of time being investigated, not the period in which the articles were published. For the most part, the articles remain as they first appeared[1]—framed around larger theoretical debates that remain relevant today. I include in the chapter titles the year of original publication, and I have indicated in the texts where ideas and politics have developed beyond what I originally wrote. I have also added this introduction and conclusion to tie the chapters together. Part II of this introduction and book focus on the early history of the European Court of Justice—when the ECJ was both a typically ineffective international court in some ways, and exceptionally activist and influential court in other ways. It adds to well-known accounts a chapter on the ECJ in the context of the ECSC (from 1951–2002), and an analysis of the role of transnational jurist advocacy movements in promoting early European legal integration. By the end of Part II, we have the ECJ of today—a constitutional court for Europe in all but name, with the supremacy and direct effect of European law, and national courts as willing enforcers of ECJ jurisprudence. Part III focuses on factors that generate variation in the influence of this court on European politics and policy. Part IV puts the ECJ in a contemporary comparative perspective, identifying how the ECJ is similar and different compared to other international courts.

Those unfamiliar with the basic outlines of the legal and political transformation I am investigating may want to stop for a moment to consult Chapter 2. I wrote this essay for an encyclopedia on law and politics. It provides some helpful background, summarizing the ECJ's transformative rulings regarding the direct effect and supremacy of European law, and how scholarship on the ECJ has evolved. Chapter 2 ends by posing the question that animates most of the rest of the analyses—is the ECJ simply exceptional, or a harbinger of the future for international courts?

I. The European Court of Justice During the Founding Period of Legal Integration (1952–80)

The chapters in this section explain the institutional transformation of the European legal system from a weak and fairly ineffectual international court to the European Court of Justice of today. Collectively the chapters introduce a theoretically tantalizing juxtaposition. Through pretty much the entire 50-year history of the European Coal and Steel Community (ECSC), the ECJ was both timid and ineffectual at compelling compliance with ECSC rules, let alone in

[1] The Introduction, Conclusion, and Chapter 4 appear for the first time in this volume. Chapters underwent light revisions for cross-referencing, to update some citations, to minimize repetition, and to indicate changes that have occurred since the articles were first published. Chapter 11 adds a case on the ECJ that had been cut out of the original publication for space reasons.

facilitating political or policy change (Chapter 3). But at the same time that the ECJ of the ECSC was doing very little (1960s and 1970s), seemingly controlled into subservience by the interests of member states, the ECJ was bold and assertive in constitutionalizing the European Community Treaty to create a quasi-federal legal order. Chapter 4 investigates the social forces that allowed the ECJ to be so bold in the context of the early European Economic Community (EEC). Chapter 5 presents my early research on why national courts eventually went along with the ECJ's doctrinal transformation, even though it compromised both national sovereignty and their own independence and authority. Chapter 6 explains why national governments acceded to a transformation of the European legal system that they did not want, and that was arguably functionally unnecessary for their more narrow aspirations of the times. Thus together these four chapters explain how the ECJ's doctrinal innovations emerged, took hold, and eventually became political realities.

Chapter 3, *The Theory and Reality of the European Coal and Steel Community* (with David Steinberg, published in 2007) analyzes the 50-year history of Europe's Coal and Steel Community, which was established in 1951. In 1958 Ernst Haas had trumpeted the success of the ECSC, developing from the ECSC case a general theory of the dynamics animating European integration.[2] While Haas' neo-functionalist theory has been largely repudiated (Caporaso and Keeler 1995), neo-functionalism remains the dominate theoretical explanation for European legal integration (Burley and Mattli 1993; Stone Sweet 2004). The title of this chapter refers to our examination of how well the ECSC's full history coheres with Haas' early theoretical conclusions. We focus more on the economic and political arena, since not much was happening in the legal arena. Haas was right that the ECSC achieved many of its formal goals during its early history, including the elimination of tariffs and quotas. But in fact there were no tariffs or quotas protecting European coal and steel markets at the time, thus the achievement was purely formal and symbolic. We follow the ECSC's role up until 2002 finding that until the 1980s the ECSC as an institution had little influence over how the European coal and steel sectors developed and adapted to changes in the international political economy, in large part because its institutions were sidelined and its rules were never fully implemented. (In the 1980s the ECSC became the chosen forum used by states to shut down their big steel industries, a policy choice that was reluctantly forced on states by international market developments.)

A central question in European legal integration is how legal integration relates to political integration. A common view is that the ECJ is most expansionist in its interpretations when the political process is blocked (Weiler 1981). But in the context of the ECSC, the political process was blocked and the ECJ was not expansionist. The reality that the ECSC for so long had little political influence

---

[2] He went on to develop a general theory that applied beyond Europe (Haas 1964).

begs the question: Why was the ECSC of so little substantive import? Why were ECSC rules barely if at all enforced? What does the very limited role played by the ECJ in this history tell us about the dynamics shaping law and politics in the European Union?

For me the reason ECSC rules were ignored is that governments, firms, and workers had little interest in actually building a common market in coal and steel, thus the High Authority and the ECJ lacked social and political support. Neither the producers nor the consumers of steel products wanted to contribute to dismantling the true barriers to free trade—the cartels, subsidies, differential transportation rates, and manipulative market practices (e.g. deviating from published prices and delivering extra goods), which ensured that steel markets remained nationally segmented. Steel industries also preferred national help over ECSC help. As a result, Europe's coal and steel policy remained nationally defined until the mid 1980s. Knowing that ECSC rules lacked any real domestic political support, the ECJ refrained from aggressively interpreting and enforcing ECSC rules in cases that were brought.

A logical question to ask is if states did not want a common market, why did they create the ECSC in the first place? The chapter answers this question, but then argues that, even after the ECSC lost its initial purpose, it did not lack an economic or political basis to proceed. There were still benefits to be had, and actors who could have profited from creating a common market in coal and steel. But firms and governments understood labor unions' desires to create and hold high paid jobs in the coal and steel sectors. European governments and economic actors were also convinced by the conventional wisdom of the day that having a national steel industry was key for industrial development and national security. European governments repeatedly aided ailing national coal and steel industries in the 1950s, 1960s, and 1970s, holding for themselves the political benefits associated with strong government intervention in the economy. Meanwhile those actors who might have gained from a more integrated European coal and steel industry eschewed the potential advantages of using litigation to pursue their economic advantage.

What does this experience tell us about the political role of the ECJ? The ECSC had the most muscular and innovative international enforcement mechanism that existed at the time (Levi 1976: 70–71). Some ECSC cases did reach the ECJ in the 1950s and 1960s, but these cases either did not ask or failed to remedy states' general non-compliance with ECSC rules. A closer look at these cases suggests that private litigants were quite willing to challenge High Authority actions that they did not like; the ECJ responded by ensuring that the High Authority stuck close to its legal mandate. Yet ECJ judges must have surmised the lack of political or societal support for ECSC rules, and for building a common market in coal and steel more generally.

An interesting juxtaposition that *The Theory and Reality of the European Coal and Steel Community* does not explore is that the ECSC was floundering at the exact same moment in time when the EEC's legal system was taking off.[3] Stuart Scheingold published his analysis of the ECSC rule of law in 1965—after the ECJ's activist 1962 *Van Gend* and 1964 *Costa v. Enel* rulings. Scheingold found signs that the ECJ was working to build a rule of law, but it was a fairly limited and technical rule of law. While Scheingold found no evidence of the ECJ yielding to government pressure, he found a number of examples where the ECJ used technical rulings to avoid controversy. In these cases, Scheingold argued, the ECJ largely avoided making decisions of substance. Scheingold concluded from these examples that political tools to control the ECJ, including the short tenure of ECJ judges, appeared to be fairly effective in limiting ECJ activism (Scheingold 1965: 34). Chapters 4 and 5 in this volume also find that the ECJ in the 1960s avoided making decisions with a substantive impact, so as to avoid provoking a political response. But an important difference is that the ECJ was doctrinally bold in the context of the EEC, issuing rulings that clearly were not the intention of national governments. Why was the ECJ a typically timid and fairly ineffectual international court in the ECSC context while simultaneously an audacious international court in the EEC context? In neither context did member states seem to actually want to build a common market, at least not in the 1960s.

Chapter 4, *Jurist Advocacy Movements in Europe: The Role of Euro-Law Associations in European Integration (1953–1975)* offers an answer to this question. The recently written analysis returns to examine primary materials I collected during dissertation research, adding a newer theoretical lens of Bourdieusian social theory (Bourdieu and Wacquant 1992). In the 1990s I had found ample evidence that Euro-law associations had coordinated to create a hegemonic narrative about the constitutional authority of the ECJ. According to the ECJ, the Treaty of Rome itself suggested that European law must be supreme to national law (and even national constitutions), and it created a legal obligation for national courts to give effect to European rules. Euro-law scholars and European Court judges actively promoted the ECJ's constitutional narrative, explaining national court support for ECJ doctrine by stressing the 'compelling logic' behind the ECJ's decisions and the natural reverence political actors have for judges (Mancini 1989; Weiler 1991). My research, however, was revealing that the ideas underpinning this hegemonic legal narrative failed to deeply penetrate national legal systems. National judges in fact did not invoke the ECJ's reasoning, sometimes going out of their way to make it clear that they disagreed with key tenets of the ECJ's argumentation (see Chapter 5). Unable to find support for a simple constructivist narrative, wherein the ECJ's ideas helped construct legal understandings, I shelved my research on knowledge communities, removing discussion of their efforts from my 2001 book.

---

[3] Ironically, just as Haas' *Uniting of Europe* was published, France, Germany, and Italy blocked the High Authority's efforts to invoke its exceptional powers to deal with a crisis in the coal sector. From 1958–1965, European governments made a number of important decisions that basically ensured that an integrated coal and steel market under supranational authority would not emerge.

But I was too rash in that I did not stop to think about how the support of Euro-law associations influenced ECJ doctrine itself. Moreover, I did not consider that the force of Euro-law advocacy movements may not have come from their passionately defended ideas, but rather from the political positions members held within national legal systems. In the words of Pierre Bourdieu, what mattered was the capital—the cultural, social and symbolic power—of the members of the Euro-law associations. Inspired to understand the Andean Tribunal of Justice's very different experience, I returned in 2007 to re-examine my dissertation research on the role of Euro-law associations.

Jurist Advocacy Movements in Europe reconstructs the efforts of nationally based Euro-law associations to use legal means to promote a political agenda that was being thwarted by Charles de Gaulle and his supporters. The empirical contribution of this article is to document the extensive coordination behind what Stein, Weiler, Burley, Mattli, and others have suggested were individual entrepreneurial actions of lawyers, judges and scholars in the 1960s. This coordination becomes apparent when one adopts Bourdieu's method of examining the social backgrounds of actors combined with the internal politics within legal fields (Bourdieu 1987). Theoretically the article challenges the neo-functionalist narrative prevalent in the literature wherein legal actors—lawyers, judges, scholars, and litigants—are seen as atomized individuals pursuing their narrow self-interest, which through the power of some invisible hand translates into empowering supranational actors and promoting market integration. The comparison to the Andean experience serves to underscore how much the ECJ benefited from having an ideologically driven kitchen cabinet of support, and how helpful it was that association members included politically well placed individuals who could use their offices (as legal counsel, judges, scholars, and government officials) to aid the ECJ's constitutionalization project. The conclusion to this chapter links to Part III of this book by considering the larger implications of the reality that the ECJ was critically aided by an ideologically driven jurist advocacy movement.

This revisionist account of the orchestration behind the ECJ's constitutionalization process reinforces what the focus on the ECSC had also found—self-interested actors do not spontaneously arise to promote market integration. Activist litigants and judges need to be inspired by more than narrow self interest—they need to believe that their interest serves a larger social purpose. Without this shared sense, either litigants will not raise provocative cases and/or judges will not reward litigants with far-reaching rulings. The result will either be a very limited jurisprudence, one that is neither expansionist nor transformative, like the ECJ's jurisprudence in the context of the ECSC. Or, there may even be a negative feedback effect—the type of disintegration discussed in Chapter 9 (*The European Union's Legal System and Domestic Policy: Spillover or Backlash?*) where narrow rulings undermine litigant incentives, limiting the extent to which actors seek to use international courts to enforce international rules.

The last two chapters in this section are older outgrowths of my dissertation work. *The European Court's Political Power* (Chapter 5) was published in 1995, before I had even finished my dissertation. This article summarizes the main argument in my dissertation, which investigated the contestation between the ECJ's supremacy doctrine and the prevailing national legal doctrine of the day whereby the last law passed should be seen as supreme to legal rules adopted at an earlier period of time. The article makes clear that there were compelling reasons, argued strongly by national judges, to reject the ECJ's supremacy doctrine. I suggest that member states' highest national courts were most antagonistic to the ECJ's supremacy doctrine, because the supremacy doctrine was more threatening to their own institutional independence and authority. For lower courts, I argued, the ECJ offered a choice. By appealing to EC law and the ECJ, lower courts could circumvent doctrinal obstacles created by higher courts. They could also simply not consult the ECJ, which they were not legally required to do, and even challenge ECJ decisions sending a contrary interpretation up for appeal. High courts could also use EC law to circumvent national legal barriers. Or, they could avoid the ECJ and even challenge its authority. My book *Establishing the Supremacy of European Law* (Oxford University Press, 2001) is even clearer on how high courts could also embrace EC law for strategic reasons.

If I were to write this article today, I would do two things differently. First, I would work harder to embed European legal developments into larger national legal and political developments. My book is better on this account. My work was some of the first scholarship to deeply contextualize the national transformations. But my analysis is limited to dynamics at play within national legal systems. Other scholars have shown more fully the extent to which European level changes occurred in tandem with broader state institutional transformations, namely the emergence of constitutional and administrative review as fundamental elements of European democracies, and the emergence of a human rights discourse within European politics.[4]

A second improvement would have been to be clearer about what my claim actually was. A number of scholars have translated my scholarship into the rather

---

[4] For example, Peter Lindseth and Francesca Bignami have found synergies between the development of national administrative legal systems across a number of European states, and the creation of European Community administrative law (Bignami 2005; Lindseth 2002). Alec Stone Sweet has juxtaposed the story of European Community legal constitutionalization with the emergence of powerful constitutional courts within European member states (Stone Sweet 2000). Rachel Cichowski shows how interactions between the European Commission, the European Union legislative process, social movements, and the ECJ shape the substance of European policies—and thus that law and politics, national and supranational, work together in multiple venues and at multiple levels of governance to shape political outcomes (Cichowski 2007). Billy Davies has compared academic debates to newspaper coverage and inter-ministerial debates in Germany (Davies 2007). A key next step is to integrate these legal developments with political developments. Antonin Cohen shows how ECJ legal politics of the 1960s were a continuation of the political campaign to build a European Constitution (Cohen 2007). Mikael Rask Madsen's work connects the ECJ's legal history to politics surrounding the European Court of Human Rights (Cohen and Madsen 2007).

simplistic claim that competition between courts drives European legal integration. This simplistic claim has then been tested quantitatively by scholars who conclusively show that after controlling for other factors, there is little evidence that lower courts are pre-disposed to send more cases to the ECJ compared to higher courts (Carrubba and Murrah 2005; Nyikos 2000; Stone Sweet and Brunell 1998). This is an important finding, but such analyses miss what I was actually arguing. My claim is that competition between different levels and branches of national courts facilitated the penetration of *the ECJ's supremacy doctrine* into national legal orders. In other words, it is a claim about competitive dynamics as they contribute to doctrinal development and the penetration of supranational doctrine into national legal systems. My earlier work contributed to the misunderstanding in that in my youthful exuberance, I overemphasized my competition between courts argument.

I still believe that a competitive dynamic is a factor in promoting doctrinal change. This is itself a very Bourdieusian notion, though I had not read Bourdieu's work.[5] Competitive dynamics are most likely to be doctrinally significant when the legal issue touches on the issues of national or supranational legal competence. But most cases, and most legal questions, do not raise fundamental issues of state or court competence, nor do they contribute to doctrinal innovation. Moreover, competition between courts is at best only one of many factors that lead to the emergence of new legal doctrines, and probably not the largest factor at play. The various articles in Part III of this volume identify a number of factors that generate variation in the expansion and penetration of European law into national systems. These factors clearly dwarf in importance any competitive dynamic between courts. By borrowing the title of this early article for this book, I am hoping for a second chance to define more accurately what contributes to the European Court's political power.

The last chapter in this section, *Who are the 'Masters of the Treaty'?: European Governments and the European Court of Justice* (Chapter 6, published in 1998) addresses the question 'why weren't national governments responding to the ECJ's revolutionary transformation of the European legal system?' This is probably my most well-known article. I had a great foil. In 1993 Geoff Garrett and Barry Weingast drew on principal–agent theory to suggest that the ECJ was not actually an independent actor. Garrett (1995) insinuated that the ECJ made its revolutionary decisions at the behest of powerful member states. While full of problems, a lack of empirical support being just one of them, Garrett rightly challenged the suggestion that law is wholly autonomous from politics and reviews findings of studies investigating the link between power and preferences in ECJ decision-making. (Chapter 2 locates their argument in the sociology of knowledge regarding the European Court of Justice.)

---

[5] According to Bourdieu, each political equilibrium is likely to give rise to a set of actors who contest it. Any given outcome will hold only as long as the supporters of a certain outcome can keep the challengers at bay.

Who are the 'Masters of the Treaty'? takes apart piece by piece the logic under-pinning Garrett and Weingast's analysis, documenting the political dynamic that makes possible ECJ activism. In the 1960s and 1970s the ECJ was playing off the shorter time horizons of politicians, embedding its doctrinally significant rulings in politically insignificant cases, or asserting doctrine but then refrain-ing from applying it. Since there was no political affect to the decision, there was little for states to mobilize against. Meanwhile, the ECJ cultivated national allies. Once national courts had accepted a role enforcing European law supremacy, it became costly to the point of often impossible for member states to ignore ECJ decisions. Only then did the ECJ begin to reveal the full(er) political impact of its doctrines. At this point, institutional rules (the joint-decision trap) made it basically impossible for national governments to return to the status quo ante.

I thought this analysis would lay to rest any claim that the ECJ is only 'appearing' to be independent. But alas, Garrett's invocation of American Politics principal–agent theory gave the analysis legs. Pretty much every study of the ECJ has found that ECJ decision-making is not in any meaningful way shaped by the preferences of the most powerful member states (see Chapter 2). Geoff Garrett himself seemed to move away from his strong phrasing of the argument (Garrett, Kelemen, and Schulz 1998), while still seeing principal–agent theory as explaining the extent of ECJ autonomy compared to other European institutions (Tsebelis and Garrett 2001).

But empirical critiques of Garrett's claims have had little to no impact on scholars who are enthusiastic about principal–agent theory and who themselves know little about Europe. These scholars not only keep Garrett's claims alive, they suggest that Garrett provided proof of the point! These scholars adopt the same rational expectations assumptions, a tautological reasoning which was one of the flaws of Garrett and Weingast's 1993 analysis, where the mere fact that states do not sanction the ECJ is assumed to be proof that the state sought, or realized they actually desired, the outcome they got. This was exactly the claim I had tried to counter in *Who are the 'Masters of the Treaty'?* where I showed that powerful member states in fact did not want the ECJ's supremacy doctrine, did not need EC law supremacy in order to capture the functional benefits which Garrett and Weingast argue states want, but they could not reverse the doctrine. Since empirical refutations do not work, *Agents or Trustees? International Courts in their Political Context* (Chapter 11) returns to this debate to provide a more theoretically grounded reason to reject the assumptions underpinning principal–agent theory's rational expectations argument.

Findings developed in Part II

As a collection, the articles in Part II suggest much more contingency about the European experience than is often presumed. While located in Europe, in a sea of liberal states, the ECJ can also suffer from having a fragile legal authority. Indeed the ECJ, *like all courts*, must strive to stay in sync with larger societal interests—which is not to say that it must kowtow to the preferences of governments in power. Evidence for this point comes from juxtaposing the ECJ of the ECSC (Chapter 3) to the ECJ of the common market (Chapters 4, 5, and 6), and to the Andean Tribunal (Chapter 4).

Together the articles in Part II also suggest significant errors in neo-functionalist theory as it is applied to the legal realm. Most people associate neo-functionalist theory with Anne-Marie Burley (now Anne-Marie Slaughter) and Walter Mattli's analysis *Europe Before the Court* (1993), and with the work of Alec Stone Sweet (1999, 2004). Since my work is compatible with their accounts of legal integration, most scholars think that I too am providing a neo-functionalist account of legal integration. Indeed we agree on most elements of analysis.

I have always labeled my arguments as historical institutionalist accounts of legal integration. Why do I insist on asserting that my work is historical institutionalist rather than neo-functionalist? I do this because I think neo-functionalist theory is actually wrong. Neo-functionlist theory remains a package deal. One cannot use neo-functionalist theory without importing the problematic elements that led Haas to reject his own theory in 1975. Burley, Mattli, and Stone Sweet intentionally import these elements because they see them as applicable to the realm of law. By contrast, I think the problematic elements of neo-functionalist theory remain problematic for the legal realm. While it certainly makes sense to recover prescient elements of Haas work by co-opting his insights into other theories (Mattli 2005), I believe that neo-functionalist theory should remain where it is—discredited as a theory because it generates expectations that are not borne out in practice.

The crux of the issue is what animates the triangle of litigant, national judge, ECJ interaction, and what dynamic does this triangle create? We need to answer this question to understand the extent to which the European experience is unique (e.g. contingent on factors specific to Europe in the 1960s, 1970s, and 1980s), and which aspects of the European experience are likely to be replicated across time and space.

Neo-functionalist theory expects legal cases to spontaneously arise because some set of economic actors will gain from promoting international rules, and judges, lawyers, and legal scholars to embrace expansionist European law as a means of self- empowerment (Burley and Mattli 1993; Mattli 2005). The essays in Part II suggest that self-interest is neither a necessary nor sufficient motivator for litigants or judges. Self-interest was insufficient to launch market integration within the coal and steel sector. A deeper look into the role of jurist advocacy movements reveals that the core of Euro-law movements were ideologically driven, seeking to achieve through law what they had failed to achieve through politics—the creation of a European legal system capable of inducing respect for European law. Once the ECJ's doctrines existed, neither a simple empowerment narrative nor legal confusion can really explain why certain national judges rejected EC law supremacy in the 1960s while others embraced it.

Another key contribution of neo-functionalist theory is that it posits a directionality to the dynamic of subnational and supranational coordination of policy. In neo-functionalist theory, the dynamic of cooperation creates a 'one way ratchet,' leading to expansion of supranational authority, and policy changes that promote the *telos* of the treaty—economic and political integration. The theory also posits a mechanism that promotes a single direction of change—functional spillover occurs because the benefits of cooperation become recognized. When opposition arises, it is suppressed because decision-makers 'upgrade' their common interests, subordinating short-term objectives to the larger term benefits only international cooperation can achieve. It was precisely these elements of neo-functionalist theory that Haas and others ultimately rejected as false (Caporaso and Keeler 1995; Haas 1975), and that Burley and Mattli and Stone-Sweet embrace in their accounts of European legal integration.

Neo-functionalist theory was repudiated as a political theory because it was so obviously empirically wrong—European integration was not proceeding, spillover was not occurring, political loyalties were not shifting. In the legal realm, however, neo-functionalist theory is not obviously wrong because legal integration has proceeded, spillover has occurred, there has been a generally expansionist pattern to legal integration in Europe (though legal and political loyalties have not shifted). Law appears to be a better domain for neo-functionalist theory in large part because law tends to develop in path-dependent ways, and because the judiciary is more insulated from the sorts of political dynamics (e.g. elections) that contribute to governments redirecting their policies via reinterpretation (Hathaway 2001). Moreover, policy-directed litigation tends to be raised by sub-state actors, and be aimed at challenging government policy because governments do not need to bring legal suits to promote their goals. If the ECJ rewards litigants even a small percentage of the time, the outcome will seemingly support neo-functionalist theory. Indeed the only way to empirically repudiate neo-functionalist theory is to have the sort of political collapse that led Haas and others to reject the theory's political counterpart, an outcome that is highly unlikely to be brought about by courts using legal means.

But when we look at what is actually occurring, neo-functionalist theory often falters as an explanation. Actors who could raise suits promoting their self-interest often do not. Spillover often does not occur, which is to say that potential avenues of political expansion are not pursued. While long-term concerns sometimes win over short-term concerns, only politicians can determine which common interests they pursue through European integration, and ultimately their choices have a decisive impact on the extent of legal integration. And the political loyalties of those 'winning' from European integration do not seem to fundamentally shift in favor of European integration, rather we mostly observe marriages of convenience between sub- and supranational actors. In other words, the same realities that led the theory to be repudiated as a political theory are present in the legal realm as well (in Chapter 4 I develop this argument more concretely).

The alternative possibility is simple contestation where the outcome is both undetermined and contingent. Political agendas are pursued by powerful actors, which include state and non-state actors. The ECJ is sometimes brought into this contestation because it exists as a legal institution outside of everyday politics, and it has the mandate and the power to issue binding and authoritative interpretations of existing rules. Sometimes the ECJ changes the trajectory of politics by creating interpretations which political actors must either accept, unseat, or collectively circumvent. But outcomes are contingent because the ECJ may or may not be brought into contestation, it may or may not challenge the political status quo, and the distribution of political interests may or may not be such that governments can unseat or circumvent an ECJ interpretation. The analyses of Part III seek to unlock the dynamics that shape when, where, and how the ECJ will use legal interpretation to push the political arena in a different direction.

Although legal integration outcomes are likely to be empirically consistent with neo-functionalist narratives, I prefer historical institutionalism as a theoretical approach for a number of reasons. As I said, neo-functionalist theory brings with it theoretical baggage which is often unsupported by evidence. Historical institutionalism also offers a more open framework that deals better with contingency, and it captures important contextual elements and counter-forces that scholars who are looking only for the forces supporting integration will miss. By focusing on counter-forces and suprising puzzles, we may well reveal dynamics that ultimately shape long-term change, and thus that better account for important systemic transformations we have observed in Europe. The supranational constitutionalization of the European legal order is one important and far-reaching institutional transformation. But it is part of a set of important changes that include the emergence of constitutional and human rights politics in Europe and the post-war creation of an administrative state, all of which contributed to the relatively new emergence of judges as important political actors who are capable of altering political outcomes. Neo-functionalist theory is ill-suited to explain these broader shifts. Yet I believe that these broader shifts made possible the ECJ's political success, which is why it is so important to contextualize when and how European level changes are influenced by domestic level changes, and vice versa.

II. The ECJ and its Varied Influence on European Policy and Politics (1980–2005)

The chapters in Part III try to understand when and how the ECJ comes to politically influence particular outcomes. The ECJ needs more than a latent social support; to exert influence it needs to be activated by litigants and to have its legal pronouncements picked up by those actors who want its jurisprudence respected. What factors influence where and when interlocutors—litigants, judges, and the implementers of ECJ rulings—embrace ECJ interpretations and the power of the European legal system? What shapes when and where ECJ doctrine expands, when and where European law penetrates national legal orders, and when and where the ECJ comes to decisively influence national policy?

Part III examines cases from the 1980s up to the present to address these questions. Such questions inevitably require mid-level theorizing as opposed to paradigmatic discussions. Ultimately, however, the findings link up to larger theoretical debates. In examining the contours of ECJ influence, my larger theoretical interest is in understanding how making law enforceable changes law's influence in the political process. Thus I focus on how the ECJ casts a shadow over this larger process of making, interpreting, and enforcing European Union law. I tend to pick cases that are litigated because it is easier to see where courts are redirecting the trajectory of law's influence, but in doing so I am not suggesting that litigation is the only or even the main way in which law has an influence. My analyses spends more time on out-of-court politics than on what happens in court because I know that judicial decision-making is merely one way through which law comes to shape political outcomes.

My first publication as a scholar was *Judicial Politics in the European Community: European Integration and the Pathbreaking* Cassis de Dijon *Decision* (Chapter 7, with Sophie Meunier, published in 1994). Sophie and I challenge the conventional account whereby ECJ's *Cassis de Dijon* was seen as creating the European policy of mutual recognition. We also challenge the notion later argued by Geoff Garrett that the *Cassis* decision reflected the interests of dominant European states, namely Germany. Instead, we argue, the ruling became significant because it provoked a political response by the European Commission, which tried to create a general policy based on the ECJ's ruling. Member states (especially Germany!) did not like the policy advocated by the Commission, and thus they responded by legislating a more qualified policy of mutual recognition. Generalizing from the story, we argued that ECJ decisions affect policy by helping to mobilize interests in support or opposition of the law, and then by provoking political responses.

Our analysis of the *Cassis de Dijon* ruling introduces—though does not name—an idea I later develop. Legal rulings gain an influence via what I later call 'political follow-through'. The key notion is that legal victories do not per se create policy change. Rather, the coupling of a legal victory with a political strategy determines whether a legal ruling has a narrow impact (affecting primarily the case at hand) or a broad impact (creating a generally applied doctrine and/or creating significant changes in policy that apply beyond the case at hand). In the *Cassis* case, the Commission provided this follow-through. In other examples, social groups provide follow-through.

This importance of follow-through is developed more explicitly in *Explaining Variation in the Use of European Litigation Strategies: European Community Law and British Gender Equality Policy* (Chapter 8, with Jeannette Vargas, published in 2000). This chapter also thinks more generally about the factors that shape when and how the ECJ is brought into political contestation. Chapter 8 identifies four steps—thresholds of activation of the European legal system. Each threshold needs to be surmounted in order for a litigation strategy to be employed. For European level litigation to influence national policy: 1) there must be a point of European law to draw on; 2) litigants must seize on a litigation strategy as a means to promote their objective; 3) national courts and the ECJ must be willing to issue favorable rulings that support their objective; 4) there must be political follow-through—a post-ruling political mobilization that shows political actors (governments, firms) that there will be continued and mounting costs to maintaining an illegal policy. The first half of the chapter shows how these four thresholds were surmounted in the United Kingdom for the issue of gender equality. The second half draws on cross-national studies on variation in gender equality litigation to explain where and why these thresholds were and were not surmounted in other European member states.

We find a number of national barriers that limit potential litigants from employing a Euro-law litigation strategy. Every EEC member state surmounts the first threshold, since the EC's gender equality law applies in all member states. But national rules of standing and national procedural rules can make litigation strategies difficult to pursue, which could explain why there were so few French equality cases. The second threshold was also not automatic—even though actors might have benefited from litigating against a discriminatory practice, they often chose not to. Why didn't potential winners embrace European law litigation? We focus on how womens' groups are organized within member states. The United Kingdom and the Netherlands had single issue actors—Equal Opportunities Commissions—whose sole mandate was to promote gender equality. Denmark had unions whose membership included mostly women, thus the issue of gender equality was important for these unions. In other European countries, however, unions saw gender equality as sapping resources without delivering benefits for their larger constituency of workers. Meanwhile women's groups were focused on a broad range of issues that affected the life of women and their ability to work; promoting equal pay in the workplace was hardly their highest priority (and it was arguably the job of unions).

Competition between courts was a motivator for British courts to make a reference—equality activists sought out judges who wanted to circumvent appellate court interpretations. But it was more important that activists were committed to a legal strategy aimed at policy change, and that the activists were able to forum shop to find sympathetic judges. It also mattered that organizations were committed to the litigation strategy, since organizations more than individual litigants are likely to combine a legal victory with a political strategy to encourage policy change (the fourth threshold). Thus we find that individuals pursuing narrowly defined interests matter less than larger group conceptualizations in translating litigation into larger scale political change.

It is interesting to note, however, that governments also draw on legal outcomes to push through policy changes they desire. Chapter 11 discusses a later ECJ decision that applied the principle of equal treatment to require Germany to expand the types of roles women could play in its military. I am aware of no movement supporting Tanja Kriel in her efforts to find employment in the German military. The time, however, was clearly ripe for political change, something the German government and its military recognized when they seized on the ruling to push through constitutional and organizational changes in their volunteer military.

While not highlighted very much in the analysis, jurist advocacy movements were part of this story too. Elaine Vogel Polsky, a former European official, first published an article where she suggested that European law could be a tool to dismantle national policies that contributed to gender discrimination (Vogel-Polsky 1967). When no case raising the issue appeared, Vogel-Polsky went in search of a litigant. Her test case, *Defrenne v. Sabena,* established the direct effect of European gender equality provisions.[6] Vogel-Polsky then wrote articles suggesting that the *Defrenne* ruling could be generalized to other gender equality cases (Harlow and Rawlings 1992: 283; Vogel-Polsky 1985). The Commission took up where Vogel-Polsky left off, working to disseminate information about the ECJ's equality rulings. The Commission also sought to mobilize actors in other member states to follow the British strategy. It held conferences for equality actors to exchange information, published 'how to' guides on pursuing gender discrimination cases, and conducted the studies I drew on in our analysis. The tremendous energy the Commission put into the issue makes all the more interesting the finding of significant cross-national variation in the actual usage of litigation to promote gender equality. This finding again suggests that litigants often fail on their own to construct legal suits that might further their interests. The case also shows the importance of follow-through when governments are disinclined to change their policy. *Defrenne* was a Belgian case. But Defrenne had disassociated herself from the case, and Belgian unions were also uninterested in promoting gender equality. By all appearances, the *Defrenne* ruling had a limited political impact in Belgium.[7]

I created a more general version of this argument as part of a project that became a special edition on 'Legalization in World Politics', published in the journal *International Organization.* For the specific goals of the international legalization volume, *The European Union's Legal System and Domestic Policy: Spillover or Backlash?* (Chapter 9, written in 2000) summarizes how the ECJ was itself an actor generating greater precision in European legal rules, and making European legal rules more binding. The analysis suggests that a formal analysis of whether

---

[6] *Defrenne v. Sabena* [1976] ICR 547; *Defrenne v. Société Anonyme Belge de Navigation Aérienne Sabena* [1978] ECR 1365, ECJ.

[7] Many scholars have gone on to investigate the transnational dimensions of the ECJ's influence on gender equality policy. For a particularly strong analysis, see Cichowski (2007: ch. 3).

legal rules are precise and binding is insufficient for explaining variation in where international rules have political effects.

I then build on the analysis in Chapter 8 by canvassing the European law scholarship to identify a number of factors that create variation at each of the four-threshold steps that are integral to using European litigation to influence national policy. The result is a series of hypotheses that could account for both cross-national and cross-issue variation in the influence of European law on domestic policy, and a series of expectations for where European law is most likely to be transformative of domestic policy. These hypotheses, summarized in a long table in the chapter, can help explain variation in the reach and scope of ECJ influence over European domestic policies.

An additional contribution of this chapter is to consider reverberation effects across the four thresholds. Neo-functionalist theory focuses on the positive interactive effects, what I call virtuous cycles and what neo-functionalist theory calls spillover. In a virtuous feedback cycle litigants and judges learn from victories in one area, raising similar yet different legal suits to extend the reach of European law across countries and issue areas. But backlash driven vicious cycles are equally possible. Each threshold presents an opportunity to derail legal integration in a way that will discourage future litigation on a subject. Governments can learn from previous experiences to write the law so as to preclude litigation that could challenge cherished national policies. Litigants can learn that bringing a case expends resources for little gain, or worse yet, produces a legal outcome they do not want. National judges can learn that sending a case to the ECJ causes delays, creates more work, and saddles a judge with a ruling they do not like thus undermining their own autonomy and influence. And victorious plaintiffs can fail to follow through to ensure that a legal victory leads to a policy change, or learn that litigation strategies are an uncertain way to foment policy change. In other words, that a litigant must surmount four thresholds suggests that there are many opportunities to derail the process, and thus many veto moments . These moments do not create the opposite of spillover (e.g. disintegration), but they hinder spillover. Even where a virtuous cycle is established, the cycle can actually be reversed by legal and political contestation that shapes ECJ jurisprudence, so that European law does not become a one-way ratchet ever eroding state authority or ever promoting market liberalization.

The final chapter in Part III, *Banana Splits: Nested and Overlapping Regimes in the Transatlantic Banana Trade Dispute* (Chapter 10, with Sophie Meunier, published in 2006) investigates how European politics is influenced by the reality that the European Union is embedded in the World Trade Organization. The article asks why the banana dispute, where neither Europe or the United States had significant banana industries, and where the legal issues were not very contested, became so difficult to resolve. We explain how the contemporary banana regime was embedded in a number of institutions and how the EU's 1993 banana regime was crafted to provide pay-offs to a variety of interests. The main loser in this deal ended up being the American banana firm Chiquita Bananas.[8] While the challenges to the banana regime looked 'German'—Germany challenged the regime in front of the ECJ, and German firms continued to raise challenges in German courts—the cases were really inspired as much by Chiquita, acting through its German subsidiary *Atlanta*.

The German litigants were perceived as narrowly focused on their own concerns. They found support by some German courts, but not in the German Constitutional Court. I discuss the German banana cases more fully in my book *Establishing the Supremacy of European Law*. The European Union's banana policy, like the European Union's television policy, very likely violated German constitutional provisions (2001: 110–17). But in both cases the German Constitutional Court recognized that Germany is part of a union, and that the German government probably got the best arrangement it could achieve. The German Constitutional Court took the pragmatic position of refusing to be dragged into the controversy, developing a rather unbelievable legal argument that as long as European law *generally* does not violate the German constitution, the German Constitutional Court will leave it to the ECJ to review the compatibility of European law with German law in specific cases.[9] The ECJ adopted a similarly pragmatic response for the German argument that the banana regime was illegal because it violated WTO rules, to which Germany was equally bound. Not wanting to create legal limits on the EU that other WTO member states do not face, the ECJ found that it lacked the competence to even consider if European law conflicts with WTO rules.[10] In other words, the ECJ refused to expand its reach to include interpreting WTO rules. The comparison suggests that the more politically multi-layered the issue, and thus the more polycentric political authority is, the less able a court is to find a solution that will satisfy a broad constituency.

With both German and European Union high courts refusing to unseat the banana policy, the case became increasingly complicated. We explain the many litigation steps along the way—in Europe and at the WTO level. Europe adopted a number of strategies to avoid complying with GATT rules, showing a flexibility in using legal means to avoid political change. The EU's behavior is quite analogous to US practices, suggesting that there is no fundamental

---

[8] Chiquita had bet that the Single European Act would open up the European market to dollar bananas. It had invested heavily in an expanded European market, and was disappointed when Europe harmonized its banana policy around the French and Spanish system, which advantaged African-Pacific-Caribbean bananas.

[9] The argument that generally protecting basic rights is somehow sufficient for a constitutional court flies in the face of the whole enterprise of constitutional review. Indeed, this argument directly contradicts the German Constitutional Court's earlier *Solange* doctrine where the Constitutional Court put basic rights protection over any goal that might be furthered by European integration. The Constitutional Court has seemingly reversed this doctrine in a recent case where it found a European arrest warrant to be unconstitutional. See *Europäischer Haftbefehl* (2005) 113 BVerfGE 273, reprinted in (2005) 32 *Europäische Grundrechtezeitschrift (EuGRZ)* 387–408.

[10] *Re: Banana cases* ECJ Opinion 3/94 [1995] ECR I-4577 (Bourgeois 2000).

difference in how the EU and the US use international law and international legal mechanisms.

The article is noteworthy for employing a technique I use in many of the analyses in this volume—a sort of hallmark of my scholarship on the ECJ. Sophie and I employ counter-factual analysis where we imagine what politics would look like if one of the variables were removed. In this case, we imagine how the banana dispute might have unfolded if either the World Trade Organization or the Lomé Convention did not exist. This technique allows us to break theoretical ground by investigating the general question of how nesting and overlapping of international commitments is in itself shaping of politics. Sophie and I have gone on to hold two conferences on this larger topic, leading to a symposium that investigates the politics of international regime complexity in general (Alter and Meunier 2009 forthcoming). Thus this article continues the bridge to examining the EU in a comparative context.

Findings developed in Part III

Together the articles in this section help to explain variation in where we find social support for ECJ activism, and thus in the ECJ's political power. The analysis offers insight into the dynamics that generate variation in legally enforced compliance with international rules, and that limit functional spillover via legal integration. The expectations point in different directions, identifying factors that make it both more and less likely for litigation to be used as a means to induce changes in state behavior. Variation in each factor mentioned can also be a source for cross-national and cross-issue differences in the influence of international rules and international courts over specific issues and across countries, as I discuss in Chapter 9 and in a review article that extracts from a wide variety of literature potential hypotheses for how international courts may or may not contribute to increased compliance with international rules (Alter 2003).

Threshold 1: Enforceable law (a.k.a. preliminary and permissive conditions for the ECJ or any other international court (IC) to influence national policies and politics)

Compulsory jurisdiction and access for injured parties: When we start comparing the ECJ to other international legal systems, the fact that the European legal system has compulsory jurisdiction, Commission access for non-compliance suits, and private access becomes relevant. Without these design features, politically inconvenient cases would not reach the European Court. National courts can create a functional substitute, but as the banana dispute revealed, national judges tend not to want to create legal barriers that governments in other countries do not face.

Substantive law on the books: There has to be law that can be invoked by litigants (for private actor cases, the international law must create direct effects). For the IC to be brought into domestic political issues, international/European law must prima facie conflict with domestic practices.

Threshold 2: Interested litigants

Given the central role of litigants in bringing the ICs into policy debates, much of my work has focused on explaining litigant mobilization. Narrow self-interest (the possibility of profiting through litigation) is neither necessary nor sufficient for potential plaintiffs to emerge.

Political commitments to the larger objectives the rules represent: Legal victories can reveal the disjuncture between government's formal commitments and its actual practice (Risse, Ropp, and Sikkink 1999: 23–5). Litigants are more likely to mobilize around a litigation strategy where there is deep social commitment to objectives the rules promote, because judges are more likely to reward litigant efforts in such cases and because a legal ruling will be more embarrassing for the government. Where governments and public opinion appears uninterested in the larger objectives (e.g. building a common market, promoting European level human rights norms), litigants are more likely to be perceived as narrowly self-interested and judges are less likely to issue far-reaching decisions because they will lack broader social support for their rulings. Thus political support for the rules themselves, and the objectives the rules promote, increases the chance of litigant mobilization.

Group mobilization v. individual private actor mobilization Part 1: Because group actors conceive of individual cases as part of a bigger project, they are more likely to find cases with clean fact patterns and to frame their legal questions in broad generalizable terms.

The way collective actors (movements, interest groups, etc) are organized shapes whether litigation is an attractive strategy: Individuals, groups, and judges would much prefer that governments on their own choose to comply with the law. Litigation is thus often a tool of the weak, used because actors cannot use the political system to address their concerns. More narrowly focused groups and more politically marginalized actors are more likely to turn to litigation strategies. Thus national variations in how group mandates are defined (broad versus narrow mandates), who is part of a group (broad versus narrow constituencies), and the type of access the group has to policy-makers will shape whether litigation is embraced as a tool of political influence. (Chapter 9 offers more specific hypotheses.)

Threshold 3: Judicial Support (national and/or international)

It is not true that judges will seize every chance to self-empower, or that judges shared affinity to enforce 'the law' will lead national actors to embrace a role enforcing international rules.

Judicial intervention in polycentric contexts (i.e. where there are many centers of authority and control): Judges are more likely to be legally assertive when there is a clear hierarchy of authority. The more political authority is diffused across institutions (domestic and international), the more risky and thus unlikely it becomes that high court judges (including international court judges) will try to impose a legal solution by siding with the plaintiff based on far-reaching legal reasoning. International institutional complexity can thus limit the political role ICs come to play.

Judicial intervention in contexts of sub-state preference divergence: Judges are most likely to contribute to significant political change where governments are internally divided (which can block the political level) but where there is significant social support for law on the books. Judges are particularly well-suited to aid in norm cascades where there is a disjuncture between political outcomes and public sentiment, and where there are actors within the state who prefer the path the court advocates.[11]

Issues involving the independence of courts and the rule of law: The more the issue touches on the independence and authority of national judges, the more likely the judge is to be legally bold even if doing so is politically controversial.

Threshold 4: Political follow-through

Legal pronouncements are rarely the end of the story. Where national courts will enforce legal rulings, and where government actors want to comply with legal rulings, we can expect fairly automatic compliance with legal rulings. Broader policy shifts are usually a result of post-ruling politics where the costs of maintaining contradictory policies are revealed.

Group mobilization v. individual private actor mobilization Part 2: Individual litigants are likely to be satisfied with a legal remedy that applies just to them. Cases where group actors are mobilized are more likely to have an amplified political impact because group members encourage each other to be bold and activist, and because groups are better able to follow legal victories with political strategies—advertising legal victories, finding copycat cases, and showing governments the cost of maintaining illegal policies. Sometimes groups seize on to cases that were raised by unaffiliated private actors. Also, because groups often lack standing, and because legal narratives play better when there is an actual person involved, often members of groups shed their affiliation for the purpose of raising a legal case. But unless a group actor (an institution, powerful state, or an NGO) mobilizes behind a legal ruling, the ruling is unlikely to have broad political impact.

What do these conclusions mean in terms of the political power of ICs? Courts are tipping point political actors. Where there are powerful actors on both sides of an

---

[11] On norm cascades see Sunstein (1996).

issue, but governments have for whatever reason privileged an arguably less law-compliant outcome, courts can be invoked to tip the balance in the opposite direction. Courts are willing to aid groups in achieving their agenda when the law in question is extremely clear, and when their legal authority is clear. Judges generally will not substitute their own interpretations for politically constructed outcomes, however, where the political terrain is a minefield sown with intensely held deeply divided political beliefs, and where their own bases of legitimacy are weak.

III. Beyond European Court Politics—The ECJ in a Comparative Perspective

These arguments developed in Part III do not, however, tell us why in Europe a number of factors came together to enhance the role of European Courts in European politics. My recent scholarship puts the ECJ in a comparative perspective to understand what is general and what is unique to the ECJ's experience. Since the conclusion to this volume focuses more on this question, my discussion of the chapters here focuses on how the chapters contribute to the larger explanation of how ICs influence international politics.

Agents or Trustees? International Courts in their Political Context (Chapter 11, published in 2008) suggests that ICs other than the ECJ can have an important political role, helping to alter the political terrain and shape political outcomes. In comparing the ECJ to other ICs, the chapter shows how the ECJ is not exceptional—it is not the only international court that can act independently of the desires of powerful states, or be a tipping point actor, and thereby influence politics.[12]

As mentioned, I wrote this article to build on Chapter 6 by providing a theoretical as opposed to empirical challenge to principal–agent (P–A) approaches. P–A theory urges scholars to focus on how states are able to influence IC decision-making. This is an important question. But I don't think P–A theory offers a useful way forward. My main frustration is how supporters of P–A theory tend to assert that we should assume ICs reflect the interests of powerful states until proven otherwise. I find this demand to be both absurd and a huge time waster, especially given how little evidence P–A scholars have themselves mustered to support their arguments. I wish there was more scholarship examining how appointment politics shape IC decision-making[13] and believe that it only makes sense to include in any study of judicial decision-making an investigation of what national governments want. But I don't think that P–A theory itself offers

---

[12] The published version of this article included an example from the ICJ and WTO; I had to edit out the ECJ example because of word limits. For this volume, I have added back an ECJ case study that examines the ECJ's role in shifting German policy with respect to women serving in combat-related roles in the military, a policy area that remains under national sovereign control.

[13] Eric Voeten has some excellent work on this topic. See Voeten (2007).

a way to ascertain what governments may want, or that it offers a useful starting point to understand how governments influence judicial decision-making,
because nearly all of the so-called tools for principal control are either intentionally made or de facto rendered too blunt to shape IC behavior (Alter 2006).

   In *Agents or Trustees? International Courts in their Political Context*, I develop a
theoretical argument to counter the 'rational expectations' claim underpinning
P–A theory. Essentially, I provide a reason to assume that ICs are acting independently of the preferences of state principles. The analysis fundamentally desta-
bilizes P–A theory by introducing the concept of a beneficiary. States delegate
decision-making to Trustees to enhance their credibility in the eyes of a set of
powerful actors in civil society and/or in the economy (the so-called 'beneficiary').
The reason governments delegate authority is that politicians are presumed to be
overly expedient actors, more concerned with helping their friends and promoting their own short-term gains than making well reasoned decisions based on the
larger and more long-term interests of the beneficiary. This different motive to
delegate reflects the political reality that for some issues, disinterested Trustees
are seen as *better* decision-makers than politicians. For delegation to Trustees to
be credible, the principal must select as an agent an actor with expert and moral
authority, and design the delegation contract so as to convince the beneficiary
that the Trustee will have the power to make independent decisions. The different motives shaping the decision to delegate explains why the principal is not the
Trustee's main audience. Rather, both governments and the Trustee are interested in convincing the 'beneficiary' that their decision represents the public's
best interest. Governments remain powerful actors, because they have their own
moral authority and political power. The way governments influence Trustees,
however, is through their attempts to convince the Trustee of the virtue of their
perspective. When governments are disappointed in their efforts, the next step
is to try to convince the 'beneficiary' that the government represents the public
interest better than the Trustee. I then explain how ICs are trustee actors who
attempt to influence outcomes by allying with those social actors within states
that favor policies that are more consistent with legal rules.

   This article is most helpful as a theoretical explanation of why the ontology of
principal–agent theory is not very useful in thinking about how states and international organizations interrelate. I believe the analysis provides a reason to reject
the rational expectations argument, and thus a reason to presume that ICs are
independent and capable of influencing governments and politics more generally.
Also, in de-emphasizing the importance of sanctioning tools, the analysis provides a theoretical bridge to studies that emphasize the importance of rhetorical
and legitimacy politics.

   But this analysis ultimately raises as many questions as it answers. To be a
Trustee is to have some legitimate authority. Trustees gain this authority by being
seen as better protectors than the principal in the eyes of the 'beneficiary,' but
I say nothing about how these actors are constituted—only that constituted

Trustees are different from constituted agents. I also present Trustees as a mono-lithic category into which I locate international courts. Clearly not all ICs have legitimate authority, thus I leave unaddressed the question of how an IC becomes a legitimated Trustee. In this context, the articles in Part I return in importance, since they do explain how the ECJ became an unusually powerful politically legitimated Trustee–actor.

Also, to argue against P–A theory, I needed to select on the dependent variable—to focus on cases where ICs made rulings that states had not intended and where ICs disappointed powerful actors. In selecting on the dependent vari-able, I lose any ability to investigate variation in the level of IC influence. In this context, the articles in Part II of this book return in importance since they do help explain variation in the influence of Trustee courts.

Up until now, I have been suggesting that the ECJ is part of a general story. But the ECJ is also clearly an outlier. It is far more active, and far more influen-tial than any other IC—with the possible exception of the European Court of Human Rights. Chapter 12, *Private Litigants and the New International Courts* (published in 2006) makes the European Court's outlier status abundantly clear. Chapter 12 draws on data I have been working with regarding international courts more generally,[14] focusing in on a puzzling aspect of delegation to inter-national courts. Most analysts expect that allowing private actors to raise cases directly will make an IC more active and independent. If states remain concerned about losing sovereignty, how can we explain a trend in creating international courts with private access provisions?

For this volume, three elements of this analysis are worth underscoring. First, I draw a bright line between what I call 'old style' international courts like the International Court of Justice—which are intended as interstate dispute resolu-tion bodies—and what I call 'new style' courts which are intended to play roles beyond interstate dispute resolution. With this bright line, we can see that old style courts are unlikely to follow the ECJ trajectory, but that most ICs these days are 'new style' ICs. Second, focusing on IC design will not explain varia-tion in the influence and role of an IC in international politics. I will return to this idea in the conclusion of this volume. Third, the empirical analysis reveals that the ECJ and the ECHR are outliers. I examine usage of ICs where litigants are empowered to raise complaints. There are eight international courts where private actors can initiate disputes (if you count the ECJ and Tribunal of First Instance separately, as I do in this article). Ninety-six per cent of all the private access initiated cases were raised in the European context. In other words, you can build ECJ clones in other contexts. But that does not mean that litigants will use these courts to influence policy.

---

[14] I have not worked out the categories fully. For example, in this analysis I coded enforcement roles as also allowing private access, but I will not continue to code enforcement courts as allowing private access if individuals are only present as defendants.

This finding begs the question: Why is it mainly in Europe that litigants have turned to supranational courts? To answer this question, it is useful to return to Chapter 4, *Jurist Advocacy Movements in Europe,* which concludes by investigating the implications of a finding that the ECJ was critically aided in its endeavor by the support of a politically well-placed jurist advocacy movement. The conclusion suggests that international law and international courts are most likely to be transformative political actors when law enforcement can be linked to a larger ideological agenda, and thus when the issue in question is more than simply enhancing compliance with international rules. I suggest that international courts can only succeed if they can connect with politically powerful actors, either by supporting the efforts of powerful governments or by connecting with social movements and actors within states to promote a common objective. Such a conjecture would need to be fleshed out, but it may explain the variation that *Private Litigants and the New International Courts* documents.

The next step is to develop the argument that different judicial roles (administrative review, constitutional review, dispute adjudication, and enforcement) generate fundamentally different politics, which will build on by qualifying the argument that ICs are Trustees. I begin in this direction in an article that has just been published where I focus on how certain IC roles self-bind states, whereas other judicial roles are primarily other-binding and thus not sovereignty compromising for states (Alter 2008). The implication of the analysis is that new insights will be revealed when we study the ECJ as three separate courts—as an administrative court, and an enforcement court, and a constitutional court. The ECJ may act as a Trustee in each role, but how it plays its Trustee role, and how it shapes politics, likely varies by role.

Findings Developed in Part IV

The ECJ is clearly not unique, but it is unusual. At this point, I can say that my work on the ECJ presents a few ideas that surely travel:

- *The four thresholds discussed earlier suggest the variety of ways in which ICs can be kept from being influential political actors.* The existence of an IC can on its own extend the shadow of the law into political decision-making, but usually ICs need to be activated by litigants to have any direct influence. At each of the four thresholds ICs can be thwarted from playing a significant political role, thus by limiting the binding nature and justiciability of international rules, by dissuading actors from using legal tools to enforce international rules, by influencing judges not to demand compliance with international rules, and by not following up a legal victory with a political strategy that makes non-compliance costly, the political influence of ICs can be minimized.
- *Even the most powerful ICs will only be activist where there is some basis of social support for the rules themselves.* It is worth repeating that social support is different

than government or state support. Most international law aims to influence governmental (e.g. public) decision-making. Where international rules have broad sub-state support, ICs are more likely to be assertive in demanding that governments respect international rules. This is why IC politics are more likely to be transnational politics. International-relations style realism (including P–A theory), offers hypotheses to investigate alongside other explanations, but because it focuses exclusively on the preferences of governments, it is not a useful starting point of analysis.

- *Compulsory jurisdiction (more than private access) makes ICs independent. IC independence is not, however, the same thing as IC effectiveness.* Chapter 11 investigates cases where the defendant government clearly disagrees with the Court's ruling. These cases would have been blocked if the court lacked compulsory jurisdiction. Of the three cases examined, only the ECJ allows private actors to initiate disputes. This suggests that private access may not be the key attribute making ICs independent from state interests. Independence is not the same thing as effectiveness, however. It may still be true that private access makes ICs more effective, though this is far from proven.

These are modest take-away findings to be sure. Real progress will occur when we can better explain *why* the ECJ was such an exceptional court. The conclusion of Chapter 4 starts to develop such an argument as it investigates how jurist advocacy movements differ from trans-governmental networks and from uncoordinated atomized entrepreneurs. The conclusion to this volume goes a bit further.

IV. Conclusion—Where We Stand in Understanding the ECJ's Political Power

This introduction sought to reveal the connections I see in my various analyses of the politics of the ECJ, and how they build to be a more general framework for understanding the politics of international courts across time and space. But others will surely take different insights away from the different chapters.

I have focused here, and in most of my work, on considering the ECJ as a laboratory in which one can find potential answers about how international law influences domestic and international politics. This focus leaves many important questions about the ECJ in particular uninvestigated. I have looked more at the ECJ's influence on politics and political outcomes than on how the ECJ operates as a political institution. I have left entirely unexplored one of the most interesting chapters of the ECJ's experience—how enlargement is changing the ECJ, including how it changes the political role the ECJ plays. The conclusion also does not delve into these questions, but it does suggest that the way to explore them is not simply to repeat how we have studied European legal integration in the past. Rather we should take some issues as settled. For me, these issues include the following:

(1) *Legal interpretation usually has a political element to it.* It is thus usually point-less to assume that there is some unambiguous unique legal solution that appears to judges and lawyers. Instead, one should investigate the factors shaping legal interpretations, considering the interpretive avenues argued yet not chosen, so as to better understand how legal interpretations represent contested outcomes.

(2) *Courts do not transform politics simply by issuing legal edicts.* Courts are tipping point actors, akin in some ways to Max Weber's switchmen who mediate pol-itics and who through their rulings can alter the dynamics of political con-testation. Courts are intriguing tipping point actors because they sit outside of regular politics, largely immune to the types of electoral dynamics that shape the behavior of politicians, and available to sub-state actors who are unable to obtain their objectives via regular political channels.

(3) *Neo-functionalist theory is probably not the best theoretical framework for under-standing legal integration*—the theory overpredicts the extent that actors will turn to international processes to promote their objectives, it overpredicts functional spillover, and it leaves uninvestigated the counter-forces which can redirect legal integration. Instead one should investigate how the key actors in legal integration (those who make the rules, the state and non-state actors affected by the rules, judges, and litigants) shape the legal process, and how critical opportunities and moments arise to reopen set understandings so as to redirect and reinterpret existing rules on the books. One should also investigate the larger structures that shape legal contestation, identifying the ways in which these structures change and evolve so as to influence legal outcomes.

(4) *Principal–agent theory is not a useful meta framework for thinking about how governmental actors influence judicial decision-making (or Trustees in general).* The theory is too myopic in considering only governments (principals) and agents/Trustees as if no other actors or concerns mattered. The theory's focus on recontracting tools fails to capture more important resources govern-ments have at their disposal. We should reject P–A theory's rational expecta-tions assumption, instead assuming that courts can be both powerful and autonomous political actors. We should also recognize that Trustee actors can create constraints on states that are politically irreversible if governments lack political support to ignore the Trustee, pass new legislation, or change the constitution.

(5) *While I believe that certain theories are simply wrong, I think it is important to consider all plausible explanations for any outcome.* Overall, it is through the heterogeneity of scholarly approaches that intellectual progress occurs. In this respect as well the ECJ serves as a model. My research keeps returning to the

ECJ as a laboratory because its rich history has been deeply (though far from completely) investigated, using a multiplicity of scholarly approaches. The scholarship on the ECJ thus serves as an excellent starting point for thinking about how ICs become powerful political actors. The conclusion begins to do this by building on what we know about the ECJ's unique experience. I hope that collecting my essays in a volume provides a way for scholars to dip into this rich scholarship and history.

2

The European Court and Legal Integration: An Exceptional Story or Harbinger of the Future? (2008)

Established as part of the European Coal and Steel Community in 1950, and later adapted as part of the 1957 Treaty of Rome, three design features distinguished the European Court of Justice (ECJ) from international courts of the time. First, member countries could be compelled to participate in proceedings (in the parlance of international law, the ECJ had 'compulsory jurisdiction'). Second, the ECJ's 'preliminary ruling mechanism' provided a means for private actors to access the ECJ via national court references. Third, there was a process whereby a supranational actor (the Commission) could raise non-compliance charges against states. There were reasons for these design features, but neither the Treaty negotiators, nor the governments who signed the Treaties founding the European Communities, nor European Community officials anticipated how legally, politically, or institutionally transformative these design features would be.

The most important feature proved to be the 'preliminary ruling mechanism'. This mechanism was intended to provide national courts with technical support in interpreting complex European law. In practice, preliminary ruling references provided a means for the ECJ to insert itself into national debates regarding the relationship of European law to national law, and to harness national courts as enforcers of ECJ decisions. The 'Transformation of the Europe' began in 1962 when a Dutch Tariff Commission sent a preliminary ruling reference to the ECJ, asking if the article of the Treaty of Rome in question could be seen as self-executing. Whether or not treaty provisions are self-executing is a question of domestic law, not European law, and the governing Dutch law implied that the particular provision in question was not self-executing (Claes and De Witte 1998). The Dutch government argued that the reference should be rejected as inadmissible, because it concerned a question of domestic law. The ECJ disagreed, issuing a provocative ruling that turned traditional legal reasoning on its head. Whereas in the past a direct internal effect of treaty provisions was an exception that had to be shown to be implicitly intended (Donner 1968: 72), the

ECJ argued that provisions reasonably capable of having direct internal affects should be presumed to have it. Its *Van Gend en Loos* ruling made the case as follows:

> The objective of the EEC Treaty, which is to establish a Common Market, the function of which is of direct concern to interested parties in the Community, implies that this Treaty is more than an agreement which merely creates mutual obligations between the contracting states...the Community constitutes a new legal order of international law for the benefit of which the states have limited their sovereign rights, albeit within limited fields, and the subject of which comprise not only Member States, but also their nationals ... Independent of the legislation of Member States, Community law therefore not only imposes obligations on individuals but is also intended to confer upon them rights which become part of their legal heritage. These rights arise not only where they are expressly granted by the Treaty, but also by reason of obligations which the Treaty imposes in a clearly defined way upon individuals as well as upon Member States and upon the institutions of the Community. (*Van Gend en Loos v. Nederlandse Administratie Belastingen*)

Two years later, an Italian citizen challenged his $3.00 electricity bill because, he claimed, the Italian electricity company ENEL had been nationalized in contravention of the Treaty of Rome. The small claims court sent its reference simultaneously to the ECJ and the Italian Constitutional Court. The Italian Court ruled first, finding the reference invalid. The ECJ accepted the case anyway, issuing a ruling that challenged the Italian doctrine that the 'last law passed' takes precedence. The ECJ asserted that:

> By contrast with ordinary international treaties, the EEC Treaty has created its own legal system which, on entry into force of the Treaty, became an integral part of the legal systems of the Member States and which their courts are bound to apply. By creating a Community of unlimited duration, having its own institutions, its own personality, its own legal capacity and capacity of representation on the international plane and, more particularly, real powers stemming from the limitation of sovereignty or a transfer of powers from the States to the Community, the Member States have limited their sovereign rights, albeit within limited fields, and have thus created a body of law which binds both their nationals and themselves.
>
> ...It follows from all these observations that the law stemming from the Treaty, an independent source of law, could not, because of its special and original nature, be overridden by domestic legal provisions, however framed, without being deprived of its character as Community law and without the legal basis of the Community itself being called into question. (*Costa v. ENEL*)

These early rulings were remarkable in their audacity, but if one looked at the full picture of ECJ authority in the 1960s, this is what it would have looked like. On paper, there was an ECJ with unusual jurisdiction and authority. But states fully controlled the process of making European law, and were quite capable of stopping integration where they did not want it. While the ECJ had asserted the direct effect and supremacy of European law, the rulings themselves were of little practical import. The ECJ avoided substantive rulings that would upset states, meanwhile the Italian Constitutional Court and the French Conseil d'État had both rejected the ECJ's doctrinal assertions.

These rulings, however, worked their way into national doctrines regarding the relationship of European law to national law (see Chapter 5), and the ECJ became more willing to make substantive rulings affecting important state interests. The ECJ's 1979 *Cassis de Dijon* ruling declared that member states must recognize as valid one another's product standards (see Chapter 7). In 1987 the ECJ struck down Germany's historic Beer Purity Law as an impediment to trade *(Commission v. Germany 'Beer Purity case')*. Three years later the ECJ forced the Conservative government of Margaret Thatcher to equalize its retirement age for men and women *(Barber v. Guardian Group)*. In 1991 the ECJ ruled that Ireland could not stop the advertisement of British Abortion Clinics' services *(Society for the Protection of Unborn Children v. Grogan)*. In 2000 the ECJ found that provisions of the German Basic Law limiting the types of roles women could fulfill in the military contradicted European rules regarding gender equality *(Tanja Kriel v. Bundesrepublik Deutschland* (Case 285/98)—see Chapter 11). Each of these rulings triggered fundamental shifts in national policies that would not have otherwise occurred.

This transformation of the European legal system is the stuff of fairytales. Off in the Grand Duchy of Luxembourg, supranational judges teamed up with lawyers in contrived cases to turn an international convention into a constitution for a new supranational polity. They did this in contradiction to the will of member states, whose leaders were in the 1960s busy making deals designed to put a halt to the process of European integration (Weiler 1991). They did this in a political context in which only a handful of European courts—national or supranational—even had authority to undertake judicial review of government policy (Stone 1990).

The question for this chapter is: How do we understand the ECJ's role in European integration? Section I summarizes a vast scholarship regarding the role of the ECJ in European integration. Section II locates the ECJ's remarkable experience in the larger context of international courts and international law.

I. Scholarship on the ECJ and European Integration

The literature on the ECJ puts forward three different narratives about its role in European integration. Legalist scholarship puts the ECJ in the center of their narrative, portraying the ECJ as a heroic actor capable of pushing European governments and institutions in the direction of greater European integration. International Relations scholars assume that states are at the center of international relations in the EU, thus they examine the ECJ as a tool of states to accomplish their objectives. Comparative politics approaches focus on the relationship between ECJ and actors above and below the state that use the European legal system to promote their own objectives. There is an element of truth in all three narratives, though today the comparative politics approach is the most widely shared of the narratives.

The legalist narrative: The ECJ as the hero driving European integration

Legalist accounts are correct in that the European legal system was transformed by a relatively small group of judges and lawyers. But legalist accounts of the 1960s and 1970s were disembodied from the actors involved, using a positivist logic that supported a myth that the ECJ was merely using legal interpretation to work out the details agreed to in the Treaty of Rome. Asked to comment on a typical legalist analysis of the period, Martin Shapiro characterized the scholarship this way:

> Professor Barav's Article is a careful and systematic exposition of the judicial review provision of the 'constitution' of the European Economic Community, an exposition that is helpful for a newcomer to these materials. But it represents a stage of constitutional scholarship out of which American constitutional law must have passed about seventy years ago (although remnants of it are still to be found). It is constitutional law without politics. Professor Barav presents the Community as a juristic idea; the written constitution (the treaty) as a sacred text; the professional commentary as a legal truth; the case law as the inevitable working out of the correct implications of the constitutional text; and the constitutional court (the ECJ) as the disembodied voice of right reason and constitutional teleology.... we must bear in mind that particularly in the European tradition, professional writing is simultaneously an act of scholarship and an act of law-making—that is to say an act of politics. In this light there is much to be said for Professor Barav's unspoken, but none the less emphatic, assertion of the autonomy of law and the teleological inevitability of the Community's legal system ... To treat the law as autonomous is to accentuate the positive; that sort of accentuation is important to institutional building. (Shapiro 1980: 538)

Today we know that there was a jurist advocacy movement backing the ECJ in its efforts. The transformation of Europe began when Robert Lecourt was essentially exiled to the Duchy of Luxembourg because French President Charles de Gaulle did not want him in Paris. Ensconced in the irrelevant ECJ, Lecourt penned the *Van Gend en Loos* and *Costa v. ENEL* rulings described above, in an intentional strategy to promote integration through law.[1] Lecourt was joined in

---

[1] An ECJ judge from 1962 to 1976, Lecourt published articles explaining how he saw the role of judges in promoting integration through law. See 'Le rôle du droit dans l'unification européenne' [1964] *Gazette du Palais* 49–54; 'La dynamique judiciaire dans l'édification de l'Europe' (May 1965) 64 *France Forum* 20–2; *L'Europe des Juges* (Brussels: Etablissements Emile Bruylant, 1976); 'Le rôle de la Cour de Justice dans le développement des Communautés' (1976) 24 *European Yearbook* 19–41; 'Quel eût été le droit des Communautés sans les arrêts de 1963 et 1964?' In *Mélanges en Hommage à Jean Boulouis: L'Europe et le Droit* (Paris: Editions Dalloz, 1991).

his mission by Pierre Pescatore,[2] and Federico Mancini, firm Euro-federalists who also penned legal rulings, wrote articles, gave speeches, and told tales of champagne brunches wherein national judges were convinced of the endeavor of constructing Europe through law.[3] The work of these judges, and the promulgation of 'heroic' narrative, was facilitated by national associations of academics and practitioners. Each country had its own association, and collectively associations came together as part of the umbrella Fédération Internationale de Droit Europeen (FIDE). As lawyers and judges, FIDE members helped create cases that the ECJ could rule on. They debated legal ideas with the ECJ judges and Legal Service advisors. They founded legal journals dedicated to European law, wrote articles in national journals to inform national legal communities about European law, wrote critical analyses of national court rulings that challenged ECJ doctrine, and even engaged in private diplomacy with skeptical national judges (see Chapter 4).

In the 1960s and 1970s, just about the only scholarship regarding European law was legal positivist in nature. A less involved group of scholars, coming from countries that were not part of the original European integration project, began writing about European legal integration in the 1980s (Stein 1981; Rasmussen 1986; Weiler 1981). While one can still find 'law without politics' accounts of ECJ jurisprudence in contemporary scholarship, the legal debate has mostly moved beyond these accounts. For example, Renaud Dehousse's 1998 analysis of the European Court and legal integration takes as given that the ECJ is a strategic political actor, and that political forces shape legal integration (Dehousse 1998). It is also now widely accepted that ECJ rulings take political mediation before they become a reality, that not all ECJ rulings do become instigators of change, and that it is not the quality of the rulings or the boldness of the ECJ that determines which rulings become instigators of change and which do not. To the

---

[2] As Luxembourg's appointee to the ECJ, Pescatore served on the ECJ from 1967 to 1985. In addition to legal rulings, P. Pescatore wrote articles and books addressing issues of concern within national legal systems. A small sample of his writing includes: 'Die Menschenrechte und die europäische Integration' [1969] *Integration* 103–36; 'L'attitude des juridictions nationales à l'égard du problème des effets directs du droit communautaire' (1970) 2 *Revue trimestrielle de droit européen* 296–302; 'Aspects of the Court of Justice of the European Communities of interest from the point of view of international law' (1972) 32 *Zeitschrift für auslandisches öffentliches Recht und Völkerrecht* 239–52; 'Community law and the national judge' (January 1973) *Law Guardian*; 'L'exécutif communautaire: Justification du quadripartisme institué par les traités de Paris et de Rome' (1978) 4 *Cahiers de droit europeen* 387–406; 'The doctrine of "Direct effect": An infant disease of community law' (1983) 8(3) *European Law Review* 155–77.

[3] F. Mancini was appointed as an Avocat Général in 1982, and became a judge from Italy from 1988 to 1999. His writings include: 'Politics and the judges—the European perspective' (1979) 43(1) *Modern Law Review* 1–17; 'The incorporation of community law into the domestic laws of the member states of the European Communities', Paper presented at the International Uniform Law in Practice, Rome 7–10 September 1987; 'The making of a constitution for Europe' (1989) 24 *Common Market Law Review* 595–614. With D. Keeling: 'From cilft to erta: The constitutional challenge facing the European Court' (1992) 11 *Yearbook of European Law* 1–13 and 'Democracy and the European Court of Justice' (1994) 57(2) *Modern Law Review* 175–90.

extent that scholars continue to put the ECJ in the center of their narrative, 'sophisticated legalists' examine how the ECJ uses its office as part of a political and legal strategy to build the foundations of its own political authority (Burley and Mattli 1993; Helfer and Slaughter 1997; Slaughter 2000).

International relations narrative: The ECJ as states' agent

Probably because the scholarship on the ECJ was so heavily tilted towards the heroic apolitical legalist narrative, a counter-narrative was championed by political scientists. Geoffrey Garrett and Barry Weingast adopted the ontology of principal–agent theory, asserting that ECJ, like all courts, was an 'agent' of the actors that delegated authority to it. If courts were simply agents of their 'principal' masters, the challenge was merely to define the hidden 'tools' states were using as their levers of control. Garrett and Weingast's analysis amounted to an assertion:

> Courts whose rulings are consistently overturned typically find themselves and their role in the political system weakened. As a consequence, the actions of the courts are fundamentally 'political' in that they must anticipate the possible reactions of other political actors in order to avoid their intervention... Embedding a legal system in a broader political structure places direct constraints on the discretion of a court, even one with as much constitutional independence as the United States Supreme Court. This conclusion holds even if the constitution makes no explicit provisions for altering a court's role. The reason is that political actors have a range of avenues through which they may alter or limit the role of courts. Sometimes such changes require amendment of the constitution, but usually the appropriate alterations may be accomplished more directly through statute, as by alteration of the court's jurisdiction in a way that makes it clear that continued undesired behavior will result in more radical changes the possibility of such a reaction drives a court that wishes to preserve its independence and legitimacy to remain in the area of acceptable latitude. (Garrett and Weingast 1993: 200–1)

Garrett originally believed that the ECJ based its decisions on the interests of the most powerful states (Garrett 1995). In subsequent writings, he distanced himself from his most strident claims, recognizing that ECJ doctrine can provide an element of political autonomy as do institutional rules that make reversing ECJ decisions difficult (Garrett, Kelemen, and Schulz 1998). The tradition of applying principal–agent theory is still alive in international relations scholarship, but now the focus is more on the determinants and limits of state control over agent decision-making (Tsebelis and Garrett 2001; Hawkins et al. 2006).

Garrett and Weingast's assertion of state control spawned an extensive effort to examine the extent to which state preferences shape the ECJ's docket and its decision-making. Bernadette Kilroy set out to test the principal–agent expectation that the ECJ responded to sanctioning threats, coding ECJ decisions to see if they were biased in favor of the more powerful states (Kilroy 1995, 1999). Kilroy herself found that the ECJ responded more to the threat of non-compliance than the threat that states might sanction the ECJ. Considering Kilroy's analysis, Mark Pollack finds that despite her efforts Kilroy cannot rule out other explanations of ECJ decision-making—such as the argument that the ECJ decides the case purely on the basis of law, without varying its rulings according to the power or intransigence of member states, or the likelihood of state compliance (Pollack 2003: 200).

Pollack investigated Garrett, Kelemen, and Shultz's claim that the *Barber Protocol* forced the ECJ to retreat from activism (Garrett, Kelemen, and Schulz 1998). The *Barber Protocol* was inserted into the 1993 Maastricht Treaty with the intent of limiting the impact of the ECJ's *Barber v. Guardian Group* ruling equalizing pension policies for men and women. While not a legislative reversal of the *Barber* ruling, the Protocol was seen as a political rebuke of the ECJ because political bodies were acting before the ECJ had a chance to itself address the issue of retrospective effects, and because it emerged at the same time that efforts to sanction the ECJ were underway (see Tallberg 2003). Reviewing the ECJ's pre- and post-*Barber* rulings regarding gender equality, Pollack finds:

only partial support for Garrett, Kelemen and Schultz's claim that the Court has 'retreated' following the Barber protocol ... Indeed one might argue that the Court's post-Barber jurisprudence, rather than constituting a generalized retreat, represents a return to the pre-Barber pattern in which the Court generally, but not always, opts for a broad interpretation of Article 141, most often over the objections of one or more ... member governments.

Pollack suggests that the political factor shaping ECJ decision-making is a concern for non-compliance, but he also acknowledges that it is equally plausible that legal factors and not concerns about non-compliance shape ECJ decisions (Pollack 2003: 200).

Derek Beach also finds limited support for Garrett, Kelemen, and Schultz's hypotheses that variations in the legal clarity of European law, variation in the potential cost of adverse rulings, or institutional barriers explain variation in ECJ decision-making. Where Pollack suggests that compliance concerns provide a tool of state influence, Beach argues that the ECJ mainly is responding to concerns voiced by national courts—which are the ECJ's crucial constituency (Beach 2001).

Jonas Tallberg examines the mixed messages states convey to the ECJ, noting that at the same time as states were complaining about ECJ activism, they were also giving it more power. Tallberg argues that states want to stop ECJ decisions they do not like, but they also want the European legal system to help enforce compliance with EU law. Like Pollack, Tallberg finds that principal–agent factors can account for the Commission's lesser autonomy compared to the ECJ. Tallberg argues that principal–agent factors also explain why the Commission and ECJ are best able to impart their vision at the interpretive stage compared to the legislative stage. While Tallberg believes that principal–agent analysis is useful and insightful, he admits up front that it does not explain ECJ decision-making (Tallberg 2003: 12).

At this point, all that is left of the Garrett-Weingast state control thesis is that concerns about non-compliance with ECJ decisions may shape ECJ decision-making. Tanja Börzel finds the problem of non-compliance is overstated—compliance with EU law is generally high. Her research, which reviews Commission enforcement of European law and quantitative studies of national court reference rates, suggests that the Commission is not skewing its investigations based on the power of the state, and that there is little relationship between the overall level of compliance and whether a country undertakes to sanction the ECJ for activism (Börzel 2001; Stone Sweet and Brunell 1998).[4]

Despite a lack of empirical support, Garrett and Weingast's arguments about states influencing the ECJ remain widely cited to support the claim that principal–agent theory is explaining ECJ decision-making. Elsewhere I have examined more systematically why the tools of political control are not as influential as Garrett and Weingast expected them to be (Alter 2006).

Comparative politics narrative: The ECJ as an interlocutor

The hardest forms of the 'hero-ECJ' and 'agent-ECJ' have been repudiated. There is now a convergence around the view that both legal and political considerations influence ECJ jurisprudence, and that the European legal system provides a legal mechanism that other actors—private litigants, national courts, or EU institutions—can use to promote their policy objectives (Weiler 1994). In some respects, this convergence represents the maturation of European law scholarship. It is no longer necessary to construct myths that justify the ECJ's authority. Meanwhile, since the ECJ now has a lot in common with other constitutional courts, it makes sense to examine the ECJ's role as one examines that of other constitutional courts.

If the ECJ is mainly an interlocutor for the efforts of other actors, then the actions or non-actions of potential litigants and those actors who channel cases to the ECJ will shape where the ECJ expands European law and influences national policies. Chapter 8 identifies four distinct steps involved in the ECJ influencing European politics. First, since the ECJ only rules in concrete cases, some actor must first raise a complaint before the ECJ can insert itself in the political process. Because cases raised in national courts or brought to the attention of the Commission are not necessarily referred to the ECJ, the second step is to understand which cases get referred to the ECJ for resolution. Third, one must understand when the ECJ is willing to provoke a political response through its rulings, and when it refrains from interjecting itself in areas where the law is

---

[4] Britain spearheaded the efforts to sanction the ECJ (Tallberg 2003). France and Germany at different times supported efforts to sanction the ECJ. These efforts are discussed in Alter (2001).

not fully clear. Fourth, we must understand when and how other actors 'follow through' on legal victories, creating pressure on political bodies to respect ECJ jurisprudence.

The 'hero-ECJ' and 'agent-ECJ' narratives only focused on step three, implicitly suggesting that the key to legal expansion is how the ECJ rules in cases. The 'interlocutor-ECJ' narrative tells you that steps one, two, and four are equally if not more important in understanding the ECJ's role in legal integration. There is extensive scholarship on each of these questions (see Chapter 9). The original version of this essay summarized newer scholarship on the four thresholds. See the introduction for an account of my current thinking about these four thresholds. For a broad literature overview related to these thresholds, see Lisa Conant's 2007 review article.

II. The European Court of Justice: The Exception or the Rule?

Scholars disagree on whether the European experience could occur elsewhere. As long as the ECJ was itself *sui generis,* one could not get traction on this question. But the end of the Cold War ushered in a period of expansive legalization of international politics that has clarified many international rules and led to a proliferation of international legal mechanisms to enforce these rules (Goldstein et al. 2001; Romano 1999). I started this essay noting design features that were unique to the ECJ when it was created. Table 2.1 below reveals a number of ICs that replicate the unusual features of the ECJ's design which many scholars see as contributing to its influence. By my count, there are now at least 15 ICs with compulsory jurisdiction, 13 which allow private actors to be a party to the suit either directly in front of the IC or in national courts that will refer the case to the IC, and 17 that can hear non-compliance suits raised against state actors either by a commission or by private actors.

Will these courts replicate the ECJ's experience ? One can look to the various narratives about the ECJ to speculate.

The early explanations of the transformation of the European legal system were heroic narratives about astute judges transforming a legal system through their rulings. If all it takes is bold rulings, then any of the courts listed above could replicate the ECJ's experience. Anne-Marie Slaughter and Laurence Helfer drew insights from the ECJ's experience, crafting a proto-'Theory of Effective Supranational Adjudication'. Effective supranational courts, they argue, are able to convince domestic political institutions to comply, either through direct persuasion or via pressure from supra and sub-state actors. Helfer and Slaughter create a list of steps that states can take in setting up an IC to aid its effectiveness (such as appointing judges with strong reputations and aiding the court in making sound legal rulings) and factors that the judges themselves can control (such as how they craft their rulings to build their own authority and to reach

Table 2.1 International Courts' design and caseloads organized within each section by date established

International Courts	Date established	Compulsory jurisdiction	Access for non-state actors help enforce international rules	Total cases (last year included in figures)[a]
Courts without private access to initiate disputes				
International Court of Justice (ICJ)	1945	Optional Protocol		111 contentious cases filed, 80 judgments 20 advisory opinions (2006)
Inter-American Court of Human Rights (IACHR)	1969	Optional Protocol	Commission can raise cases	162 judgments, 19 advisory opinions, 245 orders for provisional measures (2006)
General Agreement on Tariffs and Trade (GATT)	*1953–1993*[d]	—		*229 cases, 98 rulings*
World Trade Organization Permanent Appellate Body (WTO)[d]	1994	X		357 disputes formally initiated, 79 appellate rulings, 192 panel reports in WTO era (2006; 2005 for panel reports)
International Criminal Tribunal for the Former Yugoslavia (ICTY)	1993	X	International Prosecutor can raise cases	73 public indictments, 31 completed cases, 46 judgments by the Trial Chambers, 24 judgments by the Appeals Chamber (2006)
International Criminal Tribunal for Rwanda (ICTR)	1994	X	International Prosecutor can raise cases	27 cases in progress, 27 completed cases, seven awaiting trial (2006)
International Criminal Court (ICC)	2001	X	International Prosecutor can raise cases	Four situations under investigation; six warrants for arrest issues (2007)
International Criminal Tribunal for Sierra Leone (ICTSL)	2002	X	International Prosecutor can raise cases	13 indictments proceeding, two withdrawn due to death (2006)
Courts with Private Access				
European Court of Justice (ECJ) including its Court of First Instance (CFI)	1952	X	Commission can raise infringement suits. Private actors can raise suits in national courts CFI—5,227 cases completed from 6,256 cases filed	5,765 cases referred by national courts, 7,908 direct actions, 822 appeals, 342 applications for interim measures, 2,860 infringements (2006)

Continued

Table 2.1 (*Continued*)

International Courts	Date established	Compulsory jurisdiction	Access for non-state actors help enforce international rules	Total cases (last year included in figures)[a]
European Court of Human Rights (ECHR)	1950	X	Commission abolished in 1998. Now private actors raise cases directly	12,310 cases deemed admissible, 7,528 judgments (2006)
Benelux Court (BCJ)	1965	X	Via national court referrals	137 preliminary references filed (10 rejected), (2006)
Court of Justice of the Cartagena Agreement (Andean Pact) (ATJ)	1979	X	Secretariat and private actors can raise infringement suits	25 nullifications, 79 infringement cases, 1,163 preliminary rulings (2006)
Judicial Tribunal for Organization of Arab Petroleum-Exporting Countries (OAPEC)	1980	So qualified as to be meaningless[b]	Private actors can raise cases only if defendant state consents	two cases (1999)
International Tribunal for the Law of the Seas (ITLOS)	1982	Optional Protocol	Private actors can challenge the decisions of the Seabed Authority. With their government's permission, private actors can challenge another state's seizing of their vessel	14 judgments (2006)
Central American Court of Justice (CACJ)	1991	X (some exceptions)[c]	Secretariat and private actors can raise cases	78 cases, 23 advisory opinions, 55 rulings (2006)
European Free Trade Area Court (EFTAC)	1992	X	Secretariat, states, and private actors can raise cases	90 opinions (2006)
Economic Court of the Commonwealth of Independent States (ECCIS)	1993	X	Private actors can raise cases	83 decisions and opinions (2006)
Court of Justice for the Common Market of Eastern and Southern Africa (COMESA)	1993	X	Secretariat and private actors can raise cases	five judgments, two orders (2006)

Common Court of Justice and Arbitration for the Organization for the Harmonization of Corporate Law in Africa (OHADA)	1993	X	Secretariat and private actors can raise cases. Private actors can appeal national court rulings	six opinions, 111 rulings (2006)
Caribbean Court of Justice (CCJ)	2001/2005	X	(still unclear)	Began operation April 2005

Table is adapted from Alter 2008: 58–60. I have excluded from consideration private access when it only includes suits brought by employees of the IO. * Indirect means that cases with private litigants would come through national courts references to the IC. ** = no data.

[a] Data compiled by author, based on the best information available on the PICT website, updated by visiting the websites of the international courts and consulting scholarship where available. ECCIS data from (Dragneva 2004).

[b] There is an implicit compulsory jurisdiction, but only so long as the disputes do not infringe on the sovereignty of any of the countries concerned. Also, for cases involving firms, jurisdiction must be consented to by the state.

[c] As a general rule, consent to the CACJ contentious jurisdiction is implicit in the ratification of the Protocol of Tegucigalpa. However, consent must be explicitly given in the case of: (i) territorial disputes (in which case consent to jurisdiction has to be given by both states party to the dispute); (ii) disputes between states member of the Central American Integration System and states which are not members; (iii) cases in which the Court sits as arbitral tribunal.

[d] GATT does not meet PICT's definition because there was no permanent court. This is the reason that NAFTA is not included on the table as well.

out to potential interlocutors) (Helfer and Slaughter 1997). Their analysis creates a checklist of factors one could examine as potential sources of variation in the impact and influence of international courts. The checklist is a helpful way to start sorting through the list of courts above, as it suggests that not all courts will have what it takes to replicate the ECJ's experience. But it is not enough. The Andean Tribunal of Justice seemingly has every tool on the checklist, yet it operates in a political context that creates inherent limitations on how activist or effective it may be (see Chapter 4).

International relations explanations suggest that ICs that promote the interests of key governments are likely to be more effective. To some extent, this is a counter-explanation to the legalist accounts in that it suggests that the actions of judges themselves are largely epiphenomenal. International relations explanations have not weathered well empirical scrutiny in the ECJ context, and the table above does not bear them much support either in that international judicial activity let alone IC effectiveness does not clearly map on to what we might expect the interests of powerful states to be.

Comparative politics literature suggests that we need to look at attributes within states to understand where ICs may replicate the ECJ expereience. Looking in the area of human rights, Andrew Moravcsik argues that supranational legal systems are far more likely to be effective if members are liberal democracies (Moravcsik 1997). The Andean Tribunal has struggled in many ways, but it also flourished in the area of intellectual property law, notwithstanding that Andean states are far from stable liberal democracies (Helfer, Alter, and Guerzovich 2009). In any event, we would need to investigate more which attributes increase the likelihood that domestic actors will turn to international courts to influence political outcomes. The conclusion to this volume begins to take a step in this direction.

There remain a number of unanswered questions raised by the ECJ's experience. It is now 'taken for granted' that the ECJ has political autonomy, and can influence European politics. Is the same true of other ICs, or is the ECJ unusually activist? If the ECJ is unusual, why is it more activist than other courts? After all, there is little in the appointment mechanism of ECJ judges, or the terms they serve in office, that separate the ECJ from other ICs. The mechanisms of 'follow-through' are different in the European context, where ECJ legal rulings are applied by national courts. But clearly there are other ways to follow up on international court rulings, other ways to amplify or limit their impact.

The debate about what the ECJ's incredible experience implies for other courts is just now beginning. International courts are proliferating. We are also witnessing the proliferation of constitutional courts in newly emerging democracies (Unger 2002; Schwartz 2000). And there are efforts underway around the world to promote the establishment of domestic rules of law (Hammergren 2007). Thus the question of why the European Court was able to develop its authority and influence is perhaps even more relevant today than it was when the ECJ was embarking on its own revolution.

PART II

THE EUROPEAN COURT OF JUSTICE DURING THE FOUNDING PERIOD OF LEGAL INTEGRATION (1952–1980)

3

The Theory and Reality of the European Coal and Steel Community (2007)

With David Steinberg

European integration began in 1950 with the Schuman Plan, which launched the ECSC. The Schuman Plan was designed to alleviate concerns that Germany's dominance in coal and steel could be used to harm European reconstruction efforts or to build another war machine. Jean Monnet, the Plan's chief architect, also wanted to shore up the French planning process for reconstruction by Europeanizing the technocratic planning approach. Most supporters of the ECSC project expected integration to expand beyond coal and steel, and hoped that it would serve as a first step toward deeper European integration.

European integration theory began with the ECSC as well. Inspired by Monnet's vision that technical functional integration could lead to political transformation, Ernst Haas created a neo-functionalist theory that specified the mechanisms through which integration would be politically transformative. With governance transferred to the European level, Haas expected the stakeholders associated with the sector to come to see their fate as linked to the ECSC's success. He predicted that firms, unions, and workers benefiting from ECSC policies would support the ECSC. Success would breed success. As other industries observed the benefits of supranational coordination, they would demand integration in their sectors, leading to the realization of Haas' hope of moving 'politics beyond the nation-state' (1958, 1964).

After the EEC was launched in 1958, theoretical and practical interest in the ECSC declined. Integrating European economies was a more ambitious goal, and it was clear early on that agriculture—not coal and steel—would be the first large policy nut that had to be cracked for the European project to succeed. Thus by 1958, practically and politically speaking, the success of the coal and steel project was no longer a bellwether for the larger integration efforts. A number of studies of the ECSC were published in the late 1950s and early 1960s (Haas 1958; Diebold 1959; Scheingold 1965), but then scholarly focus shifted after the 1960s (see Dudley and Richardson's article (1999) for a noteworthy exception).

This chapter examines the experience of coal and steel integration during the ECSC's 50-year history, focusing on the extent to which practice coincided with theory. Like others, we find that ECSC rules were regularly ignored. Our question is: What does it mean for integration theory that the ECSC was mainly a paper tiger? Why did Haas' integration theory not materialize in this case par excellence? Why was the ECJ not the integrating actor in the ECSC that it came to be in the EEC and EU?

We argue that the ECSC failed because the situation for which it was created never materialized, and absent that situation member states actually preferred market segmentation to market integration. Its early failure put to rest the technocratic functional integration approach that inspired the ECSC, and in doing so assured states that integration *did not* mean ceding power to the High Authority (HA). The ECSC did prove useful when external forces created benefits for working collectively. When the United States was concerned about dumping of European steel products, the ECSC assumed its role as foreign representative for the member states. When a global oversupply led to a collapse of the price of steel products, the ECSC was a useful means to manage the painful but necessary market adjustment. However even when the ECSC assumed the role Monnet had envisioned, the ECSC did not trigger a shifting of loyalties, spillover, or an entrenchment of supranational institutions and policies. Instead, the ECSC performed its task and was disbanded.

Section I discusses the ECSC at its founding. The next section divides the ECSC into historical periods demarcated by changes in the economic terms of trade in coal and steel, and thus by critical junctures in which changes in European policy could have and sometimes did occur. Finally, reviewing the entire time trajectory, the chapter evaluates the role the ECSC played in postwar European steel and integration politics.

I. The ECSC at its Founding

In the immediate postwar period, Germany's European neighbors were concerned that Germany might regain its dominance in steel, and that they would lack the steel they needed to rebuild their economies. While the Allies were occupying Germany, the International Ruhr Authority monitored and controlled Germany's industry. But by 1949 it was clear that the US planned to create a sovereign Germany largely free of international oversight and control. Schuman proposed the ECSC to avoid German sovereign control of its industry (Milward 1984).

At the time the ECSC was proposed, states were concerned about coal and steel scarcities. In a context of scarcity, Germany could abuse its dominant position in the market affecting other European states' economic rebuilding efforts. Jean Monnet drafted the ECSC Treaty with the problem of scarce supply in mind, but with the idea that the ECSC could eventually engage in supranational sectoral planning (Duchene 1994). During negotiations over the Treaty of Paris, it became clear that countries were not interested in coordinated sectoral planning. Instead, countries wanted resources they could use to rebuild national industries. French producers fought for favorable access to German coal (Duchene 1994: 221; Rittberger 2001: 686–8). Belgian, Dutch, and Italian firms demanded adjustment subsidies and time to build up their industry (Kipping, Ruggero, and Dankers 2001: 81–5). The Dutch foiled Monnet's plan to have a highly independent supranational planning body, insisting on creating a Council of Ministers to control the HA (Dinan 2004b: 51). The end result was a treaty that was far less ambitious than what Schuman had originally proposed (Haas 1958: 251; Milward 1984: 380–420; Groenendijk and Gert 2002: 602).

While the Treaty of Paris ended up an inter-governmentalist bargain, it did establish supranational institutions with real powers, at least on paper. The Council of Ministers, composed of ministers from member countries, had to assent formally to policy measures initiated by the HA, but decisions would originate from the HA, based on a majority vote of the six members. The HA could fine firms and withhold transfer funds to encourage compliance with ECSC rules. There was also a supranational ECJ to arbitrate disputes among participants including member states, European institutions, and affected private actors (e.g. firms, unions, and so on). The Treaty also created a 'common assembly' made up of national parliamentarians, and umbrella associations for each industry, for employers, and for unions.

In addition to its institutions, the Treaty created a framework of rules that could be used to shore up the competitive nature of the market. Elements of this framework included:

- *Transparency with respect to prices:* firms were obliged to publish prices, and price discrimination was forbidden.
- *Management of investment:* the HA could help fund or prohibit investments to avoid illegal subsidization of industry.
- *Banning cartels:* cartels were generally forbidden and the HA had to approve that mergers were aimed at increasing efficiency and not at market dominance.
- *Eliminating subsidies:* subsidies were generally illegal, though exceptions were permitted so long as they were gradually reduced.
- *Labor policy:* information provisions aimed to create transparency in labor practices.
- *Transportation:* the same transport rates had to be applied to all steel firms, regardless of nationality, and rates had to be published.

- *Foreign relations:* under the supervision of the Council of Ministers, the HA could negotiate and establish diplomatic relations with foreign governments regarding matters related to coal and steel.
- *Crisis measures:* in the event of a 'manifest crisis', production quotas would be established by the HA.[1]

While Monnet and Schuman had not achieved all they had wanted, the Treaty did establish institutions that could be used to coordinate European coal and steel industries. Monnet saw sectoral planning 'as above all a "method" of mobilizing people for collective effort' and the Schuman Plan as the 'first step to a united Europe' (Duchene 1994: 157, 199). Schuman claimed that the ECSC would 'simply and speedily [create] that fusion of interests...that will be the leaven from which may grow a wider and deeper community' (quoted in Groenendijk and Gert 2002: 602). Analyzing its first ten years of existence, Ernst Haas found evidence of HA influence, of the interpenetration of European steel markets, and of actors below the state organizing to promote common goals. Haas argued that 'political integration is taking place' (Haas 1958: 485). But these interpretations were quite disputable.[2]

II. Critical Junctures in Coal and Steel Integration

This section assesses the reality of what happened in the ECSC over time. Were the substantive rules followed? Did the institutional mechanisms work as Haas and Monnet expected (e.g. did policy come to be set at the European level, did the peak associations created to oversee coal and steel market integration assume the political role of supranationalizing political representation and loyalties)? Our empirical analysis is oriented around four periods, each with a crisis that presented an opportunity to declare a 'manifest crisis' which would trigger the ECSC's provisions to set policy at the European level.

1950–58—Searching for a *raison d'être*

The common market for coal, iron ore, and scraps was officially opened in February 1953,[3] when members agreed to eliminate tariffs and quotas in accordance with the Treaty. But in fact there were no tariffs or quotas at the time protecting markets (Haas 1958: 60–2; Gillingham 1991: 268), so this vote

---

[1] For a comprehensive and detailed description of ECSC policies and institutions, see Haas (1958), Lister (1960), and Diebold (1959).

[2] For an excellent discussion of problems in Haas' theory, see Moravcsik (2006). For a discussion of how Haas' thinking evolved over time, see Mattli (2005).

[3] A market for 'ordinary steel' opened in May 1953 and after delays the market for 'alloyed steel' opened in August 1954.

was mainly symbolic. To create a real common market, the HA would need to tackle the policies and institutions that created barriers to trade, which required Council assent. European governments were most concerned with protecting jobs and facilitating industrial growth—defined exclusively in national terms. These objectives led governments to prefer market segmentation over unleashing competition via market integration. European governments blocked the HA's efforts to dismantle barriers to trade, and aided their firms, often in contravention of ECSC rules.

France

The French government granted low interest state-guaranteed loans to help its industry. Convinced that economies of scale would make its industry competitive, the French orchestrated mergers that arguably cut against the ECSC's anti-cartel policies (Daley 1996: 58). While French consumers of steel wanted open markets to gain access to cheaper steel, the government continued to control domestic steel prices, in violation of the ECSC Treaty (Kipping 1996: 16). The government offset high prices with discounted investment credit, but it did so differentially to develop targeted regions; in some places steel prices were higher than prices in neighboring ECSC states, but in other locations prices were lower than they might have been if there were an integrated European market (Daley 1996: 64).

Germany

Germany was the only country with highly concentrated ownership in the 1940s. While the German government negotiated with Allies regarding deconcentration and complied with ECSC rulings pertaining to German industry, it dragged its feet when it came to implementing the anti-cartel spirit of the ECSC's provisions. Its strategy succeeded. By 1952, efforts to deconcentrate German industry were loosened; by 1958, they were abandoned (Warner 1996: 236). Germany did not have explicit subsidization policies for its steel industry, relying instead on indirect subsidization via special tax credits, relaxed regulatory standards, and favorable credit terms (Esser and Fach 1989: 239). These investment tax incentives were the 'private equivalent to the publicly sponsored heavy industry modernization program of the French Plan' (Gillingham 1991: 284).

Italy

Italy's industry was among the least internationally competitive in Europe, though the high cost of transporting German, Belgian, or French steel provided a buffer for Italian firms. Italy grew its steel industry in the 1950s through a combination of heavy public sector investment, tariffs, subsidization of scrap inputs, and increased concentration of ownership to create economies of scale (Villa 1986: 169; Kipping, Ruggero, and Dankers 2001). The legal authority for these policies was negotiated as part of the ECSC negotiations, where Italy and Belgium won the right to maintain protection during a five-year transition period (Milward 1984: 408). Italy's exceptions to ECSC rules continued, however, past the five-year transition period. Italy was thus able to develop its industry rapidly, increasing production from 3 million metric tons in 1951 to 9 million plus tons in 1961, to 12.7 million tons in 1965 (Kipping, Ruggero, and Dankers 2001: 86).

The ECSC

So what were ECSC institutions doing while its rules and provisions were bypassed? In the 1950s, European countries were not focused on exporting steel. Rather, national industries primarily served national markets. This made it easy for the ECSC to eliminate national policies on the books that were blatantly discriminatory (e.g. formal rules setting different taxation rates or prices for national vs. foreign steel, export subsidies, and so on). The HA also monitored markets and worked to increase transparency in transportation and selling prices, requiring that prices be posted. Despite its efforts, discriminatory railroad rates continued providing a hidden subsidy for local producers (Diebold 1959: 1757). Firms also continued to sell their product at prices that differed from the advertised price. The HA also conducted studies and published reports. In a 1954 report the HA admitted that its price transparency efforts were failing as non-compliance with ECSC price policies was more the norm than the exception. Unable to crack down on cheating, the HA instead created the 'Monnet Margin' for prices to deviate up to 2.5 per cent from the published prices. William Diebold saw the policy change as a sign the ECSC was unable to implement its rules (1959: 258); Haas by contrast argued that the Monnet Margin showed the ECSC was flexible (1958: 195, 203). French and Italian steel producers did not like the Monnet Margin, and they challenged it in front of the ECJ, which declared the Monnet Margin illegal (Scheingold 1965: 54–70). Indeed many contentious HA decisions were challenged by firms and states, ending up as cases heard by the ECJ, creating an irony—the only actor truly being held to ECSC rules was the HA.

Why were the ECSC policies not enforced? First, as an empirical reality, the problems the ECSC was created to solve quickly disappeared on their own. The 1950s was a buyer's market for steel; supply was not critically scarce. Access to German coking coal—France's main economic motivation for establishing the ECSC—did not prove to be important because technological advances reduced transport costs, and American coking coal became abundant and cheap (Gillingham 1991: 188, 230, 357). While German industry remained cartelized, and implicitly subsidized through cozy relationships with banks (Zysman 1983; Katzenstein 1987), German industry was in no position to dominate the European market. Second, the ECSC was not set up to deal with government policies that created the main sources of market distortions—exchange rate policy, national regulatory rules, and government's low-interest loans to industry. Finally, there was simply no real interest in creating market competition. As long as national policies did not create negative externalities that flowed across borders, member states saw no role for ECSC institutions in facilitating market adjustments.

The political momentum created by the early ECSC was far different than what Monnet had expected. In 1954, France rejected treaties aimed at creating a European Political Community and a European Defense Community, refusing to accept greater supranationalism. The model of technical functional integration was also rejected when proposals for a transport community and an atomic energy union were refused (Moravcsik 1998: ch. 2). Instead, states agreed to build a broader EEC. EEC institutions were weaker than their ECSC counterparts. For example, where the ECSC allowed the HA to create fines for non-compliance, and withhold transfer payments to non-complying states and firms, the Treaty of Rome only allowed the Commission to raise infringement suits, which could lead to a toothless ECJ declaration that a 'member state had failed to fulfill its obligation'. Chapter 6 identifies a number of options available to member states had they wanted stronger enforcement mechanisms for the common market. That they chose none of the options was no accident. Member states wanted for the EEC less, not more, supranationalism than they had in the ECSC.

1959–74—National management of industrial modernization

In 1959, the European steel sector entered recession and the European coal sector experienced a severe crisis of oversupply and falling world prices. The HA asked member states to declare a 'manifest crisis' for the coal industry. Belgium, Luxembourg, and the Netherlands wanted ECSC help in dealing with the coal crisis, but Germany, France, and Italy refused to authorize the HA action plan. They agreed to aid measures for Belgium but argued that national governments, rather than supranational actors, should determine the best way to deal with the crisis.[4] Their veto, issued just at the time of publication of Ernst Haas' *The Uniting of Europe,* in some ways was the death knell for the ECSC. The HA could not enforce ECSC rules, nor adjust them, nor could it make itself useful when a European-wide crisis erupted.

In the 1960s, Europe faced more challenges—a continued oversupply of coal, then iron ore, then steel followed by the rise of foreign competition in raw inputs and in steel outputs. At the same time as international competition increased, car firms switched to thinner sheet steel, and concrete construction began using less iron.[5] The ECSC was created for robust demand combined with scarce supply, not falling demand. Member states refused to adapt ECSC institutions to the changing market realities. In the face of a proposal to merge the three

---

[4] 'La France, l'Allemagne et l'Italie repoussent définitivement le plan de la Haute Autorité' *Le Monde* 4,451 (16 May 1959) 1. Available at <http://www.ena.lu/mce.swf?doc=914andIg=2>.

[5] 'L'acier casse l'Europe' *L'Express* 799 (10 October 1996) 62–4. Available at <http://www.ena.lu/steel_splits_europe_express_10_october_1966–020200699.html>.

EEC Treaties (the Common Market, EURATOM, and ECSC treaties), the HA published a document, informally known as 'the last will and testament of the ECSC'.[6] Member states responded by declaring the importance of the ECSC, yet refusing to work with the HA to address challenges in the steel industry. Each of the large countries had their own reasons for rejecting a supranational approach. De Gaulle opposed supranational solutions in principle, claiming a preference for different plans for each country. Germany did not want a move toward a centrally controlled economy. Benelux and Italy disagreed about the specific policies and tools the HA recommended, in part because their market competitiveness differed.

France

Despite investments in modernization, French firms entered the European recession uncompetitive compared to their European neighbors. For example, in 1966, French firms took 16.4 hours to produce a ton of steel, but Germany only needed 12.7 hours and Italy 10.0 hours (Daley 1996: 61). Among the sources of French inefficiency were a failure to specialize, a refusal to close plants using outdated technology, combined with an unwillingness to invest in new technologies (Daley 1996: 61–3). Market forces might have forced rapid economic rationalization, but with a growing desire to protect jobs, the French government instead poured more resources into its industry. It kept uncompetitive firms alive with state subsidies or loans; meanwhile it encouraged modest consolidation and rationalization in the industry by orchestrating mergers that closed some uncompetitive production while injecting investment funds into 'national champions' using the latest production technologies (Howell et al. 1988).

Germany

The German government generally let the coal and steel industries, in consultation with German banks, work out difficulties they encountered. Government subsidies to industry were fairly low from 1960 to 1970, at least relative to others, such as Italy (Harris 1983: 179). The exception to this rule was the German government's rescue of the ailing Krupp firm in 1967.[7] German firms rode out economic upheaval through 'market coordination', which resembled cartel policy-making. Banks would lend to steel industries in times of crisis, and firms signed multi-year arrangements where they agreed to share rather than compete for the market. German firms regularly agreed to reduce or postpone production in return for other firms agreeing to buy from them or withhold production in the future (Shoenfield 1969: 256–7).

---

[6] Ibid.

[7] The German federal government provided a loan of DM 400 million and the Saar government gave a loan of DM 150 million to Krupp which agreed, in return, to transform itself from a private empire into a limited liability company. See Esser and Fach (1989).

Italy

Italy lacked domestic sources of raw inputs for steel, and thus large integrated steel firms. Firms in the north focused on electric furnace technology, creating small 'mini-mills' that specialized in the production of simple products for local and regional usage.[8] Mini-mills flourished at the same time integrated steel suffered, because they focused on the most profitable needs of local consumers (Barnett and Crandall 1986: chs 1 and 2). But consumption demand outstripped supply of steel in Italy in the 1960s (Villa 1986: 169). Italy could, of course, have relied on the international market for this supply. Indeed with a fall in transportation prices, it would have been cheaper for Italy simply to import the products it needed. But with a national demand unmet, the Italian government opted for a more interventionist investment strategy that created jobs and economic growth in the Christian Democrats' political stronghold—the Mezzogiorno South.[9] This decision created an economic liability Italians would be saddled with for the next thirty years (Brusoni and Orsenigo 1997).

The ECSC

If all countries were pursuing their own policies, what was the ECSC doing? The HA developed recommendations to deal with the crisis, but most of its efforts were rejected by member states.[10] It could find support for small, isolated projects. For example in the 1970s, the ECSC helped address a lack of iron ore by helping build private harbors for imports.[11] The HA also found some funds to grant modernization loans, and it created a system of welfare guarantees for workers who lost their jobs.[12] Its studies on the labor market provided information for unions to use to support their case for retraining programs, worker compensation, and improved worker conditions (Collins 1975: 100–7). According to Gilbert Mathieu, the HA's policies did not affect industrial development, but its coordination (and, one might add, blind eye) arguably made it easier for each

---

[8] There are three types of steelmaking plants: basic oxygen systems, open-hearth furnaces, and electric furnaces. The first two types are located close to raw materials, and employed by integrated steel plants that produce a great variety of steel products (Barnett and Crandall 2002; Villa 1986). Germany and France had raw inputs sources, and in the 1950s and 1960s focused on creating and innovating around the technology used in integrated plants. Italy did not have raw inputs, thus small northern producers innovated mini-mill technology in the 1960s. Between 1959 and 1970, mini-mill production grew in northern Italy by a factor of five (Kipping, Ruggero, and Dankers 2001).

[9] In the 1960s a new steel plant was built in Taranto, owned by Finsider which was 99.82 per cent owned by the state holding company IRI (Istituto per la Ricostruzione Industriale) (Howell et al. 1988).

[10] 'La Haute Autorité de la CECA explore toutes les possibilités du traité pour surmonter la crise' (November 1966) 11/10 *Communauté Européenne* 6.

[11] Based on interviews with the Deputy Head of the Commission Unit for steel, non-ferrous metals and other materials in the 1970s, 7 September 2004, Brussels.

[12] Op. cit. note 10.

country to obtain supplies when short, while avoiding cutbacks during periods of oversupply (Mathieu 1970).

Beyond these specific policies, the ECSC played two roles in this period. First, from 1953 to 1963 ECSC institutions (mainly the ECJ) provided a forum for actors to challenge policies in other countries that harmed them. In a number of cases, firms or governments of one country were challenging policies that conferred competitive advantages on firms in another country.[13]

Second, the ECSC was the external voice of European countries in negotiations over dumping steel. In the 1960s, declining transportation rates and the rise of new production technologies created problems for all traditional producers of steel (Warren 1975). Responding to the economic distress of US steel producers, the United States (US) pressured Europe and Japan voluntarily to restrain their exports of steel to the US. The US negotiated this agreement with the EEC; presumably member states agreed to common representation to avoid a US retaliation that might affect them all (McClenahan 1991).

This period ended with a boom phase (1968–74)—rising prices, rising consumption, extensive expansion plans, and bright horizons for the industry. Countries could well imagine that their intervention had contributed to the recovery. Buoyed by optimistic market projections in the 1970s, national governments redoubled their efforts to invest in and modernize their steel industries, contributing to a vast overproduction and the crisis of the 1970s.

1974–86—The HA (now the Commission) Gets Support for Market Coordination

The international iron and steel industry faced a worldwide crisis starting in 1974, triggered by the rising price of energy, decreased world consumption of steel, and worldwide overcapacity as developing countries created their own steel industries and began exporting cheap steel. Oversupply created a collective problem for European countries, which was exacerbated when the UK joined the EEC in 1973. Firms wanted to protect jobs, and the incremental cost of producing steel was such that firms had an incentive to keep producing even though it contributed further to the collapse in the price for steel. In the first year of the crisis,

---

[13] German steel producers engaged in a five-year legal battle against Italy for the latter's failure to publish trucking rates—a policy which benefited Italian producers at the expense of German ones (Scheingold 1965: ch. 8). The Dutch Coal Association successfully challenged the German 'miners' bonus' in 1956, which conferred a considerable competitive advantage on this industry relative to others. Still, even after the ECJ ruled the subsidy illegal in 1961, it took years of prodding from the HA before Germany finally repealed the policy in 1964. See Scheingold (1965). The stream of coal and steel cases pretty much dried up in the 1960s. The ECJ heard 226 coal and steel cases from 1953 to 1963, and an average of 31 cases per year from 1958 to 1963. The ECJ averaged 5.5 ECSC cases from 1964 to 1969, perhaps because the HA was not making much policy worth contesting. See Scheingold (1971).

internal EU steel prices fell by 40 per cent and export prices dropped 50 per cent (Tsoukalis and Strauss 1985: 212).

A number of European countries wanted to follow the US approach to over-supply: setting minimum prices combined with quotas to avoid firms overproducing. Germany opposed strong market intervention, so the ECSC's 1976 'Spinelli approach' mainly monitored the market, with the expectation that the crisis was merely a cyclical adjustment (Tsoukalis and Strauss 1985: 215). Needing a stronger policy, the 1976–77 'Simonet Plan' included regional aids, protection against third countries, and recommended steel prices (Daley 1996: 149; Tsoukalis and Strauss 1987: 199–201).

To help reach price targets, a European Confederation of Iron and Steel Industries, EUROFER, was created in 1976. Working through EUROFER was voluntary, but to create a real power for EUROFER the Commission agreed only to bargain and distribute production quotas via negotiations with EUROFER.[14]

As reality set in that the steel market would not recover to pre-1974 consumption levels (let alone consumption growth), member states came to support a communal approach to deal with oversupply of steel in Europe and the world. EC Minister Davignon's 1977 Plan marked a new era for the ECSC: the steel industry became actively managed at the Community level and the Commission for the first time became a 'relevant actor' from the perspective of national firms and policy-makers (Grunert 1987: 233–4).

Davignon's first plan created common external trade barriers; required detailed production, employment, and delivery forecasts from firms; set minimum prices and production quotas; and granted aid on the condition it was coupled with capacity reductions. These efforts were only partially successful. Competitive firms in the Bresciani region of Italy, as well as some French and German firms, refused to follow the restrictions, creating 'rebates' and 'accidentally' delivering more steel than was requested (Jones 1979: 50–1).[15] While national governments voiced support for European policy-making, they continued to bail out their industries, in the hope that the market would recover. In 1980, the US accused European firms of 'dumping' steel, causing a decline in exports to the US at the same time that auto companies further reduced the amount of steel in their products to obtain fuel efficiencies. These two events led the European market into another price war (Howell et al. 1988: 80), which prompted the Commission to ask the Council to declare a 'manifest crisis'.

The 1981 vote declaring a manifest crisis led to the second Davignon plan, and the creation of EUROFER II. From a legal standpoint, a manifest crisis authorized the adoption of extensive measures, such as mandatory production quotas covering about 80 per cent of all steel products and regulations regarding

---

[14] Based on an interview with the director of the European Steel Association (EUROFER), 7 September 2004, Brussels.
[15] The Commission fined about 20 firms in 1978–79 for infringing on price rules.

subsidies (Grunert 1987: 235). The resurrection of cartels as a major component of the Davignon strategy shows how far the ECSC strayed from the hopes of Monnet, for whom eliminating cartels was a chief aim (Gillingham 1991: 232; Duchene 1994: 213).

From a political standpoint, it is not clear what changed with the declaration of a manifest crisis. Compliance with ECSC rules regarding prices, quotas, and subsidies remained problematic because national governments contin-ued to rescue their own industries. According to Kent Jones, only a market readjustment, raising input prices so that firms' profit-maximizing price fell in line with ECSC rules, ended the cheating regarding European price policies (Jones 1986: 127–8). Indeed it is quite telling that in a general book on 'Steel and the State', the chapter on 'The European Community' spends 48 pages talking about European-level policies and then 80 pages describing the steel policies of the member states that are basically unrelated to ECSC policy. For example, the ECSC, under German pressure, created rules limiting subsidies at the same time as the French nationalized their industry so as to bail it out, and the Italians poured aid into its firms owned by the state holding company IRI (Howell et al. 1988).

The crisis did not per se make a growing Commission role inevitable. The HA's request that the Council declare a manifest crisis for coal in 1958, its numerous policy suggestions in the 1960s, and even the French request for such a declar-ation in 1975 had been rejected despite having the support of different member states at different times. Declaring a manifest crisis was easier in 1981 for a few reasons.

First, it had become clear that demand for steel would not recover to its pre-1974 levels both because consumption patterns had changed and because developing countries could now compete in the international marketplace. With this realization came a common diagnosis of the problem and agree-ment about what was needed to deal with the crisis. All agreed that European production of steel needed to be permanently reduced, and integrated steel pro-duction—being no longer economically profitable—was where reductions had to occur (Tsoukalis and Strauss 1985; Grunert 1987; Daley 1996: 148; Dudley and Richardson 1999: 245).

Second, the duration of the crisis meant that governments had a chance to attempt to solve the problem on their own. National policies from 1976 to 1981 were both expensive and ineffective. Governments were frustrated that firms continually undermined their efforts through continued production. With little good news to claim credit for, European governments became more willing to turn the problem over to the European level, which allowed national politicians to pin the blame for the pain inflicted on unelected EEC officials (Tsoukalis and Strauss 1985, 1987).

Third, an international politics of steel had emerged. Falling transportation prices had created a competitive international market in steel for the first time in the late 1960s. When supply outstripped demand in Europe, European firms had looked for international outlets for their goods. They faced strong rebukes from countries that charged European countries with dumping products on their markets. The political bargaining regarding dumping and countervailing duties took place in the context of the General Agreement on Tariffs and Trade (GATT). Within GATT, the European Economic Community (EEC) was treated as a regional organization, which provided EEC states with beneficial exemptions. Its status as a regional organization also put the EEC on the potential receiving end of collective dumping and countervailing duty charges. Within the GATT, the Commission continued its role begun in the 1960s as the interlocutor in negotiations with foreign governments—a role which dovetailed with the general trend to grant trade negotiation authority to the Commission in this period (Meunier and Nicolaidis 1999; Meunier 2003).

Fourth, there was a sunset clause of the ECSC Treaty that was not too far off. As long as the ECSC Treaty was not extended beyond its original 50 years, states could grant the Commission extraordinary powers without being concerned that the Commission would continue to erode member state authority. In yet another irony, it was not the promised effectiveness of the ECSC's supranational institutions that led to their usage, but nearly the opposite—the fact that the Commission could not be as powerful in the future—that facilitated the granting of extraordinary powers to the Commission.

Europe used its massive intervention in the 1980s to shut down its integrated steel plants, restructure local economies, and develop mini-mill capacity to produce highly specialized steel products. The interventionist policies continued until 1986, and a bit longer in member states that joined the EEC in the mid-1980s. The bailout was stated as the last and final major subsidy to the industry, and was coupled with privatization policies that allowed governments to extricate themselves from direct involvement in steel production.[16]

1987–94—Downsizing the European effort

By the 1980s, the ECSC's intervention had finally achieved some of the goals Haas had identified in 1958. There were true EEC-level peak associations representing industry and workers, with real power to negotiate with the Commission to set price and output targets. There were coal- and steel-related labor policies that improved the welfare of workers (Collins 1975: 100–7). Finally, there was momentum behind the ECSC, and coincidentally behind the integration endeavor more generally. Thus, at the conclusion of the crisis, many observers expected the demand for ECSC intervention to continue and for the experience of collective industrial management to spur on supranationalism and European

---

[16] Based on interviews with the deputy head of the Commission Unit for steel, non-ferrous metals, and other materials in the 1970s, 7 September 2004, Brussels.

integration (Grunert 1987; Mény and Wright 1987: 91). But this episode did not foment more of the same. Schuman's expected 'fusion of interests' and Haas' expected 'shifting of loyalties' never materialized despite clear government support for ECSC policies.

When steel once again went into recession in the early 1990s, firms in Italy, Spain, Portugal, and eastern Germany demanded Commission intervention. They were not ECSC converts as much as they were, as always, wanting state support. This time, however, states refused to empower European institutions to act. In the 1980s, Germany had been alone in its opposition to the Davignon Plan's heavy market intervention.[17] But Margaret Thatcher had assumed power in the United Kindgom, and Francois Mitterrand had embraced the market in France, providing Helmut Kohl with political allies. With neo-liberal free market ideas in ascent, advocates of free markets, who viewed the supranational interventions associated with the Treaty of Paris as a thing of the past, became dominant in both the Commission and most national governments (Dudley and Richardson 1999). Thus in this crisis the coalition favoring free markets was able to prevail over advocates of supranational interventionism.

In March 1991, the Commission declared that the ECSC would end on schedule in 2002, and the coal and steel sector would be absorbed into the EEC (Groenendijk and Gert 2002). National governments gladly assented as they were tired of supporting steel and were looking for a way out of their expensive subsidization policy.[18] By 1994, the ECSC ceased granting loans to industry for investment. By the time the Treaty of Paris reached its 50-year end, little subsisted of it anyway. Its competition policy and external representation in international negotiations were fully absorbed into the Common Market structure. Because it no longer gave industry any loans, the ECSC's remaining financial mechanisms were generating funds that were disbursed for research and development, and objectives distantly related to coal and steel. The ECSC disappeared, largely without notice, as member states focused on the monetary union, enlargement, and their many other policy concerns.

III. What Role Did the ECSC Play in Postwar European Politics?

Assessing the role of the ECSC in European integration is challenging. Ernst Haas noted an increasing interpenetration of coal and steel imports as evidence

---

[17] Germany alone had opposed compulsory production quotas in 1981. It withdrew opposition in exchange for a policy on phasing out state aids to steel. See Tsoukalis and Strauss (1985).

[18] Based on interviews with the deputy head of Unit in Trade Defense instruments, and a member of the Commission's DG Enterprise, who was involved with the EC's steel policy in the 1980s, 7 September 2004, Brussels.

that a common market existed (1958: 63). But writing on the history of the ECSC up until 1958, William Diebold found little evidence that the ECSC per se changed either the pattern of production or the pattern of European trade in coal and steel (1959: 590). Writing on the same topic 30 years later John Gillingham agreed:

[The ECSC] neither reformed prevailing business practices, produced a new relationship between public authority and private power, nor shifted the locus of economic policy, even as regards heavy industry, from national state to supranational agency. The economic impact of the community was slight. Few of its policies had demonstrable effect. (Gillingham 1991: 300)

Even after the heavy intervention of the Commission in the 1980s, it is hard to say that the ECSC has left a stamp on the face of the European steel industry that would not exist otherwise. Thus asking the counterfactual question of 'how would EU steel industries look different were there no ECSC' does not reveal a significant institutional imprint.

One can identify several ways in which the ECSC experience mattered. The prime purpose of the ECSC was to assure European countries that Germany would not again become an abusive dominant force on the continent. While there were many factors contributing to Germany's postwar industrial and political policies, the assurance the ECSC provided remained politically important. John Gillingham points out that despite the many failings of the ECSC, the 'Schuman Plan . . . ended the competitive bids for heavy industry domination that had wrecked every previous large-scale attempt to reorganize the Continent since 1918, led to *Westintegration* and Franco-German partnership, and resulted in the creation of a new entity, Europe' (Gillingham 1991: 364).

Foundational elements of the ECSC's institutional blueprint also endured. The Treaty of Paris became the 'boiler plate' text in negotiations for the common market. While subsequent agreements tended to strip away elements of the supranational bodies' powers, features of European coal and steel integration endured. For example, the ECJ's preliminary ruling mechanism was transferred wholesale from the ECSC to the European legal system (Pescatore 1981), a transfer that proved extremely important in the development of the EU (see Chapter 5). The legacy of HA failure was also a potential benefit. The ECSC showed that the Council of Ministers could control the HA (now Commission), and that rules would only be enforced to the extent countries wanted them enforced.

The ECSC did become a venue in which policies toward steel were discussed and sometimes implemented. But the ECSC remained throughout its entire history a framework of convenience, to be used when there was a coalition of support for collective responses and ignored when the support faded. Indeed weaving the ECSC into the story of European integration more generally reveals 'critical disjunctures'. The drive to deepen integration signaled by the ratification of the Treaty of Rome was coupled with a decision not to grant the HA's wish to declare a manifest crisis to deal with the coal crisis of 1958. The agreement to declare a manifest crisis in 1981 came well before the Common Market was relaunched, and by the time the SEA was going forward, support for significant ECSC intervention in the economy had evaporated. These couplings represent a shifting over time in the taste for market forces versus government intervention, not for more or less integration. They also reveal that the coalitions of support for integration were not that deep; there was no constituency for integration per se, just a constituency for or against specific policies. These disjunctures may also have been politically significant. The HA's willingness to step back, and look the other way when states did not want intervention may have provided assurance that made further integration more palatable.

The history of the ECSC teaches us two main lessons. First, the actual history of the ECSC highlights the role of external forces in promoting European cooperation. The impetus for the ECSC was internal to European politics. If not for the larger geopolitical concern about German dominance, it is doubtful that states would have been negotiating about the details of a common market in coal and steel. Once the threat of German dominance in coal and steel was gone, there was no impetus to integrate. Firms were quite happy to segment European markets to avoid competition, and European governments were happy to protect and subsidize national production. The HA only came to play its supranational role in response to externally imposed challenges. When the United States wanted a partner to coordinate with to avoid 'dumping' by European firms in its market, the HA assumed its foreign affairs role. When global oversupply created a need to coordinate production and close segments of the industry, the ECSC again played a role. Thus the actual history of the ECSC followed a 'second image reversed' process, where the realization of the ECSC's political structure and policies were caused by forces emerging from the international political economy of the steel sector (Gourevitch 1978).

Second, the existence of multilateral mechanisms cannot be taken as evidence for multilateral politics. Today the active and powerful role of the ECJ in European politics has led many scholars to suggest that European culture and position in the world leads Europeans to like international law and international approaches that Americans do not (Kagan 2002; Rubenfeld 2003). In this light, it is interesting to note the HA did not set European steel policy, nor did the ECJ serve as force of integration. In other words, in a collective polity of liberal democratic European states, with common rules and powerful supranational institutions, law and legal institutions were not an integrating political force. The ECSC's legal and political history suggests that there is nothing uniquely 'European' about the international rule of law working—when it suits them, European countries are quite capable of ignoring common rules, avoiding legal mechanisms, pursuing national interests, and maintaining a reality that is quite distant from what exists on paper.

4

Jurist Advocacy Movements in Europe: The Role of Euro-Law Associations in European Integration (1953–1975) (2009)

It is well established that the European Court of Justice transformed the original European Community legal system through the creation of revolutionary legal doctrines turning the Treaty of Rome into a constitution for Europe, and that this transformation created the bases for the ECJ's expanded political role in European politics (see Chapter 5). This paper challenges previous accounts of this early period of European legal integration, situating individual entrepreneurs and far-reaching ECJ decisions into the social context of the times—namely the organized and activist Euro-law associations. The activities of Euro-law associations are known among European law scholars, though seldom written about.[1] Ignoring the role of legal associations served a purpose. Especially while the ECJ was seeking to establish its authority, revealing the extensive coordination that gave rise to the ECJ's early legal successes could have implied conspiracy potentially undermining the effort to portray support for an active European court as spontaneously spreading. But given that the ECJ is often seen as a model to follow (or avoid), it is important to understand how the ECJ orchestrated its legal revolution. Thus we must add back in the role of Euro-law associations.

Section I of this chapter documents the activities of Euro-law associations, formally constituted member organizations that planned activities related to European law. Section II explains how the activities of Euro-law associations contributed to European legal integration, invoking Bourdieu's framework of the politics of legal fields (Bourdieu 1987). Both Bourdieusian and neo-functionalist accounts stress how the promoters of European legal integration drew on law's capital—they justified their cases and the ECJ's rulings using legal argumentation so as to envelop their political agenda in law's putative neutrality and accepted authority (Burley and Mattli 1993; Weiler 1991). But neo-functionalist theory offers an essentially liberal story in which integration

---

[1] Hjalte Rasmussen already in 1986 discussed the cozy relationship between the ECJ and legal scholars (Rasmussen 1986: 265–7).

succeeds by playing to the self-interest of individuals. Walter Mattli paraphrased Haas idea:

> The 'good Europeans' are not the main creators of the … community. The process of community formation is dominated by nationally constituted groups with specific interests and aims, willing and able to adjust their aspirations by turning to supranational means when the course appears profitable … the groups driving the process of integration are rational maximizers of their narrow self interest; they hail from the word of business, politics and science and their actions or beliefs need not be infused with pan-regional ideology or commitment. Deeper integration is the intended as well as unintended consequence of their self-serving actions. (Mattli 2005: 330–1)

The liberal narrative suggests that merely transplanting European style legal institutions will spur legal integration because at least some set of self-interested actors will benefit from legal integration and be likely to exploit the opportunities international litigation offers (Stone Sweet 1999).

The Bourdieusian approach of examining politics within legal fields considers jurists to be self-interested in that lawyers, judges, and legal scholars are jockeying to advance the position of law so as to increase their own power and influence. It is not, however, a liberal vision in that actors are not atomized 'rational maximers of their narrow self-interest'. Instead, Bourdieusian approaches investigate the social backgrounds of and connections between legal actors, assuming that larger group interests guide the political behavior of individuals and expecting the 'capital' of actors—e.g. their power bases—to be key to whether or not they achieve their objectives. Because politics in the legal field is characterized by contestation—clashing interests and objectives, which generate actions and counter-reactions—political outcomes are constructed, contingent on the balance of interests and power among actors, and thereby subject to change when the balance changes.

Part II shows how Euro-law associations coordinated the actions of individuals to propel legal integration in a constitutional direction, identifying four contributions of Euro-law associations. The community that Euro-law associations fostered coordinated and encouraged individual actions. The success of Euro-law associations, however, was in large part a result of the political capital of association members. Inspired by the meetings, members of associations used their offices to help the European legal integration project—lawyers found test cases; judges promoted European arguments before national courts and referred cases to the ECJ; professors wrote supportive arguments, planned conferences and imparted ECJ doctrine to the next generation of academics and practioners. The core members of the jurist movement were more ideologically driven than self-interested, inspired by the larger historical idea of overcoming war and enmity via European integration. In their view, a Europe united under a rule of law provided 'the most reliable and durable way to establish a harmonious political union' where the preponderance of larger European powers could be managed

(Madsen and Vauchez 2005: 19). This larger agenda, rather than narrow self-interest, unified members and spurred them to action.

Part III imagines legal integration absent the support of an organized jurist movement by examining the ECJ's clone, the Andean Community Tribunal of Justice (ATJ). In 1984 Andean countries created the ATJ, modeled explicitly on the ECJ. The ATJ is now the third most active international court in existence, having issued over 1,400 rulings to date. Yet outside of the issue of intellectual property law, an island of effective international adjudication that I explore in another co-authored paper (Helfer, Alter, and Guerzovich 2009), the Andean Tribunal has not transformed national legal systems or Andean politics. Indeed the ATJ and its doctrine are largely unknown. This brief section explores how the absence of a jurist advocacy movement combined with the weakness of national legal fields impedes the ATJ from developing bold legal doctrines and limits Andean law from penetrating national systems.

Part IV concludes by considering what the European experience suggests more broadly about the importance of jurist advocacy movements for transnational law. The European and Andean cases together suggest that jurist advocacy movements need to do more than disseminate information about legal best practices. They also suggest that neither the prospect of advancing narrow self-interests nor of collective functional gains provide enough of an incentive if individuals are to act iconoclastically. Legal movements need a combination of ideology and affiliation with political power to succeed.

I. Founding National Euro-Law Associations and the Fédération Internationale de Droit Européen (FIDE)—1952–1975

The founding of the European Community in 1958 provided an impetus to organize pro-integration lawyers into national associations dedicated to the study and promotion of European Community law. Euro-law associations, including the *Wissentschaftliche Gesellschaft für Europarecht, Association Belge pour le Droit Européen, Association Française des Juristes Européens, Associazione Italian dei Giuristi Europei, Association Luxembourgeois des Juristes Européens, Nederlandse Vereniging voor Europees Recht,* formed in each European Community member state in the 1950s up through 1961. According to the founders, the nearly simultaneous emergence was not directly coordinated, but it was a natural outgrowth of practices within national legal communities where diplomat-jurisconsults in the 1940s and 1950s had been actively involved in national and international political and legal developments (Madsen and Vauchez 2005). Indeed the Mouvement Européen had always seen law as an integral part of European integration.[2]

---

[2] The Mouvement Européen, a group of activists seeking European integration, had in 1952 established a Comité des Juristes. In the 1950s a separate Comité des Juristes, a transnational group

Euro-law associations served as gathering grounds for jurists (lawyers, legal scholars, and governmental actors with legal backgrounds) interested in the European integration project. Euro-law associations included politically connected and well-placed individuals. For example, the *Association Française des Juristes Européens* (AJE) was founded in 1953, by 'gentlemen-politicians of law' including Pierre-Henri Teitigen and Maurice Roland (Sacriste and Vauchez 2007: 91). Teitigen was, among other things, a government minister in the immediate postwar period, and a deputy and then head of the centrist French Mouvement Républicain Populaire (MRP), which captured a quarter of the French vote in the immediate postwar period. He was part of the French delegation to the Comité des Juristes, and rapporteur for the Committee on Legal and Administrative Questions in the negotiations for the Council of Europe (Madsen 2007: 141). Roland was a high magistrate at the Cour de Cassation. The German association the *Wissentschaftliche Gesellschaft für Europarecht* (WGE) was founded in 1961 by academics including Hans-Peter Ipsen, Gert Nicolaison, and Ernst Steindorff. Ipsen, a lifelong academic, was the intellectual father of European law in Germany. The leadership included Reimer Schmidt (an academic and early author on European legal issues), lawyers Bodo Börner and C. F. Ophüls (the latter was an advisor to Konrad Adenauer and Walter Hallstein, and he had participated in negotiations regarding the Treaty of Rome), and Walter Roemer from the Federal Ministry of Justice (Ipsen 1990: 335).[3] Employees of European institutions (the Court of Justice, the Commission, and its Legal Secretariat) were implicit and at times explicit members of national Euro-law associations. For example, Walter Hallstein (President of the European Commission), Otto Riese (a Former German Supreme Court judge and ECJ judge from 1959 to 1964) were members of the WGE (Davies 2007: 54) Many ties held this emerging European legal field together—members had been active in the resistance, worked together in national government ministries, participated in the construction of the legal order for the Council of Europe, and participated in drafting the United Nations Charter, the Council of Europe, and the European Coal and Steel Community. A common commitment to the larger objective of European integration, under a rule of law, provided an ideological cohesion to the group (Madsen and Vauchez 2005: 17–23).

Forming an organization dedicated to a particular legal topic (e.g. European Community law) was hardly novel. According to Hans-Jürgen Rabe, an early member of the WGE and later its secretary, in Europe it is quite

---

of lawyers (scholars, practioners, and government officials), was charged with helping to write and advise negotiation of a European constitution based in law, protected by legal institutions (Friedrich 1954: xxvi). Members of these early committees later joined or helped found national Euro-law associations.

[3] Antoine Vauchez and Antonin Cohen have been documenting the political background of Europe's early legal pioneers. See their work in the bibliography, and check for ongoing publications for more information.

common to establish associations when there is a new area of law.[4] Indeed the WGE was founded as a working group of the pre-existing Gesellschaft für Rechtsvergleichung. Associations helped lawyers learn about legal developments so that they could better advise their clients, and they helped judges learn about legal developments within other parts of the judiciary. It is also quite normal for practioners to have seminars on new areas of law, to write briefs for legal journals, and to be consumers of journals that published rulings and notes regarding developing law. Thus in some respects the activities undertaken by Euro-law associations were within the normal range for the European legal profession.

But Euro-law associations had a specific political objective of promoting the larger European project of integration (which included the human rights work of the Council of Europe). The new Euro-law associations actively sought to wrest the topic of European law from specialists in coal and steel law and from international law experts whose traditional doctrines about the relationship between national and international rules were too limited given the aspirations of association leaders (Davies 2007: 50–69). These larger objectives of associations were explicit. The French AJE's stated goal was to 'help those outside of the organization understand the necessity of creating Europe and to identify the role jurists can and must play in the creation of a United Europe.'[5] ECJ judges also spoke clearly about the role of judges in building European legal integration (Donner 1968; Lecourt 1964; Mancini 1989; Pescatore 1983). The common objectives united the members into a largely homogenous 'policy community' all working in the same direction (Schepel and Wesseling 1997). One participant summarized the environment as follows:

in Europe around 1950 the idea of European unification was capable of evoking almost religious enthusiasm among young lawyers. We believed in the United State of Europe. Hardly anybody had any doubts about the possibility of achieving this aim within a few years. The reality turned out to be very different indeed.

Yet, in spite of this state of affairs, the vast majority of West German teachers of 'European Law' remained faithful to this ideal of their youth and passed on this ideology to their assistants, who now hold their chairs of 'European Law'. (Seidl-Hohenveldern 1984: 282–3).

Euro-law associations were immediately successful in organizational terms. The WGE reached 200 to 300 members by the early 1960s, with a core membership of 30–40 practioners including academics, in-house lawyers for large corporations, members of European and national governmental institutions, and interested professionals. According to the WGE's Secretary Hans-Jürgen Rabe, within this 'core group' there was intense contact with the eight German lawyers of the

[4] Interview with Dr Hans-Jürgen Rabe, Secretary of the *Wissentschaftliche Gesellschaft für Europarecht*, Brussels, 11 January 1994.
[5] Reprinted in a 1994 publication about the Association Française des Juristes Européens. On file with the author.

Commission's legal services.[6] In 1963 the AJE had 70 active members, including an Avocat Général of the ECJ and the Secretary of the European Commission on Human Rights (Maurice Lagrange), 34 lawyers, 11 French judges, five members of the Conseil d'État, eight professors of law, the president of the Tribunal de commerce de la Seine, and a variety of well-known individuals from government and the private sector (Vauchez 2007b: note 22).[7] The meetings of the Belgium association also regularly drew 50 participants.[8]

With financial support from the European Commission, organizations were able to host a number of conferences. The WGE, with its scholarly focus, put its energy into planning conferences where issues of European law were debated, and in writing analyses of the law. According to the AJE's President Dr Lise Funck-Bretano, the French association was more distant from academics because 'academics were involved in the teaching in Universities, not in the development of law'. Thus the AJE organized smaller meetings, lunches, and seminars for national lawyers and judges, sometimes meeting within national courts and often bringing in high officials from the European legal system.[9] The European Commission also helped develop the European legal field by establishing the Fédération Internationale de Droit Européen (FIDE), an umbrella organization connecting national associations. FIDE sponsored conferences every two years in the 1960s, providing a means for pro-integration lawyers from different countries (including the United Kingdom) to get to know each other and to coordinate activities.

Hans Peter Ipsen identified 41 scholarly meetings of the WGE, FIDE, and a number of institutes from 1961 to 1973 (Ipsen 1972).· This number does not include the smaller meetings, like those organized by the ATJ, which created a discussion-forum for practioners regarding specific legal topics. Meetings were well attended. According to Hans-Jürgen Rabe, at least throughout the early 1970s everyone who was anyone in European law attended WGE's conferences. Ipsen notes that the 1963 FIDE meeting in the Hague had over 200 participants, including 20 WGE members (Ipsen 1964: 339). H. V. Brinkmann

---

[6] Interview with Hans-Jürgen Rabe, the Secretary of the WGE, 11 January 1994, Brussels. By 1990 the WGE made up 45% of its parent organization the *Gesellschaft für Rechtsvergleichung*, with 516 members, 60% of whom were practitioners and 40% scholars. See Ipsen (1990).

[7] By the 1990s, the head of the Association said it had 300 members, and that between 100 and 250 turned out for its events. Interview with Dr Lise Funck-Brentano, President of the Association des Juristes Européens, 26 May 1994, Paris.

[8] Interview with Michel Gaudet, Director of the Legal Services of the European Commission, 7 July 1994, Brussels.

[9] Interview with Dr Lise Funck-Brentano, President of the Association des Juristes Européens, 26 May 1994, Paris. This distance between practioners and the teaching of European law may be why politicians— Pierre-Henri Teitigen and Walter Hallstein (Former President of the European Commission)—created a separate organization for academics. Teitigen founded the Commission pour l'Etude des Communautés Européennes (1964) and Walter Hallstein the German Arbeitskreis für Europarecht, both academic associations that worked to integrate European law studies into legal education. Interview with Gerard Nafylan, Treasurer of the Commission (CEDEC), 16 May 1994, Paris.

notes that a conference at the Gustav-Stresemann Institute in 1965 had 40 judges, public attorneys, and clerks (Brinkmann 1965).

Euro-law associations were fonts for briefs about European legal developments. For example, within a little more than a year of the ECJ's seminal *Van Gend en Loos* decision, scholars published at least 13 notes in national legal publications discussing the ruling, many if not most of which were written by Euro-law association members.[10] That there were so many legal venues to report in (13 is just the tip of the iceberg) is already a sign of the existing legal infrastructures European law associations could use to their advantage. Association members also wrote reference books about European law that interested lawyers could consult to learn about the European legal system. Members of the WGE started a quarterly series in the most widely read legal journal, the *Neue Juristischen Wochenzeitshrift,* to inform the German bar about European legal developments.[11] They addressed the German Juristentag to inform its members about European law.[12] On occasion, WGE members telephoned judges who issued rulings counter to European law, explaining to them what they should have done. According to Rabe, this was a gentler approach than writing critical commentaries, but they also wrote critical commentaries.[13]

Members of the European Commission's Legal Services helped in these efforts. Michel Gaudet, Director of the Commission's Legal Service from 1958 to 1970, explained that the Legal Services tried to meet with as many lawyers as possible to convince them to use European law. The goal, according to Gaudet, was to get people used to referencing European law and European institutions as part of the normal legal debate.[14] The Commission also sent representatives and developed materials for training meetings on specific legal subject areas, and ECJ

---

[10] *Recueil Sirey* (1963) 29–33 (by Jean Robert, lawyer at the Cour de Paris), *Diritto Internazionale* (1963) No. 3 Part I, 247–8 (by Italo Telchini, legal counsel to the High Authority), *Giustizia Civile* (1963) No. 6 Parte Prima, 1225–31 (by Mario Berri); *Giurspruenza Italiano* (1963) Disp. 4a, Parte IV (by Paolo Gori, attaché to ECJ); *Common Market Law Review* (1963) Vol. 1, 88–92 (by Samkalden); *Der Betrieb* (1963) No. 20, 683–5 (by Andreas Hammann, lawyer*); Juris-Classeur Périodique, La Semaine Juridique* (1963) No. 19 II Jurisprudence No. 13177 (by Fernand-Charles Jeantet, an active private business lawyer, identified at the time as a judge at the Cour d'Appel de Paris); *Le Barreau de France* (1963) No. 147–8, juin–juillet, 25–6 (also by Jeantet); *Rivista di diritto processuale* (1963) No. 4, 651–7 (by Alessandro Migliazza, professor), *Journal des Tribunaux* (1963) No. 4397, 190–2 (by Fr. Rigaux), *Revue générale de droit international public* (1963) No. 2, 421–2 (by Ch. R), *Il Foro Padano* (1963) No. 3 Parte Quinta, 33–42 (by Nicola Catalone, former legal advisor to ECSC, ECJ judge 1958–61) *The International and Comparative Law Quarterly* (1963) Vol. 12, 1411–16 (by Norman Marsh).

[11] The first article explains the intent. See Ophüls (1963). Ipsen also discusses the series in his 25th year retrospective in the journal *Europarecht* (Ipsen 1990).

[12] Ipsen spoke to the Juristentag group in 1964. The 1966 meeting had a section focused on European law. After that, European law was not an explicit theme, though it was frequently in the background of discussions. Only in 1992 was there again an explicit focus on the European legal system. See *Verhandlungen des Neunundfünfzigsten Deutschen Juristentages* (1992).

[13] Interview with Hans-Jürgen Rabe. See citations to legal criticisms in Alter (2001: 80–98).

[14] Interview with Michel Gaudet, Director of the Legal Services of the European Commission, 7 July 1994, Brussels.

Justices and Commission Directors attended meetings, visited national judges, and penned introductions to important works concerning European law, lending the prestige of their office to fledgling publications and to association activities.

With seed money from the Commission, associations founded European law journals including: *Rivista di dirritto europeo* (1961), *Cahiers de droit européen* (1965), *Revue trimestrielle de droit Européen* (1965), *Europarecht* (1966) (Gaudet 1963; Ipsen 1990). The stated goals of these journals was to provide a venue for discussion of European legal issues (including Human Rights law), and to keep practioners abreast of European legal developments. FIDE helped to found the *Common Market Law Review* (1964)—a joint venture of the British Institute of International and Comparative Law and Europa Institute in Leyden. Like its national counterparts, the *Common Market Law Review* had a trans-European editorial board, drawn from national associations and European officials.[15] But it was written in English so as to facilitate Great Britain's accession to the European Community.

Academic association members founded institutes at a number of universities and trained doctoral students who later became active members of associations (indeed Hans-Jürgen Rabe, the long time secretary of the WGE, wrote his thesis under Hans Peter Ipsen). The European Commission helped by providing grants for doctoral students, funding the publication of dissertations, giving subsidies to professors who taught seminars in European law, and funding university meetings where scholars could exchange research and teaching insights. The Commission also financed institutes for European studies, then built associations of institutes, and general associations for the study of the European Community, subsidizing meetings, newsletters, and events held by these groups. It created documentation centers that brought resources and prestige to the universities that were repositories of European documents, and it provided resources so European officials could spend time in national universities.[16] With these and other policies, the Commission helped ensure that nationally based universities had faculty members focused on European issues.

In addition to participating in the activities of associations, European officials undertook their own public relations. Members of European institutions were active writers on European legal issues. Harm Schepel and Rein Weisseling found that 32 per cent of the 1,181 articles published in the *Common Market Law Review*, *Europarecht*, and *Cahiers de Droit Européen* from their founding through 1995 came from people who worked for European institutions—the Commission, the ECJ, and the Tribunal of First Instance—a level of involvement in scholarship

---

[15] Ernst Steindorff, co-founder of WGE, was on the board, as was Nicola Catalano, a former legal advisor for the Coal and Steel Community, and an ECJ judge from 1958 to 1961. Other members included Lord Diplock, H. Drion, W.L. Haardt, G. Van Hecke, Andrew Martin, Jonkheer F. van Panhuys, Jean Robert, and Wilberforce L.J.

[16] Interview with Jaqueline Lastenouse, Director of Academic Affairs, the European Commission, 11 July 1994, Brussels.

that significantly exceeds the norm for public actor participation in legal debates (Schepel and Wesseling 1997: 172–3). With its docket fairly empty in the 1960s, the ECJ used its time to cultivate support within national legal communities. It welcomed every reference from national courts, working with national judges to refine the formulation and substance of questions they sent. Justices regularly participated in scholarly conferences and workshops on European law, and they organized *stages* where their national colleagues could visit the ECJ, to be wined and dined. The ECJ took its show on the road, holding sessions in national capitals to generate news coverage and expose their workings to national audiences. In a somewhat unusual practice, European judges also wrote articles, speeches, and op-eds promoting the idea of lawyers helping to build integration through law (e.g. Donner 1968; Lecourt 1964, 1965; Mancini 1989).

While association members shared a general affinity for the project of European integration, members came from a variety of backgrounds (Vauchez 2007a) and were free thinkers who often disagreed about the means of promoting integration and about specific legal questions. Emil Noel stressed that the Commission encouraged free thinking. Academics and lawyers could not be controlled or indoctrinated, thus it was best to encourage open debate. Ultimately, Noel argued, the influence of European law would come from the persuasiveness of legal arguments, thus European officials were best off developing sound legal opinions.[17]

Written together, these efforts look extensive. But European Community law remained an esoteric topic in the 1960s, and the advocates of European law knew they were fighting an uphill battle. The ECJ's doctrines of the Supremacy and Direct Effect ran counter to established international and national legal doctrines (Donner 1968). Especially if one considers that many early ECJ cases only existed because association members sought out ways to facilitate European legal integration, there were relatively few national court references to the ECJ in the 1960s (75 references from 1960 to 1969). And there were newly issued high court rulings in Italy (1964), France (1964, 1968), and Germany (1967) that directly contradicted the ECJ's doctrine of the day.[18]

---

[17] Interview with Emil Noel, longtime member of the European Commission, 9 June 1994, Paris. According to one website, Noel was employee number 32 of the European Commission, and the right hand man of Walter Hallstein: <http://www.nyulawglobal.org/events/emilenoellecture/EmileNoel.htm>.

[18] *Costa v. Enel and Soc. Edisonvolta*, Italian Constitutional Court Decision 14 of 7 March 1964, [1964] CMLR 425, [1964] I Il Foro It. 87 I 465; *Re Tax on Malt Barley* (Case III 77/63) FG Rhineland-Palatinate decision of 14 November 1963, [1963] EuR 10 130, [1964] 10 CMLR 130. BVerfG decision of 5 July 1967, BVerfG 2 BvR 29/63, [1967] 2 EuR 351, [1967] 27 CMLR 302; *Société des pétroles Shell-Berre et autres, Sociétés 'Les Garages de France', Société Esso-Standard, Société Mobil Oil française, Société française des Pétroles B.P.*, Conseil d'État, decision of 19 June 1964, [1964] Recueil Lebon 344; [1964] 5 RDP 1019, 1991; *SA des Etablissements Petitjean et autres*, Conseil d'État decision of 10 February 1967, [1967] Recueil Lebon 63, [1967] AJDA 267, [1967] RTDE 681; '*Semoules decision' Syndicat General de Fabricants de Semoules de France*, Conseil d'État

Indeed the 1960s the ECJ resembled the mouse that roared.[19] It was a small and rather powerless supranational court, asserting doctrines with constitutional aspirations that challenged entrenched legal practices so as wrest power away from powerful state actors. Associations worked to magnify the mouse's actions, and to seize the topic of European law from the leading international law minds of the day who seemed quite willing to keep European law quite limited in its reach.[20] Their objective was epic, and the resources Euro-law organizations had at their disposal were modest in comparison to the larger budgets funding universities and other political and economic projects in European countries. But compared to jurist movements in other contexts, European actors were well resourced. The immediate organizational success of Euro-law associations in planning events, turning out participants and influencing the legal press—made possible in no small part by funds from the Commission—suggests that there was a constituency of activists eager and able to support the European project. It also suggests that Europe of the 1960s had fairly vibrant national legal fields populated by lawyers and scholars with both the means and practice of participating in transnational legal debates and publishing articles that debated and disseminated legal developments. In many developing country contexts it is hard to imagine that newly established member-organizations could have such a broad and quick presence.

II. The Impact of Euro-Law Advocacy Movements on European Legal Integration

How were Euro-law associations helpful to the larger process of legal integration? The neo-functionalist notion of legal integration is that lawyers, judges, and professors are working on their own or as independent interest groups, promoting their narrow self-interest. In Anne-Marie Burley and Walter Mattli's account of European legal integration, the political system was rigged as a 'one way ratchet.' Since plaintiffs could only ask the ECJ for help enforcing EC rules and the ECJ could only empower itself by obliging such requests, the supranational pursuit of self-interest led ineluctably to the development and penetration into national

---

decision of 1 March 1968, [1968] Recueil Lebon 149, [1970] CMLR 395. These cases are briefly discussed in Alter (1996: 461–6).

[19] *The Mouse that Roared* is a 1955 book by Leonard Wibberley that was made into a film in 1958. In the book and film, the fictional Duchy of Grand Fenwick wages war on the United States expecting to lose in the hopes that the United States will then help it rebuild its economy. Instead, through a series of strange events and coincidences, it captures a nuclear weapon and the great super power capitulates to the tiny country.

[20] Eyal Benvenisti aptly summarizes the reasons why international lawyers have maintained a deferential approach of leaving international law to political actors to interpret (Benvenisti 2008: 245–7).

systems of the European law (Burley and Mattli 1993: 60–5), or in Stone Sweet's terminology, the judicial construction of the rules of international governance (Stone Sweet 1999). Certainly Euro-law associations contained self-interested members, and hoped to mobilize and inspire more self-interested non-ideological actors. But the core association leaders were not themselves such actors, and their goal was not simply to help European rules penetrate national orders. Rather, Euro-law activists wanted to achieve what they had failed to win politically, creating a constitution for Europe (Cohen 2007).

This section shows how Euro-law associations helped define the larger legal field of contestation, making possible the ECJ's constitutionalizing doctrines by creating test cases to facilitate the development of far-reaching European legal doctrine, by acting as the ECJ's and Commission's kitchen cabinet, by spurring individuals to bold action, and by creating an impression of a momentum favoring the ECJ's doctrinal creations. The implication of the argument is that Euro-law associations critically defined what European legal integration became. The counter-factual claim is that without the activities of Euro-law associations, a far more limited type of legal integration would have existed in Europe of the 1960s. Thus I am challenging the notion that there is an automaticity in the international legal process, a sort of invisible hand that channels internationally oriented self-interested litigant and judicial behavior in the political direction of ambitiously expanding the reach and scope of international rules.

1. Creating test cases for the ECJ to use to develop far-reaching legal doctrine

The majority of cases referred to the ECJ in the 1960s concerned the complicated formula for calculating social security benefits for migrant workers and the classification of customs categories. These cases represented how the European legal system was designed to work—national courts would refer to the ECJ technical questions about European Community rules that arose as litigants raised suits involving European law. But these spontaneous cases were not per se helpful in building the ECJ's authority as an important legal and political actor. The references asking far-reaching questions, and thus provoking rulings of doctrinal significance, took orchestration by association members.

The ECJ's constitutionalizing process began with two early rulings, *Van Gend en Loos* (1962) and *Costa v. Enel* (1964), which established the direct effect and supremacy of European law (see Chapter 5). Euro-law associations were key in constituting these rulings. The Dutch legal system offered the most hospitable environment for European law because the 1953 Dutch constitution allowed for the supremacy of international law.[21] Moreover, in Dutch law international rules

---

[21] Fifteen of the first 18 preliminary references to the ECJ came from Dutch courts (Vauchez 2008: note 25).

that are self-executing can be applied by domestic courts (Claes and De Witte 1998: 173–6). In November 1961, the Dutch Euro-law association established a working group to identify which provisions of the Treaty of Rome might be seen as self-executing, which under Dutch law would mean that they would be directly applicable by domestic courts and supreme to conflicting Dutch rules. L. F. D. Ter Keile, a young Dutch lawyer and member of the Dutch Euro-law association, fashioned the test case *Van Gend en Loos* where the Dutch judges queried the ECJ as to whether the European provision in question could create direct effects (Vauchez 2008: 9). The case concerned the reclassification of a customs duty which, according to L. F. D. Ter Keile, had the effect of raising the existing tariff in contravention of the Treaty of Rome. A similar fact pattern would appear twenty years later in the Andean context. The *Van Gend en Loos* reference, which came from a tariff commission, was significant for a few reasons. There was a clear and well-established answer to the legal question at hand—given that the European Treaty provision in question was not addressed to individuals, it should not create direct effects (Claes and De Witte 1998: 176). Referring the question to the ECJ could help legal activists procure a different answer than what a more conservative Dutch judge might on their own give. The reference also suggested that the ECJ had the authority to speak to the effect of European law within national systems, thus providing the ECJ an opportunity to assert a reach for European law that would apply beyond the Netherlands. The ECJ's *Van Gend en Loos* ruling is famous for asserting that some European Treaty articles generate direct effects which individuals can invoke in front of national judges.[22]

For the Dutch system, if European law created direct effects, it was *ipso facto* supreme to conflicting domestic rules. But in other European legal systems, legal primacy went to the last law passed, which meant that even if European law created direct effects, it could be supplanted by national rules passed later in time. The ECJ's *Costa v. Enel* decision spoke to the supremacy of European law over subsequently enacted national laws.[23] The lawyers behind the *Costa v. Enel* case were not pro-integration activists, rather they created the case to challenge what they saw as excessive government intervention in the Italian economy (Vauchez 2008: 17). The lawyers had raised the suit in a small claims court, using a $3 electricity bill as the legal basis to challenge the nationalization of the Italian energy industry. The small claims court also referred the case to the Italian Constitutional Court that ruled first, finding that the case raised no question related to European integration. Nonetheless the ECJ went on to find

---

[22]   Case 26/62, *Van Gend en Loos v. Nederlandse Administratie Belastingen* [1963] ECR 1, [1963] CMLR 105.

[23]   It is not clear if the lawyers—Flaminio Costa and Giangaleazzo Stendari—were members of Euro-law associations, though they did write about European legal issues (Vauchez 2008: 17).

that European law is supreme to national law, but that the nationalization of the Italian energy industry did not violate European law.[24]

The ECJ decision in fact upheld the validity of the Italian law in question, and given the Italian Constitutional Court's prior ruling, it was moot in any event. It was the pro-integration advocates that made the *Costa* ruling legally significant. From within their offices as EC officials, Euro-law association members situated the *Costa* reference into the context of a handful of recent adverse national court rulings, suggesting a dangerous trend of national courts finding limitations to the effect of European law within national systems. Framed in this way, the need to assert EC law supremacy seemed more pressing. European judges and Euro-law associations then followed up the ECJ's *Costa v. Enel* pronouncements with writings and speeches that both advertised the legal rulings and manufactured the far-reaching implications of the decisions. According to Vauchez, participants were engaged in a sort of ventriloquism. Before the ruling academics and practioners spoke about what European law should mean. Then ECJ judges pronounced in the rulings what European law did mean, though they did so with ambiguity. Then the very same set of actors summarized what the ECJ had said, offering less ambiguous interpretations of the ruling, and thereby manufacturing a meaning and import to the decisions they themselves had helped author (Vauchez 2008b).

There were a number of other test cases constructed through association meetings and then trumpeted for their importance. The ECJ's *Cassis de Dijon* ruling, which is the focus of Chapter 7, was a test case constructed following an association meeting where a member of the Commission leaked to a German lawyer that it had settled a case involving the French liqueur *Anisette*. Euro-law association member Gert Meier, the in-house counsel for Rewe Zentrale, simply changed the type of liqueur to Cassis de Dijon, and brought his own test case.[25] As Chapter 7 shows, the Commission's reaction to the ECJ ruling, more than the decision itself, triggered legal and political contestation, the end result of which was arguably a retrenchment of the ECJ doctrine of mutual recognition, broadly interpreted. Still, the ECJ's interlocutors had achieved a huge victory. They had transformed a legal decision that applied only to alcohol imported into Germany into a widely known legal doctrine of general significance, and helped to surmount a political impasse by forcing member states to actively alter the ECJ's mutual recognition doctrine through passing their own legislation on the topic.

---

[24] *Costa v. Enel and Soc. Edisonvolta*, Italian Constitutional Court Decision 14 of 7 March 1964, [1964] CMLR 425, [1964] I Il Foro It. 87 I 465.

[25] In total Meier brought at least 12 cases that were ultimately referred to the ECJ. Meier estimated that national judges referred only 10% of the cases where he argued that European law was relevant. But, where Meier's goal was to have a case referred to the ECJ, Meier estimated that he succeeded 90% of the time because he would bring the case to sympathetic judges. Sometimes judges even asked Meier to find cases to address issues. These types of requests, he noted, usually were made at FIDE, WGE, and Gesellschaft für Lebensmittel conferences. Interview with Gert Meier, the in-house lawyer for Rewe Zentrale, 26 April 1993, Cologne.

European officials also influenced legal integration by shedding their official positions and assuming the role of a private actor. While a member of the European Commission, Elaine Vogel-Polsky published an article suggesting the provision of the Treaty of Rome guaranteeing equal pay for men and women could create direct effects, and thus provide a basis to challenge national practices that discriminated on the basis of gender (Vogel-Polsky 1967). Vogel-Polsky helped write the EC's Equal Treatment Directive. As a private lawyer, she later found the plaintiff Defrenne (who gave Vogel-Polsky her case but did not participate beyond) and constructed the test case against Sabena airlines which established the direct effect of Article 119 (now Articles 141 and 142) (Harlow and Rawlings 1992: 283).[26]

Such activism does not always work in the ECJ's favor. Bourdieu's concept of a legal field involves contestation—actors react to each other with the actions and counter-actions propelling political developments. But legal strategies can also be counter-reactions to political activism. The WGE co-founder Bodo Börner actually supported the German Constitutional Court's *Solange I* ruling that asserted that the German Constitutional Court could find European law invalid in Germany if it conflicted with German Basic Law. Börner felt that ignoring German concerns regarding a lack of basic rights protections in European law would be counterproductive and even dangerous for European integration (Seidl-Hohenveldern 1984: 283). Later still, when political developments were proceeding uncomfortably fast, four members of the European Parliament from the German Green Party and a member of the European Commission became litigants opposing the constitutionality of the Treaty of Maastricht, which led to the German Constitutional Court's decision that again asserted limits to the reach of European law inside of Germany (Alter 2001: 94–117).[27] Most recently, the German Constitutional Court actually rejected the constitutionality of an EU arrest warrant, though it did so on narrow grounds suggesting that the greater problem was implementation of the EU Directive, not the Directive itself.[28] Such contestation, inherent in the politics of legal fields, ensures that European legal integration is not the 'one-way ratchet' neo-functionalist theory expects.

2. Associations served as the ECJ's and the Legal Secretariat's kitchen cabinet

The American term 'kitchen cabinet' refers to President Andrew Jackson's practice of circumventing his real cabinet (the one approved by the Senate) to instead plan policy with like-minded friends. National governments are arguably the ECJ's

---

[26] *Defrenne v. Sabena* [1976] ICR 547; *Defrenne v. Société Anonyme Belge de Navigation Aérienne Sabena* [1978] ECR 1365, ECJ.

[27] *Brunner and Others v. The European Union Treaty, 'Maastricht decision'*, 2 BvR 2134/92 and 2 BvR 2159/92 of 11 January 1994 [1994] 1 EuR 95, [1994] CMLR 57.

[28] *Europäischer Haftbefehl*, 113 BVerfGE 273 (2005), reprinted in 32 *Europäische Grundrechtezeitschrift* (EuGRZ) 387–408 (2005).

statutory cabinet, since they write the laws the ECJ is interpreting. Euro-law associations were the ECJ's kitchen cabinet, providing a means for European officials to test out ideas and seek informal advice, which was especially important given that in the 1960s national political leaders were challenging the supranational aspects of European integration.

It is hard to underestimate the benefit to the ECJ of having such a discussion forum. In the 1960s the ECJ had a handful of judges who were ardent European federalists, but they were also pragmatic about the obstacles they faced (Mancini and Keeling 1995: 403). The European legal system by design provides ECJ judges with legal advice. The ECJ has a system of Advocats Généraux who offer legal interpretations for the ECJ to consider. In addition, the Commission's legal secretariat usually weighs in during legal proceedings. These insider suggestions, which are publicly available before the ECJ itself rules, serve as a sort of trail balloon where the ECJ can gauge support for different legal arguments. Association members and events provide the audience, keeping track of legal developments and providing real time feedback (Rasmussen 1986: 265–6). Associations helped ECJ judges gauge how far they could push their federalist agenda.

Hans-Jürgen Rabe, secretary and early member of the WGE, recalled a conference in Vienna, shortly after the ECJ's *Van Gend en Loos* decision where conversation kept returning to the *Van Gend* ruling.[29] Even though the Avocat Général in the *Van Gend* case had pointed out that a finding that European law created direct effects implied that European law was also supreme to national law, Rabe recalls that the ECJ's president André Donner vigorously denied that the *Van Gend* ruling spoke to the supremacy of European law. Rabe interpreted Donner's denial as an effort by the ECJ to tread carefully. Inspired by the exchange, the WGE's leadership put the issue of supremacy on the agenda for its next meeting, held on 10 July 1964 in Bensheim. The date proved highly fortuitous. On 24 June 1964, just two and a half weeks before the WGE's conference, the ECJ's Avocat Général Maurice Lagrange (an AJE member) made his oral argument on the *Costa* case. Lagrange had argued that national judges should find ways within their constitutions to give effect to European law, or national governments should change constitutions to facilitate legal integration. At the 10 July meeting, Ipsen critiqued Lagrange's widely shared perspective, urging instead that ECJ judges should find that the Treaty of Rome itself implied European law supremacy. The advantage of this interpretation was that the Treaty of Rome was already part of national law. Also, basing EC law supremacy on the Treaty ensured that the origin of the supremacy doctrine was uniform and independent from national constitutional limitations (Ipsen 1964). Rabe notes that three European judges were at the meeting 'listening with red ears,' wanting to know if the leading academics

---

[29] *Van Gend en Loos* was issued 5 February 1963. The dates correspond to a meeting held in Vienna from 18–21 September 1963 organized by Würdinger and Wohlfarth.

of EC law would accept Ipsen's argument. Five days later, the ECJ issued its famous *Costa* ruling, going beyond Lagrange's argument to base the supremacy of European law in the Treaty of Rome.[30]

With a friendly set of critics willing to engage doctrinal ideas, in an oral context where there are no written records and where opinions can be gauged in real time, the ECJ gets important insight into the reception its rulings may receive within national systems. In the case of the supremacy debate, the ECJ learned that there was support for a bolder legal assertion of the supremacy of European Community law over national law. European officials kept track of these debates. The ECJ had employees who compiled dossiers on national legal decisions and who culled national legal journals for articles on these decisions and on ECJ decisions. The conversation in Bensheim was deemed of great enough importance to be reported to the President of the EC Commission, Walter Hallstein, via a memo that summarized the debate and noted most people in the audience had sided with Ipsen's perspective (Davies 2007: 65).

3. Associations created community, which inspired and emboldened members

The two previous points—that association members fashioned test cases and advised the ECJ on doctrinal issues—suggests a third contribution of Euro-law associations. Associations provided community, which helped inspire individuals to bold action. Association meetings were places that the Commission leaked to lawyers the legal issues that it had chosen not to pursue through infringement proceedings (which led to the *Cassis de Dijon* case discussed above). They were places where lawyers could identify friendly national judges, and where lawyers and judges could learn about the types of cases the ECJ would welcome. The discussion earlier about the 1964 WGE Bensheim conference shows how the interactions of like-minded supporters egged on each member, encouraging the ECJ to make the bolder legal claim that the Treaty of Rome itself suggested the supremacy of European law. This community was important because the steps needed to develop the supremacy of European law were larger than any one actor. The ECJ needed cases so it could issue rulings; its ruling had to be well received within legal communities; and follow up efforts were needed to create a reality that reflected legal doctrine. Associations fostered a sense that the different components of the process would work in tandem, which helped individual actors to play their part in the larger scheme. When the ECJ rewarded litigants, and scholars then praised the ECJ for its rulings, there was confirmation that bold actions lead to good results. Such

---

[30] Interview with Dr Hans Jürgen Rabe, Secretary of the WGE, Brussels. For more on this conference, see Vauchez (2008a): manuscript 15–16: Davies (2007: 61–9).

positive reinforcement helps activists be entrepreneurial by suggesting that bold ideas are not merely crazy ideas.

4. Creating the perception of momentum in favor of European legal integration

European law and ECJ doctrine were more frequently ignored than followed in the 1960s and 1970s (see Chapter 5). National judges unaffiliated to Euro-law movements were reluctant to refer cases to the ECJ, there were national high court rulings that seemed to contradict ECJ doctrine,[31] and the common market objectives of a free movement of goods, services, capital, and people remained a distant dream. Euro-law movements sought to change the legal perception regarding European integration while the political will and thus the political reality of European integration lagged. Already mentioned are the numerous legal briefs heralding the importance of the ECJ's *Van Gend* and *Costa* rulings, which helped manufacture the sense that the rulings were of great constitutional importance. Euro-law associations also manufactured the national court decisions that created the sense that the ECJ's doctrines were spreading within national legal systems. The French Cour de Cassation's *Cafés Jacques Vabre* is an example; it would not have become important were it not for Euro-law supporters using their offices to aide European legal integration.

The *Cafés Jacques Vabre* ruling was important because France's two other high courts had established a record of opposing ECJ authority and European law supremacy. In the 1964 *Shelle-Berre* and 1967 *Petitjean* cases, Commissaire du Gouvernement Questiaux (who played the equivalent role of the ECJ's Avocat Général) urged the Conseil d'État to assert that it could interpret even rather unclear European law on its own—which the Conseil d'État implicitly did by not referring the cases to the ECJ (Alter 2001: 137–40).[32] In 1968 the Conseil d'État issued its *Semoules* ruling, which refused to consider whether European law was supreme to the French law in question, suggesting that the Constitutional Council was responsible for enforcing the French constitutional provision that granted supremacy to international rules.[33] Then, in 1975 the French Conseil constitutionnel found that it lacked the authority to consider whether or not

[31] See note 18.

[32] *Société des pétroles Shell-Berre et autres, Sociétés 'Les Garages de France', Société Esso-Standard, Société Mobile Oil française, Société française des pétroles B.P.,* Conseil d'État decision of 19 June 1964, [1964] Recueil Lebon 344, [1964] 5 RDP 1019. *S.A. des Etablissements Petitjean et autres,* Conseil d'État decision of 10 February 1967, [1967] Recueil Lebon 63, [1967] AJDA 267, [1967] RTDE 681.

[33] *Syndicat Général de Fabricants de Semoules de France,* Conseil d'État decision of 1 March 1968, [1968] Recueil Lebon 149, [1970] CMLR 395.

French laws conflicted with international rules, so that it appeared as if no French courts were obliged to enforce the supremacy of European law.[34]

Adolphe Touffait, the former chef de cabinet of Pierre-Henri Teitigen (see p. 66 for more), was an active member of AJE, and ultimately a judge on the ECJ from 1976–82. He used his offices to imply that there was movement in the prevailing French position, which by all appearances opposed both ECJ authority and the ECJ's Supremacy doctrine. As President of the 'ordinary' Cour d'Appel de Paris, Touffait sent references to the ECJ. Indeed between 1965 and 1969 nearly half of the references by French courts (three out of seven) to the ECJ came from the Cour d'Appel in Paris.[35] These were not important cases, but at least they signified that some French courts recognized the ECJ's authority. By the time the *Cafés Jacques Vabre* case reached the Cour de Cassation (France's highest ordinary court), Touffait had been promoted to the position of Procureur Général of the Cour de Cassation (the equivalent of the administrative system's Commissaire du Gouvernement and the ECJ's Avocat Général) where he used his office to great effect.

In the *Cafés Jacques Vabre* case, the coffee-maker had refused to pay a tax arguing that the tax in question violated EC law. If the coffee-maker wanted to challenge the legality of the tax, the coffee-maker would have had to go to the Conseil d'État, which, given its *Semoules* doctrine, would have meant that he would have lost the case. But because Café Jacques Vabre was being pursued by the tax authority for non-payment, and because the tax law in question had been issued subsequent in time to the Treaty of Rome, the case became one of the rare 'ordinary court' cases raising the question of European law supremacy. The first instance court had sided with the coffee-maker suggesting the supremacy of European law but basing the legal decision on other inaccuracies in the government's calculations of the tax. The appeals court had also sided with the coffee-maker, but suggested that the issue at stake was a French regulation, not a law, thus it ducked the question of whether European law could be supreme to French law.[36] If the Cour de Cassation had taken either of these routes, the legal outcome would have been the same but the ruling would not be famous.

Procureur Général Touffait avoided any obfuscation, framing the case in historic terms. He suggested that the French Conseil d'État's *Semoules* ruling was made in the context of an exceptional situation (the independence of France's former colony, Algeria), and thus not of general significance. He offered a questionable interpretation of the French Constitutional Council's 1975 ruling, suggesting that

[34] Conseil constitutionnel decision 74–54 of 15 January 1975, [1975] Recueil des Décisions du Conseil constitutionnel 19, [1975] Dalloz-Jurisprudence 529.

[35] In an interview, a French legal scholar discussed how Touffait used his position at the *Cour d'Appel* in the late 1960s to send references to the ECJ (interview with Marie-France Buffet-Tchakaloff, 6 June 1994, Paris). For more, see Buffett Tchakaloff (1984).

[36] *Administration des Douanes v. Société Cafés Jacques Vabre and J. Weigel et Compagnie Sarl*, Tribunal d'instance decision of 8 January 1971 [1976] 1 CMLR 43. *Administration des Douanes v. Société Cafés Jacques Vabre and J. Weigel et Compagnie Sarl*, Cour d'appel decision of 7 July 1973 [1975] 2 CMLR 22.

the ruling implied that reviewing the compatibility of French law with EC law was merely 'applying' the constitution, not conducting judicial review of national laws which only the Constitutional Council could do. Touffait summarized the state of European law doctrine in other member states and argued that the French court should base the supremacy of European law on the Treaty of Rome, not the French constitution. He finished his argument saying 'It is in this context that the judgment you are to deliver will be read and commented upon; its audience will extend beyond the frontiers of our country and spread over the whole of the member states of the Community.'[37] (For more, see Alter (2001: 145–51.)

References to the ECJ and supportive national court decisions were trumpeted by European officials and legal scholars as signs that the European Court's doctrine was beginning to take hold. Really, what was happening was that activists were finding opportunities, doing what they could to make the rulings seem important and portentous. Euro-law scholars were then heralding pro-EC law national rulings as indications of new thinking in national systems. The *Cafés Jacques Vabre* case was trumpeted by Euro-law scholars as actively supporting the ECJ's supremacy doctrine. The Cour de Cassation ruling itself actually says very little—it is not what students or scholars focus on. Rather, for many years Touffait's argument has been used in European law case books as an exemplar of a national court applying European law supremacy.

A similar story could be told about the famous Belgium *Le Ski* decision which asserted for Belgian judges a role enforcing the supremacy of European law. This decision was famous in no small part because of the arguments of Ganschoff Van de Meersh, a member of the Belgian Euro-law association, who played the analogous role Adolpe Touffait had played in the *Cafés Jacques Vabre* case.[38]

The overall effect was intimidating. German judge Helmut Friedl was not a member of the WGE. As a tax judge, Friedl believed he was obliged to refer to the ECJ questions that concerned European tax directives. Friedl estimated that he referred at least 40 cases to the ECJ over his years at the Finanzgericht München, yet he still believed that there was little legal basis supporting the supremacy of European law. Friedl said that the supremacy doctrine crept up on national judges who did not pay much attention to the ECJ's rulings or the pro-Europe doctrinal debates. Friedl was aware of the ECJ's *Costa* decision, but he emphasized that the ECJ had said that the ruling applied *as far as European law was concerned*. But by 1970 there was a 'governing opinion' in the literature supporting EC law supremacy. Judges, he said, avoided the criticism that would come with contradicting the governing opinion by sidestepping the issue, which was easy to do since few

---

[37] *Administration des Douanes v. Société Cafés Jacques Vabre and J. Weigel et Compagnie Sarl*, Cour de Cassation decision of 24 May 1975, [1975] 2 CMLR 343. Quote at p. 367.

[38] *État Belge v. S.A. 'Fromagerie Franco-Suisse Le Ski'*, decision of the Cour de Cassation, 1ere Chambre, 1971. *Journal des Tribunaux* 460 2. CCH CMLR 8141. See 'Conflicts between Treaties and Subsequently Enacted Statutes in Belgium: État Belge v. S.A. 'Fromagerie Franco-Suisse Le Ski' 1973.

cases involved an issue of European law supremacy. Friedl also observed that after 1968 there was not nearly as much literature challenging the supremacy doctrine, surmising that authors were avoiding being labeled 'anti-European.'[39]

ECJ judges and early European legal integration scholars explained the success of the ECJ's doctrine by focusing on the persuasive authority of ECJ decisions (Mancini 1989: 605–6; Weiler 1991: 2428). But it was not the ideas of the ECJ that made the difference. The legal interpretations propounded by the ECJ, and stridently supported through publications penned by association members, did not gain much traction within national legal communities. Numerous national judges and unaffiliated legal scholars told me that they discounted the opinions of pro-Europe lawyers and scholars, seeing them as more ideological than legal. And in fact national high courts have not accepted the argument that the Treaty of Rome requires the supremacy of European law—not even France's Cour de Cassation (Alter 2001: 149 note 50). Instead, they have found ways within national systems to accommodate European law supremacy, without ceding the supremacy of their own constitutions or their own judicial authority (Alter 2001).

The key to Euro-law associations' success was the social and political capital of its members. Antoine Vauchez, Antonin Cohen, Guillaume Sacriste, and Mikael Rask Madsen document the many ways in which the legal pioneers of Europe had political capital. They served in government ministries and high courts and were members of political dynasties and thus close relatives of ministers and high officials. They were professors who chaired dissertation committees and thus had sway over the prospects of young academics. They served as lawyers to industries, which allowed them to find test cases (Madsen and Vauchez 2005; Sacriste and Vauchez 2007; Vauchez 2007a, 2008). They switched offices, rotating their roles—one day being a lawyer, another a commentator, and another a judge or legal advisor—to magnify their actions so as to appear greater in number and effect than they actually were. The cumulative result of their actions as participants—lawyers, judges, scholars, and government officials—was the monopolization and ultimately the construction of what European law meant. How their constructions were then diffused across national systems is a different question that I take up elsewhere (see chapter 5).

III. Imagining Legal Integration without Jurist Associations—The Case of the Andean Tribunal of Justice[40]

If a tree falls in the forest, does anyone know? Absent Euro-law associations, would ECJ decisions have been trees that fell largely without notice? Would the

---

[39] Interview with Dr Helmut Friedl, former Judge at Finanzgericht München, Clerk at the Bundesfinanzhof from 1967–72, 22 February 1994, Füßen.

[40] This section is based on research conducted in collaboration with Laurence Helfer and Maria Florencia Guerzovich.

ECJ have even issued its bold rulings without the clear signals that they would be welcomed? A brief comparison with the Andean Tribunal of Justice—the ECJ's clone—reveals how a lack of an advocacy movement inhibits supranational doctrinal development.

The Andean Community Tribunal of Justice (ATJ) was created in 1984, 15 years after the creation of the Andean Pact. The ATJ was explicitly modeled on the ECJ, including among other similarities an infringement process and a preliminary ruling mechanism (Keener 1987: 49). Andean legal integration was in some ways advantaged in that all member states shared a common language and the ATJ had the model of the ECJ to emulate. But the ATJ has lacked cases raising significant constitutional legal issues. With the notable exception of the issue of Andean intellectual property rules (Helfer, Alter, and Guerzovich 2009), Andean law has been slow to penetrate national legal systems, and the ATJ has itself been timid about asserting its authority and about providing purposive teleological interpretations of Andean rules (Saldias 2007).

The ATJ initially lacked cases. In the 1980s member states refused to authorize the Andean legal secretariat to proceed with cases, even the type of technical non-controversial cases the European Commission raised in the 1960s.[41] Luis E. Pochet tried to overcome this blockage, bringing to the ATJ an infringement suit on behalf of Reynolds Aluminum. The case greatly resembled the *Van Gend en Loos* suit where the litigant invoked an article of the Treaty of Rome prohibiting member states from raising tariffs against each other to challenge the Dutch customs administration's reclassification of product. Article 41 of the Andean Treaty called for the progressive elimination of internal tariffs, and thus it arguably prohibited raising any tariffs. Pochet argued that a Colombian regulation 75/86 had the effect of increasing the tariff, which in his view violated Article 41 of the Cartagena agreement. In November of 1987 the ATJ rejected the suit because private actors were not authorized to raise infringement suits.[42]

Shortly afterwards, the ATJ received its first preliminary ruling reference. The reference came from a case brought by Germán Cavelier, who had served as Secretary General of the Ministry of Foreign Affairs in 1968 and 1969

---

[41] Based on an interview with Alfonso Vidales Olviedo, legal council for the Andean Junta 1970–83 and 1986–91, 22 June 2007, Lima, Peru. The original Andean Tribunal Treaty only allowed the Junta to pursue infringements that were identified by member states. The Court Treaty was revised in 1996 through the Cochabamba Protocol. From 1996 on, private actors could bring to the Secretariat charges that states were infringing Andean rules. Private actors were also authorized to bring infringements directly to the ATJ. The Secretariat started bringing infringement suits on its own, arguing that if it did not raise the suit, the private actor would raise it on their own. The original Andean Tribunal Treaty is published in 18 *Int'l Legal Materials* 1203, 1979. The Cochabamba Protocol, signed on 28 May 1996, substituted the original Andean Tribunal Treaty with a revised text. The revised Treaty Creating the Court of Justice of the Andean Community is available at: <http://www.comunidadandina.org/INGLES/normativa/ande_trie2.htm> (visited 1/8/08).

[42] 1-AI-87.

when the Andean Pact was negotiated.[43] Dr Cavelier was an internationalist, writing his doctoral thesis on international law, followed by numerous treatises on international law. According to lawyers in the law firm Cavelier established, Cavelier believed in integration of the countries as a way to strengthen law, though he himself was not involved in legal negotiations regarding the Andean Pact.[44] Cavelier challenged a Colombian administrative decision denying Volvo's application for a trademark, taking the bold step of asking for a preliminary reference. Cavelier did not simply make a legal argument; he talked with former judges who personally lobbied Colombian Council of State judges to change their position regarding referring cases to the ATJ. This case became the first national court reference to the ATJ.[45]

The ATJ used case 1-IP-87 to explain the preliminary ruling process. Invoking terminology that was nearly identical to the ECJ's it asserted that Andean rules create direct effects and are supreme to national rules. Its decision 2-IP-88 explicitly embraced the ECJ's *Costa* and *Simmenthal* jurisprudence. Neither ruling turned on these assertions, perhaps because they were framed in terms of the legally authorized self-interest of litigants, rather than intentionally constructed to frame a broad legal issue. (The narrower framing may have also been needed to convince the Colombian Council of State to refer the case.) Rather, the ATJ took the opportunity of having a reference to instruct Andean Tribunals on the legal system, using the ECJ's language to insist that the relevant national agencies were required to refer cases and enforce Andean rules. The ATJ followed with numerous other decisions where it reasserted these principles within the ruling— though none of the cases actually turned on constitutional issues related to the ATJ's pronouncements.

Pochet's case—which had been rejected as an infringement suit—later reappeared as a preliminary ruling reference brought on behalf of Reynolds Aluminum Santodomingo and Sociedad Aluminio Nacional. Article 41 of the Andean Treaty called for the progressive elimination of internal tariffs and thus it arguably prohibited raising any tariffs. The Colombian government urged the Andean Tribunal to focus on Article 55, which allowed for a list of exceptions. The plaintiff stressed that even though the Andean treaty allowed temporary exceptions, this did not mean that governments could raise tariffs in the meantime. The ATJ, however, sided with the Colombian government finding that

---

[43] The five founding members of the Andean Pact were Bolivia, Chile, Colombia, Ecuador, and Peru. Venezuela joined the group as a sixth member in 1973. Chile withdrew from the Andean Pact in 1976. These countries committed to integrating their markets. The Andean Pact's legal and institutional architecture mirrored that of the EC. But the substantive policies of the two regions were quite different. Whereas the European integration project focused on liberalizing trade and creating a common market, the Andean Pact's *raison d'être* was import substitution—promoting regional development as an alternative to purchasing goods and technologies from foreign firms.

[44] Interview with German Marin and Emilio Ferraro, Cavelier Abogados, 11 September 2007, Bogota Colombia.

[45] Case 1-IP-87.

Andean governments could in essence do as they wanted regarding goods included on the list of exceptions. Moreover, it left to national courts the task of determining which goods were part of the list of exceptions (Saldias 2007: 11–12)!

Pochet and Cavelier were legal entrepreneurs, though they did not appear to be following a constructed plan nor is there any evidence that they were working as part of a larger group of actors.[46] The ATJ was relatively bold in asserting the supremacy and direct effect of European law, but its 1-IP-90 decision avoided a chance to issue a *Van Gend en Loos*-like ruling.

All of these rulings fell into almost complete silence. The Andean Tribunal did not set up a system to disseminate its rulings. Indeed even highly motivated individuals would have found it hard to access an ATJ decision in the 1980s and 1990s.[47] One can find a few articles on the Andean legal system, which appear far later in time, are mostly penned by lawyers with degrees in Europe or the United States, and/or are published in Europe or the United States.[48]

This different context changes how the actors perceive and play their roles. Gallo Pico Mantilla was President of the ATJ when the ATJ's first ruling asserting the supremacy of Andean rules was issued (1987), and he served on the ATJ until 1993. A gentleman-politician lawyer who was once Secretary of the Minister of Industry and Ambassador to Venezuela, and later as a judge at Ecuador's Supreme Court (1997–2004), Mantilla sought to emulate the European legal integration strategy. Mantilla was committed to Andean integration as an end in itself, having been a participant in negotiations involving Andean integration and in the negotiations that led to the founding of the Andean Tribunal.[49] As President of the ATJ, Mantilla probably penned the 1-IP-87 ruling, and he helped convince the first Ecuadorian courts to start making reference to the ATJ.[50] Later, Mantilla joined the Ecuadorian Supreme Court that in 1999 issued a ruling ordering an Ecuadorian court to refer the case in question to the ATJ, as it was required to do

---

[46] Members of Cavelier's law firm were not aware of any movement or group that Cavelier might have been connected to. In their view, he was a true entrepreneur: German Marin and Emilio Ferraro, Cavelier Abogados, 11 September 2007, Bogota, Colombia.

[47] An Andean Tribunal judge recounted a meeting he had with a student who wanted to write a thesis on the Andean legal system. The student was stuck on the doorsteps of the Andean Tribunal, having been refused access to review the Court's decisions. The judge provided access to his copies, and presumably the student wrote his thesis. Interview with Ugarte del Pino, 22 June 2007, Lima, Peru. Web access became available around 2004.

[48] There are writings in Spanish that mainly summarize aspects of Andean law or ATJ decisions. Far harder to find are analyses that consider the doctrinal implications of legal rulings, or their contribution to legal integration. A few exceptions to the trend include: Baquero-Herrera 2004; Rodriguez Lemmo 2002; Saldias 2007; Tremolada 2006.

[49] While in the Economics ministry, Mantilla participated in a working group regarding the Andean Pact. Mantilla later held various positions in the Ecuadorian government, including as the Secretary of the Minister of Industry and Ambassador to Venezuela. Mantilla was an early advocate of creating a court for the Andean Pact.

[50] The big turning point in terms of Ecuadorian courts sending references to the ATJ came after Mantilla's time (Helfer and Alter 2009). Proctor and Gamble brought an infringement suit against the Ecuador Supreme Court for failing to refer a tax dispute to the Andean Tribunal (ATJ ruling 24-AN-99). After that case, the number of references from Ecuadorian courts rose significantly.

under Andean law.[51] Mantilla was an integration activist, who like Pochet and Cavelier used his offices to aid Andean legal integration. But he had few other interlocutors to work with.

Juan Vincente Ugarte del Pino, the Peruvian judge on the Andean Tribunal from 1990 to 1995, is more typical of appointments to the ATJ. Ugarte del Pino did not put his energy into the Andean integration system; for example he did not work to educate the Peruvian judiciary on their responsibility to refer cases to the ATJ, nor did he write treatises on the Andean system for Peruvian lawyers and judges. To some extent, his lack of energy is understandable. Ugarte del Pino recounted the basic struggles he faced as a judge on the Andean Tribunal—since the Ecuadorian government did not supply a building, judges had to spend time finding a building to work in. Andean judges lacked a staff or a system of Avocat Général to help them analyze legal issues or draft decisions, and early on the Andean Tribunal spent time dealing with labor disputes from employees whose contracts were never fulfilled because promised resources were not supplied by Andean governments. The picture one gets is of a judge lacking the basic means to do his job.[52] Time has overcome these logistical difficulties, but still the ATJ has very limited resources and ATJ judges remain relatively inactive legal diplomats.

There do not appear to be as many outlets for legal articles. ATJ judges and members of the legal secretariat have written chapters for books commemorating each other's years on the court. Some have written treatises on Andean law, but legal writings are primarily technocratic, including mostly replication of relevant legal texts and descriptions of legal procedures. The writing of Andean judges, Mantilla included (Mantilla 1992), is in sharp contrast to the speeches and writings of European Court judges (Donner 1968; Lecourt 1964; Mancini 1989; Pescatore 1983).

There is a University of the Andes, located in Bolivia, which presumably focuses on Andean integration. Andean officials have also taught courses on Andean integration at local universities, but they have not created a burgeoning field of integration studies populated by their students. Andean officials have also served as lawyers bringing cases involving Andean law.[53] There is also a regional association, the *Comisión Andina de Juristas*. This association is over 25 years old, but only recently has it started to work to help the Andean legal integration process. Its involvement has been limited: it was contracted by the Andean Community to help create a website to help distribute Andean Tribunal Rulings, and to work with Peruvian and Bolivian legal systems so that they might start referring cases

---

[51] Claim No. 13–99; Res. No. 468–99, Recurso de Casacion, Third Civil and Commercial Law Courtroom of the Supreme Court of Ecuador, 5 October 1999.

[52] Interview with Ugarte del Pino, 22 June 2007, Lima, Peru.

[53] A former member of the legal division of the General Secretariat (Alfonso Vidales Olviedo) served as the lawyer for the Peruvian generic pharmaceutical industry in the suit against a Peruvian decree regarding second use patents. Marcel Tagareife Torres has been a norm entrepreneur with respect to legal cases involving agro-chemicals.

to the ATJ. According to the lead association member involved it the projects, Andean integration had not been part of the *Comisión* area of focus because the Andean Pact and Andean Community were seen as economic projects, distant from the organization's core objectives of promoting human rights, democracy, and respect for international law more generally.[54] The absence of interlocutors has starved the ATJ of legal advice that could have been useful. Also, without an active debate about ATJ rulings, the Andean legal system remains largely unknown within larger national legal and political systems.

The lack of a larger movement perhaps contributes to making the ATJ less bold than its European counterpart. The ATJ's 1-IP-87 preliminary ruling decision was written in bold terms, but the ATJ has hesitated to innovate through legal doctrine or to encourage more entrepreneurial legal behavior by lawyers and national judges. I already mentioned how ATJ decision 1-IP-90 avoided issuing a *Van Gend en Loos*-type interpretation. The ATJ's ruling of 2-IP-90 refused to follow the ECJ in asserting a doctrine of implied powers—ruling instead that where Andean rules are not clear or complete, legal and political authority resides at the national level. In 3-IP-93, the Reynolds company had dropped out but the Sociedad Aluminio Nacional tried again to get the ATJ to issue a more purposive ruling regarding the Colombian regulation in question, but for the third time the ATJ refused to find that the Andean Treaty created inherent limits on what governments could do (Saldias 2007: 13–14).[55] When in 1999 the Peruvian intellectual property agency *INDECOPI* asked the ATJ to consider a legal question sent by itself, the ATJ refused because *INDECOPI* was not part of the Peruvian judiciary.[56] In refusing this case, the ATJ shut off an avenue for requests involving Peru—and indeed it took until 2005 for Peruvian courts to start regularly sending references to the ATJ.[57] In Decision 87-IP-2002 the Andean Tribunal excluded from its jurisdiction practices that, even though restrictive, do not create external effects involving other member states.

Many elements keep Andean judges from more assertively developing and expanding their authority. One could claim that the ATJ's greater restraint in its legal interpretations reflects the intent of member states as revealed in the Court

---

[54] The association is a regional offshoot of International Commission of Jurists. For many years, the association had institutional funding to allow it to pursue its own projects. Beginning around the year 2000 it was contracted by the Andean Community for a handful of projects. Phone Interview with Salvador Herencia Carrasco, Comisión Andina de Juristas, Asesor jurídico, 20 May 2008.

[55] The other two opportunities were those raised by Pochet, discussed above.

[56] Interview with Teresa Mera Gomez who worked in the INDECOPI trademark office from 1993 to 2005, Member of INDECOPI Tribunal (2006 to present) 21 June 2007, Lima, Peru.

[57] Ugarte del Pino explained the reasoning for the ATJ's decision. Dictators had a history of politicizing the judicial function by locating judicial review in executive agencies. For Ugarte del Pino, rejecting INDECOPI's request to send references, and perhaps also interpreting the ATJ's mandate narrowly, helped insure the independence of the judiciary. The decision was reasonable, but not one that the ECJ would have taken. Interview with Ugarte del Pino , 22 June 2007, Lima, Peru.

Treaty[58] and the many Andean rules that have loopholes that make them hard to legally enforce (Helfer, Alter, and Guerzovich 2009). Also, national judiciaries in the Andean context have historically been politically weak, often afraid to assert their independence or challenge political authority (Dezalay and Garth 2002: 222–7; Merryman and Pérez-Perdomo 2007: 36–7; O'Donnell 1998). These legal attributes, however, probably do not fully explain the ATJ's reticence. In Europe as well state negotiators did not intend the ECJ to transform the preliminary ruling system as it did. Moreover, it is easy to forget that European founding states were all civil law countries with limited traditions of judicial review, formally committed to the principle that judicial rulings apply only to the case at hand and that the last law passed reigns supreme. In other words, just like the ATJ, the ECJ needed to break out of the legal tradition of its time in order to succeed, and it needed to do so without the blessing of national governments.

My point is not that there are no jurist movements in the Andean context, or that Andean lawyers in general lack political capital. In Latin America lawyers with prestige are associated with the leading families within a country, which tend to hold positions of power in both business and government (Dezalay and Garth 2002: 198–203). And one can find signs of emerging legal fields in Latin America to support the free market and human rights agenda (Dezalay and Garth 2006; Lutz and Sikkink 2000; Sieder, Schjolden, and Angell 2005; Sikkink 2003, 2005). The Andean Tribunal's problem is that lawyers with prestige have not embraced Andean integration. Rather the political context of Andean integration, more than formal legal and political constraints, creates a reality where Andean legal integration lacks the support of an activist, politically well connected jurist movement. For more see Alter and Helfer (2009).

The exception is that Andean lawyers have coalesced behind Andean intellectual property rules, a puzzle I explore elsewhere. Over 90 per cent of the Andean Tribunal's docket (1,303 out of 1,338 preliminary rulings) concerns Andean IP rules (Helfer, Alter, and Guerzovich 2009). Said differently, there are fewer than 100 Andean legal rulings regarding issues other than intellectual property, suggesting little grass roots or upper level political demand to enforce the Andean Community's common market rules. While there was also little demand in Europe of the 1960s for a common market, Euro-law advocacy movements entered the legal breech for the ideological reasons noted above.

---

[58] The Andean Tribunal's statute was written with 20–20 European hindsight, and negotiators took pains to circumscribe the preliminary ruling mechanism's role. Andean Tribunal Treaty, Article 30 defines a division of labor where the ATJ is not supposed to consider the facts of the case in rendering preliminary rulings. This provision was revised in the Cochabamba Protocol. States added a suggestion that the ATJ can refer to the facts of the case 'when essential for the requested interpretation'. Still the ATJ has avoided delving into specifics in the case, and thus it has avoided making decisions with clear implications for the merits of the case. See note 42 for citations of Andean legal texts.

IV. Does Transnational Law Need Advocacy Movements and Transnational Legal Fields to Flourish?

To investigate the role of advocacy movements is to question the forces driving international legal integration, meaning the spread and penetration of international rules within national polities. It is well established that advocacy movements use litigation domestically and internationally to promote their causes (Cichowski 2007; Harlow and Rawlings 1992), and that cause lawyers actively promote political agendas (Halliday, Karpik, and Feeley 2007; Sarat and Scheingold 2001). It is also well established that national advocacy movements can latch onto international rules to great effect (Keck and Sikkink 1998; Risse, Ropp, and Sikkink 1999). This article's contribution is to think about how uniting like-minded actors together in a coordinated fashion—in this case via Euro-law associations—facilitates the entrepreneurship of legal actors.

One way to think about the role of advocacy movements is to contrast the dynamic of having coordination by an ideologically cohesive politically well-placed set of actors with other forces for the global spread of rules. One oft-credited source of the global spread of common international rules is information. The theoretical suggestion is that ignorance keeps individuals and collectivities from adopting best practices, in which case knowledge is all that is needed to create a global convergence around common rules and standards. Certainly there is a much greater awareness about the benefits of using international rules to promote political agendas in 2008 than there was in 1960. The Internet also makes it easier for lawyers to publish their views, and if they choose, to blog about legal issues. There is also an emerging trend of high court judges meeting each other, providing opportunities to share their solutions to the problems that judges face (Slaughter 2000, 2004). Thus we can see that the opportunities to exchange information have grown over time, which might suggest that we no longer need the type of coordination Euro-law associations provided in the 1960s. The analysis in this article, however, suggests that Euro-law associations did not simply share information, they built communities of like-minded actors. The contrast to the Andean case also suggests that the new information technologies are an insufficient substitute for the sort of community building that Euro-law associations provided.

There is also growing recognition that international coordination increasingly occurs via trans-governmental networks which bring together national administrators and judges who are engaged in similar policy enterprises (Sikkink and Walling 2006; Slaughter 2004; Turner 2005). The theoretical suggestion in this literature is that functional imperatives (e.g. the need to build relationships with their counterparts in other countries and coordinate internationally to achieve domestic goals like fighting money-laundering or terrorism) generate the emergence of transnational networks. The analysis offered here suggests that including actors with political capital is very important for the process of legal integration, which is why trans-governmental networks are important. But the functional imperative to work together is probably not a sufficient basis for cooperation, something Ernst Haas and the early proponents of neo-functional theory long ago recognized (Haas 1975) and that experience of the Andean Tribunal of Justice reinforces. Euro-law associations were far more than trans-governmental networks are likely to ever be. They included governmental actors, but they also reached beyond these actors. They brought together ideologically cohesive groups united by a political agenda—integration via a constitutional legal structure.

Others have recognized the role of ideology in unifying movements. Margaret Keck and Kathryn Sikkink adopt the term advocacy movement to indicate that a commitment to a common agenda provides the critical glue unifying members. They also suggest that certain issues are inherently more amenable to being influenced by transnational advocacy networks, because certain issues have a greater ability to connect with and resonate within political actors who are not part of the advocacy movement (Keck and Sikkink 1998; Risse, Ropp, and Sikkink 1999). The scholarship on epistemic communities is similar in that it recognizes that group cohesion is furthered by the existence of shared beliefs about cause-and-effect relationships, and that it is the shared epistemes that provide epistemic communities with cohesion and ultimately with power (Haas 1992). This analysis concurs in that it suggests that self-interest alone provides too narrow a basis to sustain collective action aimed at ambitious and fundamental objectives. The ideology of unifying Europe so as to create peace helped unite the core membership of Euro-law associations. By contrast, the Andean Pact's import substitution ideology, and the Andean Community's liberal economic ideology have failed to mobilize a group of jurists to aid the Andean integration project.

The Bourdieusian approach adds in an examination of the social backgrounds of actors and thus an investigation of power. Investigating the backgrounds and connections among actors reveals how in Europe, jurist advocacy movements connected a well-placed set of actors personally, ideologically, and strategically. The contrast with the Andean integration process also suggests the importance of a larger movement of jurists in generating international judicial activism. Notwithstanding the similar structure of the legal system, and even though the Andean Pact also had legal provisions that were supposedly would automatically lead to the reduction of internal barriers to trade (Avery and Cochraine 1973; Vargas-Hidalgo 1979), neither the desires of some ideologically motivated actors, knowledge of what had occurred in Europe, or the behaviors of a small number of self-interested actors, have managed to spread Andean legal integration much beyond the issue of intellectual property law. While the ATJ is the third most active international court, it is neither an activist court nor a legal actor capable of surmounting the political obstacles hindering Andean integration.

Euro-law associations are not unique in the history of international law, or domestic law for that matter. In the United States, the judicial turn to constitutional originalism reflects the active efforts of jurists to found a conservative Federalist Society (<http://www.fed-soc.org/>) which has penetrated academia, the bar, and the judiciary. Internationally, Yves Dezalay, Bryant Garth, and others have noted how groups of lawyers have influenced international economic and human rights legal developments in Latin America and beyond (Dezalay and Garth 2002, 2006; Halliday, Karpik, and Feeley 2007; Sikkink 2005). There are also emerging movements of lawyers—in Europe and beyond—that are formally or informally working to promote the development of international criminal law (Hagan and Levi 2005). The question remains, however: What are the keys to such movements being successful?

This study suggests that there must be a mixture of ideology and power fueling legal integration. International law is most likely to inspire dogged activism when it is seen as linked to a project that is significantly larger than the substance of the cases being litigated, and thus when actors are motivated by more than narrow self interest. Moreover, transnational jurist movements need to include powerful actors, and/or be allied with the agendas of powerful actors, if they are to succeed. This study suggests that one can build an international court in other contexts, but without the larger ideological motivation, and without a community of legal activists with political and social capital, even the most entrepreneurial legal activists are unlikely to be able to replicate the type of legal revolution that occurred in Europe in the 1960s.

5

The European Court's Political Power: The Emergence of an Authoritative International Court in the European Union (1996)

International law and international courts have always been weak. While many aspects of international law may be respected, when controversy emerges national governments often interpret international agreements as they see fit, prioritize national goals over international obligations, and violate international law. National practices within the European Union stand in sharp contrast here. Member states can not 'interpret' their way out of compliance with European Community law, governments which do not comply with European law are brought in front of the European Court of Justice, and European Court decisions are usually respected. Even the threat of bringing a case to the European Court can be enough to influence national governments to back down on important national issues, and to give way to the authority of European law.

This chapter asks how the European Court of Justice (ECJ) came to be an authoritative legal and political institution, and how an international rule of law which actually works was created within the European Union. The ECJ, and the legal system designed by the Treaty of Rome, by all accounts started out quite weak. When confronted with alleged Treaty violations, politicians used political channels to circumvent the legal mechanisms of the Treaty, giving the ECJ little opportunity to wage into national or EC debates over economic integration, and the purely declaratory nature of ECJ decisions made them easy to ignore. The bottom line was that a legal declaration regarding a technical issue of Treaty compliance, issued by an obscure court in Luxembourg was often not enough to embarrass a member state into compliance. With few cases and no means to elicit compliance with its jurisprudence, the ECJ was a marginal political actor in Europe.

But this has changed, and the ECJ has emerged as one of the strongest of the European Union's political institutions, with the authority to declare illegal national law and policy which conflicts with EC law. The European legal system has been used to remove national non-tariff barriers to trade, to stop national governments from illegally subsidizing national industries, and to enforce EC directives in areas such as environmental policy and social policy. The ECJ has also come to influence policy debates in areas which would seem to be issues of domestic policy. How can we understand the transformation of this weak international court into one of the most influential political institutions in Europe?

Legal scholars explain the authority of the ECJ by pointing to key legal decisions of the Court in 1963 and 1964, which created the doctrine of direct effect and the doctrine of EC law supremacy. The doctrine of direct effect implied that EC law could create rights that individuals can claim in their national courts. The doctrine of EC law supremacy implied that EC law is supreme to national law passed either before or after the coming into force of EC law, so that national governments are prohibited from applying any law or policy that violates the Treaty of Rome. Together these two doctrines established the legal basis for individuals to use EC law to challenge in national courts national policies that violate EC law, and for national courts to set aside laws and policies that violate EC law.[1]

The importance of the Court's revolutionary legal doctrines in fundamentally transforming the EC legal system cannot be underestimated. But simply declaring that EC law created direct effects and was supreme to EC law was not enough to create a rule of law in Europe. To put it bluntly, the Court of Justice can say whatever it wants, the real question is why anyone would follow. The Court's legal doctrines were very controversial, both legally and politically. They clashed with national legal practices, threatened to subjugate national high courts to the ECJ, and implied a great compromise of national sovereignty. Especially in the political context of the 1960s and 1970s, when supranationalism was being rejected by politicians, and when national sovereignty concerns were largely winning out over European integration, the Court's legal declarations were easy for national courts to reject and politicians to ignore.

This article explains why national judiciaries and politicians came to accept the ECJ's controversial legal doctrines. Gaining national judicial acceptance of the direct effect and supremacy of EC law was key to the development of an effective rule of law in Europe. With individuals able to bring cases involving EC law directly in national courts, and national courts referring these cases to the ECJ, all sorts of legal disputes that the Commission or a member state would have never raised actually made it to the ECJ for decision. National court support also made ECJ decisions enforceable. Disobeying an ECJ decision now meant disobeying national courts, and all the enforcement power of the national courts could be

---

[1] In general, private parties are not allowed to bring cases directly to the ECJ. Instead private parties gain access to the ECJ through national courts. The procedure works as follows. A private party challenges in a national court a law or policy which potentially violates EC law. The national court uses the 'preliminary ruling procedure' (Article 177 of the Treaty of Rome) to send a question of interpretation to the European Court, which renders a ruling on the meaning of EC law. The national court then applies the ECJ ruling to the case. For more on EC legal procedure, see Brown (1994). For more on the legal and political importance of the Court's revolutionary legal doctrines of Direct Effect and Supremacy see Hartley (1994); Weiler (1991).

used in the enforcement of EC law. With national courts willing to enforce ECJ jurisprudence against national politicians, the ECJ became emboldened. Since the 1970s the ECJ has increasingly made decisions with significant political and material impact and politicians have come to find themselves constrained in ways and in policy areas that they had not expected, by the interpretations of the ECJ and the force of EC law.

With the support of national judiciaries, the European Court has emerged as one of the strongest courts in Europe. But it is not only a strong legal authority; it has become a political actor in Europe as well. The EC legal system has been used to pressure France to open Orly airport to other European carriers, Germany to accept beer produced in other countries, and Britain not to revoke the license of Spanish fishing boats. The Court has influenced European Union policy on issues such as who represents member states in negotiations of international agreements, and if countries can make bi-lateral trade arrangements with third countries. EC law has also become part of domestic political debates such as the debate over the provision of equal pay for men and women. For many areas of European and national policy, knowing the position of the ECJ is as important as knowing the position of the member states and national interest groups. Part I of this article examines why national courts agreed to accept a role enforcing EC law against their governments. Part II of this article originally explained why politicians did not stop an institutional transformation that they clearly did not support. This topic is now covered in Chapter 6. Part III concludes.

I. Turning National Courts into Enforcers of International Law

The debate over the role of national courts in enforcing EC law took the form of a legal doctrinal debate about the supremacy of EC law over national law. To simplify greatly, the issue of EC law supremacy came down to the questions of whether national courts had an obligation to ensure national compliance with international law and if the European Court had jurisdictional authority to decide on national court references involving national law. If EC law was not supreme to national law, or if plaintiffs did not have legal standing to call on EC law, then national courts could ignore the whole question of whether national policy violated EC law. But if EC law was supreme to national law, then national courts would be legally compelled to disregard any national law which conflicted with EC law, and to apply EC law instead.

The ECJ's interest in the supremacy and direct effect of EC law was clear. With individuals raising cases in national courts and national courts referring cases to the ECJ, the ECJ had more opportunities to rule on national law and to expand the reach and scope of its jurisprudence, thereby expanding its own jurisdictional authority and influence in the policy-making process. The ECJ could also draw

on the authority of the national courts to make its decisions more legally binding and authoritative. Less clear, however, is why national courts would want to
facilitate the expansion of ECJ authority and the penetration of EC law into the
national legal system.

Within the national legal communities, the Court's assertion of the direct
effect and supremacy of EC law were extremely controversial. Many legal scholars and judges questioned the legal basis of the ECJ's decisions and one German
legal scholar even called the Court's doctrine 'wishful thinking,' with no foundation in either international law, the EC Treaty, or national law (Rupp 1970: 356).
The ECJ's jurisprudence on EC law supremacy challenged many well accepted
tenets of international law and national law. International law is traditionally
interpreted narrowly, sticking to the clear intent of the negotiating partners. But
nowhere did the Treaty of Rome say that European citizens had a legal right to
have the Treaty implemented; nowhere was it written that EC law was supreme
to national law; and nowhere in the Treaty were national courts empowered to
enforce EC law against their governments. There was also no national legal basis
for courts to apply the supremacy of EC law. In most European legal systems,
international law was applied according to the legal principle *lex posterior derogat
legi priori*—the last law passed trumps all previous law. To the extent that an
international treaty was the last law passed by the national parliament, national
judges did not have a problem applying Treaty law over prior national legislation.
But any subsequent national legislation was supreme to all previous legislation,
including international treaties. The ECJ was authorized to interpret EC law. But
many politicians and legal scholars felt that in telling national courts to apply EC
law over subsequent national law the ECJ had exceeded its legal authority and
meddled into an issue of national law. It is interesting to note that national judiciaries continued to resist the reasoning offered by the ECJ as the legal bases for
EC law supremacy.[2]

In countries without a tradition of judicial review, the ECJ was asking national
courts for nothing short of legal revolution. In order to accept a role enforcing EC
law supremacy, national judges would have to change how they interpreted their
constitutions, alter entrenched national legal precedents regarding the relationship of international law to national law, and embrace a new judicial role as an

---

[2] The ECJ based the supremacy of EC law on the 'special' nature of the EC Treaty, arguing that
'By contrast with ordinary international treaties, the EEC Treaty has created its own legal system
which, on the entry into force of the Treaty, became an integral part of the legal systems of the
member states and which their courts are bound to apply. By creating a Community of unlimited
duration, having its own institutions, its own personality, its own legal capacity and capacity of
representation on the international plane and, more particularly, real powers stemming from a
limitation of sovereignty or a transfer of powers from the States to the Community, the member
states have limited their sovereign rights, albeit within limited fields, and have thus created a body
of law which binds both their nationals and themselves' (Case 6/64, *Costa v. Ente Nationale per
L'Energia Elettrica (Enel)* [1964] ECR 583). National judiciaries have not accepted that the EC
Treaty is special in nature, or that the Treaty itself provides a legal basis for the supremacy of EC
law over national law. For more see Alter (2001).

enforcer of international law. While the objections to EC law supremacy were usually stated in legalistic terms, underlying the doctrinal differences regarding the supremacy of EC law were different conceptions of the role of the judiciary in the political system.

Within almost every European country the Court's supremacy doctrine raised fundamental issues of political authority. The doctrine touched on the limits of parliamentary sovereignty, the sanctity of the national constitution, the separation of authority between the Parliament and the executive, the separation of authority between regional and federal governments, and the role the judiciary should play in the political process. For the French and the British, applying EC law supremacy went against the very essence of democracy as embodied in the notion of parliamentary sovereignty. Lachaume explained French judicial reticence saying:

The national judge should not have doubts in the face of a statute posterior to a treaty that contradicts it, because this statute expresses, if one dare say, the latest state of the general will. He would therefore, that is according to his historical and normal mission, apply [the law]. If the law contradicts the treaty, without admitting that it is inconceivable that the legislature did not know what it was doing, this is the general will which—right or wrong—has decided and the judge can not but yield: his function as judge consists of applying the law, and not of judging it; above all, if in doing so, and in establishing the incompatibility of a law with a previous treaty, he is disposed to disregard the law. (Lachaume 1990: 386)

The Germans had different concerns with EC law supremacy. Having experienced what could happen when judges did not adequately supervise what politicians did, they feared that EC law supremacy could undermine national court ability to ensure respect for the German constitution and for democracy. A judge in Rheinland-Pfalz argued:

The most important aim of the Constitution is to avoid a repetition of the developments which, in the Weimar Republic, led to the abolition of the separation of powers, and thus to the collapse of the rule of law. The path to the complete surrender of the doctrine of the separation of powers through the Special Powers Act of 24 March 1933 took its first open form in the excessively wide interpretation of Art. 48 (2) of the Weimar Constitution in favor of the executive. As early as this, the thinking of leading academic lawyers had reached the highly dangerous stage, in which an inadequately circumscribed clause in the Constitution had itself become a gap in the Constitution. The undermining and destruction of the rule of law for a second time can be avoided only by the courts opposing every attempt to interpret another inadequately circumscribed constitutional provision so as to weaken...the Constitution's protection of the principle of separation of powers, and reduce the significance of the rule of law to a sham.[3]

---

[3] Case III 77/63, *Re Tax on Malt Barley* FG Rhineland-Palatinate decision of 14 November 1963, [1963] EuR 10 130, [1964] 10 CMLR 130. Quote CMLR p. 163.

National high courts were also concerned about ceding interpretive authority to the European Court of Justice. Not wanting to admit that they were looking out for their own institutional interests, high courts cloaked their concerns in legalistic arguments about respecting the constitution, protecting constitutional guarantees and legal certainty, and respecting parliamentary prerogatives. While the arguments were not wholly without merit, many legal scholars found them exaggerated and legally inconsistent, revealing ulterior motives behind the legal arguments.[4]

Finally, there were political factors that judges had to consider. The transformed EC legal system implied a significant loss of national sovereignty; a foreign court could rule on national law and policy in areas seemingly tangentially related to creating a common market. National judges were sensitive to issues of national sovereignty, and were accustomed to deferring to national parliaments while leaving foreign policy to the government. Indeed the 'last law passed' doctrine was an attempt on the part of courts to respect international treaties without crossing national parliaments. Insisting on the supremacy of international law over contrary and subsequent national law would in many respects be a thankless task that would likely engender controversy among political bodies. National courts do not necessarily run from controversy, but it was far from clear that EC law supremacy was an issue worth fighting for.

ECJ justices and pro-EC law academics tend to dismiss these concerns of national judges, implying that they are relatively isolated anachronisms of small-minded people who fear change. But the ambivalences of national judiciaries were not only well founded, in the 1960s and 1970s they were widely spread, and much of the fears of the national judges have become realities. Pioneering national courts that enforced EC law over the will of politicians were denounced and their independence was threatened. ECJ jurisprudence has also directly encroached on high court prerogatives, providing ample fodder for high courts concerned that they would lose authority to the ECJ. The ECJ instructed lower courts to ignore the jurisprudence and rules of higher courts if it hindered them from applying EC law supremacy, indeed certain national high courts have, for all practical purposes, become completely subjugated to the jurisprudence of the European Court. Former German Tax Court judge Voss argued that given the advanced development of EC taxation law 'the Chamber of the Bundesfinanzhof, that is the five judges who are in charge of VAT jurisdiction, would hardly be needed any more' (Voss 1987: 65). The Employment Appeals Tribunal in Britain has also found its authority in certain legal issues to have been compromised because of EC law supremacy (Vargas 1995).

Given the controversy surrounding the legal reasoning offered by the ECJ in support of the supremacy of EC law, and its incompatibility with national legal doctrine and traditions, there was ample legal basis for national judges to reject

---

[4] For example see Cohen-Jonathan (1975); Dehaussy (1990); Ehlermann (1975); Lachaume (1990); Sabourin (1990).

the ECJ's doctrine of EC law supremacy. While most national judges did not want to create legal barriers to the political decision to integrate Europe, and they did not wish ill on the European Court, they did not want the ECJ stepping too far on their legal turf or upsetting the national administration of law. As some high court judges argued, just because politicians did not create an adequate enforcement mechanism for the Treaty of Rome that did not mean that national judges must take on a role enforcing EC law supremacy.[5]

During the years following the ECJ's supremacy declaration, a virtual battle over legal interpretation was waged at the national level. Many national courts refused EC law supremacy, sticking to established constitutional interpretations. But some national courts accepted EC law supremacy, re-interpreting national constitutional provisions to support their position. As national courts went different ways on the issue of EC law supremacy, a variegated pattern of national judicial adherence and non-adherence to EC law emerged. Within the variation in national court practices and legal reasoning regarding EC law are significant clues as to how the process of legal integration at the national level came to unfold, how EC law supremacy took hold within national legal systems, and thus how the national doctrinal battle was resolved in favor of EC law supremacy.

The legal concerns about EC law supremacy and the challenges to ECJ authority were often given their strongest voice by higher national courts. This is not so surprising when one considers that higher courts had the most to lose by the extension of ECJ jurisdictional authority over national legal issues. As courts of last resort, high courts traditionally enjoyed dominant influence over the development of national law and were the final interpreters of national law.[6] Any time a new area of EC law was declared to create 'Direct Effects', the supreme interpretive authority over that area of law became part of the European Court's jurisdictional authority. Higher courts were also concerned with policing the overall functioning of the national legal system, making them inherently more conservative than lower courts. The concerns of high courts are manifest in their jurisprudence regarding EC law supremacy, where high courts reject ECJ legal arguments, refuse the authority of the ECJ, try to limit the reach and scope of ECJ jurisprudence, and try to keep lower courts from making referrals to the ECJ. It is also manifest in the referral patterns of high courts to the ECJ. Even though high courts, as courts of last instance, 'must' refer questions of EC law to the ECJ, the Constitutional Courts in Germany, Italy, Belgium, and France have never made a referral to the ECJ. Other national high courts have sent relatively few referrals

---

[5] For example see *Molkerei-Zentrale Westfalen/Lippe GmbH v. Hauptzollamt Paderborn* BFH reference of 27 July 1967 to the ECJ.

[6] High courts are courts where the jurisdictional authority over substantive, constitutional, *or* procedural legal interpretation is not subject to appeal. Most European legal systems have multiple high courts. For example, in Germany, there is a federal supreme court for each substantive area of law. In France, Belgium, and Italy there is a high administrative court, and a high court for civil and penal systems, and a high constitutional court.

to the European Court compared to the number of referrals coming from lower courts. More important than the number of referrals being made, however, is the type of referrals being made. High courts' referrals to the ECJ are much more likely to be narrow technical questions about EC law, questions which do not allow the ECJ to expand the reach or scope of its jurisprudence. Commenting on the French and German high courts' use of the *Acte Clair* doctrine, where national courts declare EC law to be sufficiently clear so as to avoid a referral to the ECJ, Gerard Bebr wrote:

The *acte clair* doctrine is of course not systematically used by the [French High Administrative Court] or by the [German Federal Tax Court] to block off a reference to the Court. These courts did make references but they did so primarily in those cases which concerned rather technical questions. It is typical for their attitude that precisely in matters of principle, particularly those concerning the supremacy of Community Law, the delimitation of Community and State competence, or the nature and effect of directives, they have avoided, under the cover of this doctrine, a mandatory reference. In these instances, they so vindicated their jurisdiction to interpret Community rules and to 'overrule' the jurisprudence of the Court, defied the supremacy of Community law and reasserted thereby State powers...In this respect the practice of the *Conseil d'État* and of the *Bundesfinanzhof* seeking to reserve questions of fundamental importance to themselves in fact challenges the exclusive interpretative jurisdiction of the Court. (Bebr 1983: 456–7)

Reserving for themselves difficult questions about the relationship of European law to national law is a sort of 'don't ask and the ECJ can't tell' policy, which limits the ECJ from expanding its jurisdictional reach at the expense of national high courts by denying the ECJ the opportunity to do so. It is not, however, universally true that high courts do not send issues of substance to the ECJ or accept ECJ jurisprudence. Sometimes high courts embraced EC law to further their own competitive battles against other high courts or other political bodies. For example, Imelda Maher argues that the House of Lords made referrals to the European Court to deflect criticism from itself when it made constitutional changes affecting parliamentary sovereignty. Joseph Weiler and Burley and Mattli have argued that to the extent that EC law accords new powers of judicial review, national courts have an incentive to embrace ECJ jurisprudence. Sometimes high courts have made referrals because they expect a decision in their favor, and they wanted to avoid having lower courts circumvent them and make the referral themselves (Burley and Mattli 1993; Weiler 1991).[7]

While EC law supremacy posed a threat to the influence and authority of high courts and implied a significant compromise of national sovereignty, lower courts found for themselves few costs and numerous benefits in making referrals

[7] For a review of the alternative explanations of national court participation in legal integration, see Alter (1998). Jonathan Golub also reviews limitations in dominant approaches to explaining national court participation in legal integration (Golub 1995).

to the ECJ and applying EC law. Being first instance courts, lower court judges were used to having another court hierarchically above them, and to having their jurisprudence rewritten by courts above them. They also did not have to worry about how their individual actions might upset legal certainty or the smooth functioning of the legal system. Thus they were more open to sending to the ECJ broad and provocative legal questions about the reach and effects of European law in the national legal order. There were also many benefits for lower courts in seizing the ECJ and invoking EC law. It allowed lower courts to circumvent restrictive jurisprudence of higher courts, and re-open legal debates which had been closed, and thus try for legal outcomes they preferred either for policy or legal reasons. For example, appealing to EC law allowed pro-women industrial tribunals to circumvent the Employment Appeals Tribunal and the Conservative government, and to get legal outcomes which helped them promote equal pay for men and women (Vargas 1995: 65–72). Having an ECJ decision also magnified the influence of the lower court decisions in the legal process, as the decision became part of established legal precedence, sometimes led to journal articles on decisions which otherwise would not have been publicly reported, and could decisively contribute to the development of national law.[8] Having an ECJ decision behind a lower court decision also made it less likely to be reversed by a higher court, thus it actually bolstered the legal power and influence of the lower courts. For the lower court, the ECJ was like a second parent when parental approval wards off sanction. When the lower court did not like what they thought one parent (the higher national court) would say, or did not agree with what the parent said, it would go ask the other parent (the ECJ). Having the other parent's approval decreased the likelihood that they would be sanctioned for challenging legal precedence or government policy. If the lower court, however, did not think that it would like what the other parent might say, it would follow the 'don't ask and the ECJ can't tell' policy and not make a referral.

The different strategic calculations of national courts vis-à-vis the ECJ created a competition-between-courts dynamic of legal integration, which fed the process legal integration and came to shift the national legal context from under high courts. The limitations on interpretation of national law created by high courts provoked lower courts to make referrals to the ECJ, so that the lower courts could deviate from established jurisprudence or get to new legal outcomes which they preferred. In using EC law and the ECJ to achieve outcomes that they were institutionally and politically unable to achieve through the domestic legal process

---

[8] In European civil law systems legal doctrine and legal periodicals play a more important role in the legal process than in the United States. As a case-book on comparative legal traditions wrote:

The bar tends...to rely on the editors of the privately published legal journals who select and print what they consider to be the important cases. Typically each case is followed by an annotation written by an expert...Though not a formal source of law, the weight of scholarly authority, known in civil law terminology as 'the doctrine', is everywhere taken into account by legislators and judges when they frame, interpret or apply law (Glendon, Gordon, and Osakwe 1985: 162–3).

alone, lower courts created opportunities for the ECJ to expand its jurisdiction and jurisprudence, and in some cases lower courts actually goaded the ECJ to expand the legal authority of EC law more and more. In this respect, one can say that lower courts were the motors of legal integration, driving legal expansion through their referrals to the ECJ, and bringing ECJ jurisprudence into the national legal order.

Higher courts tried to stop lower courts from making references to the ECJ so as to stop EC law from encroaching in their legal domain. In Britain, the Court of Appeal and the House of Lords developed narrow guidelines about when a lower court referral to the ECJ was justified (Bermann et al. 1993: 264–7), and in Italy the Constitutional Court said that all issues of the validity of European law and national law were constitutional issues, so that only it could decide if EC law was supreme to subsequent national law.[9] In other cases, high courts issued their own narrow interpretations of EC law to limit its applicability in the national realm and ward off referrals to the ECJ.[10] Sometimes high courts even quashed lower court decisions to refer a case to the ECJ, or directly challenged ECJ jurisprudence.[11] But the ability of higher courts to stop lower court referrals was limited. The decision to refer a case to the ECJ had to be appealed to the higher court in order for a high court to be able to quash a referral, and often decisions were not appealed. And lower courts often simply ignored the rulings of the higher courts, and made referrals anyway to provoke the ECJ to issue an alternative interpretation.[12]

The ECJ for its part encouraged the competitive dynamic between lower and higher courts. It defended the right of lower courts to refer any question they wanted, and encouraged lower courts by giving serious evaluations of their questions, while dismissing higher court refutations of their own authority. In direct challenge to the Italian Constitutional Court, the ECJ even instructed lower courts to ignore the constitutional rules, guidelines, or jurisprudence of higher courts if such rules would lead the lower court not to give effect to EC law.[13]

---

[9] *Costa v. Enel and Soc. Edisonvolta* Italian Constitutional Court decision of 7 March 1964 Judgment No. 14, Foro Italiano 87 I 465.

[10] For example, in the Turnover Tax Struggle covered in more detail in (Alter 2001: 80–7) Case 57/65, *Alfons Lütticke GmbH v. Hauptzollamt Saarlouis* BFH decision of 15 January 1969.

[11] For example *Minister of Interior v. Daniel Cohn-Bendit* Conseil d'État decision of 22 December 1978, [1980] CMLR 545–62; Case V B 51/80, *Re Value Added Tax Directives* BFH decision of 16 July 1981, [1982] 1 CMLR 527.

[12] To name but two examples, lower finance courts in Germany ignored Federal Finance Court's jurisprudence on the direct effect of directives, making references to the ECJ to challenge the Federal Tax Court's jurisprudence (FG Munster decision of 24 May 1984, EFG 1985 310; FG Niedersächsen decision of 9 February, 1984 , EFG 1984 527–8; FG Hessen decision of 24 April 1985) and British industrial appeals tribunals ignored the Employment Appeals Tribunal's jurisprudence on pregnancy dismissals, relying on EC law instead (op. cit. Vargas).

[13] Case 106/77, *Amministrazione delle Finanze dello Stato v. Simmenthal SpA (II)* [1978] ECR 629, ECJ.

Because of the actions of lower courts, EC law expanded into new issue areas and came to influence national law. Since all it takes is one court referral to allow the ECJ to expand its jurisdictional authority, the possibilities for legal expansion presented by the preliminary ruling system were abundant. The influence of EC law spread to areas never envisioned by national politicians, such as the provision of education grants to non-nationals, the provision of equal pay to men and women, industrial relations, and the advertisement of British abortion services in Ireland.[14] As legal questions were appealed up the national judicial hierarchies, higher courts were put in the position of either quashing ECJ doctrine, or accepting it. High courts freely accepted ECJ jurisprudence so far as it did not encroach on their own authority. When the ECJ encroached too far into their own jurisdictional authority, high courts rejected the aspects of ECJ doctrine that undermined their own jurisdictional authority. The confrontational responses of high courts to ECJ jurisprudence that asserted ECJ authority over national legal issues led legal commentators to invoke the terminology of 'war' to describe the relationship between the ECJ and higher national courts, and in some cases the commentators baldly concluded that higher national courts had chosen war over cooperation. Since ECJ jurisprudence did not affect all high courts equally, there was seldom a unified opposition by national courts to any given ECJ decision. Thus a varied pattern of acceptance and refusal of ECJ jurisprudence and jurisdictional authority by national high courts emerged within and across national legal systems.

Lower courts referred to the ECJ questions high courts would not have asked and the actions of the lower courts came to actually shift the national legal context from under the high courts. It shifted the context in two ways. The acceptance of EC law supremacy by some courts and the rejection of ECJ legal authority by other courts within the same national system created problems of legal consistency which, in legal communities committed to legal logic and legal reasoning, was alarming. Observing the legal inconsistency created by the different positions of the French Conseil d'État and Cour de Cassation regarding EC law supremacy, French legal scholar and member of the legal order of the Conseil d'État Ronny Abraham wrote:

This discord is very troublesome ... a disputant can receive a different solution depending on if the case involves administrative or civil jurisdiction: in one case it will be decided by the rules of the legislature and in the other by rule of the treaty. But intellectually, such different treatment is not justified by any account. It is without relation to logic that should rule over the division of competences between the two legal jurisdictions. That one jurisdiction would apply private law and the other public law, which corresponds to

---

[14] Case 9/74, *Casagrande v. Landeshauptstadt München* [1974] ECR 773, [1974] CMLR 158, 423; Case C-159/90, *Society for the Protection of Unborn Children Ireland Ltd v. Grogan* [1991] 3 CMLR 849.

the logic of the system. But that one would apply the treaty and the other national law, that doesn't correspond to any logic. (Abraham 1989: 120)

In Germany, concerns about legal inconstancy motivated the German Constitutional Court to actually address legal issues which it had avoided or allowed to languish in its docket, deciding the issue in order to restore legal order.[15] But in France the divergence in the legal positions of the Conseil d'État and the Cour de Cassation was maintained for fourteen years, and there is no evidence that the legitimacy of either institution was seriously damaged or that the consistency concerns were enough to encourage one of the two courts to change their jurisprudence.

More important seems to be that at a certain point it became clear that high courts had failed in their efforts to stem the legal tide of EC law, or to decisively control the development of national law in certain legal issues. As the French Commissariat du Gouvernement argued in the famous *Nicolo* case:

It cannot be repeated often enough that the era of the unconditional supremacy of internal law is now over. International rules of law, particularly those of Europe, have gradually conquered our legal universe, without hesitating furthermore to encroach on the competence of Parliament...In this way certain entire fields of our law such as those of the economy, employment or protection of human rights, now very largely originate genuinely from international legislation.[16]

It was not merely the fact that there was more EC legislation, but rather ECJ doctrine had made more areas and types of EC law directly binding. As ECJ doctrine expanded and was applied to more issue areas, more and more areas of national law came to be influenced by EC law and the ECJ. Pinpointing the ECJ's doctrine as a source of legal expansion, former House of Lords judge Lord Denning re-configured his famous metaphor of EC law as an incoming tide, arguing:

Our sovereignty has been taken away by the European Court of Justice. It has made many decisions impinging on our statute law and says that we are to obey its decisions instead of our own statute law...It has put on the Treaty an interpretation according to their own views of policy...the European Court has held that all European directives are binding within each of the European countries; and must be enforced by the national courts; even though they are contrary to our national law...No longer is European law an incoming tide flowing up the estuaries of England. It is now like a tidal wave bringing

---

[15] Legal scholars have argued that mounting conflicts over legal interpretation among German ordinary courts will provoke the German Constitutional Court to enter into the legal debate, if only to resolve the legal issue. See Alter (2001: 85, 104).

[16] Despite what the name would imply, the Commissaire du Gouvernement is not a representative of the government. He/she is a member of the Conseil d'État who offers a reasoned opinion to the Conseil to consider. Since Conseil d'État decisions are short and cryptic, the argument of the Commissaire is often printed along with the Conseil's decision, and used to help interpret the legal basis for Conseil judgments. *Raoul Georges Nicolo and another,* Conseil d'État decision of 20 October 1989, M. Frydman, Commissaire du Gouvernement, [1990] 1 CMLR 173–91.

down our sea walls and flowing inland over our fields and houses—to the dismay of all. (Denning, 1990)

Because so much national law touched on EC law, and so many lower courts were following the ECJ rather than their own high courts, opposition to ECJ jurisprudence lost its influence and effectiveness. National high courts repositioned themselves to the new reality, reversing their jurisprudence that challenged EC law supremacy and adjusting national constitutional doctrine to make it compatible with enforcing EC law over national law. But they did not accept the legal reasoning offered by the ECJ. By basing the supremacy of EC law on national constitutions and not tying themselves to the ECJ's legal reasoning regarding EC law supremacy, high courts left open legal avenues through which they could refuse the authority of the ECJ in the future without contradicting their jurisprudence on EC law supremacy.

The legal process in general, and legal integration more specifically, is not only about courts competing against each other. Clearly judges also care about policy outcomes, legal logic, and legal certainty, and the relationships between courts are not so adversarial that judges mainly want to challenge each other. But since EC law supremacy involved the question of who decides and who is the highest authority, the doctrinal issue of EC law supremacy was more contentious than most EC legal issues. The competition dynamic was instrumental in establishing the supremacy of EC law over national law and it continues to be an important component shaping the development of EC legal doctrine and fueling the process of legal integration in Europe.

Without the competition dynamic, it is difficult to understand why national legal doctrines shifted from *lex posterior derogat legi priori* to doctrines compatible with the supremacy of EC law. The debate over the relationship of national law to international law was an old one for national legal communities, and while tensions still remained by the time the ECJ declared EC law supremacy, the national legal debates in many countries had settled at an equilibrium around the principle *lex posterior derogat legi priori*. Given that there was no clear legal basis for EC law supremacy, and there were solid and entrenched legal reasons to refuse a role enforcing the supremacy of international law, there was seemingly no reason to reverse this long-standing doctrine. Indeed many national courts refused to change national doctrine in light of ECJ rulings for many years, picking apart the legal reasons in support of EC law supremacy offered by courts embracing EC law supremacy or by pro-integration legal scholars.

At the same time, to the extent that national courts had an interest in embracing a role enforcing international law over national law, because it empowered them or because they thought it was the right thing to do, they had all they really needed to make such a change long before the ECJ told them that they could. In many European countries, the new post-war constitutions created legal opportunities to assert a new role controlling the compatibility of national law with international law (Lagrange 1968), and the failure of the legal profession during fascist rule made judicial review acceptable in German and Italy. But it took lower courts making referrals to the ECJ, and invoking ECJ jurisprudence in their decisions for national doctrine to shift. Had the ECJ not been there as a willing actor which could support lower court deviation from higher court legal precedent, it is highly unlikely that lower courts would have been so bold in their challenges to established jurisprudence and their refusals to follow high court jurisprudence. Had lower courts not incorporated EC law, seized the ECJ and ignored higher court jurisprudence, it is also unlikely that higher courts would have overturned historic traditions and doctrines and accepted a role enforcing international law in the national realm. Without the ECJ as a common reference point for national court competition dynamics, it is also doubtful that the national legal systems of all the member states would have evolved to similar doctrinal positions regarding the supremacy of European law over national law.

Competition between courts continues to be an influence in European legal integration so far as concerns over jurisdictional authority make some national courts reticent to send questions to the ECJ to decide, and lower courts more willing to send cases. Competition is also involved in high court threats of non-compliance with ECJ jurisprudence, which they use to influence the development of EC law.[17] Just as Pierson and Leibfried find that competition among layers of government was important in shaping the content of EC and national social policy (Pierson and Leibfried 1995), competition over who decides and how they decide seems to be important in shaping EC legal doctrine, the development of the EC's legal institution, and the outcome of judicial decision-making.

In trying to establish a federal system in the United States, it took many years before the US Supreme Court's authority to review state law and state court decisions was accepted by the state supreme courts.[18] In Europe, the process of

---

[17] High courts learned that they could influence ECJ jurisprudence by holding out threats that they might find EC law and ECJ jurisprudence inapplicable, while clearly indicating to the ECJ which legal expansions and interpretations they would object to. These threats clearly work; for example in light of national court non-compliance and reticence the ECJ did not expand the reach of its doctrine regarding the direct effect of directives (Morris and David 1987). In light of the German Constitutional Court's criticism of the basic rights protections in EC law, the ECJ has developed a doctrine on basic rights protection (Mancini and Keeling 1992). Recently the German Constitutional Court has sent the message that it will reject future expansions of EC law if such expansions amount to a re-writing of the EC Treaties, calling on the German government and the ECJ to better protect the subsidiarity rights of member states and regions. We can already see the effect of this threat as the ECJ makes greater pains to recognize member state rights and limit the reach of EC law (see *Brunner and Others v. The European Union Treaty* BVerfG decision of 13 October 1993 2 BvR 2134/92 and 2 BvR 2159/92, CMLR 57–108).

[18] 'Between 1789 and 1860 the courts of seven States denied the constitutional right of the United States Supreme Court to decide cases on writs of error to State courts—Virginia, Ohio, Georgia, Kentucky, South Carolina, California and Wisconsin. The Legislatures of all these states adopted resolutions or statues against this power of the Supreme Court. Bills were introduced in Congress on at least ten occasions to deprive the Court of its jurisdiction—in 1821, 1822, 1824, 1831, 1846, 1867, 1868, 1871, 1872, and 1882.' (Warren 1913: 516) Leslie Goldstein has since written more on this topic, see Goldstein (2001).

establishing the supremacy of EC law over national law took fewer than 25 years. The competition dynamic in legal integration could well explain the rapidity through which this fundamental legal transformation came about.

II. Eliciting Political Acquiescence and Political Support?

The original version of this chapter included a section on how the ECJ co-opted politicians. Chapter 6 covers this topic more completely, thus I have edited the section out. I did, however, move a few pieces of the analysis to Chapter 6, which was written with strict space limitations.

III. The Emergence of a Rule of Law in Europe

The acceptance of EC law supremacy by national judiciaries created an institutional basis for an effective international rule of law in Europe, providing the opportunity and the capacity for the ECJ to influence many areas of EC and national policy. Once the ECJ had national courts to implement its jurisprudence, the largest political threat against the ECJ—non-compliance—was gone, giving the ECJ more latitude in its decision-making. National court support also changed the default outcome of political non-action. When ECJ decisions were unenforceable, a member state could ignore an ECJ decision and simply maintain an 'illegal' national policy. But with national courts enforcing ECJ decisions directly, political non-action could mean significant political and financial costs. Taking legislative action to reverse unwanted decisions is much harder than dismissing or ignoring the decision, and if legislation requires the assent of other member states, legislating over an ECJ decision might be impossible. Because the ECJ knew that politicians would probably not be able to create enough consensus to reverse activist jurisprudence or to attack the Court for its excesses, it was emboldened to make decisions with more significant material and political impact. In these respects, national judicial support contributed indispensably to the legal and political authority of the European Court.

Stripped of its legal attributes, the account of the transformation of the EC legal system is a classic story of bureaucratic politics in response to the creation of a new political institution. As Terry Moe has argued:

A new public agency is literally a new actor on the political scene. It has its own interests, which may diverge from those of its creators, and it typically has resources—expertise, delegated authority—to strike out on its own should the opportunities arise. The political game is different now: there are more players and more interests to be accommodated. (Moe 1990: 434–5)

The interests of the ECJ were to be an authoritative voice on issues of EC law, which meant having cases and interesting legal questions to rule on and creating a means to elicit compliance with its decisions. The Court used the resources it had to help realize these interests, and in the case of the EC legal system the resources it had were above and beyond that of a traditional court—national or international.[19] But what proved critical in the establishment of a rule of law in Europe, was the preliminary ruling procedure. The preliminary ruling system was new for most national legal systems, and was unique as far as international law went. By allowing national judges to stop legal proceedings to get a legally authoritative decision from an international court outside of the national legal and political system, the preliminary ruling procedure introduced a new layer of politics that could be appealed to when domestic channels of influence were foreclosed.[20] In the words of Moe, because of the preliminary ruling procedure, the national legal process, indeed national politics, was now a different game. Preliminary ruling cases came to dominate the Court's docket, and the most significant of the Court's rulings still come through the preliminary ruling procedure.[21]

The new game remained largely a game of domestic politics with plaintiffs and judges following domestic political incentives and working to influence domestic law and policy. Indeed the vast majority of preliminary ruling cases attacking national law were not instigated by exporters trying to enter new markets, but rather by importers, national firms, and domestic interest groups trying to gain advantage over their competitors, gain tax refunds, create escapes from restrictive national legislation, or change national policy. National legal actors did not appear particularly interested in legal integration per se, indeed in interviews

---

[19] For more on the European Court's resources, see Burley and Mattli (1993); Weiler (1991).

[20] By invoking EC law and the ECJ, domestic interests could transform the domestic politics of certain issue areas, actually shifting the domestic balance of power between groups and the government to obtain outcomes unattainable through domestic politics or the national legal process alone. For a discussion of when and how this works, see Chapter 8.

[21] By 1991 national courts had referred 2,324 cases to the ECJ, as compared to 868 cases raised by the Commission during the same time. Most of the Commission's cases were brought in the 1980s. The exponential increase in Commission cases can be explained by the increasing authority of the ECJ combined with the completion of the single market. Most of the infringement cases raised by the Commission in the 1980s dealt with the timely and correct implementation of directives passed to help complete the common market. The more authoritative nature of ECJ decisions (especially in light of the ECJ's doctrine on the direct effect of directives) made using the infringement procedure to challenge the late or incorrect implementation of directives made it a successful strategy.

	1960–1969	1970–1980	1981–1991	Total 1960–1991
Cases brought to the ECJ by Commission	27	87	741	855
Cases brought to the ECJ through national courts	75	666	1583	2324

Data updated and reprinted in Alter (2001: 15). For more on the Commission's use of the infringement procedure see Börzel (2001).

European lawyers and judges said that they were not especially interested in the goal of promoting European integration nor did they see themselves as Community judges.

Legal experts and ECJ judges have expressed significant doubt that the EC legal system could have become effective if it had to rely on an infringement procedure initiated by the Commission or a member state (Lecourt 1991; Mancini and Keeling 1994; Stein 1981). But the transformed preliminary ruling system allowed the ECJ to create a political constituency, indeed a political power base, of its own: the national judiciaries. Because of this political alliance between the ECJ and the national judiciaries, judicial politics in Europe has been transformed. National sovereignty has been fundamentally redefined so that national parliaments and governments are no longer necessarily the highest authority. The ECJ has become an important and influential actor in Europe and courts have become political actors in all sorts of policy areas. Given that lower national judiciaries in Europe have historically played a much less significant role in policy-making than they have in the United States, this transition is especially significant. How the ECJ will use its position and authority to influence EC and national politics in the future remains to be seen. But its success in establishing the political and legal authority of an international court is unprecedented. No longer can it be said that an international court cannot significantly influence national and international politics.

6

Who Are the 'Masters of the Treaty'?: European Governments and the European Court of Justice (1998)

Few contest that the European Court of Justice (ECJ) is an unusually influential international court. The Court can declare illegal European Union (EU) laws and national laws that violate the Treaty of Rome in areas traditionally considered to be purely the prerogative of national governments, including social policy, gender equality, industrial relations, and competition policy; and its decisions are respected. Nevertheless, there is significant disagreement about the extent of the Court's political autonomy from member states and the extent to which it can decide cases against their interests.

Legal and neo-functionalist scholars have asserted that the ECJ has significant autonomy by virtue of the separation of law and politics and the inherent legitimacy of courts as legal actors, and that it can use this autonomy to rule against the interests of member states (Weiler 1991; Burley and Mattli 1993). Such an analysis implies that virtually any court, international or national, can decide against a government's interests because it is a legal body.[1] International relations analysts have argued that member states have sufficient control over the Court so that it lacks the autonomy to decide against the interests of powerful member states (Garrett and Weingast 1993). This implies that the ECJ, as an international court, is particularly dependent on national governments and must bend to their interests.

Both accounts contain significant elements of truth. The legal nature of ECJ decisions affords the Court some protection against political attacks, but member states have significant tools to influence it. Neither theory, however, can explain why the Court, which was once politically weak and did not stray far from the interests of the European governments, now has significant political authority and boldly rules against their interests. The nature of the ECJ as a court

---

[1] This generalization follows from the logic of the argument, with an important caveat that this argument applies to liberal democracies where the rule of law is a political reality. If domestic courts in general lack political authority, an international court is also likely to lack political authority (Burley 1993).

has not changed, nor have the tools the member states have to influence judicial politics. This article is an attempt to move beyond the categories of legalism, neo-functionalism, and neorealism, drawing on theories from comparative politics literature to explain the nature of ECJ–member state relations.

Member states intended to create a court that could not significantly compromise national sovereignty or national interests, but the ECJ changed the EU legal system, fundamentally undermining member state control over the Court. A significant part of the 'transformation' of the EU legal system has been explained by legal scholars who have shown how the Court turned the 'preliminary ruling system' of the EU from a mechanism to allow individuals to challenge EC law in national courts into a mechanism to allow individuals to challenge national law in national courts (see Weiler 1991 and Chapter 5). But important questions remain. How could the Court expand the EU legal system so far from the desire of the member states and beyond their control? Once the ECJ had transformed the EU legal system, why did member states not reassert control and return the system to the one they had designed and intended? If member states failed to control the transformation of the EU legal system or the bold application of EC law by the ECJ, what does this mean about the ability of national governments to control legal integration in the future?

Through an investigation of how the ECJ escaped member state control, I develop a general argument about ECJ–member state relations. The argument has three components. First, I argue that judges and politicians have fundamentally different time horizons, which translates into different preferences for judges and politicians regarding the outcome of individual cases. By playing off the shorter time horizons of politicians, the ECJ developed legal doctrine and thus constructed the institutional building blocks of its own power and authority without provoking a political response.

Second, I argue that the transformation of the European legal system by the ECJ limited the possible responses of national governments to its decisions within the domestic political realm. In the early years of the EU legal system, national politicians turned to extralegal means to circumvent unwanted decisions; they asserted the illegitimacy of the decisions in a battle for political legitimacy at home, instructed national administrations to ignore ECJ jurisprudence, or interpreted away any difference between EC law and national policy. The threat that national governments might turn to these extralegal means, disobeying an ECJ decision, helped contain ECJ activism. With national courts enforcing ECJ jurisprudence against their own governments, however, many of these extralegal avenues no longer worked. Because of national judicial support for ECJ jurisprudence, national governments were forced to frame their response in terms that could persuade a legal audience, and thus they became constrained by the legal rules of the game.

Third, national court enforcement of ECJ jurisprudence also changed the types of policy responses available to national governments at the EU level.

Member states traditionally relied on their veto power to ensure that EU policy did not go against strongly held interests. The ECJ, however, interpreted existing EC laws in ways that member states had not intended and in ways that compromised strongly held interests and beliefs. As member states began to object to ECJ jurisprudence, they found it difficult to change EU legislation to reverse court decisions or to attack the jurisdiction and authority of the ECJ. Because there was no consensus among states to attack the authority of the ECJ, member states lacked a credible threat that could cow the Court into quiescence. Instead, the institutional rules combined with the lack of political consensus gave the ECJ significant room to maneuver.

In the first section I identify the functional roles the ECJ was designed to serve in the process of European integration and show how the Court's transformation of the preliminary ruling process went beyond what member states had intended, significantly compromising national sovereignty. In the second section I explain how the ECJ was able to transform the EU legal system during a period when the system was inherently weak, developing the time horizons argument and the argument about how national court enforcement of ECJ jurisprudence changed the policy options of national governments at the national level. In the third section I explain why member states were not able to reform the EU legal system once it was clear that the Court was going beyond the narrow functional interests of the member states, developing the third argument about the changes within the EU political process. In the conclusion I develop a series of hypotheses about the institutional constraints on ECJ autonomy and discuss the generalizability of the EU legal experience to other international contexts.

I. The ECJ as the Agent of Member States?

Before looking at how the ECJ escaped member state control, I first consider the role the ECJ was created to play in the EU political system. Geoffrey Garrett and Barry Weingast use principal–agent analysis to explain how the ECJ is an agent of the member states, serving important yet limited functional roles in the EU political process and politically constrained by the member states. The principal–agent framework is useful in identifying the interests of national governments in having an EU legal system at all. But the emphasis of Garret and Weingast on the Court's role in enforcing contracts and dispute resolution is historically misleading. It attributes to the ECJ certain roles that rightfully belong to the European Commission, and it misses the main role the member states wanted the ECJ to play in the EU political system: keeping the Commission from exceeding its authority. Why is Garrett and Weingast's historical inaccuracy important? It overlooks entirely the role of the courts in a democratic system of government where courts provide checks and balances against abuse of executive authority and thus overlooks a whole area for judicial influence in the political process. And, importantly for this article, focusing on enforcing contracts and dispute resolution misrepresents the interests of the member states in the EU legal system and misrepresents the role the preliminary ruling system was intended to play in the EU legal process, thereby giving the impression that the preliminary ruling system existed to help enforce EC law. This impression is wrong, and it leads one to overlook the importance and the meaning of the transformation of the preliminary ruling system, missing the essence of the Court's political power.

The ECJ was created to fill three limited roles for the member states: ensuring that the Commission and the Council of Ministers did not exceed their authority, filling in vague aspects of EC laws through dispute resolution, and deciding on charges of non-compliance raised by the Commission or by member states. None of these roles required national courts to funnel individual challenges to national policy to the ECJ or to enforce EC law against their governments. Indeed, negotiators envisioned a limited role for national courts in the EU legal system.

The ECJ was created as part of the European Coal and Steel Community in order to protect member states and firms by ensuring that the supranational high authority did not exceed its authority.[2] When the EU was founded, the Court's mandate was changed, but its primary function remained to keep the Commission and the Council in check. Indeed, most of the Treaty of Rome's articles regarding the Court's mandate deal with this 'checking' role, and access to the ECJ is the widest for this function: individuals can bring challenges to Commission and Council acts directly to the ECJ, and the preliminary ruling system (Article 177 §2) (now Article 234 §2) allowed individuals to raise challenges to EU policy in national courts.[3] The most significant expansion of the Court's authority by national governments since the Treaty of Rome has also been in this area. The creation of a Tribunal of First Instance, which was long opposed because it was seen as a stepping stone to a federal system of courts, was finally accepted so that the ECJ could better review the Commission's decisions in the area of competition policy.

A second role of the Court is dispute resolution when EC laws are vague (or, in the language of Garrett and Weingast, filling in incomplete contracts). In the EU, the Commission is primarily responsible for filling in contracts in areas delegated to it (competition law, agricultural markets, and much of the internal market), and national administrations fill in the principles in EU regulations and directives they administer. The ECJ may be seized in the event of a disagreement between

---

[2] The ECJ was modeled after the French Conseil d'État, which controls government abuses of authority. In France individuals can bring charges against the government to the Conseil d'État. They cannot challenge the validity of a national law, but if they think that the law was implemented incorrectly, or that a government official exceeded their authority under the law, they can challenge the government action in front of the Conseil. For more on the history of the ECJ, see Kari (1979: ch. III); Rasmussen (1986: 201–12); Robertson (1966: 150–80).

[3] Articles 173–176, 177 §2, 178–179, 181, and 183–184 of the Treaty of Rome pertain to the checking function of the ECJ (now Articles 230–233, 234 §2, 235–236, 238, and 240–241).

member states or firms on the one hand, and the Commission or national governments on the other, about how the treaty or other provisions of EC law should be interpreted.[4] The ECJ resolves the disagreement by interpreting the disputed EC legal clause and thus by filling in the contract through its legal decision. The preliminary ruling procedure (Article 177 §1 and 3 (now Articles 234 §1 and 3)) allowed individuals to challenge in national courts EC law interpretations of the Commission or of national administrations (for example, an individual could challenge the government's administration of EU agricultural subsidies). Article 177 (now Article 234) challenges were to pertain only to questions of European law, not to the interpretation of national law or to the compatibility of national law with EC law.

The ECJ was not designed to monitor infringements of EU agreements (in Garrett and Weingast's terms, monitoring defection), which has always been the Commission's responsibility (1993).[5] In the Coal and Steel Community, the Commission monitored compliance with ECSC policies on its own, and the ECJ was an appellate body hearing challenges to Commission decisions. Under the Treaty of Rome, the ECJ was designed to play a co-role in the enforcement process. The Commission was still the primary monitor, but the ECJ mediated Commission charges and member state defenses regarding alleged treaty breaches. The ECJ was to play this role, however, only if diplomatic efforts to secure compliance failed. The preliminary ruling system was not designed to be a 'decentralized' mechanism to facilitate more monitoring of member state compliance with the treaty.[6] Indeed, the ECJ clearly lacks the authority to review the compatibility of national law with EC law in preliminary ruling cases.[7]

---

[4] Articles 183 and 177 §1 and 3 (now Articles 240 and 234 §2) of the Treaty of Rome pertain to the filing in incomplete contracting role of the ECJ.

[5] The Commission's first task, as enumerated in Article 155 EEC (now Article 211), is 'to ensure that the provisions of [the] Treaty and the measures taken by the institutions pursuant thereto are applied'.

[6] Negotiators of the Treaty confirm that member states intended only the Commission or member states to raise infringement charges, through Article 169 EEC and Article 170 EEC (now Articles 226 and 227) infringement cases, based on interviews with the Luxembourg negotiator of the Treaty of Rome (Luxembourg, 3 November 1992), a commissioner in the 1960s and 1970s, 9 June 1994, Paris, France, and a director of the Commission's legal services in the 1960s who also negotiated the treaty for France, 7 July 1994, Paris, France. National ratification debates for the Treaty of Rome also reveal that member states believed that only the Commission or other member states could raise infringement charges; document 5266, annex to the verbal procedures of 26 March 1957 of the debates of the French National Assembly, prepared by the Commission of the Foreign Ministry; 'Entwurf eines Gesetzes zu den Vertragen vom 25 Marz 1957 zur Gründung der Europaischen Wirtschaftsgemeinschaft und der Europaischen Atomgemeinschaft' Anlage C; report of representative Dr Mommer from the Bundestag debates of Friday, 5 July 1957, p. 13391; Atti Parlamentari, Senato della Repubblica; Legislatura II 1953–57, disegni di legge e relazioni-document, N. 2107-A, and Camera dei deputati document N. 2814 seduta del 26 marzo 1957.

[7] The preliminary ruling system is designed to allow questions of the interpretation of EC law to be sent to the ECJ. The original idea was that if a national court was having difficulty interpreting an EC regulation, it could ask the ECJ what the regulation meant. It was not designed to allow individuals to challenge national laws in national courts or to have national courts ask if national law is compatible with EC law. For more see Alter (2001: 9–11).

II. The Transformation of the Preliminary Ruling Procedure into an Enforcement Mechanism

Member states continue to want the ECJ to keep EU bodies in check, fill in contracts, and mediate oversight, which is why they have expanded the resources of the ECJ with respect to these narrow functional roles.[8] But none of these roles requires or implies that EC law is supreme to national law, that individuals should help monitor member state compliance with EC law through cases raised in national courts, or that national courts should enforce EC law instead of national law and national policy. These aspects of the Court's jurisdiction were not part of the Treaty of Rome; rather, they were created by the ECJ, which transformed the preliminary ruling system from a mechanism to allow individuals to question EC law into a mechanism to allow individuals to question national law.

The Court's doctrine of direct effect declared that EC law created legally enforceable rights for individuals, allowing individuals to draw on EC law directly in national courts to challenge national law and policy. The doctrine of EC law supremacy made it the responsibility of national courts to ensure that EC law was applied over conflicting national laws.[9] In using the direct effect and supremacy of EC law as its legal crutches, the ECJ does not itself exceed its authority by reviewing the compatibility of national law with EU law in preliminary ruling cases. Indeed, the ECJ usually tells national courts that it cannot consider the compatibility of national laws with EC law but can only clarify the meaning of EC law. But it intentionally encourages national courts to use the preliminary ruling mechanism (Article 177 (now Article 234)) to do this job for it, by indicating in its decision whether or not certain types of national law would be in compliance with EC law and encouraging the national court to set aside incompatible national policies. ECJ Justice Federico Mancini candidly acknowledged the Court's complicity in this jurisdictional transgression:

> It bears repeating that under Article 177 national judges can only request the Court of Justice to interpret a Community measure. The Court never told them they were entitled to overstep that bound: in fact, whenever they did so—for example, whenever they asked if national rule A is in violation of Community Regulation B or Directive C—, the Court answered that its only power is to explain what B or C actually mean. But having paid this lip service to the language of the Treaty and having clarified the meaning of the relevant Community measure, the court usually went on to indicate to what extent a

---

[8] As already mentioned, in 1986 the Treaty of Rome was amended to allow for the creation of a Court of First Instance to allow the ECJ to examine in more detail competition policy decisions of the Commission. In 1989 the role of the ECJ in checking the Commission and the Council was expanded by allowing Parliament to also challenge Commission and Council acts. Also in 1989 the Commission was given the authority to request a lump sum penalty from states that had willfully violated EC law and ignored an ECJ decision. For more see Tallberg (2003).

[9] For more on the doctrines of direct effect and EU law supremacy, see Weiler (1991).

certain type of national legislation can be regarded as compatible with that measure. The national judge is thus led hand in hand as far as the door; crossing the threshold is his job, but now a job no harder than child's play. (Mancini 1989: 606)[10]

Having national courts monitor Treaty of Rome compliance and enforce EC law was not part of the original design of the EU legal system. The transformation of the preliminary ruling system significantly undermined the member states' ability to control the ECJ. It allowed individuals to raise cases in national courts that were then referred to the ECJ, undermining national governments' ability to control which cases made it to the ECJ. Individuals raised cases involving issues that member states considered to be the exclusive domain of national policy, such as the availability of educational grants to non-nationals, the publication by Irish student groups of a how-to guide to get an abortion in Britain, and the dismissal of employees by recently privatized firms. The extension of direct effects to EC Treaty articles also made the Treaty's common market provisions enforceable despite the lack of implementing legislation, so that EC law created constraints member states had not agreed to. Finally, the transformed preliminary ruling system made ECJ decisions enforceable, undermining the ability of member states to ignore unwanted ECJ decisions.

One might think that member states would welcome any innovation that strengthened the monitoring and enforcement mechanisms of the EU legal system, but national governments were not willing to trade encroachments in national sovereignty for ensuring treaty compliance. Negotiators of the Treaty of Rome had actually weakened its enforcement mechanisms compared to what they were in the European Coal and Steel Community (ECSC) Treaty in order to protect national sovereignty, stripping the sanctioning power from European institutions.[11] In most of the original member states, ordinary courts lacked the authority to invalidate national law for any reason. It is unlikely that politicians would give national courts a new power that could only be applied to EC law simply to ensure better treaty compliance, especially because in some countries it would mean that the EU Treaty would be better protected from political transgression than the national constitution! Indeed, if monitoring defection were such a high priority for member states, it might have served their interests better to have made ECJ decisions enforceable by attaching financial sanctions to

---

[10] The ECJ has been known to go beyond this trick and on occasion to tell the national court exactly what to do. In 1994 Mancini acknowledged that the ECJ 'enters the heart of the conflict... but it takes the precaution of rendering it abstract, that is to say it presents it as a conflict between Community law and a hypothetical national provision having the nature of the provision at issue before the national court.' The fiction is necessary to avoid the charge that the ECJ is exceeding its authority (Mancini 1994: 184–5).

[11] In the Coal and Steel Community, the Commission and the ECJ could issue fines and extract payments by withholding transfer payments. In the Treaty of Rome ECJ decisions were purely declaratory.

ECJ decisions (as was done in 1989)[12] to have made transfer payments from the EU contingent on compliance with common market rules, or to have given the Commission more monitoring resources. This would have given member states the benefits of a court that could coerce compliance, and they would not have had to risk having the ECJ delve so far into issues of national policy and national sovereignty.

Most evidence indicates that politicians did not support the transformation of the EU legal system, and that legal integration proceeded despite the intention and desire of national politicians. As Joseph Weiler has pointed out, the largest advances in EU legal doctrine at both the national and the EU level occurred at the same time that member states were scaling back the supranational pretensions of the Treaty of Rome and reasserting national prerogatives (Weiler 1981). When the issue of the national courts enforcing EC law first emerged in front of the ECJ, representatives of member states argued strongly against any interpretation that would allow national courts to evaluate the compatibility of EC law with national law (Stein 1981). In the 1970s, while politicians were blocking attempts to create a common market, the doctrine of EC law supremacy was making significant advances within national legal systems. With politicians actively rejecting supra-nationalism, one can hardly argue that they actually supported an institutional transformation that greatly empowered a supranational EU institution at the expense of national sovereignty.

The preliminary ruling system (Article 177 (now Article 234)), the direct effect, and the supremacy of EC law remained polemic through the 1990s. The Council refused attempts to formally enshrine the supremacy of EC law in a treaty revision or to formally give national courts a role in enforcing EC law supremacy.[13] Numerous battles have ensued over extending the preliminary ruling process to 'inter-governmental' agreements. It took nearly three years after the signing of the 1968 Brussels Convention on the mutual recognition of national court decisions for member states to reach a compromise regarding preliminary ruling authority for the ECJ. For the Brussels Convention, member states restricted the right of reference of national courts to a narrow list of high courts[14]—courts that are known to be reticent to refer cases to the ECJ (see Chapter 5). In the late 1970s negotiations over inter-governmental conventions to deal with fraud against the EU and crimes committed by EU employees broke down altogether over the issue of an Article 177 role for the ECJ. The terms of the conventions had been agreed to, and little national sovereignty was at stake. Nevertheless, France refused to

---

[12] Frustrated that certain member states (especially Italy and Greece) repeatedly violate EC law and ignore ECJ decisions, in 1989 member states returned to the ECJ some of the sanctioning power it had in the ECSC Treaty granting it authority order lump sum payments.

[13] Based on an interview with a member of the German negotiating team who put forward the proposal at the Maastricht negotiations for the Treaty on European Union, 17 February 1994, Bonn, Germany.

[14] Protocol regarding the interpretation of the Brussels Convention of 27 September 1968, adopted 3 June 1971.

extend Article 177 authority for the ECJ at all, and the Benelux countries refused to ratify the agreements without an Article 177 role for the ECJ.[15] This conflict over extending preliminary ruling jurisdiction played itself out again regarding the 1992 Cannes Conventions on Europol, the Customs Information System, and the resurrected conventions regarding fraud in the EU.[16] And it was an issue again in negotiations for the Treaty of Amsterdam where national governments could not agree on the desirability of preliminary ruling powers for the ECJ in Justice and Home Affairs.

Transforming the preliminary ruling system was not necessary for the ECJ to serve the member states' limited functional interests, and it brought a loss of national sovereignty that the Council would not have agreed to then and still would not agree to today. Member states had significant political oversight mechanisms to control the ECJ. As Garrett and Weingast have pointed out:

> Embedding a legal system in a broader political structure places direct constraints on the discretion of a court, even one with as much constitutional independence as the United States Supreme Court. This conclusion holds even if the constitution makes no explicit provisions for altering a court's role. The reason is that political actors have a range of avenues through which they may alter or limit the role of courts. Sometimes such changes require amendment of the constitution, but usually the appropriate alterations may be accomplished more directly through statute, as by alteration of the court's jurisdiction in a way that makes it clear that continued undesired behavior will result in more radical changes. (Garrett and Weingast 1993: 200–1)

Member states controlled the legislative process and could legislate over unwanted ECJ decisions or change the role or mandate of the ECJ. They could also manipulate the appointments process and threaten the professional future of activist judges (ibid.). How could the ECJ construct such a fundamental transformation of the EU legal system against the will of member states?

III. Escaping Member State Control

Although the Court likes to pose modestly as 'the guardian of the Treaties' it is in fact an uncontrolled authority generating law directly applicable in Common Market member states and applying not only to EEC enterprises but also to those established outside the Community, as long as they have business interests within it.[17]

---

[15] Based on interviews with French, German, and Dutch negotiators for these agreements: 27 October 1995, Brussels, 30 October 1995, Paris, and 2 November 1995, Bonn, Germany.

[16] This time Britain has refused to extend Article 177 authority, and the German, Italian, and Benelux parliaments have refused to ratify the agreement without Article 177 authority for the ECJ. According to sources within the Legal Services of the Council, France and perhaps Spain are hiding behind the British position, laying low so that the British take the political heat for a position they too support.

[17] From 'More Powerful Than Intended', *Financial Times,* 22 August 1974.

Principal–agent theory tells us that agents have interests that are inherently different than principals; principals want to control the agent, but the agent wants as much authority and autonomy from the principals as possible (Garrett and Weingast 1993; Pollack 1995; and Moravcsik 1995). The ECJ preferred the transformed preliminary ruling system for the same reason that member states did not want it: it decreased the Court's dependence on member states and the Commission to raise infringement cases by allowing individuals to raise challenges to national law, and it decreased the Court's need to craft decisions to elicit voluntary compliance by making ECJ decisions enforceable (Burley and Mattli 1993; see also Chapter 5). In other words, it enhanced the power of the ECJ. This inherent difference of interests explains why the ECJ would want to expand its authority, but not how it was able to expand its authority. If member states had political oversight controls, how could the agent escape the principals' control?

The answer lies in the different time horizons of politicians and judges and the lack of a credible political threat that was a direct result of the transformation of the preliminary ruling system. With national courts enforcing EC law against their governments, politicians could not simply ignore unwanted ECJ decisions. They were forced to respond to the issues raised by the ECJ in a way that would be legally acceptable both to the ECJ and to national courts.

Different time horizons of courts and politicians

Legalist and neo-functionalist scholars have argued that politicians were simply not paying attention to what the ECJ was doing, or that they were compelled into acquiescence by the apolitical legal language or by their reverence for legal authority.[18] A different explanation is that politicians and judges have different time horizons, a difference that manifests itself in terms of differing interests for politicians and judges in each court decision. Because of these different time horizons, the ECJ was able to be doctrinally activist, building legal doctrine based on unconventional legal interpretations and expanding its own authority, without provoking a political response.

Politicians have shorter time horizons because they must deliver the goods to the electorate in order to stay in office. The focus on staying in office makes politicians discount the long-term effects of their actions or, in this case, inaction (Pierson 1996: 135–6). Member states were most concerned with protecting national interests in the process of integration, while avoiding serious conflicts that could derail the common market effort. As far as the Court's decisions were

---

[18] Joseph Weiler implied that being a supreme court, the ECJ had an inherent legitimacy that was difficult to politically contest (Weiler 1991: 2428). Burley and Mattli argued that it was the non-political veneer of judicial decisions that made them hard for politicians to contest. They acknowledge that this veneer is more myth than reality, but the judicial use of nominally neutral legal principles 'masks' the politics of judicial decisions, gives judges legitimacy, and 'shields' judges from political criticism (Burley and Mattli 1993: 72–3).

concerned, member states wanted to avoid decisions that could upset public policies or create a significant material impact (be it political or financial).[19] The strategy of relying on 'fire alarms' to be set off by ECJ decisions before politicians actually act has advantages. Politicians do not have to expend political energy fighting every court decision that could potentially create political problems in the future, and they can take credit and win public support for addressing the public and political concerns raised by adverse ECJ decisions.[20] But such an approach leads to a focus that prioritizes the material impact of legal decisions over the long-term effects of ECJ doctrine. The short-term focus of politicians explains why they often fail to act decisively when doctrine that is counter to their long-term interest is first established.

The ECJ took advantage of this political fixation on the material consequences of cases to construct legal precedent without arousing political concern. Following a well-known judicial practice, the ECJ expanded its jurisdictional authority by establishing legal principles but not applying the principles to the cases at hand. For example, the ECJ declared the supremacy of EC law in the *Costa* case, but it found that the Italian law privatizing the electric company did not violate EC law.[21] Given that the privatization was legal, what was there for politicians to protest, not comply with, or overturn? Trevor Hartley noted that the ECJ repeatedly used this practice:

A common tactic is to introduce a new doctrine gradually: in the first case that comes before it, the Court will establish the doctrine as a general principle but suggest that it is subject to various qualifications; the Court may even find some reason why it should not be applied to the particular facts of the case. The principle, however, is now established. If there are not too many protests, it will be re-affirmed in later cases; the qualifications can then be whittled away and the full extent of the doctrine revealed. (Hartley 1988: 78–9)

The Commission was an accomplice in the efforts of the ECJ to build doctrinal precedent without arousing political concerns. In an interview the original director of the Commission's legal services argued that legal means—with or without sanctions—would not have worked to enforce the treaty if there was no political will to proceed with integration. He argued that the Commission adopted the 'less worse' solution of compromising on principles but worked to help the ECJ develop its doctrine. The Commission selected infringement cases to bring that were important in terms of building doctrine, especially doctrine that national courts could apply, and avoided cases that would have undermined

---

[19] Rasmussen also observed that states' short-term interests influenced their participation in EU legal proceedings. States tended to participate in cases in which their own national laws were at stake, not paying attention to other countries' cases (Rasmussen 1986: 287).

[20] In their work on the US Congress McCubbins and Schwartz develop the notion of 'fire alarms' as a form of political oversight and identify the many benefits for politicians of such an approach (McCubbins and Schwartz 1987).

[21] Case 6/64, *Costa v. Ente Nazionale per L'Energia Elettrica (Enel)* [1964] ECR 583.

the integration process by arousing political passions.[22] (We now know that the Commission provided more types of aid to the ECJ, including leaking to private plaintiffs cases it decided not to pursue as infringement rulings. See pp. 69–70, 75 in this volume.) By making sure that ECJ decisions did not compromise short-term political interests, the judges and the Commission could build a legal edifice without serious political challenges.

Indeed, the early jurisprudence of the ECJ shows clear signs of caution. Although bold in doctrinal rhetoric, the ECJ made sure that the political impact was minimal in terms of both financial consequences and political consequences. Clarence Mann commented on the early jurisprudence of the ECJ in politically contentious cases, saying that 'by narrowly restricting the scope of its reasoning, [the ECJ] manages to avoid almost every question in issue' (Mann 1972: 413). Stuart Scheingold observed that, in Article 173 (now Article 230) cases, 'the ECJ used procedural rules to avoid decisions of substance' (Scheingold 1971: 21). A French legal advisor at the Secrétariat Général de Coordination Interministérielle des Affaires Européennes argued that the ECJ did not matter until the 1980s because the decisions were principles without any reality. Since there was not much EC law to enforce in the 1960s and 1970s, and since national courts did not accept that they should implement European law over national law, ECJ jurisprudence was simply marginal.[23]

Politicians may have been myopic in their focus on material consequences, but this does not mean that they did not realize that their long-term interest in protecting national sovereignty might be compromised by the doctrinal developments. The Court's *Van Gend* and *Costa* decisions were filled with rhetoric to make politicians uneasy, and lawyers from member states had argued strongly against the interpretations the ECJ eventually endorsed.[24] Indeed, some politicians were clearly unsettled by the legal precedents the ECJ was establishing in the 1960s. According to former Prime Minister Michel Debré, General de Gaulle did ask for revisions of the Court's power and competences in 1968.[25] But other member states were unwilling to renegotiate the Treaty of Rome, especially at a French request, so the political threat to the ECJ was not credible.

In the 1960s the risk of the ECJ running amok was still fairly low given the inherent weakness of the EU legal system. Most national legal systems did not allow for international law supremacy over subsequent national law (indeed, the Italian Constitutional Court and the French Conseil d'État rejected a role

---

[22] A former Commissioner called the Commission's strategy 'informal complicity'. Interview with the former director of the Commission's Legal Services, 7 July 1994, and with a former Commissioner, 9 June 1994, Paris, France.

[23] Based on an interview: 31 October 1995, Paris.

[24] The rhetoric of the *Van Gend en Loos* and *Costa* decisions (see p. 33 in this volume) do not require a legal export to recognize the broad nature of the ECJ's legal claims.

[25] Debré mentioned this in the discussion of the Foyer-Debré's Propositions de Loi (Rasmussen 1986: 351).

enforcing EC law supremacy in the 1960s),[26] and there were relatively few national court references to the ECJ. Until the ECJ began applying the doctrine in unacceptable ways, politicians lacked a compelling interest in mobilizing an attack on the Court's authority. In retrospect political non-action seems quite shortsighted. But predicting what would happen in light of the Court's declarations was difficult, and the strategy of holding off an attack on the ECJ was not stupid. EC law supremacy was at that time only a potential problem. Member states thought that controlling the legislative process would be enough to ensure that no objectionable laws were passed (Moravcsik 1995; Weiler 1981). In any event, the problem was for another elected official to face.

IV. Transformation of the Preliminary Ruling Procedure

By limiting the material impact of its decisions, the ECJ could minimize political focus on the Court and build doctrine without provoking a political response, creating the opportunity for it to escape member state oversight. What were marginal legal decisions from a political perspective, were revolutionary decisions from a legal perspective. They created standing for individuals to draw on EC law and a role for national courts enforcing EC law supremacy against national governments. Once national courts became involved in the application of EC law, it was harder for politicians to appeal to extralegal means to avoid complying with EC law. Instead, politicians had to follow the legal rules of the game.

Through the doctrines of direct effect and EC law supremacy, the ECJ harnessed what became an independent base of political leverage for itself—the national judiciaries. With national courts sending cases to the ECJ and applying ECJ jurisprudence, interpretive disputes were not so easily kept out of the legal realm. National courts would not let politicians ignore or cast aside as invalid unwanted decisions. Nor could politicians veto ECJ decisions through a national political vote, because EC law was supreme to national law. Indeed, national courts have refused political attempts to circumvent ECJ jurisprudence by passing new laws at the national level, applying the supreme EC law instead. National courts created both financial and political costs for ignoring ECJ decisions.

I have explained elsewhere why national courts took on a role enforcing EC law against their own governments (see Chapter 5). What is important is that because of national court support of ECJ jurisprudence, extralegal means to avoid ECJ decisions were harder to use, forcing governments to find legally defensible solutions to

---

[26] See 'Semoules decision' *Syndicat General de Fabricants de Semoules de France* Conseil d'État decision of 1 March 1968, [1968] Recueil Lebon 149, [1970] CMLR 395. *Costa v. Enel and Soc. Edisonvolta*, Italian Constitutional Court Decision 14 of 7 March 1964, [1964] CMLR 425, [1964] I Il Foro It. 87 I 465.

their EU legal problems. In the EU legal arena, however, member states were at an inherent disadvantage vis-à-vis the ECJ. As Joseph Weiler has argued:

by the fact of their own national courts making a preliminary reference to the ECJ, governments are forced to juridify their argument and shift to the judicial arena in which the ECJ is preeminent (so long as it can carry with it the national judiciary) when governments are pulled into court and required to explain, justify, and defend their decision, they are in a forum where diplomatic license is far more restricted, where good faith is a presumptive principle, and where states are meant to live by their statements. The legal arena imposes different rules of discourse. (Weiler 1994: 519)

The turnover tax struggle of 1966 offers a clear example of how the ECJ could rely on governments' fixations with the short-term impact of its decisions to diffuse political protests. It also shows how national judicial support shifted the types of responses available to governments to the advantage of the ECJ. When the Court's 1966 *Lütticke* decision created hundreds of thousands of refund claims for 'illegally' collected German turnover equalization taxes, the German Finance Ministry issued a statement, saying 'We hold the decision of the European Court as invalid. It conflicts with the well reasoned arguments of the Federal Government, and with the opinion of the affected member states of the EC', and it instructed German customs officials and tax courts to ignore the ECJ decision in question.[27] The decree would have worked if it were not for the national courts that refused to be told by the government that they could not apply a legally valid ECJ decision. Lower tax courts insisted on examining case-by-case whether or not a given German turnover tax was discriminatory. With national courts refusing to follow this decree, with lawyers publishing articles about the government's attempts to intimidate plaintiffs and order national courts to ignore a valid EC legal judgment (Meier 1967; Stöcker 1967; Wendt 1967a; Wendt 1967b), with legal cases clogging the tax branch and creating the possibility that nearly all German turnover taxes might be illegal, and with members of the Bundestag questioning a Ministry of Finance official on how the decree was compatible with the principles of a Rechtstaat (Meier 1967; Meier 1994)—a state ruled by law— the German government turned to its lawyers to find a solution to the problem.

The lawyers for the Ministry of Economics constructed a test case strategy, suggesting that the wrong legal question had been asked in the 1966 case, that really Article 97 EEC (now repealed) was the relevant EC legal text, not Article 95 EEC (now Article 90), and that Article 97 did not create direct effects, so that individuals did not have legal standing to challenge German turnover taxes in national courts (Meier 1994; Everling 1967). The ECJ accepted the legal argument, and all of the plaintiffs lost legal standing; thus the government won in its efforts to minimize the material impact of the Court's decision. But the strategy implicitly left the Court's precedence established in the *Lütticke* case intact. Article 95

---

[27] 7 July 1966 (IIIB.4-V8534–1/66), republished in *der Betrieb* (1966), 1160.

remained directly effective, and, even more importantly, member states became obliged to remove national laws that created tariff and non-tariff barriers to trade even though no new EC-level policies had been adopted to replace the national policies. The government was quieted because its problem (the numerous pending cases) was gone. But the precedent came back to haunt the German government and other member states in subsequent cases.

Because of national court support, politicians were forced to play by the legal rules of the game, where precedence (legal doctrine) matters, and any position must be justified in legal terms in a way that is credible within the legal community (Weiler 1994; Mattli and Slaughter 1995). Most importantly, in the legal sphere judges—not politicians—are in the power position of deciding what to do.

The doctrinal precedents stuck into the Court's benign legal decisions were in fact formidable institutional building blocks that would be applied in the future to more polemic cases. Once national courts had accepted EC law supremacy, they became supporters and advocates of the ECJ in the national legal realm, using their judicial position to limit the types of responses politicians could use to avoid unwanted ECJ decisions. Indeed, once the important legal precedents of direct effect and supremacy of EC law were established, judges were loath not to apply them or to reverse them fearing that frequent reversals would undermine the appearance of judicial neutrality, which is the basis for parties accepting the legitimacy of their decisions. If legal arguments cannot persuade either the national court or the ECJ, in the end politicians can do little to influence the legal outcome. The ECJ is after all the highest authority on the meaning of EC law, and national courts will defer to the ECJ for this reason. The only choice left for politicians is to rewrite the EU legislation itself.

The legal rules of the game limited political responses to ECJ jurisprudence, but national governments still had significant means to influence the EU legal process. Member states could influence the interpretation of the law through legally persuasive arguments, mobilization of public opinion, or political threats. They could rewrite the contested legislation and even rewrite the mandate of the ECJ, limiting access to it and cutting back its jurisdictional authority without violating the legal rules of the game. The next section considers why member states have not exercised these options.

V. Could Member States Regain Control? Why Did Member States Accept Unwanted ECJ Jurisprudence?

Our sovereignty has been taken away by the European Court of Justice. It has made many decisions impinging on our statute law and says that we are to obey its decisions instead of our own statute law.... Our courts must no longer enforce our national laws. They must enforce Community law... No longer is European law an incoming tide flowing up the estuaries of England. It is now like a tidal wave bringing down our sea walls and flowing inland over our fields and houses—to the dismay of all. (Denning 1990)

Some scholars have argued that the fact that member states did not reverse the direct effect and supremacy declarations of the ECJ shows that the Court had not deviated significantly from member state interests. The strongest argument of the strongest proponent of this view, Garrett, comes down to a tautology. He argues that, 'If member governments have neither changed nor evaded the European legal system, then from a "rational government" perspective, it must be the case that the existing legal order furthers the interests of national governments', and thus reflects the interests of national governments (Garrett 1995).[28] But the failure to act against judicial activism cannot be assumed to mean political support for the transformation of the preliminary ruling system. It is equally plausible, and more consistent with the evidence,[29] that national leaders disagreed with the Court's activist jurisprudence but were institutionally unable to reverse it.[30] For more on the problems with Garrett's tautology, see the discussion in Chapter 11 on rational expectations arguments.

Institutional constraints: The joint-decision trap

EC law based on regulations or directives can be rewritten by a simple statute that, depending on its nature, requires unanimity or qualified majority consent. A few of the Court's interpretations have been rewritten in light of their decisions, though surprisingly few. This is because ECJ decisions usually affect member states differently, so there is not a coalition of support to change the disputed legislation. Also, it takes political capital to mobilize the Commission and other states to legislate over a decision. If a member state can accommodate the decision of the ECJ on its own, by interpreting it narrowly or by buying off the people the decision affects, such an approach is easier than mobilizing other member states to relegislate. Such actions can reverse the substance of the decisions, allowing the specific policies affected by the Court's interpretation to remain unchanged. But they do not affect the Court's legal doctrine or the EU legal system as an

---

[28] Rasmussen also implies that states 'tacitly welcomed' ECJ expansions through the in-court behavior of their council and by their willingness to accept ECJ legal interpretations (Rasmussen 1986: 291).

[29] As mentioned earlier, EU authority expanded at a time when member states were contesting the Court's supranational powers, making it unlikely that they would support a significant aggrandizement of the Court's authority at the cost of national sovereignty. Lawyers for the national governments argued strongly against the Court's eventual interpretations on the grounds that they would compromise national sovereignty. Evidence indicates that de Gaulle protested the growing powers of the ECJ and tried to organize an attack on it (Weiler 1981; Stein 1981).

[30] This finding is consistent with Brian Marks, who shows how legislators may be hamstrung to reverse a legal decision. Marks argues that 'inaction is neither a sufficient nor necessary condition for acceptability [of a legal decision] by a majority of legislators. Nor can we conclude that the absence of legislative reaction implies that the Court's policy choice leads to a "better" policy in the view of the legislature' (Marks 1989: 6).

institution. Nor do they undermine the doctrines that form the foundation of ECJ authority: the supremacy or the direct effect of EC law, or the 'four freedoms' (the free movement of goods, capital, labor, and services). Reversing these core institutional foundations or any ECJ decision based on the EU Treaty would require a Treaty amendment, a threshold that is even harder to reach under the policy-making rules of the EU.

In order to change the Treaty, member states need unanimous agreement plus ratification of the changes by all national parliaments. Obtaining unanimous agreement about a new policy is hard enough. But creating a unanimous consensus to change an existing policy is even more difficult. Fritz Scharpf calls the difficulty of changing entrenched policies in the EU context the 'joint-decision trap' (Scharpf 1988). According to Scharpf, a joint-decision trap emerges when (1) the decision-making of the central government (the Council in the case of the EU) is directly dependent on the agreement of constituent parts (the member states), (2) when the agreement of the constituent parts must be unanimous or nearly unanimous, and (3) when the default outcome of no agreement is that the status quo policy continues. The default outcome is the critical factor hindering changes in existing polices. As Scharpf notes:

> What public choice theorists have generally neglected ... is the importance of the 'default condition' or 'reversion rule.' ... The implications of unanimity (or of any other decision rule) are crucially dependent upon what will be the case if agreement is not achieved. The implicit assumption is usually that in the absence of a decision there will be no collective rule at all, and that individuals will remain free to pursue their own goals with their own means. Unfortunately, these benign assumptions are applicable to joint decision systems only at the formative stage of the 'constitutional contract,' when the system is first established. Here, indeed, agreement is unlikely unless each of the parties involved expects joint solutions to be more advantageous than the status quo of separate decisions ... The 'default condition' changes, however, when we move from single-shot decisions to an ongoing joint-decision system in which the exit option is foreclosed. Now non-agreement is likely to assure the continuation of existing common policies, rather than reversion to the 'zero base' of individual action. In a dynamic environment ... when circumstances change, existing policies are likely to become sub-optimal even by their own original criteria. Under the unanimity rule, however, they cannot be abolished or changed as long as they are still preferred by even a single member. (Scharpf, 1988: 237)

States can block the attribution of new powers to the ECJ until their concerns are met. But the joint-decision trap makes reversing the Court's key doctrinal advances virtually impossible. Small states have an interest in a strong EU legal system. In front of the ECJ, political power is equalized, and within the ECJ, small states have a disproportionate voice, since each judge has one vote, and decisions are taken by simple majority. The Benelux states are unlikely to agree to anything they perceive will weaken the legal system's foundations and thus compromise their own interests. The small states are not alone in their defense of the ECJ. The Germans from the outset wanted a 'United States of Europe', and considered a more federal-looking EU legal system a step in the right direction. Although sometimes critical of the ECJ, the German government was also a supporter of a European Rechtstaat. In the period of time this chapter considers, Germany and the Benelux countries tended to block attempts to weaken ECJ authority, and they tried to extend its authority as the EU expanded into new legal areas whenever the political possibility existed. Britain and France, on the other hand, blocked attempts to expand EU legal authority.

The need to call an Inter-Governmental Conference (IGC) to amend the Treaty is an additional institutional impediment to member state attacks on the ECJ. Any member state can add an item to the agenda of the IGC, making member states hesitant to call for an IGC lest the agenda get out of control.

The reality of the joint-decision trap fundamentally changes the assumptions of Garrett and Weingast regarding member states' ability to control the ECJ through political oversight mechanisms. Recall Garrett and Weingast's argument:

> Embedding a legal system in a broader political structure places direct constraints on the discretion of a court, even one with as much constitutional independence as the United States Supreme Court. This conclusion holds even if the constitution makes no explicit provisions for altering a court's role. The reason is that political actors have a range of avenues through which they may alter or limit the role of courts. Sometimes such changes require amendment of the constitution, but usually the appropriate alterations may be accomplished more directly through statute, as by alteration of the court's jurisdiction in a way that makes it clear that continued undesired behavior will result in more radical changes…*the possibility of such a reaction drives a court that wishes to preserve its independence and legitimacy to remain in the area of acceptable latitude.* (Garrett and Weingast 1993: 200–1 (emphasis in original))

Certainly, courts have political limits, some area of 'acceptable latitude', beyond which they cannot stray. Indeed, all political actors are ultimately constrained to stay within an 'acceptable latitude'. But Garrett and Weingast imply that the political latitude of the ECJ is very limited—so limited that the ECJ has to base its individual decisions directly on the economic and political interests of the dominant member states.[31] They compare the institutional authority of the ECJ to that of the US Supreme Court to highlight what they see as the inherent political vulnerability of the ECJ and of ECJ justices, arguing:

> The autonomy of the ECJ is clearly less entrenched than that of the Supreme Court of the United States. Its position is not explicitly supported by a constitution. One of the thirteen judges is selected by each of the twelve member states, and their terms are renewable every six years. Many are likely to seek government employment in their home countries after they leave the ECJ. Moreover, there is no guarantee that the trend to ever greater European integration—legal or otherwise—will continue. At any moment, the opposition of a few states will be enough to derail the whole process. (Garrett and Weingast 1993: 201)

---

[31] Garrett has made this argument more clearly elsewhere; see Garrett (1992, 1995).

The difficulty of changing the Court's mandate given the requirement of unanimity and given the lack of political consensus implies that the Court's room for maneuver may be, in some respects, even greater than that of the US Supreme Court or other constitutional courts. Changing the authority of the ECJ requires a treaty amendment, not a simple statute. Securing an agreement on a treaty amendment from all member states could be even harder than convincing a national parliament to agree on a statute amending jurisdictional authority, especially if the parliament were dominated by one party. Because of the decision-making rules of the EU, the political threat to alter the Court's role is usually not credible. The ECJ can safely calculate that political controversy will not translate into an attack on its institutional standing, thus it will not need to reconcile its behavior with a country's political preferences. For these reasons, Mark Pollack calls amending the treaty the 'nuclear option—exceedingly effective, but diffi-cult to use—and is therefore a relatively ineffective and noncredible means of member state control' (Pollack 1997: 118–19).

The joint-decision trap also affects the ability of member states to control the ECJ through the appointment process. The relevant EU institutional feature is that decision-making takes place in the sub-unit of the member state. Using appointments to influence judicial positions is never a sure thing, but without a concerted appointment strategy on the part of a majority of member states, such a strategy is extremely unlikely to succeed. Each state has its own selection criteria for EU justices, and high-level political appointments are governed by a variety of political considerations, including party affiliation and political connections. A judge's opinion on EU legal matters is seldom the determining factor, and only a few member states have even attempted to use a judge's views regarding European integration as a factor in the selection process.[32] The individual threat to the judge's professional future may also be more hypothetical than real. Because ECJ decisions are issued unanimously, knowing if a given justice is ignoring its state's wishes is impossible. And in most European member states the judiciary is a civil bureaucracy, and judges have all the job protection of civil servants. If an ECJ judicial appointee came from the judiciary (or academia), which many do, they are virtually guaranteed that a job will be awaiting them on their return.

Garrett and Weingast raise another potential political tool of control over the ECJ—the threat of non-compliance—arguing that the ECJ must fear that a failure to implement its jurisprudence will undermine its legitimacy and thus its influence in the political process (Garrett and Weingast 1993: 200).[33] Although

---

[32] I have explored this issue in interviews with the Italian, Greek, Dutch, Belgian, French, German, British, and Irish judges at the ECJ and with legal scholars and government officials in France, Germany, and the United Kingdom. The criteria for ECJ judicial selection varied across countries but included factors such as party affiliation, ethnicity, legal background, ability to speak French, familiarity with EC law, and domestic party politics. Only in France and Germany could appointments designed to limit judicial activism be identified.

[33] See also Garrett, Kelemen, and Schulz (1996: 9).

courts do not like flagrant flaunting of their authority, as Walter Mattli and Anne-Marie Slaughter have argued, it could hurt a court's legitimacy even more to disregard legal precedent and bend to political pressure than to make a legally sound decision that politicians will contest or ignore (Mattli and Slaughter 1995). Indeed, in most legal systems a significant level of non-compliance remains: think of the many states in the United States where unconstitutional law and policy exist despite US Supreme Court rulings. Does this mean that the US Supreme Court curbs its jurisprudence to avoid non-compliance? It is hard to sustain the argument that in most cases or even in the most political of cases the fear of non-compliance shapes the jurisprudence of the ECJ. (For more on the limits of political tools of control, see Alter (2006).)

The key to member states' ability to cow the ECJ into political subservience is the credibility of their threat. If a political threat is not credible, politicians can protest all they want without influencing judicial decisions. That being said, the ECJ is more interested in shaping future behavior than exacting revenge for past digressions, especially if the past digression was not intentional (which is usually the case). Neither politicians, nor the public, nor the ECJ has an interest in a judicial decision that would cripple a government bureaucracy by filling it with thousands of claims, bankrupt a public pensions system, or force a significant redistribution of gross national product to pay back a group of citizens for past wrongs. That the ECJ takes these political considerations into account is not a sign of politicians dominating the ECJ. Rather, it is a sign that the ECJ shares a commitment to serving the public interest.

VI. Overcoming the Joint-Decision Trap? The Barber Protocol and the 1996–97 IGC and the Treaty of Amsterdam

I have argued that decision-making rules significantly undermine the ability of national governments to control the ECJ. Although reforming existing policies is made difficult by the joint-decision trap, this does not mean that policies can never be reformed. Scharpf argues that the joint-decision trap can be overcome in a given policy debate if a member state adopts a confrontational bargaining style, such as threatening exit or holding hostage something that other member states want. Thus intensely held interests by one state can lead to hard bargaining and reform of entrenched policies if the state will subjugate other issues to a single goal.

In an article published in the same edition as this article originally appeared, Geoff Garrett offered the 1993 'Barber Protocol' as an illustration of member states sanctioning the ECJ (Garrett, Kelemen and Schulz, 1998). After numerous failed attempts, politicians did for the first time seemingly achieve their goal. Stuck into the Maastricht Treaty was the Barber Protocol that limited the impact of a recent ECJ decision on equal pay in pension schemes for men and women.

The Barber Protocol clearly sent a sharp message to the ECJ. Speaking of the Protocol, one ECJ judge said:

[S]ome observers suggested that, far from being a carefully thought-out attack on the prerogatives of the Court, the Protocol was the result of last-minute brokering in some smoke-filled room of the building where the twelve Heads of State and governments were busying themselves with the destiny of Europe. This may well have been the case. However, that is of little solace to the Court, which now knows that basic constitutional rules can be undermined so wantonly. The awareness of being at the mercy of lobbies and a handful of Member-State experts multiplied the Court's misgivings. The circumstances were obviously no longer propitious to grand designs; letting sleeping dogs lie and therefore speaking in a low key was the new golden rule.[34]

The circumstances surrounding the Barber Protocol were unusual in that the Court's decision implied significant financial costs across member states and perhaps more importantly it came down at a time when member states were already in the process of amending the EC Treaty so that mobilizing against the decision was unusually easy.[35] But the Barber Protocol was not the only attack levied at the ECJ recently. During the Maastricht negotiations the ECJ was also excluded from two of the new pillars of the Treaty. And British Euro-skeptics have made it clear that they hope to 'clip the wings' of the ECJ at the 1996 Inter-Governmental Conference.[36] Fritz Scharpf tells us that the joint-decision trap can be overcome if a member state is mad enough that it is willing to adopt a confrontational bargaining style which can induce other members to give in by threatening exit or veto over decisions other member states want. The late 1990s presented such a point.

Short-term assessments saw signs of the ECJ moderating its jurisprudence in response to the Barber Protocol and the political sentiments behind it (Mancini and Keeling 1995). But in the longer term, the effects are far less clear in large part because shortly after the Barber Protocol, the ECJ survived a more serious challenge. Indeed Mark Pollack examined the policy area covered by the Barber Protocol, concluding that the Protocol had no long-term impact on the ECJ's equal pay jurisprudence (Pollack 2003: 354–9; see also Stone Sweet's discussion (2004).

More serious were the attacks on the ECJ in the context of the 1996 inter-governmental conference. British Euro-skeptics had a very intense interest in weakening the powers of EU institutions, especially the ECJ. In the Maastricht

---

[34] This quote came from a manuscript version of the paper I had. It did not reappear in the published version, though Mancini and Keeling do discuss how the political responses shocked and upset the ECJ. See Mancini and Keeling (1995: 406–8).

[35] Institutional politics also create barriers to member states opening the issue of ECJ authority. While in theory member states can call an Inter-Governmental Conference at any time (even within a Council meeting), politicians know that opening complex issues such as the authority of Community institutions is politically risky because the agenda could get out of control, and member states might try to open difficult bargains and extract favors in exchange for supporting the country that called the Inter-Governmental Conference.

[36] 'Government to demand curbs on European Court' *Financial Times*, 2 February 1995, p. 9.

Treaty negotiations the British demanded the scheduling of an inter-governmental conference to discuss the roles and powers of EU institutions, and the British made it part of their list of demands that the Court's powers be addressed. Euroskeptics wanted to make the ECJ directly accountable to political bodies and leaked to the press a proposal to allow a political body to veto or delay the effect of ECJ decisions (Brown 1995). They forced the British government to put into the negotiating process of the IGC a series of proposals to make the ECJ more politically accountable and to limit the cost of its decisions. British officials hoped to elicit German support for their proposals. There had been rumors about a potential German proposal to limit preliminary ruling reference rights to high courts. And Chancellor Helmut Kohl had become increasingly critical of the ECJ. The British challenge to the ECJ was the most serious to date because it went beyond rhetoric to articulate and specify an anti-ECJ policy.

In interviews during the fall of 1995, while meetings of the planning group for the 1996 IGC were being held, Dutch, German, and French legal advisors and members of the Council's legal services all agreed that the mandate of the ECJ, as it stood in the Treaty of Rome, was not up for renegotiation.[37] Because the other member states were unwilling to renegotiate the *aquis communautaire*, the British put forward proposals to the IGC planning group that did not directly attack the authority or autonomy of the ECJ or attempt to dismantle the preliminary ruling procedure or the supremacy of EC law. The British suggested creating an ECJ appeals procedure that would give the Court a second chance to reflect on its decisions in light of political displeasure, but according to the proposal it would still ultimately be the ECJ that executed the appeal! The British also suggested a Treaty amendment to limit liability damages in cases where the member state acted in good faith, as well as an amendment that explicitly allowed the Court to limit the retrospective effect of its judgments. Nothing in the current text of the Treaty of Rome denies the authority of the ECJ to limit the liability of member states if they have acted in good faith or to limit the retrospective effect of its decisions. Nevertheless, the British hoped that having these texts in the Treaty would encourage the ECJ to use them and open the possibility that governments could appeal ECJ findings using good faith and retrospective effects arguments. Being forced to put its ideas in legally acceptable terms that other member states might accept stripped most of the political force from the British government's proposals.

The British proposals were rejected entirely by the other member states. The existing jurisdiction of the ECJ for common market issues was not altered in the new Treaty of Amsterdam, thus the British threats never materialized. But

---

[37] Based on interviews in the British Foreign and Commonwealth Office (10 November 1995), the Tribunal of First Instance (2 November 1995), and the German Economics Ministry (correspondence from 6 January 1996). The desire to 'clip the Court's wings' was also announced in an article in the *Financial Times* and in an academic article written by a civil servant, Mr Clever, in the *Bundesministerium für Arbeit und Sozialordnung* (Brown 1995; Clever 1995).

in the new areas of jurisdiction given to the Court, the ECJ was significantly restricted. In the Maastricht Treaty, the ECJ was excluded from the new areas of EU authority: the Common Foreign and Security Policy, and Justice and Home Affairs (so-called pillars 2 and 3, respectively). This exclusion showed that member states had learned from the past, and that they were unwilling to allow the ECJ to meddle in these important policy areas. As usual, the small states were especially unhappy that the ECJ was excluded from Justice and Home Affairs. In the Treaty of Amsterdam, formally concluded in October 1997, the small states managed to have aspects of Justice and Home Affairs transferred into the realm of the ECJ, but in a restricted way. For issues of asylum law, migration policy, border controls, and the Schengen Agreement, the preliminary ruling system was extended only to the courts of last instance, which are less likely to send controversial issues of national policy to the ECJ. Officially, the explanation for excluding lower courts from sending references is that states were worried about a flood of asylum appeals to the ECJ, but EU officials admit that behind this official stance is a fear of ECJ activism based on lower court references. The ECJ was also explicitly denied jurisdiction over domestic issues concerning internal order and security, including assessments of the proportionality of state security actions (Article K.5 and K.7 §5). For issues of policing and judicial cooperation (that is, fighting terrorism and drug trafficking), each government is allowed to choose if its courts will be able to make preliminary ruling references; thus national governments can keep the ECJ out of domestic issues by denying the right of reference to national courts (Article K.6 §2). More easily overlooked is the provision stating that policies adopted under the EU framework with respect to Article K will not create direct effects, that is, individual rights that can be claimed in national courts (Article K.6 §2). Thus no individual or group will be able to draw on these EU rules to challenge national policy. This restriction will make it possible for individuals to challenge the EU agreements themselves but not national implementation of the agreements.

This outcome accords exactly with the expectations of the joint-decision trap. For existent ECJ jurisprudence and for areas of the Court's established jurisdiction, the ECJ remained virtually immune from political sanction. But in areas of new legislation and new authority for the ECJ, member states were able to block changes that they feared would undermine their sovereignty.

The ECJ has survived the most serious attack on its authority in its history. The ECJ may have retreated in some of its jurisprudence, but it has still shown a willingness to make bold decisions even at the height of the political threats against it.[38] The ECJ knew that the British government was angry over the cost of ECJ

---

[38] In an article entitled 'Language, Culture, and Politics in the Life of the European Court of Justice', Justice Mancini of the ECJ argued that there had been a 'retreat from activism', citing three reasons for this retreat: (1) the change in public opinion signaled by the debates of the Maastricht Treaty, which identified the ECJ as one of the chief EU villains; (2) two protocols in the Maastricht Treaty designed to circumvent potential ECJ decisions regarding awarding retrospective benefits for

decisions, yet in March 1996, while the IGC was still underway, the ECJ ordered the British government to pay Spanish fishermen a fine for violating European law. It also ordered the German government—the British government's desired ally—to compensate a French brewery prevented from exporting to Germany (Rice, Harding, and Hargreaves 1996). Even under the most concrete and direct political attacks to date, the ECJ continued its doctrine building—and in an area of significant concern to the attacking member states. (Subsequent studies, however, do not reveal a significant retreat. See Stone (2004).) This experience shows yet again that the ECJ continues to have the institutional and political capacity and the will to make decisions that go against member state interests.

VII. Conclusion: A New Framework for Understanding ECJ–Member State Interactions

In this article I have offered an account of how ECJ–member state relations are embedded in and constrained by institutions. I have argued that these institutional links, both at the national and supranational levels, directly shape the maneuverability of the ECJ so that its decisions do not have to be simple reflections of national interests. The account is self-consciously historical, focusing on understanding the evolution of the EU legal system over time as a window into how the present system operates.[39] Only when one considers that the current EU legal system was not intended to function as it does can we understand why member states that have an interest in maximizing national sovereignty have ended up with a legal system that greatly compromises national sovereignty. To say that this outcome was unintended is not to say that it happened by chance. The ECJ was very conscious in its strategy, as were the member states. But their different time horizons combined with a national judicial dynamic that propelled legal integration forward created a situation that national governments had not agreed to and, collectively, continued to reject.[40] Only by knowing this evolution of the Court's political power can we understand why these same countries remained very reluctant to extend the jurisdictional authority of the ECJ even in very limited areas, such as the Cannes Conventions for Europol and a common

pension discrimination and German house ownership in Denmark; and (3) recent criticism from Germany—one of the Court's historic allies—especially in light of the IGC (Mancini 1995: 12).

[39] A similar general account of this nature has been developed by Pierson (1996). I am indebted to Pierson for helping crystallize many of the ideas with which I have been working.

[40] European enlargement has changed state calculations. The European Constitution, which has been rejected many times by European populations, has sought to codify the transformations created by the ECJ. I spoke to the proposed constitutional amendments in a written testimony for the British House of Lords. See Written Testimony solicited for the Select Committee of the European Union, House of Lords, Sub-Committee E (Law and Institutions), November 2003. 6th Report of Session 2003–2004 'the Future Role of the European Court of Justice' HL paper 47. Located: <http://www.statewatch.org/news/2004/mar/hol-ecj-47.pdf>.

customs information system. Because we know the history of the European legal system, we can understand why European states, committed to a rule of law and benefiting from increased compliance with EU law, are also reluctant to agree to replicate the successful EU legal system in other international contexts or even in other areas of European integration.

The arguments advanced in this article are built on many important insights from the early literature on the ECJ. Like the neo-functionalist and legalist literature, this article stresses the important difference between the legal and the political rules of the game. Like the international relations literature, it examines the ECJ as an agent of the member states and identifies important political constraints created by the control of the decision-making process by member states. This article goes beyond these accounts, however, offering a different and even competing conception of the interests of the ECJ and member states and of the relationship between the ECJ and the member states. By moving beyond international relations approaches, I hope to widen the variables considered in evaluating EU–member state relations and contribute to the growing debate on how domestic politics influences European integration, and vice versa.

Many of the arguments raised in this article can be stated as more general hypotheses about ECJ–member state relations and about national government–judicial relations. If these hypotheses hold, there are also significant reasons to question how generalizable the experience of the ECJ is to other international legal contexts.

Different time horizons for different political actors

One of the reasons why the ECJ could develop legal doctrine that went against the long-term interests of the member states is that politicians focused on the short-term material and political impact of the decisions rather than the long-term doctrinal implications of the decisions. Member states understood that the legal precedent established might create political costs in the future, and thus they were not fooled by seemingly apolitical legalese or by the technical nature of law. But national governments were willing to trade off potential long-term costs so long as they could escape the political and financial costs of judicial decisions in the present. From this experience, one could hypothesize that legislators are more likely to act against judicial activism when it creates significant financial and political consequences and less likely to act against judicial activism that does not upset current policy.[41] In other words, the doctrinal significance matters less to national governments than the impact of decisions. If, however, the doctrine itself created a political impact by mobilizing groups, as many US Supreme Court decisions do, the doctrine alone might be enough to upset member states.

---

[41] For similar arguments, see Garrett, Kelemen, and Schulz (1998).

This time horizons argument comes from rational choice and historical institutional analysis and is, of course, generalizable beyond the ECJ or EU case (Pierson 1996).

Importance of national judicial support

National judicial support was critical in limiting the ability of national governments to simply ignore unwanted legal decisions from the international ECJ. In other words, where the inherent legitimacy of the ECJ or the compelling nature of the legal argumentation did not convince member states to accept ECJ decisions, national court legitimacy forced the government to find legally acceptable solutions to accommodate the jurisprudence of the ECJ.[42] This implies that in areas where national courts cannot be invoked, either because EC law does not create direct effects or the ECJ does not have jurisdictional authority to be seized by national courts, politicians would more likely ignore unwanted ECJ decisions or adopt extralegal means to mitigate the effects of ECJ decisions. Consequently, the ECJ would be more careful to take member state interests into account. The critical role of national courts as enforcers of ECJ decisions also implies that in countries where national courts are less legitimate, less vigilant, and a rule of law ideology is not a significant domestic political factor, politicians would be more likely to use extralegal means to circumvent ECJ jurisprudence.[43]

The EU experience highlights the importance of having domestic interlocutors to make adherence to international institutions politically constraining at home. One could hypothesize that international norms will most influence national politics when they are drawn on or pulled into the domestic political realm by domestic actors (see Chapter 9).

Creating a credible threat

If courts should start deciding against national interests, what can national governments do? In the European Union, where governments cannot selectively opt out of the European legal system, the only solution available to member states is to rewrite EU legislation or renegotiate the jurisdictional authority of the ECJ. For the many reasons discussed, doing this is not so easy. This is not to say that states can never overcome the institutional constraints. Germany and the Netherlands are pivotal countries in the coalition protecting the ECJ. If these countries turned, and all other countries agreed to go along, a credible threat could be mustered. One could hypothesize that when political support for the

---

[42] This argument is supported in survey research on ECJ legitimacy (Caldeira and Gibson 1995).

[43] This hypothesis follows from Slaughter (1995). It is also supported by a more recent comparison I am making between the European Court of Justice and the Andean Tribunal of Justice (Alter and Helfer 2009).

ECJ is waning in the key states blocking jurisdictional change, we can expect the ECJ to moderate its jurisprudence to avoid the emergence of a consensus to attack its prerogatives. But when a clear blocking contingent exists, the ECJ can be expected to decide against the interests of powerful member states.

In international contexts where states can opt out of legal mechanisms or keep disputes from even getting to an international body, it will be easier for governments to credibly threaten international tribunals to moderate their jurisprudence. Whether these threats will be enough to cow the tribunal into quiescence is another story. As mentioned earlier, in some circumstances the legitimacy of a legal body could be hurt more by caving in to political pressure than by making a legally sound decision that the court knows politicians will ignore (Mattli and Slaughter 1995).

The ECJ: A model for other international legal systems?

The ECJ began as a fairly weak international tribunal, suffering from many of the problems faced by international courts. It lacked cases to adjudicate. No enforcement mechanism was in place, so ECJ decisions were easy to ignore. The neutrality of the ECJ and its reputation for high-quality decisions and sound legal reasoning were not enough to make member states use the legal mechanism to resolve disputes or to force member states to adhere to decisions that went against important interests. The ECJ has changed the weak foundations of the EU legal system, with the help of national judiciaries. If the ECJ, by building legal doctrine, created a base of political leverage for itself, could other international legal bodies not do the same?

If national courts are the main reason why European governments adhere to ECJ decisions in cases that go against national interests, one must question how generalizable the EU experience is to other international contexts. In the EU the preliminary ruling mechanism serves as a direct link coordinating interpretation of national courts with the ECJ. As I have argued elsewhere, the preliminary ruling system also serves a political function, pressuring national high courts to bring their jurisprudence into agreement with the ECJ (see Chapter 5). In most other international judicial or quasi-judicial systems, there is no direct link between the international court and national courts, making it much more difficult to coordinate legal interpretation across boundaries. (This link exists in more places than I originally suspected. See Chapter 12.) Although it is always possible that national courts could look to jurisprudence generated from international bodies and thus enhance the enforceability of international law, without the preliminary ruling mechanism one must wonder if independent-minded national judges with different legal traditions and much legal hubris will turn for guidance to international bodies whose jurisprudence goes against strong political interests. (Note: Chapter 4 examines the Andean Tribunal of Justice which does have a preliminary ruling mechanism.)

Given that unintended consequences almost always accrue when institutions are created, it should not surprise us if politicians wake up at some other time to find their sovereignty constrained in unintended ways in other international contexts. At the same time, it could be that member states are now wise to the benefits and costs of the EU legal system, and that they will not make such a mistake in the future. Although great strides have been made in the development of international dispute resolution mechanisms, only the Andean legal system includes a preliminary ruling mechanism. Most international legal systems still have significant political controls for the member states that allow them to avoid the costs of an international judicial decision that greatly compromises national interests. Whether the success of the EU legal system is a prototype for other international legal systems is still open for debate.

[Note: My work with Laurence Helfer compares the European legal system to the Andean legal system to investigate how the political context shapes IC law-making. This volume includes a small part of this research (in Chapter 4). Two articles from this research will be published in 2009. At the time of publication, the article directly comparing the ECJ and the ATJ had not yet been submitted to peer review. See the Appendix for references to this work.]

PART III

THE ECJ AND ITS VARIED INFLUENCE ON EUROPEAN POLICY AND POLITICS (1980–2005)

7

Judicial Politics in the European Community: European Integration and the Pathbreaking *Cassis de Dijon* Decision (1994)

With Sophie Meunier

Although it is indisputable that the ECJ has issued many far-reaching decisions, there is disagreement regarding the impact of these decisions on the policy-making process of the EC. Many legal scholars portray the Court as a hero who has greatly advanced the cause of integration by intervening when the political process is stalled and no political consensus can be reached (for examples, see Lenaerts 1988: 19; Louis 1990: 48). This intervention takes the form of judicial decisions that make law that transcends current policy. These judicial decisions are seen as setting the context of political integration by altering member state preferences through the creation of de facto policies, which themselves serve as constraints on the actions of member states (Weiler 1981, 1991).

Political scientists, on the other hand, tend to discount the effect of the Court's jurisprudence, often ignoring the role of the Court when discussing EC politics. When the ECJ is not ignored, it is seen under the realist rubric where the ECJ's decisions mimic the will of dominant member states (Garrett 1992), where compliance with ECJ decisions is based on national interest calculations (Garrett and Weingast 1993; Volcansek 1986), and where ECJ decisions echo rather than shape the preferences of member states (Garrett and Weingast 1993). The tendency to underestimate the autonomy of the ECJ and to minimize the impact of its jurisprudence is reinforced by the dearth of empirical work showing how the Court actually influences the policy-making process in the EC, or how its jurisprudence affects member state policy preferences.

This study is meant to be a first step in providing empirical information on the impact of ECJ jurisprudence in the political arena. By exploring the implementation and consequences of one of the ECJ's best known judgments, the *Cassis de Dijon* (1979) decision, this article attempts to identify the role of the Court in the creation of the 'new approach to harmonization', which emerged as the cornerstone of the 1985 Single European Act. The *Cassis* ruling, decided during the period of 'Eurosclerosis', is one of the most famous ECJ decision outside of the legal community because it suggested a policy of mutual recognition whereby goods lawfully produced in one member state would be allowed to circulate freely within the European market. This case has been used by the promoters of the heroic vision of the Court who imply that, with the stroke of a pen, the ECJ changed the playing field on which technical harmonization negotiations proceeded (Jacot-Guillarmod 1989). Political scientists have also used this case as an example of the Court replicating the will of the member states (Garrett 1992). The importance and saliency of the *Cassis* case in itself makes it a good candidate for empirical research. The numerous misperceptions about this case also make it worthy of greater scrutiny.

Examining, in turn, the legal and political aspects of the new harmonization policy based on mutual recognition, this article explores the implications and consequences of the Court-made principle of 'mutual recognition' with respect to the 'new approach to harmonization'. Section I introduces the *Cassis* case, analyzing how the Court attempted to influence the EC policy-making process by writing its decision in a provocative fashion. Section II recounts the political consequences of the Court's decision and of the Commission activism following the ruling. The third section examines two competing explanations about how this decision impacted policy and puts forth a counter-explanation of how *Cassis* contributed to shaping a new harmonization policy based on mutual recognition. Generalizing from our case study, the conclusion focuses on how the ECJ can influence the policy-making in the EC and proposes avenues for further research.

I. Legal Significance and Implications of the *Cassis de Dijon* Case

Creme de Cassis, the blackcurrant elixir which transforms white wine into Kir, also transformed the nature of Europe's common market. It is largely due to a famous European Court case involving this liqueur that the 1992 single-market initiative has been able to do so much to restore progress to the European Community, but also to arouse such unease in Member States about loss of sovereignty.

'Message in a bottle that changed Europe'. *The Independent*, 6 May 1990

The *Cassis* case has become famous for its association with the policy of mutual recognition. However, the words mutual recognition did not appear in the decision and the decision itself did not mean that any good legally produced in one member country had to be allowed into all national markets. This section provides background information on the case itself, focusing on the style of the decision, the political context in which it emerged, and its legal contribution to the Court's jurisprudence on non-tariff barriers.

In the *Cassis de Dijon* case, the ECJ was asked to rule indirectly on the legality of a German law that required spirits to have a minimum alcohol content of at least 25 per cent. The effect of this law was that the French liquor Cassis de Dijon, which has an alcohol content of 15–20 per cent, could not be marketed in Germany. This German law had been previously challenged in 1974 in an infringement proceeding raised by the Commission against Germany (Commission document 373, 17 July 1975). The Commission's case was identical to the *Cassis* case, only the liquor in question was French Anisette which, like Cassis, had too low an alcohol content to be marketed in Germany. The infringement proceeding was dropped in 1975 after a political settlement was reached whereby Anisette was allowed into the German market, but the German law remained intact (Meier 1991: A1–A4).

By all accounts, the *Cassis* case was selected as a test case by the plaintiff's lawyer (Gert Meier) to challenge the Commission/German agreement and to provoke harmonization of the alcohol industry.[1] The import/export firm asked the German administrative agency to make the same exception for the Cassis liquor as was granted to Anisette. When the agency refused, the firm brought suit in a German national court, charging that the German regulation on minimum alcohol contents was an illegal non-tariff barrier. The German court suspended its legal procedure to ask the European Court for a preliminary ruling, which interpreted Article 30 EEC (now Article 28) in light of the German regulation. This process of freezing the national procedure and asking the ECJ for an interpretation of EC law in light of a national law is one of the main means through which the ECJ comes to rule on the compatibility of national laws with European law.

In the European Court proceedings, the German government defended the validity of its regulation primarily on health grounds, claiming that the law aimed at avoiding the proliferation of alcoholic beverages on the national market and, in particular, alcoholic beverages with low alcohol content, because such products might more easily induce a tolerance toward alcohol than more highly alcoholic beverages. The German government also offered a consumer protection justification based on the need to protect consumers from unfair producer and distributor practices of lowering the alcohol content to avoid paying higher taxes, thus creating a competitive advantage. Finally the German government argued that requiring Germany to accept French alcohol content laws would mean that one country could set standards for all member states, thus precipitating a lowering of standards throughout the EC.

In its decision, the Court rejected the German health argument as unconvincing. Applying the legal principle of proportionality, whereby the least restrictive measures to achieve a desired goal must be chosen, the Court dismissed the Germans' consumer protection justification as excessive to achieve the desired

---

[1] Meier actually learned of the legal issue at a meeting of a Euro-law association where a Commission official leaked news of the settlement.

goal. The Court then argued that removal of a minimum alcohol content law was not, per se, a lowering of standards. After dismissing the German arguments, the Court went on in its decision to state a general principle, now the most often cited part of the ruling:

There is therefore no valid reason why, provided that they have been lawfully produced and marketed in one of the Member States, alcoholic beverages should not be introduced into any other Member State.

This second to last paragraph, in the context of the rest of the decision, was provocative. Because the Court had already dismissed the validity of the German law for legal reasons well established in the Court's previous jurisprudence, the statement was indeed redundant. But by inserting the dependent clause 'provided that they have been lawfully produced and marketed in one of the Member States', the Court introduced the criterion of a product being lawfully produced in one member state as the basis for its admittance into the market of another member state. This implied that national regulations governing how a good was produced had to be recognized as equivalent to the regulations of the exporting member state.[2] The effect of this statement will be explored later, but it is important to note that this sentence carried no legal weight in the context of the rest of the decision. At most, the phrase signaled a general principle that the Court would use in future decisions.

The *Cassis* decision itself did not mean that any product legally produced in another member state had to be admitted throughout the European market. Instead, the Court spoke of the criterion for excluding a product, saying that there had to be a valid reason to prohibit the importation or sale of the product. Although the Court rejected the German reasons as invalid, it created a general 'rule of reason' whereby any national law with reasonable policy goals, such as environmental, health, consumer protection, and so on, would be tolerated. This rule was an extension of Article 36 (now Article 30) of the EC Treaty, which permitted national laws to impede the free movement of goods only if they could be justified on the grounds of a circumscribed list of policy objectives. The rule of reason is a continuation of the ECJ's *Dassonville* (1974) jurisprudence,[3] which established a legal basis for challenging the validity of national laws that create non-tariff barriers. To the extent that the *Cassis* decision ruled invalid a national law on the basis that it created a non-tariff barrier, it was a straight application of the jurisprudence established in the *Dassonville* decision.[4]

---

[2] Case 120/78, *Rewe Zentral AG v. Bundesmonopolverwaltung für Branntwein ('Cassis de Dijon')* [1979] ECR 649, ECJ.

[3] Case 8/74, *Procureur du Roi v. Benoit and Gustave Dassonville* [1974] ECR 837, ECJ.

[4] For more on the ECJ's jurisprudence regarding the free movement of goods, see Maduro (1998) which is brought up to date by Stone Sweet (2004: 120–49). Stone Sweet sees the *Cassis* ruling as innovating on *Dassonville* in that it suggested that national measures that did not on their face discriminate would still be subject to ECJ judicial scrutiny (p.127).

This analysis of the *Cassis* ruling raises many questions that a strict legal analysis cannot answer. Why was the *Cassis* decision seen as so important, while the *Dassonville* ruling remained largely unknown? Why has the Court's line in the end of its decision, a sentence with no real legal significance, come to dominate the layman's perception of the meaning of the *Cassis* ruling? The answers to these questions lie in the political realm, in the response generated by the decision.

II. Political Consequences of the *Cassis* Decision

The Legal Services of the Commission and the German government were stunned by the *Cassis* decision. Even the German government had expected the Court to rule against its regulation, but no one anticipated that the Court would draw such wide conclusions from the case, as the phrase at the end of the judgment seemed to imply. Still, there are many examples of ECJ decisions that shock the legal community but do not even register in the political arena. Indeed, the fame of the *Cassis* case did not come from the legal audacity of the decision, but rather from the political use and counter-use that was made of the ruling. The political debate was instigated by the Commission, which extracted from the decision those aspects useful for developing a new approach to harmonization policy, to satisfy its own political agenda of completing the internal market and furthering European integration. The flurry of reactions following the Commission's expansive interpretation of the *Cassis* ruling shed light on the Court as a major political actor in the EC and on the necessity of designing a new harmonization strategy.

The Commission rapidly drew its own conclusions from the Court judgment. Already in the fall of 1979, the internal market Commissioner, Etienne Davignon, suggested in front of the EC Parliament that harmonization policy should take a new direction, based on the *Cassis* ruling.[5] In July of 1980, with great fanfare, the Commission sent to the member states, the European Parliament, and the Council a communication that laid out its 'new strategy'.[6]

The Commission's communication posited policy guidelines, which were derived from its interpretation that harmonization policy should take a new direction, based on the *Cassis* decision.[7] The guidelines laid down the principle of mutual recognition of goods, stating that 'any product lawfully produced and marketed in one Member State must, in principle, be admitted to the

[5] Debates of the European Parliament: *Subject: Freedom of Trade within the Community* (Sitting of Monday, 22 October 1979). Answer to Written Question No. 243/80 regarding 'Consequences of the judgment in the "*Dijon Cassis*" case on the abolition of technical barriers to trade', OJCE No. C183/57 (21 July 1980).

[6] *Agence Europe*, 1980, p. 11 discussed in Barents (1981: 296).

[7] Communication from the Commission concerning the consequences of the judgment given by the Court of Justice on 20 February 1979 in Case 120/78, (*'Cassis de Dijon'*) [1980] OJ C256 (3 October 1980).

market of any other Member State'. A corollary to this principle, according to the Commission, was that member states 'may not take an exclusively national viewpoint' and must 'give consideration to the legitimate requirements of other Member States' when they draw commercial or technical rules that may affect the free movement of goods. The Commission informed the member states that the conclusions derived from the *Cassis* decision would serve as the foundation for a new policy of harmonization, according to which national laws inadmissible under the *Cassis* principle would be targeted through the infringement procedures to be raised by the Commission, and national laws that were admissible under the *Cassis* principle would be targeted through harmonization efforts.

This was the first time that the Commission tried to extract policy from a Court decision by issuing an interpretative communication.[8] Although the Commission's communication seemed only to restate the Court's *Cassis* ruling, it was indeed an artful interpretation of the ruling and a bold assertion of new policy (Barents 1981; Capelli 1981; Masclet 1980). This communication can be seen as an attempt to capitalize on the legitimacy of the Court of Justice, where the Commission used the decision as a justification to redirect its harmonization policy in a way that promoted freer trade and further integration (Gormley 1981: 454). Thus the Commission interpreted very broadly the principle of mutual recognition as the cornerstone of the new harmonization policy, stressing the 'in principle' clause while minimizing most of the restrictions posed by the Court, such as the rule of reason.

The torrent of reactions following the Commission's communication contributed to the fame of *Cassis* perhaps more than the decision itself. It also revealed a profound lack of consensus with respect to the policy of mutual recognition. One month after its formal issuance, the author of the communication published an article in which he expanded on the contents of the communication and declared that the Commission was going to apply a new approach to harmonization policy based on the *Cassis* ruling to put an end to internal protectionism and safeguard the *'acquis communautaire'* (Mattera 1980). While the member states were preparing a vigorous response to the Commission's political assertiveness, legal scholars were detecting legal flaws in the Commission's interpretation and interest groups were mobilizing for and against this new approach, thus adding to the legend of *Cassis*.[9]

---

[8] This new instrument, modeled after what occurs at the national level when a law is not clear, was created specifically to suit the Commission's needs in the *Cassis* case. Although the Commission could not frame its interpretation of *Cassis* and its new policy in the form of a directive, the communication was designed to be the most constraining and solemn instrument possible. From 1980 to 1994, approximately ten interpretative communications were issued by the Commission.

[9] Evidence for these arguments was gathered in interviews at the Commission, the German Ministry of Exports, UNICE, and the European consumers' union, the Bureau Européen des Unions de Consommateurs (BEUC). Primary sources were gathered at the archives of UNICE, the BEUC, and the French environmental movement. Proceedings and testimonies at Britain's House of Lords were also examined. See the Report of the Select Committee on the Internal Market

The member states reacted with apprehension and discontent to the broad policy implications of the *Cassis* decision drawn by the Commission. As relatively high standard countries, France, Germany, and Italy were the most vigorously opposed to the new policy. They repeated the German government's argument that the principle of mutual recognition of goods would lead to a lowering of safety and quality standards. Even the British government had some reservations, although the United Kingdom was generally favorable to the principle of market liberalization and opposed to the excess of legislation in the EC.

The Council immediately asked its legal services to analyze the *Cassis* ruling to investigate the legal foundations of the Commission's interpretation. The legal staff delivered a counter-interpretation of the case, arguing that although the definition of what fell under Article 30 differed from that of a 1969 directive on the subject (Directive 70/50/EEC), and although the decision gave the Commission more concrete guidelines under which to intensify its scrutiny of national measures, the criteria on which to determine whether a national measure is allowed remained the same as that of the 1969 Directive (Service Juridique du Conseil des Communautés Européennes: 10690/80). In addition, the Legal Services found that the Commission's generalization of the *Cassis* argument—that any product lawfully produced and marketed in one country must be admitted into the territory of another—was excessive. Instead, they argued that the compatibility of national regulations with Article 30 could only be examined case-by-case, following the criteria set by the 1969 Directive. Thus the Legal Services of the Council concluded that the *Cassis* ruling changed virtually nothing.

Conferences and seminars on *Cassis* and the Commission's communication were held by legal and business associations throughout Europe in 1980 and 1981, and articles attempting to create the definitive legal interpretation of *Cassis* and condemning the Commission's communication flourished in the legal literature (for example, see Barents 1981; Capelli 1981; Masclet 1980). The articles criticized the Commission's extensive interpretation of the *Cassis* ruling, which deliberately ignored the rule of reason proposed by the Court. Barents (1981) concluded in a *Common Market Law Review* article:

> The Cassis de Dijon judgment, while constituting a continuation of the Court's policy outlined in the Dassonville case, is not so revolutionary as the Commission wishes to believe. It has to be regretted that the Commission has used a dubious interpretation of this judgment as a weapon to revive its crusade against protectionism.

The Commission's critics were reinforced by subsequent ECJ cases that finessed the rule of reason, creating limitations on the application of mutual recognition

Memorandum on the implications of *Cassis de Dijon* by the Food and Drink Industries, Council to the House of Lords, Session of 24 February 1982.

such as the requirement of 'functional equivalence',[10] thus bringing the Court further away from the mutual recognition guidelines defined by the Commission (see Gormley 1989; Keeling 1992; Nicolaïdis 1993; White 1989).

The publication of the communication also triggered the mobilization of various interest groups. Consumer groups were torn between welcoming and rejecting the Commission's interpretation of the *Cassis* ruling.[11] Although looking forward to the greater diversity and lower prices of products implied by a common market, consumer groups were worried that trade liberalization could have negative consequences on consumer safety and jeopardize the gains previously made in consumer legislation on the national front. The EC consumer group argued that:

> it is necessary to maintain a balance between the securing of free trade, which should afford consumers a broad range of products, and the need to protect the health, safety and economic interests of consumers. We are concerned that the Commission interpretation of the Cassis ruling may jeopardize that balance.

Moreover, they declared that they did 'not consider competition to be a justification for banning national provisions relevant to the different situations found in the Member States nor for seeking harmonization at the lowest common denominator'.[12] Consumer groups also denounced the use of the judicial process rather than legislative harmonization because such a process prevents groups from having an impact on the eventual directives.

The reactions of producer groups also varied. Many exporters and producers, anticipating the economic benefits of a new policy of mutual recognition, advocated bringing more Court cases to flesh out the legal jurisprudence.[13] UNICE, the European association of industrial producers, also reacted favorably to the Commission's communication, which reflected many of their previously voiced demands. Other firms felt threatened by the removal of protectionist barriers and the foreign competition that would suddenly be introduced by this new policy.

---

[10] The principle of functional equivalence implies that states can restrict the sale of goods from country X because country X's regulation is not functionally equivalent to country Y's regulation. The classic case is one where France was permitted to apply its own safety requirements to legally manufactured German woodworking machines because the German machinery presumed a higher worker training level than was prevalent in France: Case 188/84, *Commission v. French Republic* [1986] ECR 419.

[11] By citing consumer protection in the *Cassis* decision as an example of a potential justification for national regulation under the rule of reason, the ECJ gave consumer groups a new tool to promote their cause at the national level, and a *raison d'être* at the EC level. At the EC level, the Bureau Européen des Unions de Consommateurs expanded its lobbying activity considerably. In addition, national consumer groups began communicating across borders to coordinate their actions.

[12] Opinion of the Consumers' Consultative Committee on the consequences of the judgment in the *Cassis de Dijon* case, adopted in October 1981, reported in the House of Lords, Session of 13 July 1982.

[13] We are grateful to Maria Green for providing us with evidence that some business groups discussed the possibility of designing a Court strategy to ensure that the policy principle derived from *Cassis* would be applied.

The firms enjoying a dominant (if not monopolistic) position in their own country, such as Italy's Barilla and Germany's beer companies, were the most vehemently opposed to the Commission's revolutionary policy assertions. Possessing money and political influence, these companies led a vehement campaign of attacks against the Commission and heavily lobbied their national governments to have the Commission's interpretation overturned. Producer groups in high-standard countries were especially worried that mutual recognition would put them at a competitive disadvantage compared to producers in low-standard countries. Overall, business was hesitant about the implications of *Cassis*. The British Food and Drink Industries Council, for instance, recognized that 'the *Cassis de Dijon* way to a true common market seems the most promising' but they were reluctant to halt the process of politically negotiated harmonization saying that 'there are still those national laws to which the *Cassis de Dijon* principles cannot apply and for which harmonization will remain the only way forward' (Report of the Select Committee, 1982).

In summary, the fame of *Cassis de Dijon,* one of the best-known ECJ judgments, derives less from the originality of the decision than from the flow of responses and counter-reactions it provoked. These responses were triggered primarily by the widely publicized legal and policy implications promoted in the Commission's communication, which themselves became the center of debate. Without the communication, it is likely that the fate of the *Cassis* decision would have been similar to that of the *Dassonville* decision—it would have remained important in legal circles, but have been relatively unknown in wider political circles.

III. The New Approach to Harmonization—Judge-Made Policy, Focal Point, or Political Compromise?

How did the *Cassis* decision change the course of harmonization policy in the EC? Two explanations have been suggested. Jacot-Guillarmod claimed that:

the *Cassis de Dijon* principle, presupposing the mutual recognition of national legislation [...] has rendered *ipso jure* obsolete the harmonization of law in sectors outside the exceptions of article 36 or in sectors or areas not covered by mandatory requirements within the scope of article 30 of the EEC treaty. (Jacot-Guillarmod 1989: 196)

This 'judge-made policy explanation' would imply that ECJ decisions can create policy consequences directly, by virtue of their legal legitimacy, thus obviating the need for a legislative solution.

In an alternative interpretation, Garrett claimed that the *Cassis de Dijon* decision itself was based on the policy preferences of dominant member states (Garrett 1992: 558). Along with Weingast (Garrett and Weingast 1993) he argued that the *Cassis* decision impacted the policy-making process by constructing a focal point around which the member states' interests in a policy of mutual recognition converged. This focal point explanation would imply that the Court is not an autonomous actor and that ECJ decisions have policy implications only when they accurately reflect a policy consensus (Garret and Weingast 1993).

This section will explore these explanations by posing two counter-factual and hypothetical questions—What would the judicial policy of mutual recognition derived from *Cassis* have looked like without the formal adoption of the new approach to harmonization in the Single European Act? How would the new approach have looked without *Cassis de Dijon*? By examining what did not happen, we can eliminate competing explanations and fashion alternative hypotheses

Judge-made policy of mutual recognition?

What would the judicial policy of mutual recognition derived from *Cassis* have looked like without the formal adoption of the new approach to harmoniza-tion in the Single European Act? To ask this question assumes that courts do make policy; yet judges do not see themselves as policy-makers and in a civil law system, policy-making is not considered as an appropriate role for courts. Indeed, European legal scholars vigorously refute any assertion that courts are making law, let alone making policy; discussing the Court as a policy player would be an anathema to most of them. But there are many examples where judges do actually attempt to make policy—that is, to render consistent rulings according to articu-lated guidelines so as to shape the behavior of public and private actors. The *Cassis* case is a good example of the ECJ attempting to make policy by promulgating a legal principle.

Hartley has observed that the ECJ has a general style invoked when the Court makes policy. Hartley writes:

A common tactic is to introduce a new doctrine gradually: in the first case that comes before it, the Court will establish the doctrine as a general principle but suggest that it is subject to various qualifications; the Court may even find some reason why it should not be applied to the particular facts of the case. The principle, however, is now established. If there are not too many protests, it will be re-affirmed in later cases; the qualifications can then be whittled away and the full extent of the doctrine revealed. (Hartley 1988: 78–9)

The *Cassis* decision exemplifies this style perfectly. By including the phrase 'pro-vided that they have been lawfully produced and marketed in one of the Member States, alcoholic beverages should [...] be introduced into any other Member State', the decision introduced the general principle of mutual recognition. The actual decision, however, was firmly grounded in previous case law, so that the principle was not directly applied to the case itself. As suggested by the Hartley formula, the rule of reason was offered as a potential qualification of the principle. The rule of reason also served as a sweetener to member states that seemingly gained prerogatives under the *Cassis* precedent, and as a back door of retreat for the Court.

One could imagine that a judge-made mutual recognition principle could create legal expectations that would encourage lawyers and plaintiffs to bring more cases. Furthermore, if an established Court-made legal principle was consistently applied across a body of cases, one could expect that anticipation of a specific legal outcome would shape the behavior of public administrators, who might then choose to settle before going to court. Thus it is possible that Jacot-Guillarmod could be right, and that the *Cassis* legal decision could have produced direct policy effects by creating a general principle of mutual recognition. If this principle was widely applied by national courts and anticipated by national administrators, the free flow of goods would have been greatly advanced and the old process of harmonization would have been rendered largely obsolete.

A generalization of this logic implies that court decisions, by virtue of their legal authority, create direct policy effects. Indeed, because the legal profession is trained to think in terms of what is 'the law', the Commission's Legal Services at first assumed that the decision would derail the harmonization process, and the division of the Commission responsible for harmonization policy also feared that their *raison d'être* would disappear.[14] Many legal scholars, in fact, implicitly assume that legal decisions have policy consequences. Written ten years after the decision was rendered, Jacot-Guillarmod's comment exemplifies this assumption. But such a general theory provides little room for politics.

What were the actual policy repercussions of the judge-made principle of mutual recognition? Hartley's characterization of the ECJ policy style implies that had there been no political reaction, the Court would have proceeded to 'whittle away the exceptions' by narrowly applying the rule of reason and revealing the full force of the principle of mutual recognition. Politicians, however, did not react favorably to the policy of mutual recognition. Given the political opposition mobilized by the Commission's communication, it is not surprising that the Court took the escape route of maintaining the legal qualifications in its subsequent jurisprudence (Nicolaïdis 1993). This meant that although the principle established by the Court in the *Cassis* judgment appeared on the surface to be a general rule of thumb that could be applied by all, its actual application remained quite complicated because national legislation could be defended under the rule of reason and because subsequent ECJ jurisprudence created even more qualifications, such as the requirement of functional equivalence (see note 10 and Gormley 1989; Keeling 1992; Nicolaïdis 1993; White 1989). In practice, only the European Court could apply the policy and then only on a case-by-case basis.

The ECJ's decision not to consistently apply its legal doctrine of mutual recognition undermines the first assumption of the judicial policy-making explanation.

---

[14] Based on interviews at the Commission.

Indeed, private interests protesting state regulations could not be sure of a positive outcome and thus had less of an incentive to raise cases, and public authorities had little incentive to compromise outside of Court. In fact, the *Cassis* decision did not precipitate a large increase in the number of cases involving non-tariff barriers brought before the Court. Following the *Cassis* ruling, from 1981 to 1989 there were an average of 9.3 judgments a year in cases raised by private parties involving non-tariff barriers.[15] This was slightly fewer than the average of ten cases per year from 1974 to 1980, following the *Dassonville* (1974) ruling (Barents 1981: Annex). In terms of increased Commission vigilance of national laws that could constitute non-tariff barriers, between 1981 and 1989 the Commission brought to completion 31 infringement proceedings involving non-tariff barriers, compared to 11 proceedings in the same area from 1961 to 1980. In all likelihood this greater number reflects a general trend of the Commission raising more infringement cases.[16]

How then would the judge-made policy of mutual recognition have looked without the Single European Act? Between 1980 and 1989, there were a total of 115 cases raised by private parties and by the Commission involving non-tariff barriers. Some of these cases were decided in favor of the national legislation; however even if all cases involving non-tariff barriers between 1980 and 1989 had been decided against the national legislation, at most 115 national regulations could have been declared to be in conflict with European law. This does not mean that 115 areas of legislation could have been harmonized on the principle of mutual recognition, but rather that, at the most, 115 types of products could have been allowed into one member state from which they perhaps had been illegally excluded. Although these figures do not take into account the cases decided at the national level, without being referred through the preliminary ruling process to the ECJ, interviews reveal that the application of the judge-made policy was hampered at the national level because national administrators, unaware of the ECJ jurisprudence, continued to apply obstructionist national laws. All of these factors meant that, in practice, the judge-made policy did not greatly increase the free circulation of goods.

But what if there had been no negative political reaction and the Court had proceeded to whittle away the exceptions and apply a judge-made policy of mutual recognition? This question ventures too far into the speculative to be answered with certainty; however, when wondering about the extent of the Court's ability to make policy through law in the most favorable circumstances, a few characteristics of judge-made law in general, and in the EC specifically, should be remembered. The judicial process is inevitably slow and costly because judge-made law can only be applied on a case-by-case basis and courts must wait

---

[15] Calculated by the authors from the 'Synopsis of the Work of the Court of Justice' issued by the Court.

[16] Between 1981 and 1989, non-tariff barrier cases comprised only 5% of all cases raised by the Commission, as compared to the period of 1958 to 1980 when they comprised 10% of all cases.

for cases to be raised in front of them. Judge-made law also creates biases in its application because it tends to favor those groups with the resources to raise cases through the legal system and pursue appeals of the decisions if necessary.

In the European context, these problems are exacerbated. A case that is sent to the European Court today might take as long as two years to go through the process of rendering an ECJ decision. Taking into account the time needed by the national judiciary to first refer the case to the European Court and then interpret the Court's decision, the entire process can easily take three to four years. This assumes, however, that a case will be sent to the ECJ in the first place. National judges are often reluctant to refer questions of EC law to the European Court, or to accord EC law supremacy over national law. Variation in the application of EC law across countries further intensifies the resource biases and time problems of relying on judge-made law. For example, in Britain, lower-court judges had been instructed not to refer cases to the ECJ, so the issue would have to be appealed up the entire legal hierarchy before it could reach the ECJ (Painter 1981). One can thus imagine that only the larger import/export firms would have had the resources to pursue a legal case against a national practice that created a non-tariff barrier; moreover, the willingness to pursue cases would probably vary by country.

In sum, the Court did not continue to develop its principle of mutual recognition, at least in part because of the negative political response the decision generated. Furthermore, any attempt by the ECJ to enforce a policy through law would have been greatly impeded by the limitations of judge-made law, which in the EC context are greatly exacerbated. Indeed, it is misleading to assume that Court decisions necessarily have policy effects.

The new approach and judicial politics

If judicial politics was important in creating the new approach to harmonization, one would expect to find evidence that the legal decision in some way affected the politics of harmonization policy. To evaluate the effects of the legal decision, we asked how the new approach to harmonization would have looked without the *Cassis de Dijon* decision.

Garrett and Weingast suggest that ECJ decisions can create focal points that serve as policy prescriptions around which interests converge. Underpinning this argument is the assumption that EC justices, fearing for their own professional futures and concerned about undermining the 'authority, legitimacy and independence' of the Court, are reluctant to make decisions that go against the interests of the member states. Although the constraints limiting the discretion of the ECJ are highly underspecified, Garrett and Weingast imply that ECJ decisions themselves are based on a reading of the interests of the influential member states, and they argue that ECJ decisions only have policy repercussions when they accurately reflect a policy consensus (for a discussion of their argument, see Chapter 6). With respect to the *Cassis de Dijon* case, Garrett sees the *Cassis* decision as being based on the interests of France and Germany (Garrett 1992: 558), and he deduces that the decision had policy consequences because the policy of mutual recognition was the preferred economic principle of the most powerful political and economic actors in Europe (Garrett and Weingast 1993).

There are significant empirical problems with the focal point argument in terms of its application to the *Cassis* case. Not only was there no consensus for mutual recognition before the *Cassis* decision, there was also no consensus after the decision. Interviews with the German government and the Commission revealed that mutual recognition was not the preferred policy for the majority of member states. In addition, contrary to Garrett's assertions, Germany and France were the strongest opponents of mutual recognition because, being high-standard countries, they had the most to lose. It has even been suggested that the unattractiveness of mutual recognition was actually a motivating force, encouraging member states to reach cooperative harmonized solutions rather than risk de facto harmonization at the lowest common denominator.

According to accounts of the actors involved, the Court's decision went well beyond what was being debated with respect to harmonization policy in 1978. Although the idea of mutual recognition was not totally new[17] and the notion that mutual recognition might be applied to goods had been evoked previously in some Commission circles, it was never acted on or even officially suggested because of the member states' opposition. The Court contributed to the debate by openly and visibly launching the notion of mutual recognition applied to goods, an idea that could have potentially enabled the traditional harmonization process to be circumvented and the completion of the single market to be reached earlier. The idea took off mainly as a result of opportune timing.

At the time of the *Cassis* decision, the Commission was searching for an instrument able to achieve the removal of technical obstacles to trade more efficiently than negotiated harmonization, the so-called 'old approach'. The institutional procedure for the adoption of a harmonization directive was generally very slow, drawn out, and costly. Because of the unanimity rule required by the Treaty of Rome, harmonization directives required years of negotiations. Sometimes, no political agreement was reached even after years of shuttling between the Commission and the Council, wasting time and resources. As a result, about 159 directives were adopted between 1962 and 1984, an average of only seven directives a year (Lauwaars 1988). Another major drawback of the old approach was the rigidity and the insistence on details of harmonization directives, which were valid for only one specific product and were often rendered obsolete by technical

---

[17] The expression *mutual recognition* was used in the Treaty of Rome in Article 57 with reference to diplomas and professional qualifications. It was also used during the 1970s with respect to financial services. At the time of *Cassis*, however, the expression was not used with reference to goods; only the terms *harmonization, approximation,* or *coordination* were applied to goods.

innovation (Vogel 1991). Finally, the old approach was politically hampered because it was believed to call for Euro-products, standardized goods that were associated in people's mind with a standardized way of life. The Commission's harmonization efforts had become objects of derision, if not objects of popular anger (Meunier-Aitsahalia 1993).

The problem of disparate regulations had become increasingly acute in the late 1970s and the old approach had proven unable to break the rising tide of protectionism created by the economic recession. Indeed, there were more non-tariff barriers resulting from divergences in national regulations in the early 1980s than when the harmonization policy of the EC was initiated in the 1960s. Under Commissioner Davignon's leadership in the late 1970s, the Commission increased its vigilance over barriers to trade, actively attempting to redirect its harmonization policy.[18] Whereas in 1974, the time of the *Dassonville* ruling, the Commission was still hopeful that a recently adopted directive[19] designed to confront the problem of non-tariff barriers would rectify the situation, by 1979 it was ready for a radical change. Thus the Commission was extremely eager to accept the *Cassis* decision as the basis of a new policy and therefore produced its communication.

The *Cassis* decision advanced the idea of mutual recognition, and the entrepreneurship of the Commission put the issue on the table and forced a debate. Both the decision itself and the Commission's response were necessary to produce the new harmonization policy. The legal decision was needed to encourage the Commission, an institution lacking power and authority, to issue its bold communication. Our interviews with members of the Commission revealed that without the *Cassis* decision, it would have taken significantly longer for the Commission to dare to suggest the application of the mutual recognition principle. The Commission's communication, however, was also necessary to bring the legal decision into the political arena. One can think of many important ECJ decisions that do not have policy consequences because the Commission, a member state, or an interest group does not seize on the judgment to exploit it for policy purposes (for example, the *Dassonville* decision). The *Cassis* decision became part of the political discourse because the Commission focused the political spotlight on the legal judgment.

In relying on the Court's decision as the basis of its policy, the Commission sought to use the Court's legitimacy as a neutral institution of law (Burley and Mattli 1993) and to circumvent the political process by basing the policy on the previously established law of the Community. Thus the Commission presented its new policy to the member states as inevitable, as deriving directly from the

---

[18] In 1978, the Commission complained to the member states about the increasing number of restrictive and protectionist measures and informed them that it was investigating over 400 cases of barriers to the free movement of goods (Communication from the Commission to the Parliament and the Council, 10 November 1978).

[19] Directive 70/50/EEC.

Cassis ruling, and justified the new policy outlined in the communication on the basis of the legal foundation of the *Cassis* judgment.

Neither the Court nor the Commission can force a policy on member states, however, as only the Council can adopt legislation. The Commission can propose a policy, but the member states must choose to adopt it. Given the member states' antagonism toward mutual recognition, the Commission's effort to impose a new approach to harmonization policy resting on the legal foundation of the Court's jurisprudence had very limited success. After the Legal Services of the Council had reinterpreted the communication, little remained of the Commission's policy and only a few of the ideas originally enunciated in the communication eventually became part of EC policy. Although in March of 1983 the Council passed a directive adopting the Commission's 1980 proposal to create a procedure to review newly proposed national legislation, the directive was not given real enforcement powers and therefore was only a meager victory for the Commission whose communication was much more ambitious.[20] Also following from the communication was the Commission's plan to systematically review national laws not yet harmonized, which became part of EC policy with Article 100b of the Single European Act, but remained without results.[21]

But the Commission's activism eventually proved effective in producing a new harmonization policy, which was enshrined into the EC treaties with the 1985 Single European Act. Although the communication did not convince the member states, it did mobilize interest groups that referred explicitly to the Commission's interpretation of the *Cassis* decision when they testified in front of parliaments and lobbied for and against the new policy. Because these groups were responding to the *Cassis* decision and the Commission's exploitation and generalization of the Court ruling, one can conclude that without these stimuli, the groups would not have been as rapid to mobilize, and less urgency would have been put on the issue of a new harmonization policy. This was especially true for consumer groups who were given a *raison d'être* by virtue of the *Cassis* ruling (see note 11). In addition, the fact that the political debate regarding mutual recognition continued even after the Commission's legal argument had been thoroughly undermined by the Council's own legal counter-interpretation and even after member states had politically undermined the attempt of the Commission to impose a new policy, indicates that interest groups were important in keeping the mutual recognition debate alive.

[20] Directive 83/189/EEC of 26 April 1983 [1983] OJ L109/8.

[21] Article 100b states that the Commission and the member states must draw up an inventory of national laws and regulations that have not yet been harmonized and that 'the Council, acting in accordance with the provisions of Article 100a, *may decide* that the provisions in force in a Member State must be recognized as being equivalent to those applied by another Member State' (emphasis added). This also means that member states may decide *not* to apply mutual recognition. Indeed, some commentators observed that this provision was worse than the status quo resulting from the Court decision and an actual setback compared to the procedure to combat protective national legislations available to the Commission under Article 169 (now Article 226). As of 1993, no inventory has been compiled by the Commission and this provision of the Single European Act appears to be dead.

Ultimately, the idea of mutual recognition originally suggested by the *Cassis* judgment was transformed into policy because the priorities and interests of member states had changed. As Sandholtz and Zysman (1989) and Moravcsik (1991) point out, the idea of the completion of the internal market was relaunched thanks to simultaneous changes in the governments of the major EC member states. The convergence in liberal economic thinking in Europe, which followed the comeback of the Tories to power in Britain in 1979, the return of the CDU in Germany in 1982, and the dramatic reversal of French economic policy in 1983 happened just as the *Cassis* principle was being watered down and rendered less easily applicable as a result of a restrictive legal analysis of its implications by the Council and application of the principle by the Court. At this point, the Court's and the Commission's endeavors had been taken up by the interest groups who lobbied the more receptive leaderships.

It is hard to see the Single European Act's new approach to harmonization as convergence around the Court's or the Commission's principle of mutual recognition. The Single European Act established a mixture of mutual recognition and negotiated harmonization, what has been called 'managed mutual recognition' (Nicolaïdis 1993, 1993b), which is very different from the initial mutual recognition proposed by the Court and the Commission. Whereas the Commission proposed applying mutual recognition to any unharmonized area, the new approach only applied mutual recognition on top of a base of harmonization, so as to minimize its deregulatory effects. The main contribution of the new approach was to redirect the goal of the harmonization process. Instead of creating detailed Euro-standards, harmonization endeavors were to be directed toward the broad definition of European-wide general essential objectives and requirements (such as preservation of health, safety, consumer protection, and the environment). In addition, the decision-making process for reaching the broad harmonized standards was changed from unanimity to qualified majority voting.

It should be noted that this new approach reflected the concerns of organized consumer and business groups. For example, Article 100a paragraph 3 of the Single European Act stated that 'the Commission, in its proposals [...] concerning health, safety, environmental protection and consumer protection, will take as a base a high level of protection', embodied the concerns of consumer groups. The idea that mutual recognition would only be applied on top of a base of harmonized regulation also addressed the concerns of businesses operating in high-standard countries. Similarly, the expedited harmonization process, as well as the codified mutual recognition, reflected the interest of most business groups. Rather than having to rely on a legal concept that was poorly understood by national administrators, businesses preferred codified rules, which the administrators were instructed to apply.

In sum, the Court's *Cassis* decision acted as a catalyst by introducing in the European debate the concept of mutual recognition, and thus the idea of transforming the harmonization process. The catalyst worked because it came at a time when the Commission was looking for a new approach to harmonization, and then later because member states' interests in the completion of the internal market were being revived. However, the policy that was ultimately adopted was neither the policy derived from the Court decision nor the policy advocated by the Commission's communication, but rather a compromise reflecting the concerns of mobilized interest groups and of the different member states. Although timing is very important, the idea of mutual recognition also mattered. Without *Cassis* and the debates triggered by the Commission's communication, it is likely that interest groups would not have been mobilized on the issue of non-tariff barriers to trade and that the relaunching of Europe might well have taken longer to be designed.

This 'Court as provocateur' argument differs from the other explanations in numerous ways. It implies that policy effects do not flow directly from court decisions themselves, but rather from a political process triggered by a Court decision. A political response is generated either because the decision is seized by individual actors or organized interests and used as a tool to promote a political agenda, or because the decision is so politically unpopular that it is seen as desirable to legislate a new policy instead of allowing the Court to develop and apply its jurisprudence. This argument implies that legal decisions succeed in jarring the political process precisely because they do not represent the interests of the dominant political actors, who seemingly would not need a Court decision to create a policy that serves their interests. Instead, the political process triggered by Court decisions helps to generate a counter-consensus. This process of consensus building is crucial because it greatly increases the likelihood that the policy will actually be implemented at the national level.

IV. Conclusion: Judicial Politics in the European Community

Although acknowledging the limitations of generalizing from a single case study, the saga of the political aftermath of the *Cassis* decision does offer some important insights into how judicial politics can influence the policy-making process in the EC. In the *Cassis* case, the Court played an important role in providing self-interested individuals access to challenge national policies, in proposing ideas for policy-makers, and in provoking political responses. There is preliminary evidence that the Court has played similar roles in other cases as well.

The Court as a medium through which interests can pursue individual and group agendas. The original version of this article saw the *Cassis* decision as evidence of the liberal narrative where the pursuit of self-interest leads to advances in European law. Chapter 3 notes how the *Cassis* case was actually a product of interactions among the pro-Europe jurist advocacy movement. The settlement in the *Anisette* case was leaked to Gert Meier in a meeting with the Commission.

There are other examples of individuals and groups appealing to the European legal system when political channels fail, and of the ECJ responding with decisions that promote the agendas of these plaintiffs. For instance, in Britain, the women's movement has repeatedly and systematically used the European legal system to promote equal pay for women (see Chapter 8). In France, the EC legal system has been used to challenge the petroleum distribution monopoly.

The availability and willingness of the ECJ to promote these individual agendas also implies that the ECJ can and does act autonomously of the policy interests of the Commission and the member states. This is not to say that the Court is immune to political influence. Rather, the Court is a political actor, responding to the political environment as do all political actors, but nonetheless able to act autonomously from the member states. Although the Commission may at times serve as a bellwether for the Court, signaling what will be politically tolerable to the member states and how the Court can contribute to the integration process (Stein 1981), the Court is also able and willing to go beyond the recommendations of the Commission, as it did in the *Cassis* decision. It has even been suggested that, in some areas, the Commission prefers to allow the Court to voice ideas and make decisions that might be politically unpopular (see Chapter 11).

Similarly, the Court is willing to decide against member state interests, a point that is especially significant given that public administrators are the defendants in the vast majority of cases raised through the preliminary ruling procedure. It might also be the case that member states prefer to have the ECJ disappoint domestic groups rather than be seen as supporting policies that are unpopular at home.

The Court as a provider of ideas. In the *Cassis* case, the Court influenced the policy-making process by writing its decision provocatively, so as to gently launch the idea of mutual recognition into the harmonization debate. The timing of the decision is important in understanding why this idea had such an impact, but it is undeniable that the idea itself provoked a debate about mutual recognition and the need to change the old approach to harmonization. There are other examples of the Court providing ideas of how to handle policy problems. For example, Nicolaïdis (1993) has argued that the Court created a 'road-map', which was used by negotiators for the mutual recognition of services. Legal scholars have also observed that legal reasoning offered by the ECJ has been adopted by national courts, leading to a general European convergence of certain disciplines of law, such as labor law (Bercusson 1993).

The Court as a provoker of political responses. Rather than usurping the legislative role, the Court can be seen as jarring the policy-making process by provoking political responses to its decisions. We have argued that the *Cassis* decision was written provocatively so as to test the political waters with respect to the idea of mutual recognition. The issuing of the communication by the Commission can be seen as a direct consequence of this provocation. The Court also provoked a political response from interest groups and member states by generating a principle that was seen as politically unappealing, and implying that the Court would apply this principle to rule national laws incompatible with EC law. The threat of a de facto policy of mutual recognition encouraged interest groups in higher-standard countries to support and promote the harmonization process as a preferable alternative to mutual recognition, and it provoked member states to negotiate Article 100b of the Single European Act, which allowed them to eliminate from a list generated by the Commission national regulations that should not be touched by mutual recognition. Article 100b potentially undermined the jurisprudence of the Court, as articulated in the *Cassis* case, because political agreement could now allow national laws incompatible with EC law to remain in force.

There are other instances where the ECJ has provoked a political response by issuing a decision with undesirable implications. In the area of equal pay for women and men, which was actively promoted by women's groups, the potential fiscal consequences of forcing member states to compensate for decades of unequal and illegal disparities in the payment of pensions provoked a backroom political deal, passing the Barber Protocol of the Maastricht agreement, which seeks to minimize the effects of the ECJ's jurisprudence in the area of equal pay (see Chapter 6).

Although the *Cassis* case is an extremely noteworthy example of the Court affecting EC and national policy-making, it is by no means the only example. It should be noted that the *Cassis* case managed to provoke a political response in 1979, a time when member states were not very interested in European integration and few politicians or scholars paid attention to the Court of Justice as a major political actor. This would imply that judicial politics has been an important factor in the EC for quite a long time, and that it remains an important factor even when political enthusiasm for integration ebbs. Yet it is also true that there are many ECJ decisions with huge policy implications, many of which would probably be seen as politically intolerable if there was a broader understanding of the potential implications involved. The next two chapters are a continuation of this research.

Explaining Variation in the Use of European Litigation Strategies: European Community Law and British Gender Equality Policy (2000)

With Jeannette Vargas

As the project of European integration continues to advance, it has become increasingly clear that the dynamics of this transnational process are producing secondary effects for domestic politics. Yet there is remarkably little systematic analysis about how European integration is transforming the national political process. This article identifies one effect that European integration, specifically the creation of a European legal system, has had on politics within the states. By providing domestic groups with a tool that can be used to impose new costs on their government, the European Union's (EU) legal system has transformed previously weak organizations with little leverage into political players capable of directly influencing national policy. We describe this transformative process as shifting the domestic balances of power.

The claim that the legal system can be a potent device to influence national policy is hardly novel, especially to those familiar with American judicial politics. Yet the European Community (EC) legal tool differs from a traditional litigation strategy, providing a unique means for groups to influence policy. There are different factors that influence whether an EC law litigation strategy will succeed. There are also advantages to using the EC legal tool that a domestic legal strategy does not offer. The EC legal system creates a means to circumvent opposition within the national judicial hierarchy, allowing a litigation strategy to succeed with the support of only a few lower level members of the judiciary. Furthermore, a change in policy based on EC law is much harder for national governments to reverse than a legal victory based on domestic law, because such a reversal would require legislating at the European level.

In the 1980s, the Equal Opportunities Commission (EOC) of the United Kingdom adopted a litigation strategy targeting British policies that contributed to gender discrimination in the workplace. Although activists might lament that discrimination remains a problem in the United Kingdom, the EOC had considerable success in forcing a Conservative government to accept significant changes in its equality policy based on European Court of Justice (ECJ) jurisprudence. We use this British case to identify the factors that contribute to a successful use of an EC law litigation strategy.

There are four separate steps that determine whether the EC legal tool can be successfully invoked to shift the domestic balance of power. First, there must exist a point of European law on which domestic actors can draw, and favorable ECJ interpretations of this law. Second, litigants must embrace EC law to advance their policy objectives, using EC legal arguments in national court cases. Third, national courts must support the efforts of the litigants by referring cases to the European Court and/or applying European Court jurisprudence instead of conflicting national policy. Fourth, the litigants must follow up their legal victory by drawing on legal precedents to create new political and material costs for the government and private actors. A litigation strategy can fail at any of the four steps.

Steps 2 through 4 involve significant actor agency. Others have hypothesized that litigants will draw on EC law to promote their interests whenever there is a potential benefit to doing so, with resource constraints being the primary barrier to litigation.[1] Despite the numerous situations in which a litigation strategy could have been profitably employed, however, EC law litigation strategies are used relatively infrequently. Indeed, in the area of equality policy, the British experience appears to be more an exception than a rule in terms of groups using EC law to circumvent national opposition and promote equality objectives. Resource constraints do not seem to have been the chief barrier preventing groups from embracing litigation strategies. The second half of the article examines the use and non-use of European litigation strategies to promote equal pay for men and women in other European member states. From this cross-national analysis, we develop a series of hypotheses about the conditions under which the EC legal system is likely to be seized and successfully used by groups to shift the domestic balance of power. Our focus is on the area of equal pay, but the hypotheses we develop could explain cross-national variation in the impact of ECJ jurisprudence on domestic policy in a variety of issue areas (this idea is picked up in Chapter 9).

The first section discusses how EC law allowed domestic interest groups to shift the domestic balance of power, forcing an unwilling British government to change public policy. It identifies the factors important to the EOC's success at each of the four stages of the EC legal process. The second section develops a series of hypotheses about the factors influencing the adoption of a successful EC litigation strategy.

---

[1] Though noting that resource constraints and short termism may keep potential litigants from raising cases, some researchers imply that private litigants raise European Community (EC) legal challenges whenever EC law will further their material or political interests (Burley and Mattli 1993; Mattli and Slaughter 1998; Stone Sweet, in press; Stone Sweet and Brunell 1998).

I. The EOC and the Shifting Domestic Balance of Power in Great Britain

In perhaps the most famous EC litigation success story, private and group actors committed to expanding gender equality in the workplace (and most notably the EOC) obtained progressive expansions of gender equal treatment policy in Great Britain during the Conservative Party's reign. The equality actors turned to an EC litigation strategy after other attempts at strengthening British equality policy failed. Their litigation strategy yielded dramatic results: exciting public attention with the successful expansion of the legal protections available to women workers and creating the potential of large costs for employers who discriminated on the basis of gender.

Domestic equal treatment legislation, including the Equal Pay Act (EPA) of 1972 and the Sex Discrimination Act (SDA) of 1975, had been enacted by a Labour government as a result of growing pressure from a variety of sources, including women's rights groups, unions, women's professional organizations, and women within the Labour Party itself (Carter 1988: 112–24; Mazey 1998 134; Meehan 1985: 40–65). Yet even with this favorable alignment of political actors, the original legislation contained numerous exemptions, applied only to a proportion of the female workforce, and employed a limited conception of equality of employment opportunity (Ellis 1988; Morris and Nott 1991; O'Donovan and Szyszczak 1988).

After the rise of the Conservative Party to power in 1979, even the legislation's limited aims were threatened. The EPA and SDA embodied the type of market interventionist legislation that was antithetical to the Thatcher government's laissez faire ideology. Domestic groups that supported gender equality policy retained little political influence and could not muster the support necessary to counter the Conservative government's antagonism toward equality policy.[2] The Conservative government did not enforce the existing equal opportunity legislation, weakened and withdrew legal protections that benefited women workers, and blocked efforts to legislate on social policy at the EC level (Kahn 1985: 96).

Nevertheless, equality actors obtained significant advances in gender equality policy under Conservative rule by relying on the EC legal system. The process by which politically marginalized actors shifted the domestic balance of power in their favor can be broken into four separate steps, each of which contributed

---

[2] The coalition of promotional groups that had mobilized public support for women's rights issues in the 1970s fell apart in the wake of the passage of the Sex Discrimination Act (SDA). The decline of interest in the women's movement can be attributed to internal ideological dissension, lack of momentum, and the harsh economic and political climate of the Thatcher era (Lovenduski and Randall 1993: 94–101). The Thatcher government's attack on the system of liberal corporatism also greatly diminished the political role of the unions (Marsh 1992; McIlroy 1991).

to the successful strategy. The first step—having the EC legal system and an EC legal basis to challenge national policy—was a precondition for an EC law-based litigation strategy. The last three steps—mobilizing interest groups around a litigation strategy, gaining national judicial support, and following through on legal victories to show the costs of not changing national policy—were necessary conditions for a shift of the domestic balance of power and the outcome of national policy change. We consider each step in turn.

STEP 1: The EC legal system creates a tool for domestic actors

For the EC legal mechanism to be useful to domestic policy actors, there must exist a point of EC law that litigants can draw upon. European law affects not all policy areas, and not all aspects of European law can be invoked in national courts. Equality actors in Britain were fortunate in that the EC had legislated extensively in the arena of equal employment opportunity. Article 119 (now Articles 141 and 142) of the Treaty of Rome established the principle that men and women should receive equal pay for equal work. In addition, while the Labour government was in office and under pressure from women's groups, the Council of Ministers passed 10 directives with implications for equal employment opportunity policy, including the Equal Pay Directive (EPD) and the Equal Treatment Directive (ETD) (Mazey 1998: 138).

The existence of a large body of EC law pertaining to equal opportunity in the workplace—a body of law that offered more protections to female workers than did British law—gave domestic actors a legal basis to mount an EC-based litigation strategy. Because of the ECJ's supremacy doctrine, legal victories based on EC law should negate conflicting national policy (*Costa v. ENEL* (1964)). But alone, the existence of favorable legislation was not enough. The ECJ's broad interpretations of Article 119 and the Equality Directives were indispensable in creating a legal canon more favorable to female workers than that of British law (Ellis 1991). The ECJ granted Article 119[3] and the ETD[4] direct effect, allowing private litigants to draw on these EC laws in front of national courts to challenge both government and private employers on issues encompassed by Article 119 and the ETD (Prescal and Burrows 1990: 24–45; Szyszczak 1997: 105). The

---

[3] The question of whether Article 119 created direct effects was explored in test cases constructed by an activist lawyer, Vogel-Polsky (see *Defrenne v. Sabena* [1976] ICR 547; *Defrenne v. Société Anonyme Belge de Navigation Aérienne Sabena* [1978] ECR 1365, ECJ). It took a highly motivated Vogel-Polsky five years to find a plaintiff for her test case, fighting hostility to the idea of a litigation strategy from the Belgian unions along the way (Harlow and Rawlings 1992: 283).

[4] The Equal Treatment Directive (ETD) was given direct effect in *Marshall v. Southampton and South-West Hampshire Area Health Authority (Teaching)* [1986] ICR 335. Although the Equal Pay Directive (EPD) has not been given direct effect, it has never been necessary to rely on it in national courts. The European Court of Justice (ECJ) has used the EPD to inform the principle of equal pay under Article 119, and thus, any rights contained in the EPD are by implication also contained within Article 119, which does have direct effect (Bourn and Whitmore 1997).

existence of EC law in the area of gender equality, the direct effect and supremacy of these laws in the national context, and the favorable interpretations of these laws were a precondition to domestic groups using an EC law litigation strategy to challenge national policy.

STEP 2: The mobilization of equal treatment policy actors

The mere existence of European legislation and favorable legal precedents by no means ensured policy change at the domestic level. Although the European Commission can use Article 169 of the Treaty of Rome to bring judicial proceedings against states that ignore their EC legal obligations, for many years it was reluctant to do so, allowing violations of EC law to persist (Rasmussen 1986: 238). As the EOC discovered, even when the Commission wins an Article 169 case, a national government can interpret the ECJ decision in a way that allows national policy to remain intact, and goes against the spirit of the ECJ's ruling.[5] Even when ECJ decisions are very clear, they do not carry fines or sanctions and in themselves were (until very recently) unenforceable.[6] The existence of domestic actors with incentives to litigate EC legal questions before national courts is thus important if EC law is actually going to influence national policy.

The readiness of domestic actors to pursue a litigation strategy depends on numerous variables. Litigation strategies are at best crude instruments for policy change, entailing the risk that adverse decisions could regress policy, and are thus usually adopted only after other political avenues have failed. Indeed, even a successful litigation strategy is unlikely to result in significant policy reform because the judiciary lacks the institutional capacity to produce social change (Horowitz 1977; Rosenberg 1991). As the next section will discuss, factors such as the national legal culture, the availability of resources, the organizational mandate of groups, and access to other sources of influence will shape litigant decisions about using litigation strategies.

Women's groups in England had shunned a litigation strategy, largely for ideological and organizational reasons (Kenney, 1992: 101–2). The EOC turned to a litigation strategy when its other efforts at influencing the national political

---

[5] In 1982, the ECJ ruled in favor of the Commission in the Article 169 proceeding brought against Great Britain for failing to implement the European standard of equal pay for work of equal value. In response, the British government created new procedures 'so burdensome and unnecessarily complicated—it even widened the defenses employers might use to avoid implementing equal pay policies—that many suspected the government of sabotaging the original Equal Pay legislation for which it had never held sympathy' (Vargas 1995: 30) (Case 165/82, *Commission of the European Communities v. UK* [1984] ICR 192, ECJ).

[6] In 1991, member states approved a procedure that can create fines for non-compliance with ECJ decisions. The procedure is meant to be used in exceptional cases. It is slow and cumbersome, and, in its first nine years of existence, the procedure has rarely been used. For more see Tallberg (2003).

agenda failed.[7] The EOC, created by the SDA to help eliminate discriminatory practices, was structurally and institutionally well suited to employ a litigation strategy. It had a narrow mandate to eradicate gender discrimination in the workplace, lawyers experienced in this specific area of employment law, and, as the repository for discrimination complaints against employers, a ready supply of potential complaints from which to select test cases. Furthermore, given the EOC's relatively uncontroversial statutory mandate to fund cases raising important points of law, a litigation strategy provided the EOC with a means of influencing public policy that carried little risk of exciting a negative reaction from the Conservative government (Ellis 1988: 236; Lovenduski and Randall 1993: 188).

Before turning to an EC litigation strategy, in the late 1970s, the EOC mounted a domestic litigation strategy. Working in conjunction with a small group of policy entrepreneurs, the EOC attempted to procure expansive read-ings of British equality legislation from the upper courts (Barnard 1995; Lord Lester QC 1994). This strategy failed, partly because of the explicitly limited scope of the British legislation, but also as a result of consistently narrow rulings from the Employment Appeals Tribunal (EAT), the appellate judicial body with the authority to interpret labor legislation. The EAT interpreted the EPA and SDA to impose huge procedural burdens on plaintiffs, and limited those meager rights granted by the original legislation (Bourn and Whitmore 1997: 266; Gregory 1987).

With the national strategy at an impasse, the EOC turned to EC law (Lester Q. C. 1994). EC laws provided the EOC with a legal basis for appealing unfavorable EAT decisions to the higher courts.[8] The EOC used EC law to challenge the valid-ity of legislation that contravened European law.[9] The EOC also funded test cases

---

[7] Although the Equal Opportunities Commission (EOC) had originally been granted formid-able powers, including the authority to launch formal investigations against employers, during its first decade in existence the EOC pursued a strategy of conciliation, persuasion, and high-level negotiation with both government and employers (Kenney 1992: 92–100; Sacks 1986). The early commissioners, selected from the ranks of business and union leadership, have been criticized for their apparent agenda of maintaining the current status of industrial relations (Gregory 1987: 137–8; Sacks 1986). Yet Lovenduski and Randall (1993) have pointed out that the Commission was also influenced by the pragmatic concern that any flamboyant use of its investigative powers would provoke the Conservative government to strip the Commission of what resources it did pos-sess (pp. 186–7).

[8] Although the Employment Appeals Tribunal (EAT) is normally the highest authority in labor law cases, a sufficiently important point of law can, in rare instances, be appealed to the higher British appellate courts, the Court of Appeal and the House of Lords. Appeals to the higher appel-late courts require the leave of either the court whose decision is being appealed or the court to which the appeal is being taken.

[9] The EOC brought suit against the Secretary of State for Employment, for example, for failing to amend the Employment Protection (Consolidation) Act 1978 to conform with ECJ decisions on indirect discrimination. The EOC asserted that the 1978 Act, which prevented part-time work-ers from pursuing unfair dismissal claims, violated European law, as women constituted 90% of the class of part-time workers affected. In 1994 the House of Lords invalidated the exemption of part-time workers from the 1978 Act's coverage, on the grounds that the Act violated the EC Equal

on appeal to the ECJ, playing an active role in the development of European equality law to gain binding precedents for use at the national level (Barnard, 1995).[10]

As the success of the EOC's strategy became apparent, trade unions also began
to use litigation strategies. Although unions had historically shown little interest
in women's economic concerns (Lovenduski 1986: 186–94) and preferred
collective action over litigation, EC equality law offered unions a possibility to
increase their bargaining leverage—a prospect that was especially attractive
because the Thatcher government's industrial relations policy had significantly
weakened union power in negotiations with employers (McIlroy 1991). Unions
litigated EC equality issues to bolster their broader collective action programs.
For example, the Transport and General Workers Union, UNISON, and the
General, Municipal, Boilermakers and Allied Trades Union, among others, used
decisions on maternity rights, part-time workers, pensions, and equal value to
procure better terms for their members in collective agreements (Kilpatrick 1992:
39). In 1991, the Trades Union Congress (TUC) even held a national seminar,
co-sponsored by the European Commission, which was designed to:

assist unions [to] develop a strategy in order to best exploit the potential of European legislation and case-law ... includ[ing] identifying potential test cases which could expand
domestic law for women members and identifying legislation which could add weight to
union negotiators' arguments in collective bargaining. (TUC 1991: 1)

Unions co-sponsored cases with the EOC (Harlow and Rawlings 1992: 284),
advertising for possible test cases relating to issues coming up in contract negotiations and funding the most promising through the courts. When legal decisions
favorable to their interests emerged, unions threatened employers violating EC
law with litigation (Holland 1994).

STEP 3: Eliciting national judicial support
to interpret EC equality law broadly

Given the EC's legal structure, an EC litigation strategy cannot succeed without
the support of the national judiciary. Private litigants cannot take their challenges
to national policy directly to the ECJ; they must rely on national courts to make
a preliminary reference to the ECJ. Any judge, no matter where they sit in the
national legal hierarchy, can send the ECJ a question and thereby create an authoritative and binding legal precedent for both the national and European legal systems, and national courts may also interpret and apply European law on their own.
Given that ECJ decisions are on their own virtually unenforceable, national court

---

Treatment Directive (*Regina v. Secretary of State for Employment, ex parte EOC and another* (1994)
IRLR 179, HL (UK)).

[10] Women's groups were also involved in positive action strategies at the European Union (EU)
level (Mazey 1998: 141).

enforcement may be the only hope of forcing governments or firms to comply with EC law. But there is no way to force national courts to send references to the ECJ, or to give EC law priority over national law. Parties to a lawsuit are therefore quite dependent on the national judiciary's willingness to aid their litigation efforts.

There was no assurance that the EOC would receive national judicial support for its EC litigation strategy. British courts at the time were not favorably disposed to the EC legal process. In comparison with courts in other member states, 'British judges [are] loath to make referrals and unwilling to cooperate with the ECJ in promoting European integration' (Golub 1996: 368).[11] This reluctance to rely on EC law was evident in early equal opportunity cases: The EAT only cited European law in 12 sex discrimination and equal pay cases prior to 1986.

In Britain, national judicial support came from an unlikely source: the industrial tribunals, which are the lowest rung of the judicial hierarchy. Tribunals were created in 1964 to be fast, inexpensive, and informal bodies with jurisdiction over industrial relations cases in the first instance. Tribunals were not designed for legal innovation. All tribunals are bound by the rules of law articulated by the EAT, and their decisions have no precedential value within the legal system. Given the restrictive interpretation conferred upon national legislation by the EAT, tribunals favoring expansive interpretations of equal opportunity law had no other means of promoting their policy preferences within the national judicial system. European law provided industrial tribunals with a legitimate legal basis for advancing their agendas, allowing them to circumvent the EAT and move to the forefront of policy development. For example, one Southampton tribunal awarded a sex discrimination plaintiff more than the maximum amount allowed under British legislation, arguing that EC law required a plaintiff to be fully compensated for their loss. This decision led to an ECJ ruling invalidating the legislative cap on remedies in sex discrimination cases. Furthermore, tribunals could make references to the ECJ directly, preempting the EAT and obtaining a legal precedent binding on all national courts.[12]

Several factors contributed to the disproportionate influence pro-women tribunals were able to exercise in the British legal system. First, the EOC employed a strategy of forum shopping, targeting tribunals thought to be sympathetic to the EOC's policy objectives and thus more receptive to EC law arguments.[13]

---

[11] Although Stone and Brunell (1998) refute this claim, others have also found British courts reluctant to embrace EC law (Craig 1998).

[12] A Northern Ireland tribunal did precisely that in Case 222/84, *Johnston v. Chief Constable of the RUC* [1987] ECR 1651, ECJ, an ECJ decision that has had important implications for the interpretation of the ETD, and for the ability of national governments to limit plaintiff's access to national courts (Prescal and Burrows 1990: 129–35).

[13] The largest number of cases were concentrated in South London, where the tribunal chair was a former legal director of the EOC and had sat on committees and working groups in Luxembourg concerning the future of EC equality law. Tribunals in Leeds, Gloucester, and Southampton were also found to be notably more progressive on equal treatment issues than other tribunals (based on interviews with tribunal chairs in London on 22 and 23 August 1994).

This strategy provided pro-women tribunals with strong cases to challenge established precedent. Second, a growing contingent of legal scholars supported the proposition that British equality laws must be interpreted in accordance with European principles (Gormley 1986; McCrudden 1987). Indeed, the only national reporting publication of industrial tribunal decisions applauded the tribunals who were applying EC equality law and advocated greater activism from other tribunals. Given the support conferred upon EC law by advocates, academics, and other tribunals, the majority of industrial tribunal chairs—who had no political preference in case outcomes and were concerned only with identifying the 'correct' rule of law—grew to accept European principles as guiding the cases in front of them. The tribunals' embrace of EC equality law became so pronounced that the Law Society's president, Martin Mears, declared that tribunals had been 'hijacked by the discrimination industry' (Dyer 1995: 8).

The EAT tried to limit the impact of European Court rulings or distinguish British cases to disable ECJ jurisprudence and to regain the policy initiative. But the EAT became increasingly less able to force industrial tribunals to follow its precedents. In one notable example, the EAT had clearly established that under British law the dismissal of a pregnant woman constituted sex discrimination only in certain rare instances (*Hayes v. Malleable Working Men's Club and Institute* (1985) IRLR 367 EAT (UK)). Nevertheless, when a subsequent ECJ decision established that dismissal on the grounds of pregnancy constituted per se discrimination, the majority of industrial tribunals began applying the European rule.[14] Although the EAT reaffirmed its original holding in a subsequent case, many lower courts continued to follow the ECJ precedent (*Webb v. EMO Air Cargo (UK) Ltd* (1990) IRLR 124 EAT (UK)).

The House of Lords was more friendly to ECJ jurisprudence than the EAT, but it also created barriers to European equality law. In 1988, the House of Lords held that national courts were under no obligation to interpret the British SDA in accordance with the EC ETD, a ruling that implicitly directed tribunals to follow the EAT's pregnancy ruling over that of the ECJ (*Duke v. GEC Reliance* (1988) IRLR 118 HL (UK)). Tribunals still continued to apply the ECJ standard, however. Eventually the EAT's and the House of Lords' pregnancy rulings were directly rejected by the ECJ. In the 1990s, the House of Lords recast itself as a progressive force on European law and equal treatment issues. The House of Lords began interpreting EC law broadly in light of EC Directives—usually without making a preliminary reference to the ECJ. Though it is impossible to know for sure why the House of Lords started to adopt more favorable EC law interpretations, one likely impetus was the House of Lords' desire to regain

---

[14] See Case C-177/88, *Elisabeth Johanna Pacifica Dekker v. Stichting Vormingscentrum voor Jonge Volwassenen (VJV-Centrum) Plus* [1990] ECR I-3941, (1991) IRLR 27 ECJ. Where national courts followed the *Dekker* rule, women plaintiffs were successful 93% of the time, as opposed to 57% under the EAT rule.

control of domestic jurisprudence by asserting its own supreme authority to interpret EC law.

STEP 4: Follow-through: creating new costs for national governments and firms

Although a court victory may sometimes be enough to obtain all of the litigant's goals, more often litigation strategies are part of a multipronged strategy designed to gain leverage in extra-judicial negotiations (S. M. Olson 1981).[15] The multi-pronged strategy is prudent because EC judicial decisions are seldom enough to create policy change on their own (see Chapter 7). This was certainly the case with respect to equality policy where, according to Harlow and Rawlings (1992), women's groups saw early on 'the need for political campaigning in parallel to litigation' (p. 147). We call 'follow-through' the process of making the potential political and financial costs of continued non-compliance clear. The EC legal victories were an important part of the overall strategy because they created concrete bargaining leverage for the EOC and unions. But the EOC and unions had to make it very clear to the government and employers that a failure to change their policy was likely to be costly.

For example, the EOC had unsuccessfully lobbied the government since 1988 to raise the legislative cap on awards in sex discrimination cases. British awards to compensate for gender discrimination were legislatively capped at £11,000, a low sum that discouraged most women from bringing cases (Leonard 1987) and removed the incentive for employers to end discrimination. Having failed to convince the government to change its policy, the EOC helped fund the *Marshall II* case, where the ECJ held that public sector plaintiffs must be fully compensated for detriment caused by discrimination.[16] Within months of the decision, the Department of Employment completely removed the cap for both public and private employees, exceeding the requirements of the ECJ decision.[17] A few factors explain the government's volte-face and its willingness to go beyond the requirements of *Marshall*. The EOC and trade unions advertised in trade journals for possible claims they could pursue on issues related to their lobbying agenda. This meant that the government and employers could expect legal claims to be forthcoming. Furthermore, legal claims seemingly had the support of the

---

[15] American women's groups, for example, pursued a litigation strategy not because they believed legal victories alone could change the status of women, but because the threat of legal action in a legal climate favorable to women's issues could force concessions from employers and government officials (McCann 1994).

[16] See *Marshall v. Southampton and South-West Hampshire Area Health Authority* [1993] IRLR 445. The EOC was actually a latecomer to this case. Marshall funded the first two rounds of appeals herself.

[17] The *Marshall* decision was based on a directive, and thus did not apply to private employers, but the government changed the national legislation with respect to the private sector as well (Sex Discrimination and Equal Pay (Remedies) Regulations 1993).

domestic judiciary; indeed, tribunals had begun applying the Marshall decision directly to grant awards well in excess of the cap before the Department of Employment even had a chance to amend the legislation.[18] There was also concern that under the ECJ's *Francovich (Andrea) and Bonifaci (Daniela) v. Italian Republic* (Cases C-6 and C-9/90 [1991] ECR I-5357) doctrine a private employee precluded by national law from pursuing an EC legal claim against their employer could potentially recover against the government. With the EOC and unions advertising for cases, the potential threat that the *Francovich* doctrine would make the government financially liable for private sector discrimination,[19] and a clear indication that the national judiciary was likely to award larger discrimination fines, the government decided to change its policy.

Lobbying to create political costs was also necessary lest the government respond to a legal decision by eliminating or lowering the benefit for both men and women. In another example, political cause groups found a test case where a woman was denied government benefits designed for men who leave the workforce to care for an invalid. As the case progressed, it was rumored that the Conservative government would respond to a legal loss by eliminating the benefit altogether. After winning in the ECJ, the groups launched a large media campaign with grassroots meetings and conferences, and with lobbying of both Houses of Parliament.[20] The campaign made it politically too embarrassing for the supposedly family-oriented Conservative government to deprive caretakers and the disabled from benefits. The result was the extension of government benefits to women who leave the workforce to care for disabled family members (Harlow and Rawlings 1992: 146).

The private sector is also facing increased pressure to reform business practices in light of new financial liabilities created by EC law. Prior to the *Marshall II* decision, employers found it more expensive to restructure their businesses than to pay damages to potential plaintiffs. This is no longer the case. Several companies have made headlines in the past few years by paying large settlements to women who brought sex discrimination claims against them (Foster 1996; Taylor 1996). Industrial Relations Services, an independent labor market analyst, found that in the two years following the implementation of *Marshall II*, the average award in

---

[18] These decisions surprised the government's lawyers in the Treasury Solicitor's office. In an interview, one lawyer commented: 'Once they were given the option by *Marshall* to apply higher awards, tribunals took it with open arms. They have been following the ethos of *Marshall*... applying the decision in the gap before the government legislated ... whenever thought we would have to face such large awards, because it goes against traditional legal argument on personal injury law and compensation' (interview with official from Treasury Solicitor's office, 11 August 1994).

[19] Department of Employment officials conceded that they were largely motivated by *Francovich* concerns. One official stated that 'it was seen as a straight choice—the government changes the law and the employer pays the balance, or we don't change the law, and the U.K. pays the balance' (interview with official, 20 July 1994). Another Department official agreed: '*Francovich* was one of the most important factors, if not the most' (interview with official, 4 August 1994).

[20] Case 150/85, *Drake v. Chief Adjudication Officer* [1985] 3 All ER 65, UK was funded by the EOC.

sex discrimination cases rose from £2,940 to £12,172. New penalties have translated into new victories for trade unions; the TUC reported a 50 per cent increase in collective bargaining deals following the elimination of the cap on awards (Bassett 1996).

By following through, activists have translated legal victories into social policy changes with real impacts on the conduct of employers and the government. This observed effect is in keeping with Rosenberg's (1991) contention that courts are more likely to be successful in influencing social policy when extra-judicial actors offer positive incentives for compliance, or impose costs to induce compliance with judicial decisions (pp. 33–6). If the government or business knows that they will lose in the courts, they can become more willing to adjust policies, regardless of whether a legal case is actually brought. If EC law and ECJ jurisprudence are clear, the credible threat of a national legal case can be a weapon in itself, altering the strategic calculations of the government and firms.

Table 8.1. Four factors in building a successful litigation strategy

---

EC legal system: A tool to influence national policy
Direct effect of EC law creates legal standing for plaintiffs to draw on EC law in national courts. The supremacy of EC law creates a legal basis for national courts to apply EC law instead of conflicting national law. Article 119 EEC (now Articles 141 and 142) and Equal Pay Directives create an EC point of law for national groups to invoke. ECJ found that Article 119 and the Directives on equal pay created direct effects, and gave favorable readings to these EC law provisions.

Mobilization of domestic groups
The EOC was committed to a litigation strategy based on national law, but the strategy failed when the EAT interpreted British law narrowly. The EOC turned to EC law to circumvent the EAT and hopefully get more favorable readings of EC law. In light of EOC victories, unions followed the EOC's strategy, choosing test cases on issues related to collective bargaining goals.

Gaining national judicial support
The EOC sought friendly tribunal chairs to make references to the ECJ. The preliminary ruling procedure allowed pro-women tribunal chairs to circumvent the EAT. The actions of first-instance industrial tribunals, combined with more favorable EC legal texts and ECJ jurisprudence, reverberated through the national legal system. Eventually, the House of Lords and the EAT retreated from their own narrow legal precedents, and adopted ECJ jurisprudence.

Follow-through: Creating political costs
The EOC and unions solicited copycat cases, eliminating the possibility to settle the individual case and making it clear that non-compliance would be costly. If the government or business knew that they would lose in the national courts, regardless of whether a case was actually brought, they became willing to adjust policies. The threat of an EC legal case in light of ECJ jurisprudence became a weapon in itself.

Note: EC: European Community, EEC: European Economic Community, ECJ: European Court of Justice, EOC: Equal Opportunities Commission, and EAT: Employment Appeals Tribunal.

There were four factors that made the EOC's threat credible and contributed to the EOC's success in influencing national policy (see Table 8.1). The EC legal tool created an important shift in the domestic balance of power, turning weak domestic actors with little leverage into political players capable of influencing national policy. With the power of the EC legal tool on their side, pro-equality actors won important victories, including the extension of work benefits for part-time workers and the equalization of pension benefits for men and women. They eliminated the cap on discrimination awards and obtained benefits for women dismissed because of pregnancy. The equality actors' victories were especially impressive because they were won against a Conservative government at the height of the Conservative Party's antagonism toward EC social policy and European encroachments on national sovereignty.[21] Undeniably, litigation was not the exclusive strategy pursued by activists. For example, positive action programs, many initiated at the EU level, were also used. But even with positive EU programs, the British government often had to be forced to implement the programs in full (Mazey 1998: 144; Meehan and Collins 1996). Although inequality persists and limits to the litigation strategy have become apparent, the significance of the changes in British equality policy created through litigation should not be discounted.

But how durable are these legal victories? To sustain the claim that the EC legal system actually shifts the domestic balance of power, governments must not be able to thwart a litigation strategy, or easily reverse victories won through litigation. The evidence suggests that national governments are limited in their ability to stop an EC law litigation strategy, or reverse victories won through an EC law litigation strategy. Litigation campaigns can be implemented with relatively minimal financial resources, and although the government has significant political resources with which to mount an attack against domestic interests, the source of these actors' empowerment—EC law and domestic courts—is not easily assailable.[22] Short of limiting access to the courts, there is little that can be done to directly prevent a group or individual from pursuing a litigation strategy. Although in this case the government had the power to eliminate the EOC altogether, political constraints prevented it from abolishing an agency designed to fight gender discrimination simply because the agency was successful.[23] It is also hard to stop national courts from sending cases to the ECJ. Because a single court located anywhere in the national legal hierarchy can make a reference to the ECJ and thus help create binding national legal

---

[21] On the Conservatives' agenda vis-à-vis EC social policy, see Streeck (1995). On the Conservatives' agenda vis-à-vis the ECJ, see Brown (1995) and Smith (1990).

[22] Though litigation may be costly for individuals, as group strategies they are relatively inexpensive (especially when compared to the costs of lobbying and mobilizing public opinion).

[23] Streeck (1995) notes that non-discrimination was consistent with the liberal ideology of the Conservative party. It is also doubtful whether at the point the EOC's success was apparent such a strategy would have helped. The legal precedents were there, and national courts were applying them.

precedent, trying to control national legal bodies through the appointment process is difficult at best. The Conservative government did, however, make a significant effort to limit EC law victories. The Conservatives tried to rally support among other member states to change the social provisions of EC law, and eventually opted out of the EC's Agreement on Social Policy annexed to the Maastricht Treaty and binding on all other member states. The Conservative government also tried to create a political check on the ECJ and pressure the ECJ into limiting its jurisprudence in social policy.[24] But existing ECJ decisions are hard to reverse. Because EC law is supreme to national law, a national government cannot simply legislate over an ECJ decision at the national level. Furthermore, as the Conservative government found, changing EC law at the EC level is also difficult. Even with the majority of member states in accord, a joint-decision trap makes it exceedingly difficult to change existent EC legislation when the voting rule is unanimity (see Chapter 6). Any ECJ decision based on Article 119 of the Treaty requires unanimous support to change the EC Treaty itself; thus, legislating over an unwanted ECJ decision based on Article 119 faces all the problems of the joint-decision trap. Making changes to EC directives is theoretically easier than legislating over Treaty provisions, but considering how isolated Thatcher's and Major's governments were on issues of social policy, building support among other states to change EC directives in this area was, as a practical matter, impossible.

This does not mean that EC laws can never be changed. When the ECJ's *Barber* decision threatened the financial integrity of the British, Dutch, and German social security systems, member states were able to coordinate a response. The Barber Protocol limited the retrospective effects of the ECJ's Barber judgment regarding the equalization of pensions. But it is important to note that member states were still required to change their policies and equalize pensions lest they be liable for financial claims in the future. Member states have also legislatively reversed the ECJ's Case C-450/93, *Eckhard Kalanke v. Freie Hansestadt Bremen* [1995] ECR I-3051 ruling, where the ECJ made a decision against women-owned firms, finding that national affirmative action policies were inconsistent with the wording of an EC directive. In the Treaty of Amsterdam member states redrafted EC law to make it more favorable to government policies, trying to promote women- and minority-owned firms.

The EOC and union victories have been difficult to reverse at the EC level, and the policy changes won through the litigation process have been enduring. EC legislation came to be seen as the best ally of unions and women's groups during a long period of Conservative Party rule. With the Labour government signing

---

[24] The British demanded the scheduling of an inter-governmental conference to discuss the roles and powers of EC institutions, including the Court's powers. British Euro-skeptics forced the British government to put into the negotiating process of the 1996 inter-governmental conference a series of proposals to make the ECJ more politically accountable and to limit the cost of ECJ decisions. See Chapter 6, Section VI for an explanation of what happened.

on the social protocol, an additional source of leverage for British labor and social groups is being created, a leverage that cannot be eliminated by a change in the ruling party.

Though the equality victories remain entrenched, the Conservative government has arguably had some success in influencing the ECJ's subsequent equality jurisprudence. The *Kalanke* decision was taken as a sign that the ECJ was retreating from its equality activism. The ECJ has also disappointed homosexual groups in their efforts to use EC equality law to stop discrimination against homosexuals. These decisions, however, should be seen in the larger context of the ECJ's equality jurisprudence. The ECJ has already gone further than most national courts and national governments in expanding equality protections under law, and there is no sign that the ECJ is retreating from its basic equality jurisprudence. With affirmative action policies now explicitly authorized under European law, such policies are better protected now than they were before *Kalanke*. The ECJ may well be moderating its handling of explosive social policy issues, but it is still one of the best aids for domestic policy actors challenging national policy.

II. When will Domestic Actors Embrace EC Law to Shift the Domestic Balance of Power?

The British case, because of its success, is well known. Yet despite the clear opportunities, and despite the European Commission's efforts to publicize the EOC's success, to share best strategies across women's groups and labor unions, and to build policy networks (Harlow and Rawlings 1992: 283–4; Mazey 1995), outside of the United Kingdom there has been a dearth of individuals and national actors turning to European law to promote the equality rights of women. Beyond the issue of equal pay, the apathy of organized groups in drawing on EC law is equal, if not greater. We have discussed why the EOC turned to a litigation strategy. The question remains: Why have actors in similar situations in other countries not done so?

This section investigates a number of factors that influence the steps of the legal process identified as important in the British case. We focus on equality policy, but the hypotheses are of a general nature and could explain cross-national variation in the use of EC law litigation strategies in areas outside of gender equality. We rely in this analysis on three excellent studies in which researchers investigated gender equality policy and the use of sex equality litigation procedures in EU member states (Blom et al. 1995; Fitzpatrick, Gregory, and Szyszczak 1993; Vogel-Polsky 1985).[25] The cross-national studies find that there were actors that

---

[25] The latter two studies were completed before the latest enlargement of the EU; thus, they do not include Austria, Sweden, or Finland.

could effectively use a litigation strategy to influence national policy, but most of these actors chose not to use litigation strategies. The studies cannot actually test any of the hypotheses we develop, but they do provide suggestive evidence that allows us to examine the hypotheses in a preliminary way. The evidence is provided in the footnotes and the text that follows.

STEP 1: When will the EC legal system provide a useful tool for domestic actors?

For an EC law litigation strategy to be used, there must be a legal basis in European law for a litigant to draw on, and this law must create direct effects. Where there is a relevant EC law, it should provide the same legal opportunities for litigants across member states. But whether EC law and the ECJ are seen as a useful ally may depend on the nature of the national legislation protecting gender equality in the workplace. A potential source of cross-national variation could come from variation in the nature of national equality legislation.

Hypothesis 1: In countries with strong domestic legislation protecting workers against gender discrimination, the need to draw on EC legal remedies should decrease.

All EC member states, in fact, have enshrined a fundamental right to equal pay for equal work into national law and have legislation that allows this right to be asserted in national courts (Fitzpatrick et al. 1993: ch. 5). Furthermore, according to Vogel-Polsky (1985), by 1985 a cross-national convergence in legislation and objectives regarding gender equality was apparent (p. 107). Indeed, none of the analysts find variations in national laws contributing significantly to the variation in the use of equality litigation strategies.[26] Blom et al. (1995) point out, however, that national legislation often does not address the larger social, economic, and political factors that are the main cause of gender discrimination in the workplace. With governments striving to increase labor flexibility through the use of part-time workers and temporary contracts, the number of workers (especially female workers) not protected by national legislation is growing (p. 11). In addition, a number of other national practices—such as relying on word-of-mouth recruitment, concentrating training resources on workers

[26] The one possible exception is Germany, because the German constitution arguably includes a guarantee of broad rights to protect individuals from discrimination. But German courts are not interpreting national protections as widely as some women's groups and individuals facing discrimination might hope. Fitzpatrick, Gregory, and Szyszczak (1993) find that 'advocates in Germany may be trying to exploit the possibilities of Community law in order to circumvent more restrictive interpretations on German constitutional law emanating from the Federal Labor Court and the Federal Constitutional Court' (p. 91). The German case implies that regardless of what the national legislation says, as long as national courts interpret national laws narrowly, and as long as there is a possibility that the ECJ may give or EC law may allow a more favorable reading, there is an attraction to a European strategy.

in higher grades, and requiring geographical relocation or work during off-hours—undermine the ability of women to participate in the workforce on the same terms as men (pp. 6–11). Blom et al. see opportunities for groups to use EC law to address these and other issues in virtually all member states. Although we cannot rule out a correlation between the extent of national legislative protections and the number of national cases, the fact that there is favorable national legislation does not mean that EC litigation strategies are not useful. As Vogel-Polsky (1985) argued:

It is illusory to think that the law can overcome discrimination. When legal discrimination has been formally abolished social discrimination remains and adopts new and sometimes much more subtle forms. The law must therefore...contain the principles of positive action...[which] requires a combination of promoters, forces, restraints and inducements. (p. 108)

Another way that national legislation may matter is that it will determine who has legal standing to raise cases, and thus shape how discrimination cases are pursued.

Hypothesis 2: The more limited the legal standing of private litigants or groups to draw on national law, the less able or likely individuals or groups are to mount a litigation strategy.

Many of the member states examined in the cross-national studies had restrictions in legal standing that make group litigation strategies harder to pursue. Indeed, the studies' examples provide anecdotal support for Hypothesis 2, at least with respect to group litigation.[27] Group *locus standi* limitations could be changed, given sufficient pressure. Alternatively, they could be surmounted through the simple expedient of having agency lawyers act in a private capacity. Thus, the existence of limited *locus standi* rights for groups might in itself be a manifestation of the lack of group mobilization around equality litigation strategies.

---

[27] In Luxembourg, groups are not allowed litigation rights (Fitzpatrick et al. 1993: 96), although unions have been given access to the judicial process in equal pay cases (p. 24). In France, common interest groups are only allowed to litigate autonomously in criminal courts (p. 91). In Denmark, gender equality clauses that are part of collective agreements can only be pursued by union officials. If the union will not pick up the issue, the individual is often out of luck—individuals not covered by collective agreements, however, can use labor courts (pp. 19–20). In Ireland, cases must first go to an equality officer and only after that to a labor court. The Employment Equality Agency can also investigate and fund cases, but it must be active in the case from the beginning. It cannot pick up cases raised by private litigants, even if it has been assisting in these cases (pp. 22–3). Because of the Employment Equality Agency's restricted ability to participate in equality cases, 'The body most likely to promote a reference to the ECJ is prevented from doing so and is reliant upon outside lawyers to take over a case which it has been overseeing' (p. 94). It is hard to go beyond anecdotal evidence because there is no good cross-national data on the number of equality cases. Because many national courts interpret EC law without referring the case to the ECJ, the number of references in equality issues cannot serve as proxy data.

National procedural factors might also limit the number of equality cases.

Hypothesis 3: Procedural rules concerning how complaints are filed, legal aid availability, attorney fee shifting, statute of limitations, award caps, and the burden of proof can also affect the willingness of private litigants to pursue their legal rights.

These factors seem especially relevant for private litigants in the sensitive area of discrimination policy. The emotional and financial costs to litigants, especially those bringing a case against their current employer, can be very high, and if procedural rules reduce the chance of victory, few will wish to incur those costs.[28] Procedural barriers might be more significant for private litigants than for group actors, because groups have the ability to find optimal test cases and the resources to develop those cases. Indeed, in Britain there was a cap on awards, restrictive time limits in which the cases had to be raised, provisions that shifted the costs of litigation to the losing party, and a lack of legal aid funding until a case reached the higher courts. The dedication and resources of the EOC made these barriers surmountable. This would seemingly also be possible in other member states.

Though there is significant variation in national equality legislation, all of it must comply with EC law. All countries have problems with gender discrimination in the workplace, and the cross-national reports imply that in all countries groups could benefit from drawing more on EC law litigation.

STEP 2: When will domestic groups mobilize around a litigation strategy?

Blom et al. (1995) identify many groups that could usefully employ EC law litigation strategies to promote gender equality, including unions, women's groups, and equality agencies. Most of these groups are not following the EOC's strategy, however. When can we expect litigants with an interest at stake and with legal standing to raise a case to turn to a legal strategy to promote their cause? Or, to use Harlow and Rawlings' (1992) term: What determines when there will be a 'good fit' between the goals of a group and the benefits of a litigation strategy?

A litigation strategy is generally a last-choice strategy to affect policy change, because it is hard to know if a court will decide in your group's favor or actually set back the group's cause. Also, litigation strategies are designed to remove objectionable legislation. They are not very helpful in constructing legislation that promotes a group's interests. In the area of equality policy, Blom et al. (1995) find that 'litigation is generally avoided, and considered an effective means only as a threat to unwilling employers: use is only made of it when all other alternatives have failed to produce acceptable results' (p. 18). Because of the risks involved in

---

[28] The Fitzpatrick et al. (1993) report notes that in Portugal, the heavy burden of proof limits the ability of private litigants to bring cases (p. 99).

litigation strategies, they are most attractive to actors with few other options to influence national policy.

Hypothesis 4: Groups with significant influence over the policy-making process are less likely to turn to a litigation strategy, because a litigation strategy is usually a last-choice tool. The greater the political strength of a group, and the more access the group has to the policy-making process, the less likely a group is to mount a litigation campaign.

The cross-national reports lend some support to this hypothesis. It was certainly true in the British case that the EOC turned to a litigation strategy because its other efforts had failed to influence public policy. The cross-national reports note that equality was part of the agenda of many groups, but they were adopting other means to promote equality besides litigation. Unions promoted equality in collective bargaining arrangements and supported their members in arbitration when the collective agreement was breached. Work councils were also a venue in Germany to pursue equality issues. Blom et al. (1995) also observe that:

the national authorities and their agencies often work on the presumption that a sufficient legal framework for sex equality at work has been established so that no further action in this field is necessary. This does not always mean that they ignore women's interests, but when campaigns exist they often focus on stimulating positive action programmes, and on issues concerned with family responsibilities and tend to ignore existing direct and indirect discrimination within the present labour market structure. (p. 15)

In addition, in many cases, groups that did challenge policy would in effect be challenging the rules and agreements they themselves helped fashion. Blom et al. (1995) note that unions are concerned that 'litigation could ... antagonize employers—who will have to be met again in future rounds of negotiations— and might furthermore be considered particularly odd in cases where a union challenges a collective agreement to which it is a party (a concern of Dutch trade unions)' (pp. 14, 18). This evidence is hardly conclusive, but it does suggest support for Hypothesis 4.

The ability to influence the policy-making process clearly is not the full story of why there is cross-national variation in the use of litigation strategies. Though not articulating this argument, Blom et al.'s (1995) observations about the use of litigation strategies imply a sort of Olsonian logic (M. Olson 1965).

Hypothesis 5: The more narrow the interest group's mandate and constituency, the more likely it will be to turn to a litigation strategy. The more broad and encompassing the interest group's mandate and constituency, the less likely it will be to turn to litigation strategy.

The reports provide significant evidence to support this argument. According to Blom et al. (1995), groups that were broader and more encompassing saw many disadvantages to litigation, and put other goals above ensuring equality. Blom et al. found that unions prioritize other objectives over equality, in part because they fear equal treatment objectives 'can only be achieved by the rest of the workforce forgoing a pay increase' (pp. 14–18). They also found that when the task of equality was assigned to offices that oversee all labor issues (thus broader labor offices), equality remained a low priority and litigation was seldom used (p. 15). And surprisingly, women's groups were not active in promoting gender equality. Blom et al. assert that women's groups assumed that unions handled women's workplace issues and chose to focus instead on issues affecting a broader base of women, such as family interests (pp. 17–18). Vogel-Polsky (1985) attributes the lack of women's group activism to the group's origins (the civil rights movements that led them to focus on the right to vote, civil rights, and the right to inheritance) and structure (their largely consultative status and their links to political parties) (pp. 195–7).

Litigation seemed to be most attractive to more narrowly focused groups. The EOC was a single-issue agency, focused exclusively on promoting gender equality in the workplace. And whereas unions have largely avoided litigation, the unions that embraced litigation to promote gender equality were those with narrow constituencies, such as the Danish clerical workers' union that has high female membership and the entirely female Danish Women's Workers Union (KAD) (Fitzpatrick et al. 1993: 89 –90). These examples support the hypotheses that the more narrowly focused the group, the more likely it is to adopt a litigation strategy. In addition, the recommendations put forth by Blom et al. (1995) for increasing the use of EC equality law reflect their implicit Olsonian understanding of the logic of collective action. Blom et al. suggest that the creation of more equality agencies would increase the likelihood that litigation strategies would be used.[29] They also look to women-dominated unions as the best hope for unions adopting gender equality as an objective and litigation as a strategy to achieve that objective. But they find hostility to this suggestion in many counties. The broader, more encompassing groups do not want to create rival groups, and do not want to give up their influence over equality issues even if they are not exercising all of their options to promote gender equality (Blom et al. 1995).

If it is true that narrowly focused groups with less access to policy-making are more likely to adopt litigation strategies, then cross-national variation in the use of litigation strategies could be explained by how interests are organized within European societies. Some countries have the type of narrowly focused interest groups that are likely to adopt litigation strategies, and other countries only have larger encompassing groups representing women and dealing with the issue of equity in the workplace. Increasingly, scholars are looking toward these types of factors to explain cross-national variation in the use of litigation strategies (Caporaso and Jupille 2001; Conant 2001).

---

[29] Blom et al. (1995) argued that 'where women-only trade unions have taken up sex equality issues, the results are frequently dramatic, providing a tantalizing glimpse of what could be achieved if there were to be a major policy shift within the trade union movement at both the national and local level' (p. 7).

STEP 3: When will national courts support litigants' efforts?

In theory, groups in all member states should have access to the EC legal system through national courts. But in practice, there is great variation in the willingness of national courts to rely on EC legal arguments or to make references to the ECJ. The cross-national studies did find 'a reluctance amongst the judiciary, and other adjudicators, to give effect to Community law principles' (Blom et al. 1995: 35), and saw this reluctance as influencing plaintiff calculations regarding whether to pursue litigation—especially where there was a significant risk for the litigant pursuing the case, as in discrimination cases. Indeed, in the British case there was evidence that negative EAT decisions had set in motion a vicious circle of equality cases where low rates of success discouraged would-be applicants from bringing cases, leading to a lack of expertise in the courts and more unfavorable judgments (Pannick 1985; Rubenstein 1991).[30]

Scholars have identified many factors influencing national judicial openness to EC law, including variations in how EU law affects the influence, independence, and autonomy of national courts vis-à-vis each other (influenced by the organization of the national judiciary); judicial identity and legal culture (which influence whether judges see themselves as authorized to make a referral to the ECJ); the appointment process (which determines the interests of judges); and rules of access to courts (which influence the types of cases heard). But it is hard to assess the link between these factors and cross-national variation willingness of national judges to embrace EC legal arguments or ECJ jurisprudence. Reference rates to the ECJ are not a good measure, because so many EC law cases are decided without a reference to the ECJ (and not always in accordance with ECJ jurisprudence), and many cases referred to the ECJ do not involve challenges to national policy.[31]

What is clear is that no national legal system, no judicial identity, no appointment criteria, and no legal culture is so monolithic or complete as to preclude the existence of sympathetic judges. All it takes is one judge located anywhere in the national legal system to create a favorable EC legal precedent and create pressure within the national system for doctrinal change. Indeed, the change in the United Kingdom came from a very small number of first-instance tribunals. The key is to find a sympathetic judge. Forum shopping can help, but groups may

---

[30] According to the Annual Report of the Equal Opportunities Commission in 1982, whereas in 1976 1,742 equal pay claims and 243 sex discrimination claims were brought, by 1982 that number had dropped to 39 equal pay claims and 150 sex discrimination claims. Success rates also declined from 1976 when 213 equal pay claims and 24 sex discrimination claims were upheld, to only two equal pay claims and 16 sex discrimination claims being upheld in 1982. In her study of the operation of the tribunal system in sex discrimination and equal pay cases, Leonard (1987) found that of the 6,090 claims brought during the first eight years of the legislation, most had been brought in the first two years, with a success rate of less than 11%.

[31] Clifford Carrubba and Lacey Murrah have undertaken the most thorough analysis of the factors shaping reference rates to the ECJ.

be better positioned than private litigants to practice forum shopping, because groups can seek out test cases that fall under the jurisdiction of more sympathetic judges. Private litigants may have far less options, and basically have to take who they get. From this observation, one could posit the following hypothesis:

Hypothesis 6: Groups are more likely than private litigants to find sympathetic judges because of their ability to forum shop. Where groups are actively and carefully pursuing litigation strategies, national judicial support is more likely to be found.

STEP 4: When will groups follow through and create political costs?

In the British case, groups triggered a political response by finding numerous similar cases that could be filed. We call this strategy 'follow-through', and argue that follow-through was key in showing the British government that non-action would create significant costs. There is evidence of similar strategies being used in other cases as well, though mostly in the United Kingdom.[32] When are we most likely to get follow-through?

Individuals are usually most concerned with the outcome of their particular case, and thus are less likely to follow through on legal victories. If an interest group goes to the trouble of putting together a test case strategy, it is likely that it will follow through and use the case in bargaining. Indeed, as S. M. Olson (1981) argued, groups usually employ litigation as part of a multi-pronged strategy.

Hypothesis 7: Individuals are less likely to follow through on legal victories, because a legal victory will likely be sufficient to achieve the individual's objective. Because groups are more likely to employ litigation strategies as part of a multipronged strategy, legal decisions in cases where a group is involved are more likely to generate follow-through.

Another possibility is that groups can pick up on a legal decision in a case raised by a private litigant, or by a group in another country. There is not enough evidence in the cross-national studies to evaluate this issue, but Conant's (1998) work suggests the following (Mancur) Olsonian hypothesis:

Hypothesis 8: Groups are more likely to mobilize around legal decisions where the benefits of policy change are narrowly focused and the costs of policy change widely distributed.

The main factor that keeps EC law from shifting the domestic balance of power more often is that groups tend not to mobilize around a litigation strategy. Thus,

---

[32] Environmental, trade, and consumer groups have disseminated forms that individuals can fill out as a first step in a legal case. Groups have published pamphlets advertising rights of citizens under EC law, including a pro forma complaint form; have created videos distributed to local environmental groups that explain how to use the EC legal process to enforce EC law; and have solicited complaints through mass mailings (the complaints are then simultaneously submitted to the government and the Commission with demands for legislative change) (Harlow and Rawlings 1992: 276). For more on the interaction between EU institutions and social groups see Cichowski (2007).

neither forum shopping nor follow-through occurs. Because there are relatively few examples of groups trying a litigation strategy, there is little empirical evidence to evaluate the factors shaping the last two steps of a successful litigation strategy. What we can say is that the problems of finding sympathetic judges and following through on cases would seem to be the most easily surmountable by interest groups committed to a litigation strategy.

III. Conclusion: EC Law as a Tool to Shift the Domestic Balance of Power

The EC legal system provides a tool that domestic actors can use to circumvent national policy barriers and to create new sources of leverage to influence national policy. Neo-functionalist theory has long argued that private interests pursuing their own agendas by turning to the EU realm contribute (perhaps unintentionally) to European integration (Burley and Mattli 1993; Mattli and Slaughter 1998; Stone Sweet and Brunell 1998). Our finding that the British case has been the exception in terms of group strategies to promote gender equality raises a question about the often implicit assumption in neo-functionalist analysis that where there is a potential benefit, it will be pursued. There are many factors, beyond cost and ideology, that lead groups not to use litigation, even when such a strategy might be beneficial. Though we could not definitively support or refute any of the hypotheses we proposed, there was suggestive evidence that would lead to a preliminary vetting of the different hypotheses.

There was little evidence to support Hypothesis 1 that the greater the protection of individual or group rights under national law, the less need there is to turn to EC law to promote litigant interests. And the procedural barriers identified in Hypothesis 3 seemed to be more of a problem for private litigants than for groups, and could not account for the lack of interest group mobilization. There was support for three other hypotheses we examined. Rules on *locus standi* (Hypothesis 2) did seem to hinder some group actors from pursuing litigation strategies, but it was possible that the lack of favorable *locus standi* rules was itself an artifact of low interest group mobilization around litigation strategies. The greater the political strength of a group, and the more access the group had to the policy-making process, the more reluctant the group seemed to mount a litigation campaign (Hypothesis 4). And the more narrow the interest group's mandate and constituency, the more likely it seemed to turn to a litigation strategy. However, the more broad and encompassing the interest group's mandate and constituency, the less likely it was to turn to litigation strategy (Hypothesis 5). We did not have enough evidence to investigate Hypotheses 6, 7, or 8 even in a preliminary way.

Our study also raises a question about the recent work by Stone and Brunell that shows a correlation between increased transnational activity and increased

Article 177 (now Article 234) references to the ECJ (Stone and Brunell 1998; Stone Sweet and Brunell 1998). To make an obvious point, the numerous cases involving equality policy have nothing to do with transnational activity. Equality policy might well be an exception to the rule, but Schepel (1998) also finds a number of famous EC law cases in which the objective of the plaintiff was to challenge national policy, and the link to transnational activity was tenuous at best. Indeed, it is not clear that even most of the cases referred by national courts to the ECJ involve transnational activity. Many are challenges to EC rules and questions about EC policies. And many are attempts to shift the domestic balance of power and achieve domestic objectives. Correlation does not prove causation. Even if litigants highlight a connection to transnational activities (to the four freedoms) to strengthen their legal case, this does not mean that transnational activity or a desire to capture the benefits of increased trade is the dominant factor mobilizing them to raise EC legal cases.[33]

Finally, most of the EC law literature talks about repeat players, putting individual, corporate, or group repeat players in the same category. Our study implies that one should not consider private litigant incentives in the same way as group litigant incentives. The calculation of groups to use litigation strategies differs from the calculations of individuals to use litigation strategies, and the ability of groups to use a litigation victory to change national policy also differs. One way to read our comparative analysis is that ironically, those actors who can most effectively use EC law litigation to promote national policy change (mainly groups) often have the least incentive to try an EC law litigation strategy. And those with the least incentive to follow through with their victories to effect policy change (private litigants) have the greatest incentive to adopt litigation strategies. This is not to say that litigation raised by private litigants is insignificant. If the private litigant is a wealthy or well-connected firm, or part of an industrial association that may join their cause, it may be possible for private litigants to use EC law to influence national policy. Well-targeted litigation might also lead to the elimination of a national law on the books. And private litigants may reveal to groups the potential of EC law, and create legal precedent that is later picked up by groups to promote changes in national policy. But the issue of follow-through is crucial if legal decisions are to lead to policy change, and one cannot assume that there will be follow-through on legal victories, especially for cases raised by individuals.

EC law litigation strategies are one way that European integration is changing domestic politics. But the argument we make—that domestic groups can pull in EC law in a strategy to shift the domestic balance of power—raises almost as many questions as it answers. It is time to move beyond vague statements that actors following their interests further integration. We need to develop understandings of how actors determine their interests to understand when actors will see an

---

[33] Stone Sweet nuanced his argument in his 2004 book. For a review of the empirical support of this claim see Conant (1998: 49–54).

interest in behaving in ways that intentionally or unintentionally promote integration. We also need to open up the possibility that actors following their interests might contribute to disintegration rather than integration (see Chapter 9). We have suggested a number of factors that may influence the decision-making process of national actors, almost all of which are domestic political factors. Our research shows that groups are often motivated by domestic political incentives more than they are by transnational incentives. The hypotheses we developed represent a first step. We leave it to later studies to investigate whether the factors we identify contribute to changes in interest group mobilization, in national policy, and in shifts in the domestic balance of power.

9

The European Union's Legal System and Domestic Policy: Spillover or Backlash? (2000)

The legal system of the European Union (EU) offers domestic actors a powerful tool to influence national policy. European law can be drawn on by private litigants in national courts to challenge national policies. These challenges can be sent by national judges to the European Court of Justice (ECJ), which instructs national courts to apply European law instead of national law, or to interpret national law in a way compatible with European law. Combining victories in front of the ECJ with political mobilization and pressure, litigants and groups have used the European legal system to force their governments to change national policies.

Using Europe's legal tool involves overcoming four successive thresholds: First, there must be a point of European law on which domestic actors can draw and favorable ECJ interpretations of this law. Second, litigants must embrace EU law to advance their policy objectives, using EU legal arguments in national court cases. Third, national courts must support the efforts of the litigants by referring cases to the ECJ and/or applying the ECJ's legal interpretations instead of conflicting national policy. Fourth, litigants must follow through on their legal victory, using it as part of a larger strategy to pressure the government to change public policy. A litigation strategy can fail at any of the four steps. When private litigants can surmount these four thresholds, the EU legal system can be a potent tool for forcing a change in national policy. Stated as such, these four steps may sound onerous. But litigants have used this tool successfully many times. In one of the most well-known examples, equal opportunity groups used the EU legal system to force a Conservative British government to make considerable reforms to British equality policy at the height of British antagonism toward the EU and EU social policy (See Chapter 8).[1]

Because the EU's legal tool can be so effective, some analysts have hypothesized that litigants will use EU litigation strategies whenever a potential benefit exists. Resurrecting Ernst Haas' neo-functionalist framework, Anne-Marie Burley and

---

[1] The reforms included extending work benefits to part-time workers, eliminating the cap on the size of discrimination awards, and stopping their policy of dismissing women from the military because of pregnancy.

Walter Mattli have asserted that the self-interests of private litigants, national judges, and the ECJ align such that the mutual pursuit of 'instrumental self-interest' leads to the expansion and penetration of European law into the domestic realm. They expected pursuit of self-interest to lead in a unidirectional way, toward ever further integration, positing that the ECJ was careful to create a system in which pursuing one's self-interest served as a 'one-way ratchet' advancing legal integration (Burley and Mattli 1993: 60). Alec Stone Sweet and Thomas Brunell adopt similar assumptions, with similar predictions. They posit that transnational trade, when combined with third-party dispute resolution, leads to the expansion of legal rules and the construction of supranational governance (Stone Sweet and Brunell 1998a: 64).

In this article I investigate the factors shaping each step of the litigation process. The analysis reveals many factors that keep private litigants and national courts from facilitating the expansion of European law. Furthermore, the pursuit of self-interest may also lead litigants and national courts to challenge advances in European integration. Indeed, there is much to suggest that the very factors that have led to the success of the EU legal process in expanding and penetrating the national order have provoked national courts and European governments to create limits on the legal process and to repatriate powers back to the national level. Thus the dynamic expansion created by the ECJ may well have provoked a backlash that contributed to disintegration.

I first explain how the ECJ has transformed the preliminary ruling mechanism, furthering the legalization of the EU and creating a means for private litigants to use the EU legal system to influence domestic policy. Second, I examine the different factors influencing each of the four steps, identifying sources of cross-issue and cross-national variation in the influence of EU law on national policy and summarizing a number of hypotheses about when we can expect private litigants and national judges to use the EU legal system to influence national policy. Third, I discuss the interactive effect of the four steps and suggest implications for neo-functionalist theory. Fourth, I show how the framework developed here may be generalizable outside of the EU. Many of the specifics discussed apply only to the European case, but the four-step framework and some of the factors influencing the steps are applicable in other domestic and international legal contexts.

I. Legalization in the EU and the Role of Private Litigants and National Courts

The EU is perhaps the most 'legalized' international institution in existence. It is at the far end of all three continuums for the dimensions of legalization defined in the special edition of *International Organization* in which this essay originally appeared:

Obligation: All member states are legally bound to uphold the *acquis communautaire,* the body of European law including treaties, secondary legislation, and the jurisprudence of the ECJ. A failure to fulfill a legal obligation can lead to an infringement suit in front of the ECJ, and as of 1993 the failure to obey an ECJ decision can lead to a fine.[2]

Precision: Many European rules are extremely specific, unambiguously defining how states must comply with their European obligations. When there is doubt, the ECJ is there to give a precise meaning to the rules.

Delegation: The ECJ is perhaps the most active and influential international legal body in existence, operating as a constitutional court of Europe.

The advanced level of legalization in Europe is in part a consequence of the institutional design of the EU. Member states set out to create a supranational political entity, giving the EU Council the power to pass legislation that is directly applicable in the national realm and creating a supranational Commission to oversee implementation of the EU Treaties, monitor compliance with EU law, and raise infringement suits against states. They also created the ECJ, authorizing it to hear disputes between states and the EU's governing institutions; to hear infringement suits against member states raised by the Commission; to review challenges to EU laws and Commission decisions; and to review and, if necessary, invalidate EU rules. States gave the ECJ these powers believing that the court would help them keep the other supranational bodies of the EU in check. They even created a preliminary ruling mechanism (Article 234 EEC) that allows private litigants and national courts to refer cases to the ECJ, so that they too could challenge the validity of EU law and thus hold EU legislative and executive bodies in check.[3]

Although member states created an unusual supranational court, the advanced state of legalization in Europe is in no small part a result of the court's own efforts. The ECJ was not designed as a tool for domestic actors to challenge national policies; these powers the ECJ created for itself, despite the intention of member states. In the 1963 *Van Gend en Loos* decision, the ECJ declared that European law can create direct effects in national law (individual rights that European citizens can draw upon in national courts).[4] Shortly thereafter in the *Costa v. Enel* decision, the ECJ declared that European law was supreme to national law and created an obligation for national courts to enforce EU law over conflicting national law.[5] Together these two doctrines turned the EU's preliminary ruling mechanism from a conduit for national court questions and challenges to *EU law*

----

[2] A system of sanctions was adopted as part of the Maastricht Treaty on a European Union. For a discussion of the origin and use of this sanction, see Tallberg (2003).

[3] The overall model of the ECJ was the French Conseil d'État, which holds the French government accountable to correctly implementing laws as passed by Parliament (Robertson 1966: 150). The preliminary ruling mechanism was an adaptation of a feature from the Italian and German legal systems adopted to facilitate national court reviews of EU decisions and laws (Pescatore 1981).

[4] Case 26/62, *Van Gend en Loos v. Nederlandse Administratie Belastingen* [1963] ECR 1, ECJ.

[5] Case 6/64, *Costa v. Ente Nazional L'Energia Elettrica (Enel)* [1964] ECR 583, ECJ.

into a mechanism that also allows individuals to invoke European law in national courts to challenge *national law* (for more see Chapter 5).

The transformation of the preliminary ruling system increased the extent of member state obligations under EU law, the precision of EU law, and the use of third parties to resolve disputes—significantly advancing legalization in Europe. As the following list shows, the ECJ has played a key role in increasing legalization in Europe.

Obligation: When the ECJ declared the supremacy of European law it turned national courts into enforcers of European law in the national sphere. National courts set aside conflicting national laws, award penalties for the non-implementation of EU directives, and assess fines for violations of European law, creating an incentive for firms and governments to change national policies that violate European law. In the words of Joseph Weiler, the transformation of the preliminary ruling system 'closed exit' from the EU legal system, ending the ability of states to avoid their legal obligations through non-compliance (Weiler 1991).[6]

Precision: The ECJ has used preliminary ruling cases to specify the meaning of EU legal texts. Furthermore, with individual litigants raising cases and national courts sending these cases to the ECJ, states are less able to exploit legal lacunae and interpret their way out of compliance with European law (see Chapter 6).

Delegation: By granting private litigants standing to invoke EU law to challenge national law, the ECJ increased the number of opportunities it has to rule on the compatibility of national policy with European law. Most of the court's case load, most of the challenges to national policies that reach the ECJ, and many if not most of the advances in European law have been the result of national courts referring preliminary rulings to the ECJ (Dehousse 1998: 51–2).[7]

Given the key role private litigants and national judges played in advancing legalization in Europe, Burley and Mattli's neo-functionalist explanation is quite compelling.

Although private litigants and national courts were key actors facilitating legalization of EU law in the past, they do not always play this role now. Scholars are in agreement that the transformation of the EU legal system has advanced legalization in Europe and made the EU legal system a potent tool for private

---

[6] In 1974 the ECJ extended member state obligations further by granting EU directives direct effect, making them more legally binding. In 1991 it created a financial penalty for states that failed to implement directives in a timely fashion. Case 41/74, *VanDuyn v. Home Office* [1974] ECR 1337. Cases C-6 and 9/90, *Francovich v. Italy* [1991] ECR 1991.

[7] Member states have raised only four infringement cases against each other. The Commission raised 1,045 infringement cases from 1960 through 1994, 88% of which were after 1981 and most of which involved non-implementation of EU directives in a timely fashion. National courts have referred 2,893 cases to the ECJ from 1960 to 1994, not all of which were challenges to national policy. (Data updated and published in Alter (2001: 15.)

litigants to influence national policy. There is also agreement that cases brought by private litigants continue to play a central role in the EU legal process. The question remains, however, whether the ECJ's success at transforming the system with the help of private litigant cases means that a never-ending process of legal expansion has been set in motion. When do private litigants and national court actions help to advance legal integration? To answer this question, we need to better understand the interests of the ECJ's key intermediaries (private litigants and national judges) and thus the factors shaping where, when, and why they use the EU legal system to promote their objectives.

II. How and When Do Private Litigants and National Courts Use the European Legal System to Influence National Policy?

By focusing on private litigants and national judges, I am not implying that private litigant cases are the only factor contributing to increased legalization in Europe or that EU law influences domestic policy only through private litigant suits. Member states advance legalization when they pass new legislation at the EU level and grant EU bodies new powers—of which they do plenty. According to a report by the French Conseil d'État, by 1992 European law included 22,445 EU regulations, 1,675 directives, 1,198 agreements and protocols, 185 recommendations of the Commission or the Council, 291 Council resolutions, and 678 communications. The Community had become the largest source of new law, with 54 per cent of all new French laws originating in Brussels.[8] Because national governments fear expansive interpretations of EU rules, and in order to bind each other more fully, they are also now more precise when they draft EU law. The Commission also has a key role in legalization. It offers interpretations of EU rules and raises infringement suits against member states. And even without a legal suit being raised, the EU legal system impacts national policy by creating anticipatory reactions within states. Most national governments automatically review the compatibility of prospective legislation with EU legal obligations.[9] They do this in a good faith effort to comply with EU law.[10]

But private litigant cases can in many instances be the only way to persuade a recalcitrant state to change its policies. Many cases that reach the ECJ through national courts arrive there because other avenues of influencing domestic policy failed. The litigant has tried to negotiate with the national administration about the policy. The litigant might also have worked with the Commission to address the violation, but either the Commission dropped or settled the case, or the ECJ's

---

[8] Conseil d' État 1992, Rapport Public, 16–17.

[9] For example, in Germany proposed legislation is reviewed by the Justice Ministry to ensure its compatibility with EU law. In France, the Conseil d'État conducts a similar review.

[10] Usually all that is needed is a change in language to avoid a conflict with EU law, with the overall substance and objective of the policy remaining intact.

infringement decision failed to create a change in national policy. If there were no EU legal tool for private litigants, the case would end in non-compliance. But private litigants can use the EU legal system to pressure a government to comply with EU law. Knowing that private litigants will challenge questionable national policies, member states are more likely to avoid violations of EU law in the first place. Thus the existence of the EU's legal tool is crucial to increasing state compliance, even when the tool itself is not invoked. The key is that it must be available for use.

Using the EU legal tool to influence national policy involves overcoming four successive thresholds. First, there must be a point of European law on which domestic actors can draw and favorable ECJ interpretations of this law. Second, litigants must embrace EU law to advance their policy objectives, using EU legal arguments in national court cases. Third, national courts must support the efforts of the litigants by referring cases to the ECJ and/or applying ECJ jurisprudence instead of conflicting national policy. Fourth, the litigants must follow up their legal victory to pressure the government to change public policy.

Because EU law influences domestic policy in other ways—by being directly applicable in the national realm, by being incorporated into national law by national governments, by creating anticipatory effects in the national government, or by the Commission raising an infringement suit—one cannot say that these four thresholds represent necessary conditions for EU law to influence domestic policy. But at least the first three are necessary if private litigants are to effectively use the EU legal system to influence national policy, with the caveat that if it is clear that these four thresholds are likely surmountable, then a group might be able to get its way simply by threatening to mount a litigation campaign.

In this section, building on the case-specific analysis of Chapter 8, I pull together the state of our knowledge about the factors influencing each step of the EU legal process. Lisa Conant has a literature review that overviews the literature through 2007. The claims made in this section are based on data that covers the period up until 1995, and thus the discussion does not capture changes brought by the enlargement of Europe. Still, the factors mentioned here remain relevant both for the historical record and for today. These factors can potentially help to explain cross-national and cross-issue variation in the impact of EU law on domestic policy.

STEP 1: EU law and domestic policy

The first step of the EU litigation process involves identifying a point of EU law on which domestic actors can draw. Not all national policies are affected by European law, and not all aspects of European law can be invoked before national courts.

EU law reaches quite widely. In addition, if a national policy indirectly affects the free movement of goods, people, capital, or services (the four freedoms) there might be an EU legal angle of attack. But EU law contains biases that make it more useful for some issues than for others. EU law creates significant legal rights for its citizens, but these rights are primarily economic citizenship rights directed at obtaining the four freedoms. The EU has created far fewer social rights and civil rights for its citizens (Ball 1996; Shaw 1998).[11] Indeed, women might find EU law helpful in promoting equality in the workplace but not in addressing larger issues of gender discrimination that do not affect their participation in the workplace. Furthermore, the economic rights of EU law are focused on workers and firms engaged in transnational activity. The British worker who stays at home might find EU law far less helpful in challenging national rules than the French worker who moved to the United Kingdom. There are also policy areas that fall under the EU's jurisdiction and tend to be covered by EU law, including customs law, agricultural policy, transport policy, certain taxation issues, and policy areas that have been harmonized. Farmers and shopkeepers might thus find themselves affected by EU law even though they sell all their goods on the domestic market.

In most cases EU law must create direct effects before it can be invoked in national courts to challenge national policy, meaning that the ECJ must determine if the law in question confers legal standing for individuals in national courts.[12] The ECJ decides on a statute-by-statute basis if EU law creates direct effects, taking into account the specificity of the law, whether the statute is clear and unconditional, and whether the statute leaves states significant discretion (Chalmers 1997; Folsom 1995: 86–9). Regulations are directly applicable in the national realm, allowing litigants to invoke them directly to challenge national policy. Directives only sometimes create direct effects, mainly when the obligation they impose is very specific and the time period for adoption has expired.

A separate issue is whether the ECJ would be willing to interpret EU law in the litigant's favor once a case is raised. There is relatively little research on the factors shaping ECJ decision-making, but it is clear that the ECJ makes strategic calculations in its decision-making, avoiding decisions that could create a political backlash. Geoffrey Garrett, Daniel Kelemen, and Heiner Schulz argue that the greater the clarity of EU legal texts, case precedents, and legal norms in support of a judgment, the less likely the ECJ is to bend to political pressure (Garrett, Kelemen, and Schulz 1998). In addition, the smaller the costs a

---

[11] EU law does create some citizen rights regarding consumer protection, environmental protection, and workplace safeguards. Although these rights exist, they are limited. The vast majority of the private litigant cases before the ECJ either directly concern the economic rights created by EU law or are couched in terms of economic rights created under EU law.

[12] The ECJ's *Francovich* doctrine implies that plaintiffs can challenge a state's non-implementation of a directive regardless of whether the directive itself creates direct effects. This is a small exception to the general rule that EU law must create direct effects to be invoked before national courts. I am indebted to Steve Weatherhill for pointing this out.

legal decision creates for a state, the more likely the ECJ is to apply the law even if it means deciding against a powerful member state (Garrett, Kelemen, and Schulz 1998). But as I argue in Chapter 6, even when the costs of ECJ decisions are significant, and the decisions are controversial, states usually lack a credible threat to cow the ECJ into quiescence. When a significant consensus exists among key member states against a decision, political threats can become credible and the ECJ is more likely to be influenced. George Tsebelis and Geoffrey Garrett further hypothesize that when the voting rule to overturn an ECJ decision requires a qualified majority, the ECJ will have less leeway to stray from the wishes of member states (Tsebelis and Garrett 2001). Their argument remains rather vague and they do not provide evidence to support their claim—indeed it is far from clear that the ECJ is less bold in cases involving regulations and directives that only require qualified majority votes (Cichowski 2007: 246). Nonetheless, most analysts agree that mobilizing a credible threat will be less difficult, though still difficult, when states only need a qualified majority vote to overturn the ECJ than when unanimity is required (such as when the decision is based on the Treaty itself).

Lisa Conant reviews the more recent literature on the factors shaping ECJ decision-making. There is no empirical support for the argument that the ECJ responds to the political preferences of national governments. There is, however, some support for the claim that the ECJ considers the likelihood of state compliance when it rules, although studies that do exist tend to create divergent findings (Conant 2007: 52–4).

These findings offer helpful starts, but they do not lead to many concrete hypotheses of how extralegal factors shape ECJ decision-making. What we can say for now is that systematic biases in EU law shape which national policies can be influenced by the EU legal process and which actors will find EU law most helpful to promote their objectives. EU law is mostly concerned with economic issues with a transnational dimension, and thus economic issues involving transnational elements are more likely to be affected by EU litigation. Laws that are more specific are more likely to create direct effects; and when the ECJ's doctrine is more developed, the ECJ is more likely to rule against a national policy.[13] The ECJ can be influenced by national governments to decide in favor of existent national policy, but in most situations member states lack a credible threat to cow the ECJ into quiescence. Furthermore, even when member states can muster a credible threat, the ECJ may prefer to stick to the letter of the law to maintain support by the legal community (Mattli and Slaughter 1995) or to make a ruling that encourages the Council to enact new legislation or change its legislation at the EU level.

---

[13] But when it is clear from the ECJ's doctrine how it will decide, states are also more likely to settle out of court in the shadow of the law, and thus the case may never go to court: Alter (forthcoming); Tallberg and Jönsson (1998).

STEP 2: Mobilizing litigants to use EU law
to promote their policy objectives

The Commission can raise cases against member states, but for a variety of reasons it may choose not to.[14] From 1982 to 1995, the number of complaints received by the Commission was more than three times greater than the number of official inquiries undertaken by the Commission and was 14 times greater than the number of Article 226 cases raised by the Commission (Conant 2001: Figure 1).[15] If the Commission will not raise a case, private litigants must pursue the issue on their own. This seems to be the norm; indeed, starting in the 1970s, private litigant cases overtook the Commission in the supply of cases involving conflicts between national law and EU law by a very significant margin (Dehousse 1998: 52).

There are many European legal texts and favorable EU legal precedents that remain unexploited even though they could help litigants promote their objectives and create significant financial gain. When are domestic actors most likely to turn to EU litigation to promote their objectives? Which domestic actors are most likely to find litigation an attractive strategy to influence national policy? Rachel Cichowski found that for environmental cases, litigants tended to mobilize against states that had opposed the EU environmental cooperation or were lax when it came to implementation of environmental policies (see discussion in Conant (2007: 50)).

A number of factors specific to national legal systems affect litigants' willingness to use EU law to challenge national policy. Restrictions in legal standing may make litigation harder to pursue in certain countries and certain issue areas. Other factors include procedural rules on how complaints are filed and investigated, variations in the existence of legal aid, requirements that losers in cases compensate winners, time limits for raising cases, rules limiting the size of awards, and rules regarding the burden of proof. In the United Kingdom, for example, a cap on discrimination awards limited the number of claimants willing to raise discrimination suits, but the Equal Opportunities Commission's (EOC) activism led to a number of British cases challenging UK equality policy (see Chapter 8 and Barnard 1995). Groups would be unable to follow the EOC's strategy in France, Belgium, and Luxembourg, where they are excluded from participating in equality cases (Blom et al. 1995; Fitzpatrick, Gregory, and Szyszczak 1993: 19–20 discussed in Chapter 8). In Denmark only union officials can pursue equality issues, since gender equality clauses are part of collective bargaining agreements. If the union refuses to pick up the issue, the individual facing discrimination may be out of luck. This type of variation can lead to cross-national and cross-issue variation in the impact of EU law on domestic policy.

[14] On the difficulty of mobilizing the Commission to pursue infringements, see Weatherhill (1997).
[15] For a study on the use of the infringement procedure by the Commission, see Tallberg (2003).

The litigiousness of a society also influences whether litigants use the EU legal process. Importers and exporters in Germany regularly challenge decisions of tax authorities in the tax courts, leading to many EU legal cases. Making a veiled reference to numerous German cases involving customs classifications, Adolphe Touffait, a former Procureur Général at the French Cour de Cassation, argued that French enterprises would never become preoccupied with the distinction between types of flours, especially given the reluctance of commercial groups to legally challenge acts of tax or customs administrators (Touffait 1975). Touffait's argument is supported by statistics on domestic litigation rates. As Table 9.1 shows, German citizens raise far more legal cases than do British or French citizens. Indeed, most commercial disputes in France continue to be resolved by arbitration rather than through the legal system.

A clever lawyer, however, can often find ways to surmount national legal and procedural barriers, if they or their clients are highly motivated. Which litigants are more likely to be motivated and more likely to raise EU law cases? Drawing on US public law scholarship, Lisa Conant argues that law is at the service of the privileged; litigants with financial resources at their disposal and significant legal know-how are more likely and able to use litigation to promote policy objectives. With respect to EU law, Christopher Harding and Conant find that interest groups, large firms, and lawyers who can provide their own services are the privileged actors most able and likely to pursue an EU legal claim (Conant 1998; and Harding 1992). Of the privileged actors, firms and private lawyers are more likely to use litigation than organized interests, although organized interests are often more able to use a test-case strategy, picking cases with favorable fact situations and shopping for a supportive legal forum.

Which firms and groups are most likely to use litigation, and when are they likely to use litigation? Conant argues that when the potential benefits are significant for an individual or group, litigants are more likely to mobilize to use

Table 9.1. Comparison of domestic civil litigation rates (per 100,000 inhabitants)

	Civil procedures	Cases heard in first instance legal bodies	Cases heard on appeal
West Germany (1989)	9,400	4,911	251
England/Wales (1982)	5,300	1,200	16
France (1982)	3,640	1,950	250

Source: Blankenburg 1996: 295.

Note: In Germany the total volume of litigation initiated by private actors (civil litigation) is unusually high. If the procedures raised in administrative and labor courts were added to the figures for Germany, the rate of civil procedures would increase by another 1,350 per 100,000, and the appeal rate would rise accordingly.

litigation. The more concentrated the benefits, the greater the likelihood of strategic, coordinated litigation campaigns (Conant 1998: ch. 3). The analysis in Chapter 8 suggests that independent of the size or concentration of benefits, how interest groups are organized at the national level influences whether or not specific groups employ litigation. We found the more narrow the interest group's mandate and constituency, the more likely it was to turn to a litigation strategy; and the more broad and encompassing the interest group's mandate and constituency, the less likely it was to turn to a litigation strategy to promote gender equality. This is because broad-based groups often have competing objectives. Thus it was unions composed predominately of women and single-issue agencies like the British Equal Opportunities Commission that used litigation to promote gender equality, whereas broad-based unions and women's groups avoided gender equality litigation and focused instead on broader employment and family issues.

Another important factor was whether an interest group enjoyed influence in and access to policy-making. In political negotiation, groups can usually strike a deal that will leave them at least better off than before. With legal decisions, groups could well end up with a policy that is more objectionable and harder to reverse than the previous policy. For this reason, and because of the risk and relative crudeness of litigation as a means of influencing policy, organized interests generally prefer to work through political channels (see Chapter 8). The greater the political strength of a group, and the more access the group has to the policy-making process, the less likely a group is to mount a litigation campaign. In Belgium, for example, neither unions nor women's groups use litigation to pursue equality issues, preferring instead to use their access to the policy-making process to influence Belgian policy (Fitzpatrick et al. 1993: 89).

Litigation is more likely in countries where actors commonly use litigation to challenge policy and where the rules on legal standing and procedures make EU law litigation feasible and profitable. One can expect litigation from wealthier individuals and firms or from lawyers who can provide their own legal council, especially when these actors face potential benefits of significant magnitude. Ironically, although interest groups can perhaps most effectively use test-case litigation strategies, they are the least likely actors to adopt such a strategy. But if political channels are closed, groups might find litigation their best option for influencing public policy. Narrowly focused groups and groups that do not enjoy significant influence over policy-making are most likely to find litigation enticing. These findings have been confirmed more recently by Cichowski (2007: 245–6) and Conant (2007: 58–9).

STEP 3: Eliciting national judicial support

When there is a point of EU law that creates direct effects, private litigants can draw upon this law in national courts to challenge national policy. Not all potential beneficiaries of EU rules will mobilize to challenge national policy through

Table 9.2. Reference patterns in EU member states (1961–97)

Country	1961–69	1970–79	1980–89	1990–98	Total
Germany	30 (40%)	284 (42%)	346 (28%)	463 (26%)	1,123 (30%)
France	7 (9%)	85 (13%)	285 (23%)	216 (12%)	593 (16%)
Netherlands	22 (29%)	108 (16%)	189 (15%)	174 (10%)	493 (13%)
Italy	3 (4%)	84 (12%)	125 (10%)	370 (21%)	582 (15%)
Belgium	10 (13%)	77 (11%)	142 (11%)	124 (7%)	353 (9%)
Luxembourg	3 (4%)	4 (1%)	17 (1%)	18 (1%)	42 (1%)
United Kingdom	—	20 (3%)	85 (7%)	163 (9%)	268 (7%)
Ireland	—	6 (1%)	15 (1%)	16 (1%)	37 (1%)
Denmark	—	6 (1%)	25 (2%)	47 (3%)	78 (2%)
Greece	—	—	21 (2%)	32 (2%)	53 (1%)
Spain	—	—	5 (—)	116 (7%)	121 (3%)
Portugal	—	—	1 (—)	30 (2%)	31 (1%)
Total	75 (100%)	674 (100%)	1,256 (100%)	1,769 (101%)	3,774 (99%)

Source: Based on the statistics in the 1997 annual report of the ECJ.

litigation, and even when they do, formidable barriers to changing national policy lay ahead. One challenge will be to persuade a national court to either refer the case to the ECJ or to interpret EU rules itself and set aside national law.

One can presume that national courts will be more likely to refer a case to the ECJ when asked to do so by one of the parties to the case. But even then, national courts may avoid referring a case for many reasons. Although national courts are supposed to make references to the ECJ any time a question of EU law arises and if they are a court of last instance,[16] in practice national courts cannot be compelled to refer a case.[17] A lower court's refusal can be appealed to a higher court in hopes of a reference or a more friendly interpretation, but often the most reticent courts are the highest courts. If the highest court refuses to refer the case, the litigant is simply out of luck. The varying willingness of national judges to make references and enforce EU law is reflected in part in variation in the total number of references to the ECJ by courts of different countries (see Table 9.2), a variation that cannot be explained by population size alone (see Figure 9.1).

Early studies explained the relative reluctance of some national judiciaries to refer cases by whether a national legal system was monist or dualist (Bebr 1981), whether a tradition of judicial review existed in the country (Vedel 1987), and whether the national legal system had a constitutional court (Cappelletti and

[16] Case 283/81, *SRL CILFIT v. Ministry of Health (I)* [1982] ECR 1119.
[17] In Germany it is a constitutional violation for national courts to deny the plaintiff their legal judge by refusing a reference to the ECJ. But appeals of a decision not to refer a case tend to languish on the docket of the German Constitutional Court, and in no other system is there a way to force a judge to make a reference or to apply EU law correctly.

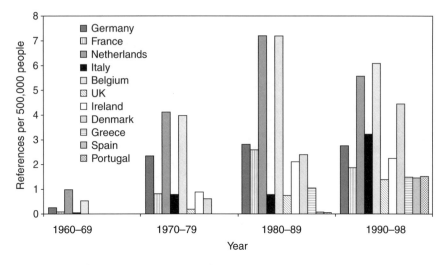

Figure 9.1. Reference per 500,000 population by country
Note: Figure excludes Luxembourg.

Golay 1986). But none of these explanations holds across countries, nor can they account for significant variation in reference rates within countries.

Clifford Carrubba and Lacey Murrah conduct the most extensive quantitative assessment of the factors contributing to cross-national variation in national court references to the ECJ. They find support for most of the explanations offered in the existing literature. In specific, they find that levels of national trade, whether or not the legal system is monist or dualist, public awareness about European integration, public support for European integration, and whether or not the legal system has a tradition of judicial review all correlate with the propensity of national courts to refer cases to the ECJ (2005). Their large N study is not, however, able to capture more subtle sub-state variation in national reference patterns. Also, as Lisa Conant points out, their data does not eliminate cases that are unrelated to trade, replicating a problem with Stone Sweet and Thomas Brunell's study of national reference patterns (Conant 2007: 49) The rest of this section considers the factors that generate variation in the willingness of specific national courts to refer cases to the ECJ.[18]

---

[18] It is hard to know how national judges deal with cases that are not referred. Damian Chalmers has made a heroic effort to find British cases involving EU law. He found 1,088 cases where British judges addressed questions of EU law. This number is nearly five times the number of British references to the ECJ (269). And Chalmers' data include only 'reported cases' that were passed on to the Registry of the ECJ or published in one of 27 publications. Lower court cases involving EU law are significantly under-represented. Chalmers analyzes these cases for the most comprehensive study to date on how national courts are applying EU law (Chalmers 2000).

As lawyers will attest, certain courts are more receptive than others to EU legal arguments. National court support cannot be captured by the number of references. Some courts accept ECJ jurisprudence without making a reference, whereas other courts reject key tenets of EU legal doctrine and thus do not make a reference. Some courts refer far-reaching questions of law to the ECJ, whereas other courts only refer narrow technical questions about EU legal texts, resolving the more significant issues about the impact of EU law in the national legal system on their own and only sometimes in accordance with ECJ jurisprudence.[19]

Case studies risk being impressionist. But given the highly aggregated nature of the ECJ's reference data, and the current impossibility of determining the number and content of national court cases that are not referred to the ECJ, it may be the only way to capture the many factors shaping judicial behavior. The following observations come in large part from my own detailed research on the French and German judiciaries. I used variation in reference rates within each judiciary to garner an overall impression of which courts were referring cases to the ECJ; and I interviewed over a hundred judges, lawyers, and government officials to gain insight into the sources of variation in judicial behavior. Research has revealed five factors that contribute to variation in the behavior of national courts vis-à-vis EU law: (1) the substance of EU law and jurisdictional boundaries; (2) rules of access to national courts; (3) the identity of a court; (4) how EU law affects the influence, independence, and autonomy of the national court vis-à-vis other courts; and (5) the policy implication of ECJ jurisprudence. The first four factors create cross-court and cross-branch variation and can cumulatively lead to cross-national variation. The last factor contributes to both cross-court and cross-national variation. I will briefly address each factor.

The influence of variations in the substance and in jurisdictional boundaries on judicial behavior. Variation in reference rates is caused in part by variation in legal substance and in the jurisdictional divisions of courts. The more harmonized EU legislation is, the more courts having to deal with this legislation will consult with the ECJ. In Germany, for example, because customs regulations of the EU were the first to be harmonized (in the 1960s) and because tax law is one of the most harmonized areas of EU law, tax courts have been more involved in legal integration from an early period than penal courts, which deal almost exclusively with national law.[20] Because the Federal Office of Nutrition and Forestry and

---

[19] For example, between 1960 and 1995 the German Federal Tax Court has sent over 140 references to the ECJ, probably more references than any other national court in the EU. But the tax court was well known for referring picky technical questions about the meaning of EU laws, wanting to know, for example, how to classify turkey tails and jeans with button flaps (Zuleeg 1993). The tax court was also well known for openly flouting the ECJ's doctrine on the direct effect of directives, reversing a lower court reference to the ECJ, and deciding important questions of legal principle on its own, without reference to the ECJ (Bebr 1983).

[20] Indeed, German tax courts, the smallest branch of the judiciary, with less than 3% of all judges, account for 49% of German references through 1994 (Alter 2001: 68).

the Federal Office for the Regulation of the Agricultural Market are located in Frankfurt, the Frankfurt administrative court hears nearly all challenges to the validity of EU agricultural policies. This helps to explain why the administrative court in Frankfurt accounted for nine per cent of all German references from 1960 to 1994 (Seidel 1987).

The influence of access rules on judicial behavior. We have seen that access rules shape litigant incentives and their ability to pursue an EU law litigation strategy. They also influence judicial behavior vis-à-vis EU law because they affect the ability of national courts to influence the development of European and national law and the incentives of judges to refer cases to the ECJ. France provides a good example of how access rules shape judicial behavior vis-à-vis EU law.

Compared with the active role played by the German and Italian Constitutional Courts in EU legal issues, the French Conseil Constitutionnel's position is bizarre: in all but a few narrow issues the Conseil Constitutionnel refuses to be involved in controlling the compatibility of French law with international law (Luchaire 1991). Access rules explain this position. Laws only make it to the Conseil Constitutionnel for review before they have actually been promulgated and only if political disagreement exists within the government or between the government and the legislature. Many laws of questionable constitutionality are never referred to the Conseil Constitutionnel, and when laws are referred, the Conseil Constitutionnel has only two months to make a decision. According to Bruno Genevois, the then Secretary General of the Conseil Constitutionnel, the Conseil Constitutionnel was concerned that a national law it found to be compatible with EU law could be implemented in a way that violates EU law or could be found to be incompatible with EU law by the ECJ or—even more embarrassing for a court charged with upholding the rights of its citizens—by the European Court of Human Rights (ECHR). Because of its inability to systematically ensure that national law complies with international law, and because of the embarrassing possibility that it could later be contradicted by the ECJ or the ECHR, the Conseil Constitutionnel prefers not to be involved in enforcing the supremacy of international law (Genevois 1989: 827).

Access rules also make it hard for French litigants to seek out the most friendly national courts for EU legal challenges. The 'ordinary courts' are clearly the most willing to make references to the ECJ (indeed they accounted for nearly 90 per cent of all French references through 1994 to the ECJ).[21] But constructing a case to challenge EU law is difficult for these courts.[22] The administrative court system deals with direct challenges to administrative acts and national law and, for most of these cases, the Conseil d'État is the court of first and last instance. For reasons that will be discussed, the Conseil d'État is not receptive to EU legal

---

[21] 'Ordinary courts' is a category in France and in other countries. Ordinary courts in France are contrasted to administrative courts and the Constitutional Council.

[22] Ordinary courts hear mainly civil and penal law cases. For a civil law case, either the case has to emerge from a dispute between private parties or from a government action against a private actor.

challenges, and in most cases it cannot be circumvented or pressured from courts beneath it.[23] The lack of judicial support from the court best placed to entertain challenges to national policy is a big reason why there are fewer litigant challenges to national policy in France and relatively few significant developments in European law based on references from French courts. For more see Cichowski (2006); Conant (2007: 58–9).

The influence of judicial identity on judicial behavior. As many scholars have argued, the identity of judges shapes their behavior vis-à-vis EU law (Chalmers 1997; Conant 2001; Mattli and Slaughter 1998: 200–1). Judicial identity is shaped by the training of judges, the selection process for judges, and the role the court plays in the legal and political process—all factors that can vary by country, by judicial branch, and by court.

Judicial training varies across countries, and even within countries there can be significant variation in how EU legal issues are taught. In most European countries, ordinary court judges participate in specialized training for judges that imparts to them a specific understanding of their role in the political system and how they are to deal with EU legal issues (this education has changed with time, creating generational differences within national judiciaries). Outside ordinary courts are a series of first instance legal bodies (some called courts, others tribunals, and others by other names) which have a different mode of appointment that does not necessarily involve training in judge schools. High court appointees may come from academia or political office, bringing a variety of training experiences and backgrounds. These different life experiences lead judges to act differently when confronted with EU legal issues.

The fairly antagonistic position the French Conseil d'État has taken vis-à-vis EU law, for example, is often explained by the identity of Conseil d'État judges, an identity imparted to them in their training at the elite Ecole Nationale d'Administration (Plotner 1998: 55–6), which teaches French high administrators to have a strong identification with the French state (Bodiguel 1981; Kessler 1986). Equally important is that members of the Conseil d'État float freely in and out of the government and private sector and the Conseil d'État. As Weil has argued:

the Conseil d'État is too close, by virtue of its recruitment, its composition, and the climate in which it is enmeshed, to the centers of political decision-making to not function on the same wavelength as [the government], to not feel vis-a-vis the authority which it is called upon to control a sympathy in the strongest sense of the word, which explains the self-censorship [the Conseil d'État] imposes on itself and the selectivity in the control it exercises. (Weil 1972, ix)

---

[23] In the 1990s the Conseil d'État was more receptive to EU legal arguments, following its change in position on EU law in the *Nicolo* case. Plotner claims that litigants have been more successful in front of the Conseil d'État since then, but it is only a matter of degree (Plotner 1998). Few would say that the Conseil d'État welcomes EU legal arguments, and reference rates from the administrative branch to the ECJ remain low.

The background of a Conseiller d'État affects its jurisprudence on a number of issues, including EU law (Loschak 1972). A similar argument was made for the German Federal Tax Court by Gert Meier, who claimed that having themselves served many years in the administration before becoming judges, Federal Tax Court judges tended to give the benefit of the doubt to the tax administration (Meier 1994).

Variation in how judges understand their legal and political mandates creates cross-national and cross-issue variation in how courts deal with EU legal issues. A number of first instance legal bodies, for example, do not consider themselves to be 'courts' and for this reason do not see themselves as qualified under Article 234 EEC to make a reference to the ECJ. In the United Kingdom, for example, first instance industrial tribunals will make references to the ECJ, whereas in the Netherlands and Ireland the legal bodies that deal with equality cases in the first instance do not see themselves as authorized to refer cases to the ECJ (Fitzpatrick et al. 1993). Some countries have legal bodies staffed by lay judges or a mix of lay and professional judges that attempt to be less formal than courts and function more like arbitrating bodies. For example, most commercial disputes in France begin and end in arbitration and thus are not referred to the ECJ (Touffait 1975). Some countries have mid-level appellate courts that, in essence, are staffed by a few law professors who review the legal basis of lower court decisions and who tend not to make references to the ECJ.

Variations in how EU law affects the influence, independence, and autonomy of national courts in relation to each other

A significant amount of evidence indicates that the more EU law and the ECJ are seen as undermining the influence, independence, and autonomy of a national court, the more reluctant the national court will be to refer far-reaching and legally innovative cases to the ECJ. As I have argued elsewhere, lower courts are often more willing to make references because a reference bolsters their authority in the national legal system and allows the court a way to escape national legal hierarchies and challenge higher court jurisprudence (Chapter 5). Lawyers attest to the greater openness of lower courts when it comes to making a reference to the ECJ, and statistics support this claim, showing that even though lower courts are not legally obliged to make a reference to the ECJ, lower and mid-level courts refer the vast majority of all references to the ECJ. Judges and scholars have also argued that lower courts have in many instances been the driving force in expanding ECJ doctrine and in promoting change in national doctrine (see Chapter 8 and Mancini and Keeling 1992; Burley and Mattli 1993; Weiler 1991).

Last instance courts are often more reluctant to make a referral to the ECJ, especially when they are threatened by the existence of the ECJ as the highest court on questions of European law or are upset at how EU law undermines their own influence and the smooth operation of the national legal process.

Indeed, courts with constitutional powers have made virtually no references to the ECJ, and doctrinal analyses reveal clear efforts by national high courts to position themselves vis-à-vis the ECJ to protect their independence, authority, and influence.[24]

Variation in the impact of EU law on national law

Judges do take into account the political implications of their decisions. Some ECJ decisions have created a divergence in the levels of legal protection and in legal remedies available under national law and under EU law, advantaging citizens who can draw on EU law over those who must rely on national law alone. ECJ jurisprudence has also resulted in great complexities for national legal systems and problematic outcomes. The seeming perversities created by the ECJ and EU law, as well as interpretations with which national courts simply disagree, can sap the willingness of national judiciaries to support the ECJ.

Many scholars (including early neo-functionalist theorists) believed that the largest barrier to national judicial support was ignorance about the EU legal system. With knowledge, they assumed, should come support. Although hearing more cases does seem to lead to more references to the ECJ, it does not necessarily lead to greater acceptance of ECJ jurisprudence. As Renaud Dehousse explains:

From the standpoint of a national lawyer, European law is often a source of disruption. It injects into the national legal system rules which are alien to its traditions and which may affect its deeper structure, thereby threatening its coherence. It may also be a source of arbitrary distinctions between similar situations... What appears as integration at the European level is often perceived as disintegration from the perspective of national legal systems... Moreover, preliminary references are one of the central elements in the inter-face between Community law and national law. The ECJ is therefore perceived as the central agent in a process of perforation of national sovereignty. (Dehousse 1998: 173)

Controversial ECJ decisions have led to rebukes by judges as well as attempts to avoid references to the ECJ and the application of EU law. For example, the ECJ's jurisprudence regarding labor law and especially its decision that employers must accept medical certificates from other member states, even when an Italian family of four working in Germany had for four years in a row all 'fallen ill' during their vacations in Italy, have led the German Federal Labor Court to openly criticize the ECJ and assert that EU law creates a danger for the consistency of codified law in Germany (Kokott 1998: 124). According to Jonathan Golub, because British judges believe that the ECJ will interpret environmental directives more broadly than necessary, British judges have withheld references to the court in environmental issues (Golub 1996). Chalmers finds a greater resistance to EU law when national judges perceive EU law to undermine the capacity of British institutions

---

[24] My study of national court acceptance of EU law supremacy shows how the highest national courts are demarcating the borders of the national constitutional order so as to limit future encroachments of European law and ECJ authority into the national domain (Alter 2001).

to promote social conformity (Chalmers 2000b). And Carol Harlow predicted a national judicial backlash against ECJ jurisprudence on state liability, possibly expanding to a larger political backlash (Harlow 1996: 31).

There is no way to ensure that a national court will refer a case to the ECJ or apply EU law as it should. If the litigant indicates a preference for a reference, presumably the likelihood of a reference will increase. If the ECJ's jurisdictional authority in the area is undisputed, and if the ECJ's jurisprudence is uncontroversial within the national legal community, it is also more likely that national courts will either make a reference or apply the ECJ's case law themselves. Lower courts appear relatively more willing than higher courts to make a reference. Courts where appointees have fewer connections to the government seem more likely to act more favorably to challenges to national policy. Lawyers have a sense of which judges are more 'friendly' to EU law arguments. Litigants who can shop for legal venues in which judges are thought to be receptive to EU legal arguments are most likely to succeed in getting their cases referred to the ECJ. Interest groups may be able to select among a variety of potential cases, and firms with numerous offices across regions and countries might have the opportunity to raise a case where judges tend to be more open to EU law arguments. The litigant should look for a court that accepts for itself a role filling in lacunae in legal texts, making references to the ECJ when necessary, and setting aside contradictory national laws. The judges must also be willing to challenge both national legal precedent and political bodies—something required when litigants use the EU legal system to influence national policy.

STEP 4: Following through on decisions: creating political and financial costs

Just because the ECJ decides in favor of the plaintiff challenging national policy, one should not assume that the government will change its policy. The government may simply compensate the litigant while leaving the legislation in effect and administrative policy unchanged. Or it can change the language of a national law to technically comply with the decision, without significantly changing domestic policy. Or it can simply ignore an adverse ECJ ruling, knowing that the plaintiff likely will not endeavor to have the decision enforced and that the government will not lose an election because it failed to respond to the ECJ's legal decision.

An ECJ decision is likely to lead directly to a change in national policy in certain cases. Anne-Marie Slaughter has claimed that the more a national political ethos supports the rule of law, the more likely groups are to castigate government actions that violate the rule of law and the more likely a government is to change its policy in light of a legal decision (Slaughter 1995).[25] Also, if a legal decision is

---

[25] Technically, all EU member states are rule-of-law liberal democracies, thus there should be little variation in compliance across them. Yet it is clear that certain EU countries have worse

made in an area of high political salience, where the government can anticipate copycat cases or political pressure, legislators are more likely to respond to the decision automatically. An ECJ decision is also more likely to influence the policy in the country that referred the case, because at least there the national court will be likely to enforce the decision.[26]

In many cases, however, translating a legal victory into a policy victory will take follow-through—a second strategy to show a government that there will be costs (financial, political, or both) to not changing its policy. Follow-through has taken a number of forms. Harlow and Richard Rawlings give examples of interest groups publishing pamphlets advertising the EU legal rights of citizens and including a complaint form and of groups distributing videos explaining how to use the EU legal process. In some cases groups have solicited complaints through mass mailings, simultaneously submitting them to the government and the Commission with demands for legislative change (Harlow and Rawlings 1992: 276; Meier 1994). Michael McCann highlighted another strategy where litigation was used to dramatize issues to strengthen political movements, and favorable decisions were invoked in bargaining with employers and public bodies (McCann 1994). Combining a legal victory with a political strategy shows the government that the legal case will not be isolated and that faced with a legal challenge, the government would likely lose.

When are we most likely to find follow-through from an EU law legal victory and thus have a legal decision that leads to policy change? Little research has been done on this question; thus most of what follows should be taken as hypotheses rather than findings.[27] Private litigants might be satisfied with winning their cases and have less incentive to make sure that the government changes its policy. However, when organized interests or repeat players use litigation with the intent of influencing public policy, the resulting decision is more likely to be invoked in bargaining with the government. From this one can hypothesize that interest group or repeat-player litigation (when successful) is more likely to create policy change than a decision in a one-shot case raised by a private litigant (Dehousse 1998: 111).

It is also possible that legal victories can be picked up by groups to create broader policy change. Drawing on Mancur Olson, Conant argues that distribution of the costs and benefits will influence whether groups mobilize in the aftermath of a legal decision. If there are significant benefits to be won by securing a change in

compliance rates than others with ECJ decisions (see Börzel 2001). Furthermore, even the clearly more law-abiding countries have been willing at times to ignore an ECJ decision.

[26] Studies have found that national courts nearly always enforce ECJ rulings they receive as a result of their preliminary ruling reference. See Dashwood and Arnull (1984); Kellermann, Levelt-Overmars, and Posser (1990); Wils (1993).

[27] Most work on the political impact of ECJ decisions has focused on the influence of ECJ jurisprudence on EU policy. Lisa Conant (2002) and Rachel Cichowski (2007) have advanced the debate since this essay was published.

policy, and these benefits fall narrowly on a group of people, it is more likely that individuals and groups will mobilize around a legal decision. When the benefits are distributed widely, an ECJ decision will garner less mobilization. Conant also points out that if the costs of policy change are narrowly focused, there can be a counter-mobilization against a legal decision. In this case the outcome will be a 'compromised acceptance' of an ECJ decision, with the government working out a compromise with the groups involved, and perhaps also with the EU institutions. ECJ decisions where the costs are distributed widely, and the benefits distributed narrowly, may lead to policy change without counter-mobilization and thus a full acceptance of the decision (Conant 1998: ch. 3).[28]

Certainly groups are more likely to mobilize when benefits are narrowly focused than when they are widely distributed, but there are numerous examples of groups mobilizing even when the benefits are unevenly distributed.[29] In each case, however, the groups mobilizing around the legal victory were preexisting. One could add to Conant's hypothesis that legal decisions in areas where there are pre-existing mobilized interests are more likely to provoke follow-through. The earlier hypotheses on group mobilization may be less important at the follow-through stage: groups with narrow mandates and single issue concerns that start a litigation strategy are likely to follow through on it; however, even encompassing groups may draw on a favorable legal decision in bargaining.

III. Interaction Effects of the Four Steps in the Litigation Process

I summarize in Table 9.3 the factors that can influence each step of the litigation process. I have categorized the factors according to whether they create cross-national and/or cross-issue variation, and, where possible, I have developed hypotheses about where and when private litigants are most likely to successfully use the EU legal system to influence national policy.

IV. A Challenge to Neo-Functionalist Theory: Negative Interactive Effects and the Process of Disintegration

While different factors influence each step of the EU litigation process, there will clearly be interaction effects across steps. Neo-functionalist theory assumes positive interaction effects. Burley and Mattli envisioned a general harmony of interest

---

[28] Conant supports these arguments with case study analyses of national responses to EU liberalization and ECJ jurisprudence involving two industries (electricity and telecommunications) in three countries (the United Kingdom, France, and Germany).

[29] See Chapter 8 and Harlow and Rawlings (1992).

Table 9.3. Factors influencing the four steps in the EU legal process

Step of legal process	Sources of cross-national variation	Sources of cross-issue variation	Where and when the EU legal system will most likely be used to influence domestic policy
Step 1: When will EU law provide a legal basis to challenge national policy?	For most EU legal texts, all states have the same legal obligations; thus these texts do not give rise to cross-national variation. Opt-out clauses in a few EU agreements could create some cross-national variation in the effect of EU law on domestic policy, but this will be the exception.	Variation based on substance of EU law. Variation based on whether EU law creates direct effects. Variation based on jurisprudence of the ECJ. Variation based on political consensus of member states. Variation based on public opinion regarding area of policy covered by EU law.[d]	EU law is mostly concerned with economic issues with a transnational dimension, but the EU has jurisdiction in some national policy areas (such as agriculture, value-added tax, and external trade); these are the areas of national policy most likely to be affected by EU litigation. Direct effects are likely to be created by laws that take the form of regulations and by directives and Treaty articles that are specific. The ECJ is more likely to rule against a national policy in areas where ECJ doctrine is well developed than where it is not.[a] The ECJ is more likely to rule against a national policy when the material and political costs of the legal decision are relatively low than when they are relatively high.[b] The ECJ is more likely to rule against a national policy when there is no political consensus against the ECJ's decision among member states.[c]
Step 2: When will litigants mobilize to use EU law to promote their policy objectives?	Variation based on national procedural and legal standing rules. Variation based on litigiousness of population. Variation based on how interests are organized at domestic level (narrow	Variation based on wealth and legal know-how of litigants. Variation based on magnitude of potential benefits of litigation. Variation based on how interests are organized at domestic level (narrow groups vs. encompassing groups). Variation based on access of domestic groups to policy-making process.	Private litigant challenges to national policy are more likely to arise in countries where citizens and businesses commonly use litigation to pursue interests and where the legal system generally works. Wealthy individuals and large firms are more likely than others to raise cases and be able to use the legal system to their advantage.[e] Private litigants are more likely to raise cases when the benefits of doing so are significant.[e]

Continued

Table 9.3. (*Continued*)

Step of legal process	Sources of cross-national variation	Sources of cross-issue variation	Where and when the EU legal system will most likely be used to influence domestic policy
	groups vs. encompassing groups). Variation based on access of domestic groups to policy-making process.		Narrowly focused groups are more likely to turn to litigation than groups with broader mandates and more encompassing constituencies.[f] Groups with limited or no access to the political process are more likely to turn to litigation to promote their objectives than groups with greater access.[f] Variation based on whether there is European law on an issue, and thus whether groups are already mobilized on the issue.[j]
Step 3: When will national judges refer cases and apply ECJ jurisprudence?	Variation in rules of access to legal bodies (influences judicial behavior toward EU law). Variation in national legal training (may influence judicial identity and judicial behavior toward EU law).	Variation in rules of access to legal bodies (influences judicial behavior toward EU law). Variation in legal substance (leads some national courts to deal with EU legal issues more than other courts, influencing number of references but not necessarily judicial openness to EU law and ECJ jurisprudence. Variation in judicial identity (influences judicial behavior toward EU law). Variation in how EU law affects the independence, influence, and authority of judges (influences judicial willingness to send references and accept ECJ jurisprudence).	If litigants indicate a willingness to pay and wait for a preliminary ruling decision, the likelihood of a referral increases. Legally uncontroversial ECJ decisions are more likely than controversial decisions to be accepted by national courts. A legal issue is more likely to be heard by the ECJ when litigants can forum-shop for sympathetic judges than when they cannot. Lower courts are often more willing than higher courts to make a reference.[g] Courts with judges who have not previously served for long periods in the national administration are more likely than others to be sympathetic to challenges to national policy.

Step 4: When will a legal victory lead to policy change? When are litigants likely to follow through on a legal victory?	Variation based on effectiveness of national legal system and political elite's belief in and general adherence to a rule of law.	Variation in the policy and legal impact of EU law on national law (influences judicial willingness to refer cases and accept ECJ jurisprudence).	The more a country tends to abide by its own court's decisions, the more it is likely to abide by a decision in an EU legal case.[h]
		Variation based on the political salience of the ECJ decision and the likelihood that the decision will mobilize domestic actors.	National legal decisions of high political salience are more likely than other decisions to provoke mobilization and thus to be respected (or legislatively overturned).
		Variation based on whether the ECJ decision was made in a case referred by a national court in the country targeted to change its policy.	Follow-through on challenges to national policy is more likely to occur in cases constructed by groups or repeat players than in isolated cases raised by private litigants.[i]
		Variation based on whether the case was brought by a 'repeat player' and/ or has interest group support.	Follow-through is more likely to occur when the benefits of policy change are narrowly focused and the costs of policy change are widely distributed.[e]
		Variation based on the size and distribution of potential benefits of policy change in light of a legal decision.	Follow-through is more likely to occur in policy areas where groups are mobilized and vigilant toward government behavior.
		Variation based on the organization of domestic interests.	Pre-existing groups are more likely than others to mobilize around favorable legal decisions.

[a] (Garrett et al. 1998).

[b] See Garrett et al. (1998); (Chapters 5 and 6).

[c] (Alter 1998); (Chapter 6).

[d] (Carrubba and Murrah 2005).

[e] (Conant 1998).

[f] (Chapter 8).

[g] (Alter, 2001).

[h] (Slaughter 1995).

[i] (Dehousse 1998).

[j] (Cichowski 2007).

among private litigants, national judges, legal scholars, and the ECJ propelling the process forward while they pursued their instrumental self-interests in a mutually reinforcing way (Burley and Mattli, 1993). Stone Sweet and Brunell expect the legal process to have its own dynamic, with litigants raising ever more cases and judges inevitably building law as they attempt to resolve disputes where the law is not clear (Stone Sweet and Brunell 1998a). It is true that the body of EU rules is expanding, driven by national governments who want to build a common market and now a monetary union. Levels of trade are expanding, driven by the completion of the common market and globalization more broadly. As a result, litigants have more opportunities and incentives to draw on European law. Furthermore, evidence indicates that one litigant's success in utilizing EU law can trigger other actors to mimic the strategy. Thus plenty of suggestive material exists to support any theory that predicts legal expansion. The key question is whether neo-functionalist theory can predict or account for the limits to the process of integration that appear along the way. The failure of neo-functionalist theory to account for these limits is what originally led Ernst Haas to abandon the theory (Haas 1975).[30]

A virtuous circle may certainly emerge: successful litigation may encourage more cases, but it is not the only possibility. Negative feedback loops may also emerge. Factors that undermine each step of the litigation process can reverberate through all four steps, leading to fewer cases involving EU law and a diminishing impact of EU law on national policy. Once litigants are stung by an undesirable ECJ ruling, they may hesitate to raise ambiguous cases in the future. And though reference rates continue to increase, the ambivalence of national courts toward EU law and their opposition to key tenets of ECJ jurisprudence are also increasing. If national courts are not receptive to EU legal arguments, lawyers may well advise their clients not to pursue an EU legal case. The less domestic actors are mobilized to capture the benefits of EU law, the less pressure states will be under to comply with EU law.

In addition to negative interactive effects, the success of EU legal integration may have instigated a larger backlash. Faced with unacceptable ECJ decisions, member states have passed protocols and laws at the EU level that reverse or qualify the effects of ECJ rulings, such as the famous Barber Protocol of the Maastricht Treaty that limits the retrospective effects of the ECJ's *Barber* ruling. Although there are relatively few examples where member states have reversed the effects of ECJ rulings, states have sought to constrain the ECJ's activism. Having seen how the ECJ used legal lacunae to seize new powers and delve into areas that member states considered to be their own exclusive realm, national governments have constructed legislative barriers to ECJ legal expansion. Member states have

---

[30] It has historically been the case that neo-functionalist theory works as long as (and only when) integration is moving forward. For a review of the rise and fall of neo-functionalist theory in the study of the EU see Caporaso and Keeler (1995).

also taken to writing clauses into EU Treaties and legislation protecting national policies, sometimes in ways that violate the spirit of the EU and contradict ECJ doctrine. For example, the Danish government insisted on a provision in the Maastricht Treaty that allows it to ban Germans from buying vacation homes, and the Irish government demanded a protocol making it clear that nothing in EU law will interfere with Ireland's constitutional ban on abortion. According to the *Economist*, EU legislation is filled with secret footnotes designed to protect national policies. For example:

[The 1994] directive on data protection attracted 31 such [exception] statements. Britain secured an exemption for manual filing systems if—work this one out—the costs involved in complying with the directive outweigh the benefits. Germany secured the right to keep data about religious beliefs under wraps. Since these and other statements are not published, Joe Bloggs will know about these maneuverings only by chance or if his government chooses to tell him.[31]

These protections are designed to limit the reach of EU law, so that states do not have to change a valued national policy. States have also excluded the ECJ entirely from some of the new areas of EU powers (such as common foreign and security policy, and issues of justice and home affairs that affect domestic security and a country's internal order). And states are writing provisions into EU law that limit the ECJ from expanding the legal effects of EU law into the domestic realm. The new Treaty of Amsterdam, for example, states that policies adopted under the EU framework with respect to Article K.6 will not create direct effects—making private litigants unable to draw on them to challenge national provisions.

Having figured out that lower courts are much more willing to send references to the ECJ, and that their references are allowing the ECJ to expand its own authority and compromise national sovereignty, member states are much more reluctant to open new access to the ECJ for lower courts. Since 1968, the extension of preliminary ruling rights to lower courts has been contested and often limited when the ECJ's legal authority has been expanded to new areas of EU law (see Chapter 6 for examples).

Member states have also sought to regain national control over certain policy issues. The Maastricht Treaty articulates a 'subsidiarity principle' authorizing the Community to undertake actions only 'if and so far as the objectives of the proposed action cannot be sufficiently achieved by the member state'.[32] This principle has provided a political/legal basis to repatriate powers back to the national level. Politicians, citizen groups, and journalists invoke the subsidiarity principle to argue against EU legislation. And member states have used this

---

[31] 'Seeing Through It' *The Economist,* 16 September 1995, p. 59.
[32] Article 3b TEU. This clause pertains to areas that do not fall under the Community's exclusive competence. For more on this clause, see Bernard (1996).

principle to reclaim power that the ECJ had claimed for the EU.[33] The ECJ has also invoked the concept of subsidiarity to revise its earlier jurisprudence in favor of national prerogatives.[34]

National high courts are also concerned that the EU and the ECJ have gained too much power, and they are creating their own limits on the expansive reach of EU law. Indeed, though early neo-functionalist theory predicted that greater experience would induce greater support for the process of integration, the opposite seems to have occurred. The more national courts have seen how the process of European integration is influencing the domestic administrative, political, and legal order, the more they seem willing to question the validity of EU law, of ECJ and Commission decisions, and even of their own governments' decisions taken at the EU level. For example, having seen the ECJ give expansive interpretations to the EU treaties in the past, in 1993 the German Constitutional Court ruled that ECJ interpretations that extend the treaty will not be valid in Germany.[35] The court warned the ECJ to protect Germany's subsidiarity rights, and it set limits on the German government's authority to transfer decision-making authority to the EU level.[36] In France the Conseil Constitutionnel has asserted its authority to evaluate the constitutionality of EU rules and declared that the French Parliament may not ratify, validate, or authorize an international (that is, EU) engagement contrary to the constitution.[37]

[33] For example, member states included Article 126 TEU, which instructs the EU to respect 'the responsibility of the member states for the content of teaching and organization of the educational system'. This clause asserts state power in an area in which the ECJ had previously denied states power (Dehousse 1998: 166).

[34] Cases C-267 and 268/91, *French Penal Authorities v. Keck and Mithouard* decision of 24 November 1993 [1992] ECR I-6097, ECJ.

[35] They stated: 'Whereas a dynamic extension of the existing Treaties has so far been supported...in future it will have to be noted as regards interpretation of enabling provisions by Community institutions and agencies that the Union Treaty...interpretation may not have effects that are equivalent to an extension of the Treaty. Such an interpretation of enabling rules would not produce any binding effects for Germany.' Interestingly, the German citizens who raised the challenge to the Maastricht Treaty were members of the European Parliament and a high-level civil servant of the European Commission. *Brunner and Others v. The European Union Treaty,* BVerfG decision of 12 October 1993, 2 BvR 2134/92 and 2 BvR 2159/92: published in CMLR, January 1994, 57–108. Quoted from p. 105 of the decision.

[36] *Brunner and Others v. The European Union Treaty,* BVerfG decision of 11 January 1994, 2 BvR 2134/92 and 2 BvR 2159/92, 57–108. For an analysis of this decision, see Alter (2001: 104–17). The German Constitutional Court went on in the Banana case to remove itself from assessing the applicability of EU law so long as the ECJ 'generally protects' basic rights (Alter 2001: 115), but then it arguably reversed this position when it found that a European arrest warrant was not applicable in Germany. See *Europäischer Haftbefehl* decision of 18 July 2005 113 BVerfGE 273 (2005), reprinted in 32 EuGRZ 387.

[37] See Maastricht I, Conseil constitutionnel, decision of 9 April 1992, 92–308 DC; and Case 91–294, Conseil constitutionnel, decision of 25 July 1991, Schengen Decision, 1991, 173. For an analysis of these decisions, see (Pellet 1998; Zoller 1992: 280–2). Both the French and German rulings are designed to position these courts to serve as a second review, a national-level review, of the validity of EU law in the national realm. Their goal is to pressure the ECJ to scrutinize the validity of EU law more carefully, to take national judicial concerns into account in its decision-making, and to be more sensitive to national sovereignty considerations. Supreme courts also hope

By opening up the possibility of national constitutional constraints to EU law, supreme courts have also created a national means for individuals, groups, and minority factions to challenge deals made at the EU level.[38] German Lander governments have drawn on the German constitution to challenge an EU directive regarding television programming that the ECJ had upheld,[39] and German importers of restricted bananas have used German courts and the German constitution to challenge the EU's banana regime (see Chapter 10 at p. 223 and Alter 2001: 112–16). These examples show that national and EU legal systems can also be used by private litigants to challenge advances in European integration agreed to by their governments.

Certainly, as long as European governments seek to facilitate more trade through drafting common rules, the present trajectory toward more integration and more EU law will continue. But negative feedback between the four steps of the litigation process can undermine the influence of EU law on domestic policy. Clearly, even in the legal realm the forces that led to increased legalization in the past are not now nearly so unidirectional. Indeed, even Burley and Mattli have backed away from their neo-functionalist argument, noting that neo-functionalism has 'no tools to determine when self-interest will align with further integration ... and when it will not' (Mattli and Slaughter 1998: 185).

Burley and Mattli suggest returning to mid-range theories about private litigant and national court behavior, like the hypotheses explored here. But there is certainly also room to theorize more broadly on the systematic factors that contribute to moves toward disintegration. There is much to suggest that the forces for disintegration are created by the process of European integration itself.[40] As European integration expands, it upsets more national policies. As more power is transferred to EU institutions, national actors (national courts, national administrators, national parliaments, and national interest groups) find their own influence, independence, and autonomy undermined. These actors may in the past have used the EU legal and political system to promote their objectives, and they may continue to do so when convenient. But they are also quite willing to use both EU and national political and legal systems to challenge EU authority in order to protect their influence, independence, and authority, and when doing so promotes specific objectives. The ECJ's intermediaries are often

to influence their governments to be more careful in what they agree to at the EU level. Alter (2001: 116–17, 170–3).

[38] Because French citizens cannot bring cases to the Conseil constitutionnel, they are less able to use the French legal system to challenge the constitutionality of EU law. Some observers speculate that the Conseil d'État may eventually create a means for private litigants in France to invoke the French constitution to challenge EU law.

[39] *Bayerische Staatsregierung v. Bundesregierung*, BVerfG decision of 11 April 1989, 2 BvG 1/89, [1990] 1 CMLR 649–55; and BVerfG decision of 22 March 1995, 2 BvG 1/89, EuGRZ 1995, 125–37.

[40] For an argument to this effect, see Dehousse (1998: 173) and Suleiman (1995).

fair-weather friends. Much to the surprise of the ECJ and pro-integration actors, they are increasingly vocal critics, too.

V. Generalizing from the European Case

The European legal system has some unusual attributes that have allowed it to contribute to legalization in Europe and that give it leverage to influence domestic policy. Access to the ECJ is far wider than for most international legal bodies, with states, the European Commission, and private litigants empowered to use the EU legal system to challenge national policy. The wide access gives the ECJ more opportunities to influence national policy, and the numerous cases have allowed the ECJ to develop EU law incrementally, a strategy that has been important in building support for its jurisprudence and enhancing the effectiveness of the EU legal system (Burley and Mattli 1993; Hartley 1994; Helfer and Slaughter 1997; Weiler 1991). But as Chapter 12 shows, increasingly there are international courts with access for non-state actors. The preliminary ruling system has been copied by the Andean Tribunal of Justice (ATJ), and a number of international courts can hear appeals of national legal decisions (e.g. the European Court of Human Rights, the court for the Organization for the Harmonization of Corporate Law in Africa, the Central American Court of Justice, the Caribbean Court of Justice, the court for the Economic Community of West African States, and the Court for the Commonwealth of Independent States).

Because of the somewhat unusual nature of the EU legal system, the EU experience is not necessarily the model of what will happen in other international legal systems. The framework developed in this article, however, can help one think about how international legal mechanisms can be used to influence national policy in other contexts.[41] The four steps of the litigation process identified in this article still need to be fulfilled for international legal mechanisms to be a tool for domestic actors to pressure for change in domestic policy. But the factors influencing each step will vary because both the source of international law and the intermediaries in the legal process will be different.

The first step in the EU litigation process involves having a body of EU law that can be invoked in a legal system to challenge national policy and an IC willing to interpret law purposively. There are many international legal texts that can be invoked by legal bodies (national and international) to challenge national policies. But the ability of litigants to invoke this law will vary depending on the binding nature of the legal text, on whether the national system recognizes the legal text as creating direct effects, and on access and legal standing rules that will influence whether or not litigants can effectively use the legal system to challenge a country's policy. As in the EU case, limitations created by the law and

---

[41] The framework could apply to domestic situations as well.

the allocation of legal standing will engender biases by which actors can benefit from the law. Because of biases, international rules may significantly advantage some domestic groups (such as economic actors favoring liberalization) over other domestic groups. This bias helps explain why some actors oppose increased international legalization. But the Andean Tribunal of Justice, discussed in Chapter 4, suggests that not all international courts will issue purposive interpretations of the law. If the IC is not willing to help out litigants, we may find that appeals to ICs decline over time (Alter and Helfer 2009).

The second step of the litigation process involves mobilizing the potential beneficiaries to draw on international law and use the international legal mechanisms. Where private litigants have access to international legal mechanisms, the factors identified in this article—such as the magnitude of potential benefits and how interests are organized—could matter. Litigation patterns in the WTO have been extensively analyzed, with scholars finding that the magnitude of potential gains as well as experience with the WTO system (being sued in the past, or having participated as a third party in a WTO suit) increase the likelihood of a country raising a WTO case (Busch and Reinhardt 2000; Guzman and Simmons 2005; Davis and Blodgett forthcoming).

Where only states have access to legal systems, the dynamics will be different. States tend to be more reluctant than private litigants or national courts to use international legal mechanisms. Governments often fear that the outcome of a legal case could be worse than a negotiated outcome, that a legal ruling could create domestic backlash, or that a legal ruling will be less flexible, tying the hands of governments in the future (McCall Smith and Tallberg 2009). This is in large part why Robert Keohane, Andrew Moravcsik, and Anne-Marie Slaughter expect legalization to progress further in transnational compared with interstate legal systems (Keohane, Moravcsik, and Slaughter 2000). National governments still might have an incentive to please a domestic group by raising a case. In this situation, domestic political factors, such as the extent to which interest groups can penetrate the political system,[42] the political strength of the domestic group desiring the legal case, and where the party in charge of the government finds its largest domestic political support, will likely be important. International level factors, such as the relations between the state raising the case and the target state and the number of other interstate issues of potentially higher priority, will also likely influence a state's calculations.

The third step in the EU case—finding national judicial support—is not a factor in legal systems where states or litigants raise their cases directly in front of an international legal body. But in some international systems an international commission or a public prosecutor acts as a gatekeeper deciding whether or not to bring a case to court (such as the original system of the European Convention

---

[42] For example, Super 301 in the United States virtually forces the executive branch to investigate and act on complaints raised by US firms.

on Human Rights, the present system for the Inter-American Court of Human Rights, and for the International Criminal Court). Where it is up to the discretion of a commission or prosecutor to pursue a legal violation, the factors shaping these actors' decisions will matter. Some of the factors identified here will surely matter, such as the legal rules defining the mandate of the commission or prosecutor, how the commission or prosecutor understands its mandate, and how a case influences the political process. In addition, the ability or inability of the commission or prosecutor to find relevant facts or gather evidence will likely shape what types of cases are pursued (Helfer and Slaughter 1997).

Follow-through, the fourth step, will also be important in other international legal contexts. Few international legal bodies are able to issue sanctions against states. In most cases a political body must authorize or take a separate action to create a penalty for a violation of international law. It cannot be assumed that states will follow through on their legal victories. Following through on a legal victory might be more costly than initiating legal proceedings. And time will certainly have elapsed between the original decision to raise a legal case and the potential decision to pressure for sanctions against the offending state, allowing other political factors to be put on the agenda and other political actors to assume control of the government. Because states—not groups, as in the European context—are the actors that must follow through, the factors influencing whether follow-through will occur will be different. But in contexts outside of Europe, this step will be no less important, and possibly even more important, than in the EU.

The European legal system is unusual in its ability to be used by domestic actors to pressure for change in national policy. But as Chapter 12 shows, increasingly there are international courts which share elements of the ECJ's design. There is great variation in the ways private litigants actually do use the EU legal system to influence national policy, and private litigants can also use the EU legal system to challenge EU policies and rules. For political scientists who prize parsimony, the answer to the questions of where and when domestic actors will use the EU legal system to influence national policy is, unfortunately, complex. Even assuming rational behavior, no human error, and full information—unsustainable assumptions to be sure—where EU law influences national policy depends on the wording of the EU law, on ECJ legal doctrine and ECJ decision-making, on private litigant mobilization, on national court support, and on follow-through. Some of these factors will matter in other international contexts. And there are likely additional factors that are important because the main intermediaries in other international legal systems differ. I have been able to suggest only a few factors that might matter in other contexts. There is fertile ground for future research.

10

Banana Splits: Nested and Overlapping Regimes in the Transatlantic Banana Trade Dispute (2006)

With Sophie Meunier

Advanced industrial democracies belong to a plethora of international institutions. Either individually or collectively, they are members of universal organizations (UN agencies), regional blocs (e.g. the European Union (EU), the North American Free Trade Agreement (NAFTA), the Association of South East Asian Nations (ASEAN)), and issue-specific institutions (e.g. the World Trade Organization (WTO), the North Atlantic Treaty Organization (NATO), the Organization for Economic Co-operation and Development (OECD), the World Health Organization (WHO)). These international institutions can be nested within each other or overlap with each other, sometimes leading to conflicting commitments for their member states. How do the nesting and overlapping of international institutions complicate the strategies of national decision-makers? Does the nested/overlapping nature of international commitments in itself generate a distinct kind of politics?

This article is an inductive exploration of how nesting and overlapping created distinctive political dynamics in the decade-long conflict over bananas between the European Union (EU) and the United States (US). The 11-year dispute is puzzling because it involved neither significant factual disagreements, nor disagreements over deep-seated values. Neither the US nor the EU has significant banana industries, and bananas account for only 0.03 per cent of transatlantic trade. In addition, many actors in Europe itself disliked the policy from the beginning. Our analytical focus is on how the nesting of the banana regime—within the EU, the Lomé Convention, and the WTO—contributed to the dispute by constraining decision-makers, thereby making a rather straightforward dispute very difficult to resolve.

Section I develops the argument for how the nesting of institutions creates shifting framing of issues by interest groups and contorted decision-making by legal and political actors. Section II shows how the EC Bananas Regulation was itself an artifact of nested and overlapping commitments, and how importers of Latin dollar bananas pursued multi-venue legal, constitutional, and political techniques to challenge the policy within the different nested layers. Section III uses counter-factual analysis that strips away each of the layered institutional levels to reveal how the nesting/overlapping of international commitments shaped actor decision-making. The analysis helps explain both the convoluted European banana policy and the difficulty in resolving the banana dispute. In conclusion, we reflect on the generalizability of our findings for the increasingly complex international environment where countries have enmeshed themselves in a variety of bi- and multilateral institutions.

I. The Nesting and Overlapping of International Commitments

'Nesting' refers to a situation where regional or issue-specific international institutions are themselves part of multilateral frameworks that involve multiple states or issues. Institutions are imbricated one within another, like Russian dolls. For instance, European states have formed the European Union, which is part of the World Trade Organization. International institutions need not be nested, however, to overlap in authority. With their multiple institutional commitments, member countries stand at the intersection of independent jurisdictions, as in the overlapping middle part of a Venn Diagram. For example, European states are members of the EU, but they also belong to the WTO and the ILO (International Labour Organization), they are part of many bilateral trade agreements with third countries, and some of them are constituting members of the G8 (see Figure 10.1). An overlapping context is theoretically distinct from a nested context, though in practice they may not differ much. In an overlapping jurisdiction context, a conflict across agreements does not per se mean that one rule is a violation of the other. When institutions are nested, however, conflicting policies of the subsumed regime constitute a violation of the more encompassing institution. As the banana dispute will show, however, the reality of international law is that there is no universally accepted hierarchy of international norms which may be used to resolve conflicts of law. Thus a conflict of international rules may be no more resolvable in a nested context than in an overlapping context.

The Complex Nesting of the Banana Dispute

Even though all nations are increasingly entangled in multiple international commitments, the issue of institutional nesting has not yet been the object of many studies. Some scholars analyze how different types of institution (e.g.

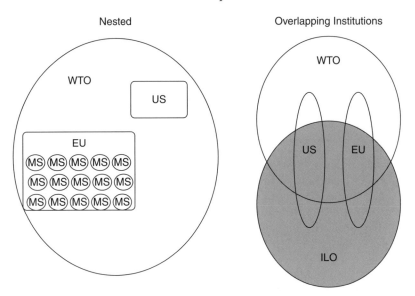

Figure 10.1. Analytical difference between nested and overlapping contexts
Note: MS: European Union member state (15 before last enlargement). Circle size is not to scale.

federal arrangements vs. multi-level governance arrangements) have different politics (Hooghe and Marks 2001: 7; Shanks et al. 1996; Tsebelis 1990). Others analyze factors influencing what type of institutional forum is chosen (Abbott and Snidal 1998, 2000; McCall Smith 2000). Other scholars describe strategies to navigate or shift from one institutional forum to another (Abbott and Snidal 2003; Helfer 2004), or the factors shaping whether new challenges are dealt with through existing institutions or generate new institutions (Aggarwal 1998). While focusing on elements related to the politics of overlapping institutions, these works do not consider how nesting matters beyond their specific question or how nesting/overlapping is a source of a specific politics.

This paper identifies one politics that nesting/overlapping institutions generate. At both the domestic and international levels, differentiation—an attempt to define the realms separately—is the first approach to resolving conflicts across rules. When differentiation fails, hierarchy becomes necessary. At the domestic level, federalism involves working out the division of authority between federal, state, and local government, so that it is eventually clear which actors have final authority over a given policy issue. State and local politics often takes place in the shadow of federal politics, with all actors understanding that disgruntled groups may appeal to federal entities, and federal actors may invalidate state and local decisions or rule that state actors have final authority. The key difference between the domestic and international context is that at the international level it is not clear who has the final authority to resolve conflicts across levels or agreements. In both the domestic and international contexts, the existence of nesting/overlapping institutions creates the opportunity for policy entrepreneurs and interest groups to choose the political forum that is both willing to adopt their policy preference and is most authoritative. Policy entrepreneurs will frame their issue to build political consensus within their chosen decision-making institution and to fit the style of the decision-making forum, with the policy outcome being a mixture of the preferences of the policy entrepreneurs and existing repertoire of policy formula within the decision-making regime.[1] Those actors wanting a different policy may respond, however, by appealing to a different forum that has overlapping authority, seeking an authoritative decision that contradicts or undermines the policy of the other institution. Thus for forum shoppers, the nested context can generate a shifting 'framing' of the issue depending on the forum in use (with different framings having substantive and political repercussions).

For decision-makers, the reality of forum shopping combined in the international context with no clear system to determine hierarchy creates dilemmas: they try to avoid being gamed by forum shoppers, while keeping their options open by adopting strategies to maximize international bargaining leverage. Political decision-makers play across forums, creating a more complex politics that includes playing multilateral institutions off against each other in addition to the traditional two-level game involving domestic and international actors (Putnam 1988). Judicial decision-makers in a nested/overlapped context may be invited by forum shoppers to weigh in, but judges know their sub-level policy decisions may be condemned, contradicted, or supplanted by the more encompassing institution. In addition, the inherently fluid and political nature of international politics makes judges far more hesitant to weigh in to resolve disputes about the hierarchy of competing rules. Thus the nested/overlapped context in itself facilitates forum shopping and leads decision-makers, legal and political, to positions on international issues that are quite different from the 'domestic' position they might advocate, when it is clear where final authority resides.

The single European banana regime, at the root of the US–EU banana dispute, illustrates the legal and political complexities triggered by the nesting and overlapping of international commitments, and how nesting complicates dispute resolution.

---

[1] Bureaucracies tend to replicate policy formulas to create internal consistency and to ease implementation. The EU chose quotas because they boosted the price of bananas, decreasing the need for subsidies to make French and Spanish bananas competitive. The particular system of import licenses replicated existing mechanisms used to distribute quotas across individual importers. Since the quotas were designed to discriminate between ACP and dollar bananas, categories of quotas (A, B, and C) were created, resulting in an incredibly complicated licensing system that caused German importers to raise legal challenges and led the EU policy to be condemned by the WTO. The difficulty of changing this system was in no small part associated with the entrenchment of the policy repertoire which bureaucracies cling to.

II. Nesting/Overlapping at the Root of the Banana Dispute

With the goal of a common market, the European Economic Community's (EEC) founding 1957 Treaty of Rome called for the removal of all internal barriers to trade and the introduction of a common external tariff for imports from third countries. Despite the Treaty's ambitious goals, national markets long remained fragmented for many goods. The 1986 Single European Act tried to remedy this fragmentation by calling for the completion of an internal market in which goods, services, people, and capital could move around freely by the end of 1992.

The creation of the single European banana regime

The banana market was particularly fragmented, with each European member state selecting its own banana regime based on past imperial relationships and present vested interests (Sutton 1997). In 1989 three distinct European banana import regimes existed. France, Italy, the United Kingdom, Greece, Portugal, and Spain offered tariff protection for the 69 African-Caribbean-Pacific (ACP) country producers, most of which were former European colonies benefiting from special trade agreements through the Lomé Convention.[2] Belgium, the Netherlands, Luxembourg, Denmark, and Ireland had an across-the-board 20 per cent tariff for banana imports. Germany relied on a special 'banana protocol' attached to the Treaty of Rome that allowed duty-free access for Central and Latin American bananas.

Unifying this regime, as required by the Single European Act, entailed reconciling the apparently irreconcilable pulls of multiple institutions and treaty obligations in contradiction with one another (Lyons 1994). How could a new banana regime simultaneously: be consistent with the Single Market; honor its Lomé Convention commitment to protect the banana exports of ACP countries; honor the 'Banana Protocol' in the Treaty of Rome guaranteeing Germany unimpeded access to bananas; and honor obligations under the General Agreement on Tariffs and Trade (GATT) to provide preferential access to imports from developing countries including non-ACP countries? The complex nesting of the EU's banana policy, as the dispute unfolded, is represented by Figure 10.2.

It took four years of intense negotiation for Europe to create its new regime involving a multi-layered system of import rules, with strong preferences for

---

[2] Signed in 1975 after Great Britain's accession to the EEC (and renewed in 1979, 1984, and 1989), the Lomé Convention is the world's largest financial and political framework for North-South cooperation. This special relationship is characterized by non-reciprocal trade benefits for ACP states including unlimited entry to the EC market for 99% of industrial goods and many other products. Of the 69 ACP countries, at least eight are significant banana producers. Lomé Conventions: [1976] OJ L25/1; [1980] OJ L347/1; [1986] OJ L86/1; [1991] OJ L229/I.

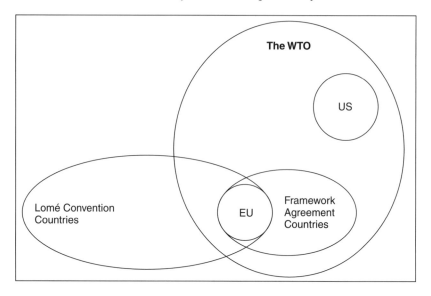

Figure 10.2. The complex nesting of the banana dispute

Note: Not all Lomé countries are in the WTO, but all EU countries are in the Lomé Convention. The Framework agreement is between the EU and other WTO states. The US was not party to any of these agreements or conventions.

EEC and ACP bananas. The import system was incredibly complex: supplies from the EEC (including overseas territories) were unrestricted; imports from the ACP countries were tariff-free up to 857,000 tons, after which they were subjected to a 750 ECU (European Currency Unit) per ton tariff; and imports from other countries (mostly from Central and Latin American producers) were allotted a yearly quota of two million tons with a 20 per cent tariff, and a 170 per cent tariff beyond this quota. The Commission kept track of this regime by issuing import licenses that allocated quotas among banana distributors: two-thirds to traditional European and ACP importers, and one-third to other importers.

The essential features of the new banana regime were adopted by a qualified majority vote in December 1992, as part of a package deal. The policy was opposed by Germany, Denmark, and Portugal whose hostile reaction led to the introduction of several changes in February 1993. These concessions were not enough for Germany who voted against it. Belgium and the Netherlands also voted against, breaking with precedent by reversing their previous position of support in December. However, the regulation was passed when Denmark, then EEC President, switched its vote. The single EEC-wide regime on banana imports (Regulation 404/93) was implemented in July 1993 (Webber and Cadot 2002: 26).

Resolving the transatlantic banana dispute

The EU's controversial policy ran afoul of WTO rules because it allowed for preferential access for some banana imports and not others. The nested nature of the member states within the EU, and of the EU within the WTO, provided multiple avenues for banana producers and importers to challenge the contested policy—complicating the situation of European legal and political decision-makers who tried to figure out how each challenge would play out. All the layers of politics made finding a compromise much harder, allowing the relatively straightforward dispute to fester for 10 years (see Figure 10.2).

Europe's banana policy was first contested in GATT while the new protocol was still under negotiation. In 1992, a group of Central and Latin American producers known as the 'dollar zone' group—Costa Rica, Colombia, Guatemala, Nicaragua, and Venezuela—tried to put pressure on the European negotiation process by requesting the establishment of a panel to examine the consistency of the various European national banana regimes with GATT. In June 1993, the GATT panel ruled in favor of the 'dollar bananas'.[3] The GATT consensus rule allowed the EU and ACP countries to block the ruling so that the panel report was never officially adopted by the contracting parties (Bessko 1996: 4). This ruling became moot when the national regimes were replaced with the unified Euro-wide banana regime.

Once promulgated, the banana policy was immediately contested—first from within the European Community (as of 1993 the European Union (EU)). France supported the new regime above all because its *départements d'outre-mer*, especially Guadeloupe and Martinique, were banana producers. The UK also supported the regime because it offered protection to the Windward Islands and preserved the interests of Geest, a major British agro-industrial company which provided shipping and support services for Windward bananas in Britain. By contrast, the member states who were forced to switch from low tariffs to the new EU system lost out in this arrangement.

Germany lost the most. The world's highest per capita consumer of bananas, Germany imported 99.7 per cent of its bananas from 'dollar zone' countries[4] and had the lowest banana prices in Europe in 1991.[5] The new EU-wide banana regime forced Germany to import more EU and ACP bananas and to go from tariff-free Latin American imports to high-tariff dollar bananas, resulting in a 63 per cent increase in the price of bananas in 1994. Given the symbolic resonance of wealth and prosperity embodied by bananas in Germany, this change hit

---

[3] Latin American bananas are often referred to as 'dollar bananas' because they are grown by American multinationals such as Chiquita and Dole on huge, efficient plantations in Latin America.

[4] With 14.9 kg/capita compared to an average EU consumption of 9.3 kg/capita (Bessko 1996: 265).

[5] In 1992, bananas cost $1.3/kg in Germany, vs. $2.07 in the UK (Sutton 1997).

Germans hard. When German Chancellor Konrad Adenauer had returned from his victorious negotiation resulting in a special 'banana protocol' attached to the Treaty of Rome in 1957, he had brought a banana to the podium of the Bundestag and hailed the fruit for '[representing] the hope of many of us and a necessity for all of us!' that the days of past privation and humiliation were behind them. In East Germany, political leaders had used bananas to 'play Santa Claus of the nation', blessing the officially atheist East Germany with a special December treat. When the Berlin wall fell, East Germans had embraced capitalist bananas, consuming twice as many bananas as West Germans—more than two per person per day (Rodden 2001: 72).

Outvoted on the European banana regime, the German government took the unusual step of airing internal EU dirty laundry by adding a written reservation to the Uruguay Round accord, joined by Belgium, Denmark, Luxembourg, and the Netherlands (Bessko 1996: 8). It then twice challenged the EU policy in front of the European Court of Justice (ECJ).[6] In its first EU legal challenge Germany, joined by Belgium and the Netherlands, raised three arguments: the regulation violated fundamental rights granted by EU law; the regulation was not covered by the provisions of the common agricultural policy (CAP); and the regulation violated GATT law. The ECJ's October 1994 ruling rejected the German arguments, declaring that the Council of Ministers had not overstepped its powers in establishing the regime and that the European judges did not have to take GATT provisions into consideration, except in special circumstances.[7]

Challenges within the GATT/WTO continued as well. After the EU implemented its new banana regime, the 'dollar bananas' producers asked for the establishment of another GATT panel. The January 1994 panel report concluded again in favor of the plaintiffs, but the Europeans once again blocked the results of the 'Bananas II' panel. Knowing that the new Uruguay Round agreement would make it impossible for the EU to block a WTO ruling, the EU offered a deal to the Latin American banana producers: if they were willing to forgo future action against the EU banana regime, they would get a higher quota for their banana exports to Europe, enjoy a lower tariff, and have a revised system of export licenses. In March 1994, four of these countries—Colombia, Costa Rica, Nicaragua, and Venezuela—agreed to the compromise known as the 'Framework agreement' (Lyons 1994: 3; Salas and Jackson 2000: 149). The agreement was concluded despite the protests of Guatemala, the United States, and Germany.

Germany then challenged the Framework agreement. Even though the ECJ had refused to consider the compatibility of the banana regulation with the GATT, Germany nonetheless asked the European Court of Justice to rule on the

---

[6] Case C-280/93, *Germany v. Council* [1994] ECR I-4973, ECJ; see para. 78. In a second case, the German government challenged the Commission's system for implementing the disputed regulation, but the ECJ dismissed this case on a technicality. Opinion 3/94 [1995] ECR I-4577.

[7] Case 280/93, *Germany v. Council* [1994] ECR I-4973.

Framework agreement's compatibility with the rules of the WTO. The ECJ again refused to consider whether or not the regulation violated WTO rules.[8]

Banana importers also raised myriad direct legal challenges in national and EU courts. Their most successful legal venue was in Germany. German judges were concerned that the EU banana regime might violate the German Constitution and troubled by the ECJ's refusal to review the compatibility of the banana regulation with GATT requirements—after all, European law and GATT law are equally binding within Germany. The German Constitutional Court at first appeared willing to consider that the regulation violated the German Constitution, allowing a lower court to decide if compensation was required for German importers.[9] By providing for a separate national review, the Constitutional Court signaled that German courts could be a rival forum to question the banana regime. German courts thus repeatedly sent references to the ECJ asking the same questions their government had raised, and lost on (Alter 2001: 110–15). Eventually the German courts backed off. The German Federal Fiscal Court found that national courts lost their competence to interpret GATT law when the EEC joined the GATT in 1968 and adopted its common customs tariffs and trade policy.[10] In addition, the German Constitutional Court refused to consider whether or not the regulation violated the German Constitution, arguing that so long as the ECJ is 'generally' ensuring respect for the Constitution, it would not consider whether specific European policies violate specific provisions of the German Constitution.[11]

In the fall of 1995, the United States joined in on the complaint, which could now be brought under the brand new dispute settlement procedure of the recently created World Trade Organization (WTO). This American involvement resulted from the intense lobbying efforts of Chiquita, a US-owned company operating in Latin America, which had made extensive investments based on their belief that the European banana market would be liberalized.[12] In September 1994, Chiquita Brands Inc. filed a Section 301 petition with the United States Trade Representative (USTR), claiming it was losing millions because of the new

---

[8] The ECJ ruled that it did not need to review the compatibility of the Framework agreement with WTO law because the Framework agreement had come into force with the Uruguay Round, and thus any assessment as to the agreement's legality raised under EEC Article 228 would be legally moot. Opinion 3/94 on the Framework agreement on bananas, decision of 13 December 1995 [1995] ECR I-4577.

[9] First Banana rulings: *Firma T. Port v. Hauptzollamt Hamburg-Jonas*, BVerfG decisions of 25 January 1995, 2 BvR 2689/94 and 2 BvR 52/95, [1995] EuZW 126. *Firma T. Port v. Hauptzollamt Hamburg-Jonas*, Verwaltungsgerichtshof Hessen decision of 9 February 1995, [1995] EuZW 222.

[10] 1996 judgment of the German Federal Fiscal Court, *Europäische Zeitschrift fur Wirtschaftsrecht (EuZW)* 126–8, cited in Gerard G. Sander (1998).

[11] Second Banana rulings: Firma T. Port v. Hauptzollamt Hamburg-Jonas (FG Hamburg order 19 May 1995 [1995] EuZW 413. Firma T. Port v. Hauptzollamt Hamburg-Jonas BFH decision 22 August 1995. Firma T. Port v. Hauptzollamt Hamburg-Jonas BVerfG decisions of 26 April 1995, 2 BvR 760/95, [1995] EuZW 412.

[12] 'Yes, we have no profits' (2001) *Fortune* 144(11): 182–96.

restrictive EU regime. Dole Foods and Del Monte, Chiquita's main competitors, did not join in the process, because they had fewer stakes in the matter as a result of different planning (Stovall and Hathaway 2003; Webber and Cadot 2002). After intense lobbying by Chiquita, the USTR filed a request for the establishment of a WTO dispute settlement panel.

The US was joined as a complainant by Guatemala, Honduras, Mexico, and Ecuador (the world's largest producer of bananas, which had become a member of the WTO in January 1996). They argued that the EU banana regime violated the General Agreement on Tariffs and Trade (GATT), the General Agreement on Trade in Services (GATS), and the Agreement on Import Licensing Procedures. The United States' complaint focused not on the preferential access accorded to the ACP countries but on the licensing arrangements and on preferential tariffs provided to the Latin American 'framework countries' which had signed banana trade agreements with the EU (Hanrahan 1999).

The WTO issued the 'Bananas III' panel report in May 1997, finding that the EU's preferential tariffs for ACP countries were not per se discriminatory because the EU had secured a special waiver for the Lomé agreement, but the three-tiered quota system was inconsistent with WTO rules. The panel ruling was reaffirmed by the WTO's Appellate Body (AB) in September 1997, and the EU was ordered to put its banana regime in conformity with WTO obligations.[13]

Beginning on 1 January 1999, the EU added an additional 353,000 tons to Latin America's quota of 75 ECU per ton tariffs (to take into account consumption in its newest member states—Austria, Finland, and Sweden), and replaced its import licensing system with one it claimed was WTO-compatible (Hanrahan 1999), but the USTR complained again because Europe retained its quotas. The WTO authorized retaliatory sanctions.[14] The US imposed tariffs of 100 per cent on $192 million worth of EU imports into the US (none of which were agricultural products), keeping the political pressure on Germany but exempting the Netherlands and Denmark 'in recognition of their voting record against the adoption of the new banana regime'.[15] Ecuador was authorized to levy tariffs on European intellectual property (McCall Smith 2005). The banana dispute was finally resolved in April 2001. The United States suspended its retaliatory sanctions when the EU agreed to implement a new regime based on a tariff-only system by 2006, after a transitory period during which bananas would

---

[13] Regime For The Importation, Sale and Distribution of Bananas, DSB Report September 2007 (WT/DS27/AB/R); AB Report May 1997 (WT/DS27/R/USA).

[14] Regime For The Importation, Sale and Distribution of Bananas, AB Report May 1997 (WT/DS27/R/USA). Aspects of the United States retaliatory system were challenged in: Import Measures on Certain Products from the European Communities, AB-2000-9, WT/DS165/AB/R (00–5330), adopted by Dispute Settlement Body 10 January 2001.

[15] USTR Charlene Barchefsky, quoted in 'USTR announces list of European products subject to increased tariffs' Document 98–113, Office of the USTR.

be imported into the EU through licenses distributed on the basis of past trade (Josling 2003; Tangermann 2003).

III. Unpeeling the Layers: Nesting/Overlapping and the Banana Dispute

In a world of independent decisions and non-nested regimes, the conflict over bananas makes little sense. The sums involved—at least for the US and Europe—were very small, whereas the protracted dispute was costly for European banana consumers, cumbersome for European importers, and very disadvantageous to importers lacking favorable import quotas. When the US retaliated by imposing tariffs on goods unrelated to bananas, additional costs were created for European exporters of these goods—from bed linen to coffee-makers. Ecuador's strategy also established a new legal precedent for cross-retaliation across WTO agreements (McCall Smith 2005).

As one of the first test cases of the new WTO dispute resolution system, the dispute also generated non-negligible legitimacy costs for the WTO. The new WTO system had made it practically impossible to block panel rulings, yet Europe still refused to change its policy even in the face of negative legal rulings and retaliation. Europe's intransigence was evidence of the weakness and unfairness of the WTO system where the powerful could ignore WTO rulings and buy their way out of compliance, while poorer countries were constrained by retaliation to comply (Alter 2003: 787). Meanwhile the banana and almost concomitant beef hormones rulings infuriated many in Europe who saw the WTO decisions as rulings by an unelected multinational body at the behest of the United States, punishing Europe because it chose to import its bananas from poor former colonies (which seemingly had nothing else to export, short of turning to drug production). Tapping into this discontent, nascent anti-globalization groups trumpeted these rulings as an unacceptable intrusion on national sovereignty in the name of economic liberalization run amok and the protection of American corporate power (Gordon and Meunier 2001). These arguments culminated in November 1999 where anti-globalization activists, some of them dressed as bananas, contributed to the derailment of the launching of the new millennium round of multilateral trade negotiations in Seattle, the first one undertaken under the new WTO.

This section uses counter-factual analysis to explore how the politics regarding bananas would have been different if a layer of the nesting—EU, Lomé, WTO—were removed. In thinking about what each layer added, we gain an insight into the politics that the nesting of the dispute generated. Of course counter-factual analysis always involves speculation, but it allows us to at least consider the possibility that the costly choices made at various points in the dispute were the result of the nesting/overlapping of institutions.

Scenario 1: No European Union regime

The revamping of the EU banana policies and the creation of a single EU-wide banana regime were part of the drive to complete the internal market. Without supranational EU politics at play, the original practices would likely have continued: countries with historic ties to ACP countries would have continued to apply tariffs to non-ACP bananas as historic agreements allowed, other European countries would have continued with their uniform 20 per cent tariff, and Germany would have kept its own policy of duty-free banana imports. Thus, one concrete effect of the EU's existence was a change in German, Benelux, Danish, and Irish policy that probably would not have occurred otherwise. The first GATT banana ruling had only condemned the French, Italian, Portuguese, Spanish, and United Kindgom discriminatory tariff, and that was before the Lomé waiver. With the WTO Lomé waiver, the unharmonized GATT banana regime would not have violated any WTO rules.

The drive to complete the common market created pressure to harmonize the EU banana policy—but such pressure did not dictate how harmonization had to occur. The justification for the banana regime was that supporting ACP banana production was part of Europe's development aid policy. Cadot and Weber hypothesize that the EU could have accomplished its aid to ACP countries by levying a 17 per cent tariff on dollar bananas instead, distributing the tariff proceeds to ACP countries.[16] Because the EU had a WTO waiver for the Lomé Convention, such a tariff would have been WTO legal. Instead, the EU crafted and then defended its banana policy, with a complex quota system that created inequalities among importers and required large amounts of administrative resources to administer and adjudicate. Furthermore, the quota system created a vested group of favored importers who fought against any change in the rules. Given all the political, legal, and administrative costs associated with the quota system, why choose the quota system? Internal EU politics made the particular form of harmonization, despite its many drawbacks, desirable nonetheless. The main disadvantage of the tariff system compared to the quota system was that EU budget rules do not allow for the earmarking of tariff revenue (Webber and Cadot 2002: 10) probably because if the EU could earmark tariff revenue, it would generate an incentive to protect. Since tariffs revenues could not be earmarked, choosing direct aid would have meant consuming part of the EU budget for

---

[16] The EU claimed that aiding the banana industry was preferable to providing direct aid. Caribbean bananas are grown on small, family-run farms, and bananas seem to be the only year-round crop that can recover quickly enough after storm or flood damage. Moreover, according to the defenders of the EU regime, the only alternative crop for these countries in the absence of markets for their banana exports would be drugs. Perhaps. But drug production is also a problem in Latin America, and Europe is also vulnerable to the effects of drug production in Latin America. In addition, a straight-up tariff on dollar bananas might have provided a sufficient benefit for ACP producers.

foreign aid. A 17 per cent across-the-board tariff on dollar bananas would also create import pressure for the few French and Spanish banana producers located in France's Dom Tom territories and in Spain's islands at a time when finance ministers were committed to trimming the common agricultural policy's budget. The EU ended up giving subsidies to local banana producers, but at the time the single EU banana regime was debated, negotiators thought that the subsidies would have been bigger without the quota system to boost the price of bananas overall, and that the Framework agreement would help Europe avoid any WTO costs for its policy. Indeed, perhaps the chief attraction of the Banana Regulation was that it generated no budgetary costs—no immediate foreign aid requirement and no immediate subsidy requirement—while satisfying those ACP and European banana importers seeking rents.

The existence of the EU layer also explains the legal and political imbroglio in which Germany found itself. German importers and consumers were the hardest hit by the changes. Past import levels were determinant in setting up import quotas for the new system. Having focused on Latin American bananas for so long, German importers lacked long-standing import relationships with ACP exporters, and thus they were disadvantaged by the EU system for allocating quotas. The distress of German importers was real enough to encourage lower German courts to order an injunction in the application of the EU banana regime, and to repeatedly ask the European Court of Justice and the German Constitutional Court to (re)consider whether or not the EU banana regime was legal, and whether it undermined the basic rights of importers by denying them their ability to exist as commercial enterprises.[17] Without Germany's overall commitment to the EU we might have expected Germany to choose defection, and thus to refuse to enforce the quota regime. With the EU, it appears that Germany accepted a deal for Bavarian farmers in exchange for the banana regime (Webber and Cadot 2002: 26).

Finally, the move towards the single European market and the consolidation of European integration were also a central reason for the involvement of the United States in the dispute. Chiquita had bet that the Single European Act would lead to a free market throughout Europe and, in the years prior to the creation of the EU-wide banana regime, had invested heavily in banana plantations in Latin America and in shipping equipment. When the EU finally adopted its banana regime, Chiquita was in a real bind. With excess capacity and huge debt, in a very real and personal way the fortunes of Chiquita's CEO became tied to the policy adopted by the EU.[18] This explains why Chiquita gave expensive political donations to both the Republican and Democratic political parties, and extensively

---

[17] First Banana rulings: *Firma T. Port v. Hauptzollamt Hamburg-Jonas*, BVerfG decisions of 25 January 1995, First Chamber of the Second Senate 2 BvR 2689/94 and 2 BvR 52/95 [1995] EuZW 126. *Firma T. Port v. Hauptzollamt Hamburg-Jonas*, Verwaltungsgerichtshof Hessen decision of 9 February 1995, [1995] EuZW 222. Discussed in Alter (2001: 112–16).
[18] 'Yes, We have no Profits' (2001) *Fortune* 144(11): 182–96; Taylor (2003).

lobbied Congress to become involved in the dispute while its competitors Dole and Del Monte stayed out of the case.

Thus the EU layer created the need to harmonize European member states' banana import rules; it led to the adoption of the convoluted quota system that ran afoul of WTO rules; it created the economic stress and legal dilemmas for Germany and its courts; and it created the incentive for Chiquita to invest in expanding its export capacities, which then led Chiquita to work so hard to challenge the EU's banana regime.

Scenario 2: No Lomé regime

A harmonized system of tariff-free bananas would have violated the Lomé Convention's promise of preferential access to the European market for bananas, forcing ACP countries to compete with Latin dollar bananas that are cheaper to produce because the climate and terrain in Latin countries is superior for bananas, and multinational corporations have invested in Latin banana production in ways that small family producers in ACP countries cannot replicate.

The larger unstated issue, however, was that the Lomé Conventions were designed to help out current and former colonies of some European states. The 1957 German banana protocol and the absence of a coordinated banana regime for so many years was a symptom of the deep antipathy European states without colonies felt towards the idea of preferences for former colonies. The Lomé Conventions offered a brilliant packaging to deal with this cleavage. Europe could boast that the Lomé Conventions represented the largest financial and political framework to facilitate North–South aid and cooperation, while member states wanting to aid former colonies (France, and then later the UK and Spain) could offer preferential treatment and thus maintain their 'special relationship' with former colonies. But the very specific Lomé promise of preferential access for ACP bananas brought the old cleavage back to the fore. John Rodden summarized the unsaid sentiment:

The new EU import regulations aimed to help banana growers in European tropical islands (e.g. France's Martinique and Guadeloupe, Spain's Canary Islands) and in former European colonies in Africa, the Caribbean, and the Pacific. Germany, which lost all of its own colonies after World War I balked: Why should its own interests be sacrificed to those of France and Spain, whose banana growing former island colonies have been the beneficiary of the 1993 (policy)? (Rodden 2001: 69)

Giving preference to very poor countries was, in itself, not the problem. The GATT had granted a waiver for the Lomé Convention in October 1994, which lasted until the end of Lomé IV (2000). This waiver became a focal point of developing countries. As the date of expiration approached, 56 ACP members of the WTO threatened to oppose new trade negotiations on non-related issues—such as environment, labor, and the 'Singapore issues' of investment and competition policy—in the upcoming Doha round of multilateral trade negotiations unless the waiver was extended. The WTO extended the waiver until 2008, covering the new Cotonou agreements that had replaced the Lomé Convention. The nesting of Lomé countries within WTO allowed ACP countries to leverage their political power. The EU could not play a two-level game telling the Lomé countries that the WTO prohibited the policy. Instead, ACP countries could play the WTO game to demand a waiver and pressure European countries to maintain their advantaged market access.

Scenario 3: No WTO regime

The WTO system differs from its predecessor, the GATT dispute resolution system, in the inability of states to block adoption of adverse panel decisions. The creation of the WTO led to an immediate change in EU behavior, though still unsatisfactory from the perspective of the US and Ecuador. Anticipating a challenge to the banana regime under the new WTO system, the EU offered a deal to the Latin American countries that were parties to the GATT case: according to the 1994 'Framework agreement', the EU would raise the global quota to 100,000 tons and reallocate unused import licenses, in exchange for the signatories dropping their claims to future GATT cases. Latin American countries started to disagree among themselves over the allocation of the quota within their group, leading the EU to drop its offer of a deal and to then block the panel report. However, soon after, Colombia, Costa Rica, Nicaragua, and Venezuela accepted a reduction in the EU tariff and an increase in their tariff quota to 2.2 million tons, leading to an arrangement that was similar to the status quo ante of the old EU banana regime. In exchange, these countries promised not to challenge the banana regime until its expiration in December 2000 (Sutton 1997). This was exactly what was supposed to happen—the new enforceability of WTO law was expected to encourage settlements in the direction of greater compliance with the law. (Ecuador, which was not a member of GATT at the time, was not part of this arrangement; nor was the US.)

European diplomats saw the quota system as an expensive pay-off scheme to compensate the 'losers' of the banana regime. Preferential import quotas were the equivalent of cash in the pockets of importers—they could buy dollar bananas at a low price, and pocket the profit reaped by selling these bananas on the price-inflated European market. Since banana companies themselves owned many European fruit-importing companies, quota profits went directly into their pockets. Every increase in the preferential quotas of Latin American producers was akin to direct compensation for firms hurt by Europe's policy. Because those most impacted by the agreement were compensated, Europeans were upset that the Framework agreement was being challenged by the US, which had far less at stake.[19]

[19] Based on interviews with members of the European Commission, 7 and 8 September 2004, Brussels.

Without the WTO layer, it is unlikely that the US would have been involved at all in the dispute. Before the WTO was formally created, the US had its Section 301 system to unilaterally retaliate against unfair trade practices, but it is not clear whether the EU would have been in violation of any trade agreement vis-à-vis the US. Since the problem was an EU policy towards third countries, and the US is not a significant producer of bananas,[20] it is doubtful that the US would have pressed the case under Section 301—especially in the absence of a means to enforce compliance. The WTO layer created a mechanism to challenge a WTO illegal policy, even if the impact in the US was only indirect. Chiquita lobbied Congressmen who in turn put pressure on the United States Trade Representative (USTR)—an executive agency that serves at the pleasure and behest of Congress. Because of the corporate interests of Chiquita and its strong lobbying power, the USTR put its negotiators under considerable pressure to aggressively pursue the banana case in the WTO (Hanrahan 1999; Stovall and Hathaway 2003; Webber and Cadot 2002).

While only Chiquita had direct interests at stake in the dispute, many US interest groups beyond Chiquita were concerned about the precedents that might be established in the banana case. For them the banana dispute was a perfect test case precisely because few American and European interests were directly at stake. US beef producers and the producers of genetically modified foods saw the case as a harbinger of what might happen when the issues of beef hormones and genetically modified foods would be litigated, and thus they wanted WTO rules enforced.

Ecuador, the world's largest exporter of bananas, was the one country with a big stake that was not compensated in the Framework agreement because it was not part of GATT at the time. The United States was keen to have Ecuador on its side because Ecuador had a clear interest in the case (where the US did not) and because Ecuador's interests were domestic, since its industry was not owned by American multinationals. According to James McCall Smith, 'officials in Ecuador decided that the case was of such paramount concern that they rushed their negotiations to gain entry to the WTO in order to ensure their status as a complainant' (McCall Smith 2005: 10). Two weeks after its accession to the WTO, Ecuador joined the US suit (McCall Smith 2005). Without US support in the form of the joint suit, it is questionable whether Ecuador would have joined the WTO until later in time. In the end Ecuador was disappointed by the dispute's outcome. While it had won the right to retaliation, Ecuador found itself unable to levy fines without harming itself more than Europe. Ecuador was so upset with the US–EU settlement that the Foreign Minister threatened to demand the

---

[20] Hawaii produces bananas for domestic consumption. It was argued that by diminishing consumption for dollar bananas in Europe, the price of Hawaiian bananas could be adversely affected. This may be true, but most commentators explain US actions by focusing on Chiquita bananas' considerable efforts to lobby Congress rather than the Hawaiian banana industry.

United States withdraw a military base from Ecuador.[21] Still, according to Smith, Ecuador got more from the settlement than it might have, had it not joined the WTO and been party to the dispute (McCall Smith 2005: 32).

On the one hand, the WTO layer 'resolved' the dispute. The threat of WTO litigation led the EU to craft the 'Framework agreement' and to ultimately change its quota system of import license allocation. On the other hand, the WTO layer exacerbated the conflict by turning it into a transatlantic battle and, ironically, by creating the incentives for political bargaining where the general public seems to be the greatest loser. The public loses twice in the case—bananas are more expensive in Europe than they would be otherwise, and banana importers get to extract rents instead of either the EU or the ACP banana producers collecting revenue to distribute. Indeed in some respects, more layers means more actors that have to be bought off and compensated. Even if the EU really does convert the system to a tariff-based system with a lower tariff for ACP bananas and an across-the-board tariff for dollar bananas, banana consumers will continue to pay 'rents'; thus one can question how much the WTO has led to a more free-trade-oriented system, or shifted the balance of power in favor of free traders over protectionist interests.

IV. Conclusion

The banana dispute was the first transatlantic dispute to be adjudicated under the newly created WTO and, as such, it created a precedent for dealing with a lack of a hierarchy of norms in the post-Cold War era. This complicated case is an example of the new trade politics—multi-layered, multi-venue, with provisions imbricated within and across multiple international agreements. As the number of international commitments proliferates, the nesting and overlapping of institutional regimes will become increasingly prevalent. How will this shape international politics? Can we derive any insights from the banana case that may be generalized to future conflicts created by nested/overlapping international regimes?

George Tsebelis reasoned from theory that 'seemingly suboptimal choices indicate the presence of nested games' (Tsebelis 1990: 248). We show specifically how nesting contributed to the choices made. In many respects the banana dispute represents a 'typically' complicated example of the consequences of institutional nesting/overlapping in the international realm. The dispute was created by nesting, since the completion of the single European market produced a clash between the EU Lomé Convention obligations vis-à-vis its former colonies and its membership in the GATT/WTO trading system. The different layers of

---

[21] 'Ecuadorian banana growers request US base withdrawal due to new import scheme', in *World News Connection*, 26 April 2001.

nesting help us understand the seemingly puzzling behaviors in the dispute—the adoption and then defense of the convoluted quota system, and the strategies of political and legal actors within the dispute.

The absence of clear hierarchy between all the layers involved—European member states, the EU, the Lomé countries, and WTO—makes the behavior of legal decision-makers more understandable. Legally and politically, the relationship of EU law to WTO law is ambiguous. EU member states have accepted unitary EU representation within the WTO, yet they still retain their individual memberships. The decision to replace member state participation with EU participation was never made because the issue of the Commission's authority over trade in services was too contentious (Meunier and Nicolaidis 1999; Bourgeois 2000: 73). Thus the problem of whether a state is obligated to the EU agreement over the WTO agreement (or vice versa) was left unresolved by political bodies. This ambiguity allowed for the internal opposition to the regime to be exploited in European member states' national courts, and to bubble over into the Uruguay Round negotiations. This ambiguity also made it hard for the ECJ to answer the question of whether WTO obligations are legally supreme to EU law. On the one hand, the ECJ's refusal to review the compatibility of EU law with WTO law is legally remarkable in that the hallmark of the legal method is the like application of reason and rules across cases. Yet here we find the ECJ refusing to do exactly what it asked national courts to do—enforce international rules at home—and we even find the ECJ interpreting similarly worded texts differently based on the political context (Bourgeois 2000). This inconsistency makes sense if we consider that the ECJ is acting like a supreme court nested in the international order. Almost all domestic courts avoid 'tying the hands' of governments, forcing them to comply with international agreements when other executive branches are not similarly bound. The ECJ tries when possible to interpret EU law consistently with WTO law. When the Council explicitly invokes international legal obligations or makes clear that the EU law is intended to bring the EU into compliance with an international obligation, the ECJ acts as the Council's enforcer, making sure that EU law and member state law comply with international legal obligations. However, it leaves the decision about whether or not to comply with WTO rules as an issue for political bodies to resolve.[22]

The nested nature of the dispute also helps us understand Europe's behavior. Not only did it take an extremely long time for Europe to change its policy; Europe's banana policy remains significantly more costly than necessary if the goal was simply to aid Lomé countries.[23] The politically and financially expensive, administratively convoluted European banana policy and the legal rulings

---

[22] The ECJ has maintained its position that it is under no obligation to consider whether EU law violates WTO law. The ECJ has denied the direct effect of WTO law, and it has rejected the notion that the community is liable when WTO retaliations affect European firms (Alemanno 2008).

[23] Part of the delay was that decision-makers waited for legal and political challenges in the different layers to play themselves out, but European actors were also buying time.

by European courts only make sense if we consider the nested context of Europe's banana policy. Otherwise Europe would have gone with preferential tariffs that would have satisfied the WTO and Germany alike.

With the ECJ position now defined through its banana and other rulings, European domestic actors may decide it is not worth trying to challenge common policies in European courts on the basis of conflicts with international treaties. How long national courts will stay out of resolving conflicts across international commitments, however, is yet to be seen. As long as conflicts of international rules represent complicated political bargains among competing interests, national courts are likely to presume that they could do no better at resolving the issue than the political or international judicial bodies. But it is hard to imagine that the German Constitutional Court would be willing to hold to its current position should an ECJ ruling create a serious and politically unpopular violation of its constitution, even if the ECJ 'generally' respects the rights of European citizens.[24]

Can findings from this study be generalized beyond the case of the EU to analyze the conditions under which nesting/overlapping is likely to result in conflictual outcomes? We can expect to find contortions and inconsistencies when actors that enforce hierarchy in the domestic realm are confronted with issues related to the international realm. This finding is significant because a number of scholars place their hope for international law in domestic courts which can become enforcers of international rules at home (Hathaway 2004; Slaughter 2004). This study suggests that the goal of domestically enforced international law may remain elusive unless political actors declare some hierarchy among the conflicting obligations they create. In addition, given the inherently nested nature of the EU, in which every deal represents a complex bargain among states and European institutions made in the shadow of the WTO, we can expect trade-related EU policy to be complicated to decipher. Where most observers blame Europe's technocratic nature for its Byzantine policies, this study suggests that the real problem is the EU's nested nature in the international system. With the number of 'regional trade bloc' exceptions proliferating in the WTO, we may well find that other regional organizations face similar realities. These regions may also follow Europe in the public being put off by the complicated nature of the region's supranational politics and policies.

How these political contortions ultimately influence international politics is not entirely clear. The banana dispute was a specific dispute about a specific policy, but it was not an 'old-style' trade dispute about protecting the domestic losers from international competition. Ecuador had direct interests at stake, but there were no powerful European or American banana producers to protect. Rather the

---

[24] Since this essay was published, the German Constitutional Court did reverse itself, finding that an EU arrest warrant was not applicable in Germany. See *Europäischer Haftbefehl* decision of 18 July 2005 113 BVerfGE 273 (2005), reprinted in 32 EuGRZ 387. This decision is discussed in Hinarejos Parga (2006).

European protection of the Lomé guarantees was about development aid through off-budget measures. The symbolic goal of maintaining the viability of Third World producers also resonated domestically. Moreover, it was not an 'old-style' dispute because the banana politics spilled over into other international arenas: Lomé countries linked their case to the unrelated 'Singapore issues' of investment and competition policy; Caribbean countries (unsuccessfully) lobbied the US to drop its banana case during the 1994 Summit of the Americas; and anger over the banana and beef hormones cases contributed to the EU's decision to pick up again its challenge to the US export subsidy regime (the FSC case). For the ongoing dispute over genetically modified crops, the likelihood of political spillover is even greater since it touches on the delicate issue of how regulators deal with scientific uncertainty, an issue that is relevant in environment, food safety, and nuclear technology politics. Because there is no clear hierarchy of international agreements, a legal victory or loss in one venue is highly likely to stir politics in another venue to try to undercut the authority of the settlement. Raustiala and Victor's discussion of the 'regime complex' seems to exemplify such politics, showing actors and countries rushing to use different forums to create different sources of authority for their preferred policy (Raustiala and Victor 2004). Raustiala and Victor hypothesize a spread of 'regime complexes', and the politics such complexes engender. Our study reinforces this finding by suggesting that the absence of hierarchy itself can be an intentional strategy, which drives a demand for international agreements that enshrine different perspectives on hotly contested issues. We continue on this line of research in a symposium that will be published in *Perspective on Politics* in 2009.

This study has highlighted an important question worthy of further investigation and systematic reflection: Under what conditions are nesting and overlapping more likely to result in conflictual outcomes? In a way, the banana dispute may be a unique case. The multiple layers of international commitments not only created the conflict, but also made it much harder to resolve. With perhaps the exception of international disputes on hormones and biosafety, most other nested issues in world politics do not explode. Understanding why in some cases the dog barks and in others it does not might usefully prevent the emergence of other protracted, potentially costly inter-institutional conflicts.

PART IV

BEYOND EUROPEAN COURT POLITICS—THE ECJ IN A COMPARATIVE PERSPECTIVE

11

Agents or Trustees? International Courts in their Political Context (2008)

Delegation of interpretive authority to International Courts is expanding exponentially. In 1985 there were seven international legal bodies meeting the *Project on International Courts and Tribunal's (PICT)* definition of an international court, meaning: (1) a permanent institution, (2) composed of independent judges, (3) that adjudicate disputes between two or more entities, one of which is a state or international organization, (4) working on the basis of predetermined rules of procedure, and (5) rendering decisions that are binding (Alter book manuscript in progress: Chapter 1).[1] Today there are 26 international courts that meet this definition and they are increasingly active, having issued 69 per cent of their over 15,000 decisions, opinions, and rulings since 1990 (see Table 2.1 in Chapter 2).

The promise of delegation to international courts (ICs) is that ICs will create a legal and political space where regular politics and the power disparities in the world do not shape how the law is interpreted and applied. The idea that ICs can take away state autonomy in interpreting international commitments, and empower actors outside of powerful states, is for many unsettling. A number of scholars have used the ideas of Principal–Agent (P–A) theory to argue that states are actually controlling what merely appear to be independent international courts. P–A theory focuses on the unique tools of political control that states have by virtue of being part of the 'Principal' body that writes, and thus can re-write, the Agent's 'delegation contract'. P–A theory posits that the ability of the Principal to 'sanction' an Agent by changing the contract (firing or not reappointing the Agent, rewriting contractual terms to undercut the Agent's realm of authority, or cutting the Agent's budget) provides states with significant political leverage that they can use to reign in Agents who go astray. P–A theory expects political control to be incomplete—some degree of 'agency slack' (unwanted Agent behavior) will be an inherent cost of delegation. The theory also expects courts to be relatively independent Agents compared perhaps to administrative agencies, if only because recontracting is harder to orchestrate with respect

---

[1] <http://www.pict-pcti.org/matrix/matrixintro.html>.

to courts compared to administrative agencies. But recontracting tools should nonetheless provide significant influence over IC decision-making. For example, Paul Stephan argues:

> Knowing that they can be replaced, the members of the [international] tribunal have an incentive not to do anything that will upset the countries with nominating authority. In those cases where the members nonetheless veer off in an unanticipated direction, the nominating state can institute a course correction within a relatively short period of time by choosing 'sounder' candidates for the tribunal. Thus one should not expect ambitious, systematic, and comprehensive law coming from an institution endowed with the authority to develop unified law on an international level. (Stephan 2002: 7–8)

Most comparative judicial politics scholars reject out of hand arguments like Stephan's, believing as a matter of course that judges are not mere Agents of the legislative actors that create them, and knowing that examples of ambitious and systematic legal construction, even by international courts, are easy to find (Burley and Mattli 1993; Stone Sweet and Brunell 1998; Weiler 1991). But one-sentence rejections fail to convince because they do not take Principal–Agent arguments seriously enough. Surely there must be some limit on the autonomy of judges. Surely contracting tools must provide some influence over international judges. Convinced of the rational basis of their theory, proponents of P–A theory place the burden of proof on judicial politics scholars, demanding they show that state Principals are not the actual puppet masters of ICs (Garrett 1995).

This article builds on the arguments in Chapter 6, providing a theoretical basis to question Principal–Agent theory, as it elucidates the nature of relations between members of the Principal and the putative Agent. Section I shows that while P–A theory appears to generate testable hypotheses, the generalized conjectures of P–A theory are unfalsifiable in practice. Since one can never prove that recontracting politics are not at play, the burden of proof rational choice scholars demand cannot be met. Instead, we need a good reason *not to presume* that recontracting politics are salient. The rest of the article provides such a reason.

Section II argues that delegation to Trustees is inherently different from delegation to Agents. Principals choose to delegate to Trustees, as opposed to Agents, when the point of delegation is to harness the authority of the Trustee so as to enhance the legitimacy of political decision-making. Trustees are: (1) selected because of their personal reputation or professional norms, (2) given independent authority to make decisions according to their best judgment or professional criteria, and (3) empowered to act on behalf of a beneficiary. Section II explains why these three factors render the Principal's recontracting tools less politically relevant in shaping Trustee behavior. While Trustees are less manipulable via recontracting tools, Trustees are not apolitical or immune to state pressure. Trustees are subject to the sorts of legitimacy and rhetorical pressures of all political decision-makers. To the extent that Trustees must rely on others to execute their decisions, they must also worry about maintaining the support of those who implement their decisions.

Section III situates international courts in the category of Trustee–Agents. The original article focused on two hard cases where ICs clearly acted against the wishes of powerful states, and in the face of clear sanctioning threats. For this volume, I have added back a third European case. The cases show how ICs respond to state sanctioning and legitimacy pressure, and how because of their independence ICs play a role in promoting political change (even when a ruling is ignored). International courts contribute to political change by delegitimizing circumspect arguments used by powerful state actors. IC rulings can shift the political status quo by providing an authoritative (re)interpretation of what the law means, and by providing incentives and resources for actors within and outside of powerful states to pressure governments to change their policy. I supplement the hard cases with additional examples where powerful and weak states engage in legitimacy and rhetorical politics with and through ICs, in an effort to facilitate political change.

International relations scholars are right that states are concerned about IC behaving in ways they did not intend, and do not want. But Principal–Agent theory misleads in its emphasis on the existence as opposed to the usage of recontracting politics as a means to shape IC decision-making. The Trustee argument provides analytical boundaries that help one know when to expect Principal's sanctioning tools to be politically significant. It also redirects the analyst to look at a broader range of actors that shape Trustee behavior, showing how actors with no real ability to change the Trustee's contract may nonetheless be equally influential in shaping Trustee politics, and thus Principal politics. The ultimate goal of this analysis is to call into question the 'rational expectations' assertion that because Principals could sanction international courts, we should presume that courts are controlled Agents, self-censoring to avoid a sanction. By providing theoretical reasons to reject the Principal control presumption, the analysis aims to redirect the analytical focus towards examining how ICs interact with states (by enhancing the position of those sub-state actors favoring law compliance) and how states live with the fact that they cannot control ICs (by maneuvering to settle cases outside of court, employing rhetorical politics to influence ICs, using legitimacy politics to respond to unwanted IC rulings, and when all else fails resorting to exit in the form of non-compliance or exit from the legal system altogether).

I. Empirical and Ontological Problems Within Principal–Agent Theory

P–A theory's main attraction is its parsimony combined with the intuitive sense that delegation only makes sense if it serves the Principal's interest. Most political science P–A analyses have as a dependent variable explaining Agent discretion/ slippage—independent action that is not fully controlled by the Principal.

Highly Controlled Agent	Highly Autonomous Agent
a. Highly transparent if Agent is slacking (low levels of uncertainty, low informational advantages for the Agent)	d. Great uncertainty as to whether or not Agent is slacking (high informational advantages for the Agent)
b. Low thresholds required to recontract	e. High thresholds required to recontract
c. No employment protection and/or short-term appointments so slacking Agents can be easily replaced	f. High employment protection and long term lengths (i.e. lifetime employment) so P has little political leverage over A

Figure 11.1. P–A theory's expectations about Agent autonomy

P–A theory posits that the size and extent of discretion/slippage is a function of: (1) informational disparities that allow Agents to obscure their slippage and (2) recontracting decision rules that create costs and difficulties associated with recontracting. By focusing on these factors, P–A theory generates hypotheses that locate different Agents along a continuum of highly 'controlled' Agents to highly 'autonomous' Agents. By conjecture, informational disparities and recontracting decision rules are also seen as determining the likelihood that an Agent will act in ways the Principal does not want.

While it makes sense that some Agents would be more autonomous than others, and while P–A theory seems to generate clear predictions, as a bundle the predictions of P–A theory are highly fungible. What if the nature of the delegation contract makes it highly transparent if the Agent is slacking (a) and includes short appointment terms (c), but there are high thresholds needed to recontract (e)? The theory does not prioritize its claims, which allows scholars employing P–A theory to make contradictory claims in support of the theory. For example, proponents of P–A theory have argued that the European Court of Justice (ECJ) is not an autonomous actor because judges need to be reappointed after a fairly short term in office, and because the ECJ fears adverse recontracting (Garrett 1995; Garrett and Weingast 1993; Stephan 2002: 6–7; Tsebelis and Garrett 2001; Vaubel 2006: 133) *and* that the ECJ is a relatively autonomous actor because changing European rules requires unanimous support of states (Garrett, Kelemen, and Schulz 1998; Pollack 2003; Tallberg 2002, 2003).

Resolving which conjectures are right is harder than one might think. Who the 'Principal' is should be ascertainable by looking at which actors have authority to change the delegation contract. Yet P–A studies sometimes label the wider public, national governments, national parliaments, or other political bodies as the Principal, shifting the political actors the Agent should be responding to. Also, like all rational choice theory, P–A theory lacks a conception of preferences. Instead, most P–A theorists rely on 'revealed preferences' to ascertain what actors want, while at the same time accepting 'rational expectations' arguments that assume that Agents automatically self-censor because they can rationally expect sanctions if they act in ways the Principal does not want. The problems associated with revealed preferences are well known. Principals may be divided and unable to act, and Principals may also self-censor if sanctioning a wayward Agent will cause more grief than benefit. The 'revealed preference' would then be false. The contradictory conjectures and measurement problems mean that for the same Agent, one can generate both expectations for control and independence from P–A theory, and one can find a way to rationalize any Agent action as consistent with Principal preferences.

Since we cannot empirically falsify the expectations of Principal control thesis, we must move to the level of ontology to question the theory. P–A theory assumes that the fact of delegation defines the nature of the relationship between the Principal and the Agent. Michael Tierney, Darren Hawkins, David Lake, and Daniel Nelson provide a good and clear definition of delegation, one that is revealing of the conceptualization that animates P–A theory:

Delegation is a conditional grant of authority from a *Principal* to an *Agent* in which the latter is empowered to act on behalf of the former. This grant of authority is limited in time or scope and must be revocable by the Principal. Principals and Agents are, in the language of constructivism, mutually constitutive. That is, like 'master' and 'slave,' an actor cannot be a Principal without an Agent, and vice versa. The actors are defined by their relationship to each other. (Hawkins et al. 2006: 7)

By this definition, the Principal *will have* the power to revoke or change the contract, and thus it will have contracting power over the Agent. Because the Principal constitutes the Agent, and is the only actor with contracting power to appoint, fire, cut the budget, or rewrite the mandate of the Agent, P–A theory suggests that being a Principal confers a unique, privileged, and hierarchical source of leverage over the Agent. This shrunken universe, in which there are only Principals and Agents united by a contract, does not allow other actors to matter, or concerns other than recontracting to animate the Agent. Since recontracting is a power source that only the Principal can wield, sanctioning via recontracting becomes emphasized to the exclusion of other sources of power. Especially for international relations, conceiving of state power solely in terms of recontracting power is too limited. At the same time, to include as part of the P–A framework *any* type of state power would lose sight of the main value added of P–A theory— the notion that *being a Principal confers power.*

II. Delegation to 'Agents' Compared to Delegation to 'Trustees'

P–A theory is intuitively compelling because it hardly seems rational to delegate meaningful power to highly independent actors who do not see themselves as one's Agent. Giandomenico Majone explains this puzzle by identifying two different logics of delegation—delegation to capture efficiency gains, and delegation to increase the credibility of the Principal and of political decision-making. Where the goal is primarily to reduce transaction costs, Agents are chosen based on whether they will be faithful and the delegation contract is designed to enhance Principal control over the Agent. In fiduciary delegation, what I am calling delegation to Trustees, the goal is to convince some third party that their interests are being protected. For credibility-enhancing delegation the best strategy is to delegate to an Agent whose values visibly and systematically differ from that of the Principal, to make these Agents highly independent and to refrain from meddling because 'an Agent bound to follow the directions of the delegating politician could not possibly enhance the commitment' (Majone 2001: 110). Majone is mainly trying to explain how different reasons to delegate lead to different contract design choices (e.g. designing Trustees to be institutionally insulated from political pressure). But the difference between Agents and Trustees goes beyond contract design. The reason certain Agents are chosen, the expectations in delegation, the actual powers given to the Agents, and the Agent's constituency are different in delegation to Trustees, so that the simple fact of delegation may not result in the author of the contract having privileged influence over the Agent.

Trustees are actors created through a revocable delegation act where the 'Trustee' is: (1) selected because of their personal and/or professional reputation, (2) given authority to make meaningful decisions according to the Trustee's best judgment or the Trustee's professional criteria, and (3) making these decisions on behalf of a beneficiary. Each of these factors contributes to a different politics between Principals and Trustees.

(1) Trustees are selected because of their personal and/or professional reputation. Traditional Agents are chosen because they are expected to be faithful to the Principal; they have *delegated authority* based on the Principal having authorized the Agent to act within a certain domain. 'Trustees' are chosen because they personally, or their profession in general, brings their own source of legitimacy and authority. Thus in addition to delegated authority, Trustees can have *moral authority* that comes from embodying or serving some shared higher ideals, with the moral status as a defender of these ideals providing a basis of authority. Trustees can have *rational-legal authority* if they are disinterested actors applying pre-existing rules in a like fashion across a body of cases, thereby imparting a perception of procedural justice and neutral fairness in their decisions. Trustees can also have *expert authority* that comes from specialized knowledge that is highly respected (Barnett and Finnemore 2004: 22–9). Because a Trustee's reputation as an authoritative actor is so central to their professional and personal identity and success, Trustees care greatly about maintaining their authority and may even choose a political sanction over an action that would be seen as compromising their identity as a moral, rational–legal, and/or expert decision-maker.

(2) Trustees are delegated the power to make meaningful decisions according to the Trustee's best judgment or the Trustee's professional criteria. Agents are meant to

implement the decisions of the Principal, thereby providing efficiency gains for the Principal. By contrast, Principals delegate to Trustees to enhance the credibility of the decision by distancing themselves from the decision, and by harnessing the Trustee's decision-making authority. Because Trustees have been given the power to decide based on their best judgment, Trustees actually have a different mandate than traditional Agents. This different mandate shapes expectations and interpretations regarding whether or not Trustees have slipped. Robert Keohane and Ruth Grant capture this difference:

> The trustee model of delegation... presupposes that officials will use discretion. Hence, the implicit standard for abuse of power differs from that implied by the Principal–Agent model. Deviations of the Agent's actions from the Principal's desires would not necessarily constitute abuse of power. A representative or officeholder could defend an unpopular exercise of power as legitimate by showing that it both was within the officer's jurisdiction and actually served the purposes for which he or she was authorized to act. (Keohane and Grant 2005: 32)

(3) Trustees are making their decisions on behalf of a beneficiary. Trustees have a putative beneficiary that differs from the Principal. The beneficiary may be entirely an artificial construction; what is important is that there is a third party who the Trustee supposedly is serving. The existence of the third-party beneficiary means that the Principal's position is no longer hierarchically supreme, rather both the Principal and the Trustee are trying to convince the third party audience that their behavior is legitimate. The Trustee cannot put the interests of the Principal over that of the beneficiary without engendering legitimacy problems for itself. The Principal also cannot only care about controlling the Trustee because the Trustee may in fact be deemed a superior decision-maker, and efforts cast as 'political interference' or exceeding state or Principal authority can alienate the Trustee's constituency and members of the Principal whose support is needed for recontracting.

These three differences contribute to the different politics between Principals and Trustees. Contractual politics may well be present at the moment of appointment. Once appointed, threatening a Trustee with adverse re-contracting (e.g. threatening to fire the Trustee, cut its budget, change its mandate, etc) will be relatively ineffective for a few reasons. First, the threats themselves may not be credible. In the international political context, the 'Principal' is almost always a collective entity so disgruntled actors need to convince other members of the Principal to sanction a Trustee. Reversing a Trustee decision requires more than showing that the decision was undesirable. It requires convincing other actors that the status quo ante is preferable to the new status quo created by the Trustee's decision.[2] If disgruntled actors want to frame the policy change as a sanction

---

[2] This is the context Fritz Sharpf defines as a 'joint-decision trap' where the weight of the status quo heavily biases against change, especially in a context where unanimous support is needed to legislate (Scharpf 1988).

against a slacking Trustee, they will also need to convince others that the Trustee acted inappropriately, beyond its delegated zone of discretion. Second, threatening sanctions tends to be less effective against actors guided by strong professional norms, who believe they are acting within their mandate, and who believe that their reputation or honor is on the line (Johnston 2001). Third, threatening sticks is less likely to win hearts and minds of the beneficiary when actors (judges, the population, etc) believe that the decision itself is legitimate. Since contracting threats will be relatively ineffective, and moreover because Trustees are more concerned about their reputation and maintaining their authority than they are about Principal sanctions, the main means and modes of state–Trustee contestation will be rhetorical, persuasive, and legitimacy-based as opposed to material and threatening.

Table 11.1 highlights the different politics leading to and emanating from delegation to Trustees compared to delegation to Agents. The argument is that differences in politics stems from the selection criteria of the actor being given delegated authority, suggesting that delegation in transparent information contexts where recontracting rules are identical can nonetheless give rise to very different politics. The two categories sit at ends of a continuum. When the sole authority of the Agent is based on delegated authority, the actor is a pure Agent and the modes of politics are more likely to be focused on recontracting politics. When the Principal selects the 'Agent' because the authority and legitimacy they bring with them, we have delegation to Trustees. Meanwhile, as Daniel Carpenter, Darren Hawkins, and Wade Jacoby have shown, the more the Agents develop relationships with their constituency, creating a personal or office-based reputation for authority, the more the Agent moves towards the Trustee end of the continuum (Carpenter 2001; Hawkins and Jacoby 2006).

This conceptualization defines the terrain where we might expect the recontracting politics discussed by Principal–Agent theory to be most relevant. In delegation to Agents, the Agent chosen only has delegated authority, and is largely substitutable which contributes to recontracting politics being a politically salient source of Principal power. In delegation to Trustees, the Trustee may be substitutable, but the Trustee has an independent source of authority that provides the Trustee with an element of political protection. This conceptualization widens the types of political power that are salient in political interaction, and the circle of relevant political actors because both the Trustee and the Principal play to a wider audience (the 'beneficiary') as do other actors in the polity.

Where delegation to Agents creates the potential for exploitable slippage, delegation to Trustees actually changes the nature of the political game. The Trustee is another decision-maker whose judgment and authority can be used to challenge the behavior of others, including of members of the Principal. Trustees do not only undermine state power or the interests of the powerful; Trustees can also be a tool of the powerful promoting shared interests and goals. The political game, however, is different because the Trustee is independent. State and

Table 11.1. Agents and Trustees—two ends of a continuum in delegation

	Agent	Trustee
Core Reason to Delegate	Transaction cost reasons: Efficiency gains of having the Agent oversee the delegated task.	Credibility reasons: To capture the benefits of the Trustee's decision-making reputation and/or to remove the taint of 'politics' as shaping Trustee decision-making.
Selection Criteria	Principal will look for an Agent with similar values and views, an Agent who is trustworthy in addition to competent.	Trustee selected because of their personal reputation, and/or because the norms of decision-making in the Trustee's profession are perceived as 'good' by the wider public.
Source of Political Authority	*Delegated Authority:* Authority based on the fact of delegation. Office-holder may develop a reputation for *rational–legal, expert,* or *moral authority* to build their independence.	Authority resides in the office-holder. Trustee brings with them a personal or professional authority (such as *Moral Authority, Rational–Legal Authority,* and/or *Expert Authority*).
Expectations in Delegation	Agents are expected to do the Principal's bidding, interpreting their mandate as the Principal would have wanted.	Trustees are supposed to make decisions on behalf of a beneficiary, using the guidelines in their mandate interpreted according to Trustee's professional norms and best judgment.
Politics	*Contracting Politics:* Manipulating material incentives of Agents through sanctioning threats (e.g. Principal tools of control). Should the Agent develop expert, rational, legal, and moral authority, rhetorical and legitimacy politics will become more important.	*Rhetorical Politics:* Actors offer self-interested interpretations of existing rules, norms, and precedents and appeal to the Trustee's mandate, role and Trustee member's philosophies in an effort to persuade. *Legitimacy Politics:* Those unhappy with Trustee decisions seek to delegitimize the decision in the eyes of the beneficiary by identifying inconsistencies between Trustee mandate and professional norms and Trustee behavior. *Contracting Politics:* Appointment decisions provide a moment for Principals to exercise contracting control. Once appointed the Trustee contracting politics are likely to be relatively ineffective so long as the Trustee can defend its behavior as within its zone of discretionary authority.

non-state actors can bring the Trustee into political interactions, and the mere existence of a Trustee can jar the political process, mobilizing potential challenges and inserting the Trustee's own ideas and views into the political realm.

It is worth reiterating that calling an actor a Trustee is not the same as asserting that a Trustee is 'out there' beyond anyone's influence. Indeed no political actor is 'out there' beyond any influence or ultimate sanction. The framework above argues that a Trustee can be influenced by appointment politics, and that because a Trustee needs to be perceived as acting appropriately, and in the interest of the beneficiary, it can be influenced by rhetorical and legitimacy politics. Should a Trustee stray beyond what the power elite or body politic can accept, the option of removing a Trustee or eliminating the office altogether remains. For delegation to international actors, this 'nuclear option'[3] requires collective decision-making, and is unappealing because it destroys both the positive and the less desirable benefits of delegation. A far more likely political response is to circumvent a Trustee whose decisions one does not like; new tasks will be given to other Trustees or agents and issues will be settled outside of the realm of the Trustee to avoid their interference. The next section explains how International Judicial Trustees are influenced by their political context, and contribute to changing international politics.[4]

III. International Judicial Trustees in International Politics

The Trustee argument places great importance in the reason for which the actor with delegated authority was chosen. Bringing in a third-party decision-maker can be helpful when parties are unable to resolve a dispute on their own, but the third party can be anyone—a government or political appointee, an independent arbiter who serves as a go-between, a mediator who hears all sides and renders a decision, or an independent judge. The first question we should ask in considering IC-Trustees is: What do courts deliver which makes delegating authority to them attractive compared to alternatives such as diplomatic negotiation, arbitration, and mediation?

When a political appointee or member of the government resolves a dispute, there will be a presumption that the outcome is influenced by political factors. Arbitrators and mediators can also provide some distance, but the process of dispute resolution is still political by design. The arbitration process takes place in secret (as in diplomatic negotiations); third party appointments and settlements are pretty much one-shot deals for the arbiters and the parties alike; and there is

---

[3] Mark Pollack uses this phrasing, arguing that in the European Union context the 'nuclear option' is ineffective because it is so extreme (Pollack 1997: 118–19).

[4] Larry Helfer makes a similar argument but where Helfer temporalizes when political pressure is used (pre versus post ruling), the argument here stresses legitimacy and rhetorical tools over appointment and sanctioning tools to influence ICs (Helfer and Slaughter 2005).

no requirement that settlements cohere with the requirements of law or even bear the scrutiny of others. Delegation to courts is different.

In delegation to courts, judges are selected because of their qualifications as experts in the law and given multi-year (as opposed to ad hoc) appointments. The legal process allows for settlements along the way and aims at facilitating compromise, thus it can resemble mediation (especially if the parties decide to seal an agreement or stop before the issuing of a legal ruling). But negotiation in the shadow of a court is different than mediation. Each party knows that if the dispute continues to the point of a legal ruling, the ruling will be made by applying pre-existing rules—thus legal negotiation takes place in the shadow of the law (Mnookin and Kornhauser 1979). Legal rulings are subject to review—by higher courts, or through publication and popular scrutiny. The public and legal nature of court rulings is why even civil law judges (where rulings formally speaking apply only the case at hand) seek consistency across cases. Thus judicial decision-making is by intention expert decision-making, undertaken by disinterested actors. Unlike mediation or arbitration where the goal is to reach a settlement, judicial decision-making uses a rational–legal method of applying pre-existing rules to resolve disputes. It renders decisions in public ways, which can create precedent for the future.

This argument implies no naiveté about who judges are or what they actually do. While judges are disinterested decision-makers in the sense that they do not have a personal stake in the outcome of the case,[5] as Martin Shapiro shows judges are not actually neutral or purely legal (as opposed to political) actors. For Shapiro, the noble lie of judicial neutrality is a necessary fiction inherent to the 'logic of triadic dispute resolution,' developed and reinforced by judges and the power elite to convince the 'loser' in the case that they had a fair chance at winning, and that the decision was not subjective or 'political' (Shapiro 1981: Ch. 1). Inherent to this noble lie is the notion that the 'rule of law' serves the larger social interest. As Alec Stone Sweet argues 'legal norms derive much of their force from the perception that they represent an expression of the social interest, one that is fundamentally superior to the expression of interests of one person or just a few people' (Stone 1994: 11). Arguments like Stone's have a long lineage in the political theory (Tamanaha 2004). But even if one does not accept that judges better represent the public interest than elected politicians, one can still believe that judges who are not out for hire on a case-by-case basis are more likely than politicians or non-judicial decision-makers (e.g. mediators or arbitrators) to consider the long-term consequences of their decisions (McAdams 2005: 1113–17). And one can believe that possibility that public officials may need to defend their actions in front of an independent judge will in itself enhance the quality of decision-making by public officials and promote democratic

---

[5] Professional ethics demand judges recuse themselves from cases where they have a personal connection to the subject matter or any party in the dispute.

accountability (O'Donnell 2004). Thus even if judges are political actors, not truly neutral or even unbiased, they can still be seen as better decision-makers than politicians.

The Trustee argument opens up the question of what are the modes of political influence? In the domestic realm, the appointment and promotion process is often a potent tool to influence the judiciary, wielded by whoever has dominant control of the executive and legislative branches of government. The international constitutional order established after World War II, however, was tailor-made to ensure that any 'international' decision requires the political support of multiple states (Ikenberry 2001). Thus in contrast to the domestic process where political branches can control the nomination process, in the international realm each country chooses which individuals it nominates for international positions. Selecting from among international judicial nominees is certainly politicized (Gordon et al. 1989; Steinberg 2004); the larger point is that the overall nomination and appointment/reappointment process cannot be controlled by any one state or organized group of states. While states did choose to keep the international judiciary beyond the control of the most powerful states, the probably unintended result is that international judges are institutionally less subject to appointment politics than their domestic counterparts (Alter 2006).[6]

Given that International Courts are hard to 'stack' or control via appointments, the way to influence international judges is through appealing to judges' philosophical leanings regarding how to interpret ambiguity and to the reputational interests of the international court. Like most decision-makers, ICs

---

[6] This argument is uncontested by those who understand the international judicial appointment process. More contested is the idea that reappointment politics are unlikely to provide political leverage over judicial decision-making. Erik Voeten has found some evidence that shorter term appointment lengths for judges moderate judicial activism (Voeten 2008), and there is certainly a concern that a perception that judges might be vying for re-appointment can sow seeds of doubt regarding the independence of international judges (Meron 2005). Voeten's finding could be explained by factors other than judges angling for re-appointment—for example shorter terms on courts in a context where judges are on staggered appointments may affect activism by limiting the socialization time of judges on a court. I am skeptical that re-appointment concerns matter because often IC judges are not re-appointed, but rarely if at all is it because of the decisions they made on the bench. IC judges on universal legal bodies are regularly rotated out to create geographic representation on the court. Even where there is a permanent national seat international judges are regularly rotated out because each new national leadership wants a chance to appoint their own judge. While IC judges could in theory still worry about their life after they serve their term, in practice the international judges I have interviewed have not been very worried about this. There is no international judicial career trajectory because the pool of international judicial appointments is simply too small, and many IC judges are near retirement or see an appointment to an IC as a short-term professional experience in any event. While there may well be isolated examples where a person did not get a job they wanted because of their association with an IC (though I know of no examples), whether a judge could anticipate these situations, let alone moderate their behavior to avoid the situation, is highly questionable. Even Richard Steinberg, who believes that the US and Europe veto AB judges who they suspect will be activist, does not argue that the concerns about re-appointment lead judges to follow the wishes of the US or Europe (Steinberg 2004: 264).

are not themselves able to implement their rulings. Because judges want compliance, they are often willing to work with litigants towards the goal of eventual voluntary compliance. To be clear, non-compliance is not a 'sanction' states threaten in order to influence international judges. All courts seek voluntary compliance, and all judges make compromises towards this end (Shapiro 1981: 5–8). Judges need to balance their objectives of enhancing their authority in the eyes of their key constituency (the legal interpretive community and the population as a whole) while inspiring compliance with their rulings by those who care more about the outcomes than the legal basis of the ruling. Thus the 'strategy of judging' involves persuading interpreters of legal decision-making (including fellow judges and the legal community) of the legal merits of an interpretation while inspiring policy-makers and the broader public to comply by convincing them of the merits or the legitimacy of their ruling (Epstein and Knight 1998; Murphy 1964). Even if a legal ruling fails to convince others of the legitimacy of the ruling itself, it can shift political dynamics within a polity by mobilizing actors who favor the rule of law in itself, and by providing a legitimacy boost to actors advocating a position consistent with the legal ruling.

The philosophies of how judges should interpret ambiguity and the strategic interests judges have in inspiring compliance shape the realm in which rhetorical and persuasive politics takes place, providing constraints on judicial decision-making.[7] Governments, NGOs, and legal scholars try to convince judges and the public that certain interpretations of the law will be preferable on normative, legal, or political grounds. States play on the desire of ICs to endeavor compliance, trying to persuade judges that certain interpretations would be politically impossible or normatively illegitimate in their country. When litigants lose in their rhetorical efforts to convince the judge, they will themselves play to judges' audience using legitimacy politics, seeking to challenge the sources of judicial authority. They will question the rational legal basis of the decision by trying to portray the ruling as an interpretive outlier, beyond normal legal decision-making techniques. They will impugn the moral authority of judges by questioning whether the judges are truly neutral and expert interpreters of the law. If all else fails, they will ignore the ruling and/or seek to place themselves outside of the authority of the court.

Three aspects of this interpretive politics are worth underscoring. P–A theory expects Principals to be in a hierarchically privileged position compared to any other actor because of their unique power to recontract. But in the rhetorical and legitimacy politics of interpreting the law, judges are in a privileged position (at least once a case is in court) because they ultimately decide the case and there is a heavy presumption that their decision is legally authoritative. Second—states may have more resources than non-state actors in these interpretive politics (non-state

---

[7] This argument is similar to that made by Richard Steinberg, though he emphasizes more the desire of ICs to seek compliance by powerful states (Steinberg 2004).

actors may be excluded from arguing in court, and governments may be better able to shape media coverage than are non-state actors). But being a member of the collective Principal does not in itself lead to unique influence let alone political control over the rhetorical politics of persuasion or over how the legal ruling will be understood by the so-called 'international community.' Third—the venue and deliberative style in which interpretive politics takes place is very different than the negotiating table dominated by state actors. Courtroom politics take place in an environment highly constrained by law and legal procedure, where judges have a privileged position because they get to ask the questions, decide what is and is not relevant, and determine the outcome. The post-ruling legitimacy politics take place in the public arena where the audience is the Trustee's beneficiary as well as other members of the collective Principal. These differences reveal how creating an IC in itself opens up a new venue where a different sort of politics plays out. That the rules of the game differ in the legalized venue is itself the attraction for those who want to create ICs, and for those who want to resolve a dispute in a legal as opposed to a political venue.

The following cases suggest the validity of this alternative mode of analysis by showing the irrelevance of recontracting politics and identifying how rhetorical and legitimacy politics manifest themselves. I purposely selected 'hard cases' that belie the expectations of P–A theory because it is clear that the IC issued an interpretation that powerful states did not intend and would not want. I selected cases from the WTO and the ICJ because these institutions vary in key features that international lawyers expect to shape the independence and effectiveness of ICs.[8] The WTO has a dispute resolution mechanism that begins with what is essentially a panel of mediators whose members are appointed by the disputants. Should a disputant be unhappy with a panel ruling, the case can be appealed to a permanent Appellate Body (AB), comprised of seven appointed members rotated over time from the membership of the WTO. The ICJ is the supreme judicial body of the United Nations. Where the WTO system has compulsory jurisdiction (e.g. no consent to litigation is required for the case to proceed), the ICJ's jurisdiction is only compulsory between countries that have signed on to the 'optional protocol' that commits them to participate in any suit brought against them.[9] The third case involves the European Court of Justice. The end of this section compares the cases, and expands the analysis beyond these examples.

---

[8] There seems to be a general consensus that courts with compulsory jurisdiction are more independent, as are courts with access for non-state actors because states are less able to control which cases make it to ICs. These design features of ICs tend to be static, and thus do not provide leverage for repeated recontracting threats (Alter 2006).

[9] The ICJ can also be designated within treaties as the final interpreter of international agreements, and given compulsory jurisdiction for specific agreements. This is why the United States could withdraw twice from the ICJ's compulsory jurisdiction—once with respect to the ICJ's general jurisdiction, and then more recently with respect to its jurisdiction over issues related to the Vienna Convention on Consular Affairs.

Case Study 1: WTO Unforeseen Developments Case

Article XIX of GATT 1994 allows 'Emergency Action on Imports of Particular Products' if *unforeseen developments* lead to or threaten to lead to 'serious injury to domestic producers'. But the Agreement on Safeguards has no mention of the requirement that the disruption be 'unforeseen'. The issue at stake in this case study was who decides which of the two possible interpretations of WTO rules prevails when applying safeguards.

In a 1997 case, the EU challenged the legality of an Argentinean safeguard on footwear. Argentina defended its safeguard by arguing that it was not required to show that the damage was unforeseen, and at any rate the injury in itself was 'unforeseen'. Appealing to WTO judges inclined to protect the 'original intent' of WTO agreements, Argentina argued that negotiators had intentionally not required that injury be 'unforeseen'. Argentina pointed out that the EU itself seemed to share this understanding of the Agreement on Safeguards, since it removed from existing domestic legislation any requirement that the damage be 'unforeseen'. The panel agreed with Argentina, but the Appellate Body (AB) reversed the panel ruling, arguing that the terms of the WTO agreement must be understood together. In essence the AB created a legal hierarchy among WTO provisions, putting the language of Article XIX of GATT over that of other aspects of the GATT agreement, including over the Agreement on Safeguards, to create a requirement that users of safeguards prove that the import damage was unforeseen.[10]

The US had participated as a third party in the footwear dispute, arguing that balancing conflicting language of Article XIX and the safeguard measure was the job of politicians to be resolved through diplomatic negotiation.[11] Just about the time that Argentina's safeguard measures were condemned, the United States implemented safeguard measures for three years against Australian and New Zealand lamb imports. The US claimed that the composition of Australian and New Zealand imports had changed, creating serious damage to US industry. Australia immediately challenged the measures arguing that the US had failed to show that the lamb market disruption was 'unforeseen'. The WTO panel applied the AB's footwear precedent and determined that the US had failed to justify that the circumstances leading to the disrupted lamb meat market were unforeseen. The US appealed the panel ruling to the AB arguing that its International Trade Commission (ITC), which had issued a report authorizing safeguard measures, had established the fact that damages were a result of 'unforeseen developments'. But the AB agreed with Australia that the ITC failed to demonstrate that the import damage was unforeseen.[12]

---

[10] Argentina—Safeguard Measures On Imports of Footwear WT/DS121/AB/R Report of the Appellate Body, 14 December 1999.

[11] Ibid p. 19.

[12] WTO Appellate Body Report: United States—Safeguard Measures on Imports of Fresh, Chilled or Frozen Lamb Meat from New Zealand and Australia AB-2001–1, WT/DS177,178/AB/R (01–2194), adopted by Dispute Settlement Body, 16 May 2001.

These cases are examples of the AB 'filling in the law', or as US Senate Finance Committee Chairman Max Baucus implied, 'overstepping their bounds by imposing obligations on the United States that do not exist in WTO rules'.[13] The Lamb-Meat ruling also established a new and higher 'standard of review', requiring states to substantiate their factual findings.

Criticism of the WTO system was at a zenith right at the time the AB issued its Lamb-Meat ruling. The US was experiencing a 'losing streak', where it had been subject to more complaints than any other country, and had lost about 70 per cent of its cases (Greene 2001). In addition to losing legal suits, the US was finding that advantages it had won in negotiations were being undermined. Jenna Greene quotes an interview with US negotiator Mickey Kantor who, when negotiating the WTO safeguard agreements, had threatened to walk out 'unless our trade laws and their philosophical underpinnings were preserved'. In 2001 Mickey Kantor argued that the dispute settlement process was being used as an alternative avenue of attack: 'Clearly, they are trying to do by indirection what they couldn't do by direction', Kantor argued (Greene 2001: 1).

In response to WTO rulings, American critics of the WTO system published articles about how the WTO dispute settlement body is 'anti-democratic' with AB judges exceeding their authority (Barfield 2001, 2002). Alan Wolff of the New American Foundation stated his concerns this way: 'substitution of the outcomes preferred by judges, replacing positions taken by the decision-makers in the Executive Branch, is not acceptable. At the international level it is intolerable, and a threat to the continued legitimacy of the WTO system itself' (Wolff 2000). The rhetoric was fierce, and anger at the ruling was enough to pressure the United States Trade Representative to articulate a 'strategy' to counter what it called 'faulty WTO decisions' regarding safeguard provisions.[14] Meanwhile, the United States respected the Lamb-Meat decision, removing its safeguard protections nine months before they were set to expire at a cost of 42.7 million dollars.[15] The US has continued to comply with WTO rulings, removing in December 2003 safeguard measures on US steel in response to a WTO ruling and European threats to retaliate against products from US states where President George W. Bush was vying for reelection votes (Jung and Kang 2004).

Case Study 2: The ICJ, the US, and the mining of Nicaragua's harbors

In January 1984, the government of Nicaragua sued the United States in front of the ICJ for supporting a rebel movement aimed at overthrowing its government. Secretary of State George Shultz immediately informed the UN that the

---

[13] 'U.S. sets strategy to address "faulty" WTO decisions', *Saigon Times Daily*, 2 January 2003.
[14] Ibid.
[15] 'US ends lamb import quotas' *Agra Europe*, 16 November 2001, 7.

US was withdrawing from the compulsory jurisdiction of the ICJ with respect to Central American countries (Reichler 2001: 31) and sought to have the suit dismissed for lack of ICJ competence, signaling the US would aggressively challenge any ICJ intervention. Yet in May 1984, the ICJ unanimously (meaning even with the vote of the US judge) rejected the US summary dismissal request and ordered the US to cease and desist in its mining of the Nicaraguan harbors.[16] In the jurisdiction phase, the US government repeated its argument that Nicaragua had never formally submitted its ratification of the Statute of the Permanent Court of International Justice (PCIJ),[17] that the US had withdrawn from the ICJ's compulsory jurisdiction for cases from Central America, and that the ICJ lacked jurisdiction to decide on issues regarding the use of force, and specifically whether or not US action was 'self defense'. The US argued that it was involved in 'collective self-defense' aiding the countries in the region, including El Salvador, and tried to have testimony from El Salvador admitted to the proceedings. The ICJ refused to accept El Salvador's testimony, finding that the 'collective self-defense' argument could only be made at the merits phase.[18] By rejecting as legally significant that Nicaragua had technically not submitted its ratification properly, the ICJ willingly passed on an exit opportunity, choosing to enter the political fray in a case where it knew that the Reagan administration would be deeply unhappy. The American judge on the ICJ, Judge Stephen Schwebel, loudly dissented both on the decision to accept jurisdiction and the decision not to accept El Salvador's statement until the merits phase. While alone in his dissent, Schwebel's 261 pages (Highet 1987: 2) of passionately argued text provided fodder American opponents could use to bolster their criticisms of the ICJ's subsequent decision.

The US responded by notifying the UN that it was withdrawing from the ICJ's general compulsory jurisdiction (for all countries, not just Central American countries) and by boycotting the merits phase of the proceedings. The US and El Salvador's arguments in support of the collective self-defense were never made, contributing to legal and procedural gymnastics critics exploited in questioning the legal legitimacy of the ruling (Bork 1989/90: 40–1; Bork 2003; D'Amato 1987; Franck 1987; Moore 1987). These behaviors were predictable and telecast in advance. Still, the ICJ went on to roundly and completely condemn the US in its ruling on the merits.[19] This ruling led to retaliation; the United States withdrew from the ICJ's general compulsory jurisdiction—never again to return. The question for this study is why the ICJ was not seemingly dissuaded by the certain

---

[16] ICJ Order of 10 May 1984—Request for the Indication of Provisional Measures.

[17] Nicaragua had wired confirmation of its ratification of the statute, but the formal document had somehow never arrived in Geneva.

[18] ICJ Judgment of 26 November 1984—Jurisdiction of the Court and Admissibility of the Application.

[19] ICJ Judgment of 27 June 1986—*Military and Paramilitary Activities In and Against Nicaragua* (Nicaragua v. United States of America)—Merits.

US anger and non-compliance with its ruling. Paul Reichler—the lawyer who recruited the legal team and organized Nicaragua's legal strategy—sees the ICJ's calculation this way:

> While the reaction in most quarters was hostile to the White House for its rejection of the Court, some U.S. academics criticized Nicaragua and its lawyers, especially [Nicaragua's American lawyer Abe Chayes], for bringing a case that caused the U.S. walkout. They argued that Nicaragua's suit undermined respect for the Court by demonstrating its powerlessness—for surely a superpower like the United States would continue pursuing a foreign policy it considered vital to its national interests even if the Court ordered it to stop, and the Court had no means of enforcing its order... Does not all this weaken the Court and undermine its legitimacy—at least as to pronouncements involving peace and security? Is not the whole edifice of international adjudication, already fragile, put at risk?
>
> ...in addressing these questions, we should not forget that the legitimacy of the Court and the prospects for the rule of law in international affairs are at stake whether the Court decides or refuses to decide the case before it....And in the circumstances, it is only in The Hague that Nicaragua can face the United States on equal terms. It is the only forum where the outcome is not predetermined by the disparities of military and economic power between the parties. In the countries of the world that are possessed of neither the purse nor the sword, it would be a severe blow to the legitimacy and moral authority of the Court as well as to the claims for international law, if the door to that forum were closed. (Reichler 2001: 38)

Case Study 3: The ECJ and women in combat-supporting roles

Included in the European Community's Treaty of Rome is a stipulation that in the common market there must be equal pay for men and women (Article 119 (now Articles 141 and 142)). This social objective came to be part of the Common Market for economic reasons: France was required by its constitution to pay men and women equally, and it did not want other countries to gain a competitive advantage by relying on inexpensive female labor (Hoskins 1996: ch. 3). In the 1970s, with Social Democratic governments in power in a number of European countries, European countries adopted a directive extending equal pay to include equal treatment for men and women. Directives are binding in the end to be achieved, and they allow for national choice in how to achieve the directive's goal. Article 2(2) of the Equal Treatment Directive allowed for derogations to the requirement of equal treatment, noting:

> This Directive shall be without prejudice to the right of Member States to exclude from its field of application those occupational activities and, where appropriate, the training leading thereto, for which by reason of their nature or the context in which they are carried out, the sex of the worker constitutes a determining factor.[20]

---

[20] Council Directive 76/207/EEC of 9 February 1976 on Equal Treatment for Men and Women in Employment [1976] OJ L39/40.

Article 2(2) suggested that certain domains, such as the military, would be exempt from the reach of European gender equality rules.

In the late 1970s and 1980s, the European Court of Justice started enforcing EC gender equality provisions (see Chapter 8 for more on these developments). These doctrinal developments were unanticipated, but by the 1990s the idea that European law prohibited gender discrimination had become well accepted. Still, Article 2(2) of the Equal Treatment Directive created some absolute limits on the requirement of gender equality. In Britain, Article 85(4) of the United Kingdom's Sex Discrimination Act 1975 cleaved out aspects that were exempt from the reach of EU law noting: 'nothing in this Act shall render unlawful an act done for the purpose of ensuring the combat effectiveness of the naval, military or air forces'. In Germany, the prohibition of women in the military was part of German Basic Law, Article 12 a (4) which stated:

If, while a state of defence exists, civilian service requirements in the civilian public health and medical system or in the stationary military hospital organisation cannot be met on a voluntary basis, women between eighteen and fifty-five years of age may be assigned to such services by or pursuant to a law. They may on no account render service involving the use of arms.

These exceptions were arguably consistent with Article 2(2) of the Equal Treatment Directive, and were never challenged by the European Commission as a violation of European law probably because the realm of the national security remained firmly a national issue and a policy area where certain types of discrimination were accepted as necessary to maintaining group morale.

In 1994 Angela Maria Sirdar was denied a job as a cook in the British Royal Marines, because the Royal Marines did not recruit women except to serve in the Royal Band. Sirdar argued that her exclusion as a cook violated European Law. In the *Sirdar* Case, the ECJ accepted the argument that the Royal Marines can exclude women because they are 'special force' within the British Military relying on the military cohesion of its all male membership.[21] The *Sirdar* ruling did not require a change in British policy, but it signaled that the ECJ would be involved in reviewing employment rules within the military.

In 1996 Tanja Kreil applied for a job in the German Bundeswehr in weapon electronics maintenance. Like Sirdar, Kreil wanted a combat supportive role, but Kreil's role required working with arms—something expressly prohibited in the German Basic Law. In the suit before the ECJ, the German, Italian, and United Kingdom governments all argued that decisions concerning the organization and combat capacity of the armed forces lay outside the scope of Community law (Points 12–13 summarized in the ECJ ruling). The European Court rejected this argument, asserting that 'Although it is for the Member States . . . to take decisions on the organisation of their armed forces, it does not follow that such decisions

---

[21] Case C-273/97, *Sirdar v. Army Board* [1999] ECR I-7403, [1999] 3 CMLR 559.

must fall entirely outside the scope of Community law.' Instead the ECJ required states to justify any derogation from the general requirement of equal treatment for men and women. Whereas the ECJ accepted the derogation justification in the *Sirdar* case, in the *Kreil* case it found that the blanket exclusion of women from many roles in the German military violated the European Communities Equal Treatment Directive.[22] The equal treatment substance of the ruling was not novel, but its application to the realm of a state's military, traditionally seen as exempt from the EEC's equal treatment requirements, was surprising.

German opinion on the role of women in the military had been evolving. In the 1970s, the peace movement was a chief opponent of a greater role for women, mainly because without an army of sufficient size, deployment would not be an option. The military also did not welcome women, nor was expanding the role of women in the military a priority for women's groups. In the 1970s, notwithstanding the Social Democrats' general desire to promote 'The Year of the Woman', opposition to women in the military was such that the German Parliament could only agree to allow women in the military's medical services, thereby relieving a shortage of medical service staff in the Bundeswehr (Liebert 2002: 13). Later, in 1991 women were granted the right to serve in the band (Kuemmel 2003: 3). In the 1990s, Germany's Red–Green coalition agreed to deploy the German military as part of the Northern Atlantic Treaty Organization (NATO) operations, which in itself signified a defeat of the peace movement and a change in German attitudes. This shift also put the military under new resource constraints. By law, German conscripts may not be sent out of Germany. If the German government wanted to continue to participate in international missions, it needed to grow its volunteer army. Participation in multi-national efforts also led to attitudinal shifts within the military. While the German military initially opposed a broader role for women, in the late 1990s German soldiers got to experience serving alongside servicewomen from NATO countries.

While the time for a change was ripe, German policy would not have changed without the ECJ decision—at least not when it changed. Writing in *Die Zeit* in the week of the ECJ decision, Constanze Stelzenmüller argued that it was not a question of 'if' Germany would change its constitution—since it *must* in light of the ECJ ruling—but rather *how* Germany would change its constitution (Stelzenmüller 2000). Gerhard Kuemmel concurs with the idea that the ECJ decision was the catalyst: 'recent steps to open the Bundeswehr to women do not stem from genuinely political initiatives as one may have thought, but from a court ruling that required to political sphere to take some action' (Kuemmel 2003: 4). Changing the German Constitution did not, in the end, prove that difficult, in large part because the German government embraced the idea expanding the role of women in the military. Only one member of the Bundestag spoke against the ECJ decision as 'a clear transgression' because the domain of the military did

---

[22] Case C-285/98, *Tanja Kreil v. Bundesrepublik Deutschland* [2000] ECR I-69.

not fall under European Union authority (Liebert 2002: 16). Within 10 months of the ruling Germany had changed its constitution, and initiated an extensive transformation of the German military, allowing in women and working to shift social attitudes of soldiers so as to dismantle resistance to women in the military (Kuemmel 2003). The number of women in the military went from 4,173 in 1999 to 7,734 in 2002, with 2,752 women serving in armed troops (Liebert 2002: 9–10). We are only beginning to understand the larger impact this change will bring (Kuemmel 2003).

That Germany seemingly embraced the ECJ decision as a helpful catalyst for needed changes does not undermine the point that the ECJ decision was well beyond what states intended when Article 119 and the Equal Treaty Directive were written, and beyond what they would themselves have chosen. European countries could always, on their own, decide to integrate women into the military. Together the *Sirdar* and *Kreil* rulings forced governments to defend their choices in an area of national prerogative and made the ECJ the final judge on whether or not restrictions on women in the military are legal (Harries-Jenkins 2002: 764).

A few years later Alexander Dory invoked European law to challenge the validity of Germany's policy of compulsory military service.[23] The German government again argued that the organization of the military remained part of member state's exclusive powers, and thus was entirely outside the scope of Community law. The ECJ again rejected this argument, but it found that conscription did not violate European law and suggested that certain aspects of military organization did remain fully within national control (Rudolf 2005: 674–5).

The ECJ has not been immune to political influence in these cases, indeed there are clear signs that the ECJ is proceeding cautiously. By first allowing the derogation to equal treatment for the Royal Marines, the ECJ could reassure states that it was not going to be a radical force of change. Also, its *Dory* decision seemed to concede terrain to member states, at the cost of interpretive clarity in the ruling. Beate Rudolf notes that some commentators interpreted the *Dory* decision as a response to the harsh criticism of the *Sidar* and *Kreil* decisions, and she suggests that the ECJ avoided for political reasons the logical finding that either Germany had to also draft women or the draft itself must be eliminated (Rudolf 2005: 678). Still, given how member states have avoided a role for the ECJ in issues of security;[24] given that they have worked to keep the issue of equal treatment separate from issues related to the military, and given the symbolism involved in any EU decision that touches on national defenses, it is highly doubtful that, if asked, European states would have agreed to let the ECJ be involved at all with decisions regarding the organization of domestic security.

---

[23] Case C-186/01, *Alexander Dory v. Federal Republic of Germany* [2003] ECR I-2508 (decided 11 March 2003).

[24] The ECJ was excluded from any role in the Common Foreign and Security Policy, and its role in reviewing issues regarding asylum and immigration is circumscribed so as to allow states to maintain final authority where issues of state security are concerned.

The intervention of the ECJ spilled over to the European Court of Human Rights (ECHR). In its 1999 *Smith and Grady* decision, the ECHR condemned the British practice of dismissing homosexuals from the military.[25] The British government responded by changing its policy. This ruling is just an example of the door that was opened by the ECJ finding that its jurisdiction reaches into the domain of the military, even if there are significant limitations on how far it reaches.

IV. Taking the Cases Together

These are 'hard cases' in that it is clear that ICs interpreted the law in ways that were unwanted by powerful actors, and thus were unlikely to have been agreed to by the collective Principal either before or after the IC ruling. Important for this analysis is that there was no formal sanction of any of the courts—judges were not replaced, the court's mandates were not rewritten, the law in question was not rewritten, nor were budgets cut.[26] Whether the ICJ suffered from its Nicaragua ruling is in the eye of the beholder. Eric Posner argues that the ICJ was explicitly sanctioned (by the US withdrawal from its compulsory jurisdiction) and implicitly sanctioned by declining usage (Posner 2004). In making this argument Posner focuses on the 'relative' decline in the ICJ's docket, that the ICJ's docket did not grow in tandem with the expansion of states in the international system meanwhile great power use of the ICJ decreased over time. While we cannot know what the ICJ's case load would have been absent the Nicaragua ruling, the ICJ's case load continues to grow even at a time of proliferating legal venues that can siphon off demand for ICJ rulings.[27] Compliance with ICJ decisions also appears largely constant over time, and certainly not declining (Paulson 2004; Schulte 2004). Posner's claim for declining ICJ legitimacy is based on great power usage of the ICJ. Meanwhile Constance Schulte sees growing ICJ legitimacy as measured by the rise in non-great power use (Schulte 2004: 2, 404). We can also see that the ICJ was not cowed by the US response to its Nicaragua ruling. When Iran turned to the ICJ to condemn the US's 1987 attacks on its oil platform, the ICJ accepted jurisdiction in the case although the basis of jurisdiction was perhaps more questionable than it had been in the Nicaragua case.[28]

---

[25] Judgment in the case of *Smith and Grady v. United Kingdom*, ECHR (Applications nos 33985/96 and 33986/96) (27 September 1999).

[26] The US withdrew from the ICJ's compulsory jurisdiction, which altered the mandatory jurisdiction of the ICJ to some extent. One may see this as a change of contract, but it should be noted that most ICs do not have optional protocols for compulsory jurisdiction. Thus most countries do not have this option in the face of unwanted IC rulings.

[27] Not counting the 10 cases dismissed by the ICJ during the Yugoslavian war, 44 ICJ rulings in contentious cases were issued in the 20 years since its Nicaragua ruling (an average of 2.2 cases per year), compared to 51 rulings in the 38 years before the Nicaragua ruling (an average of 1.3 rulings per year).

[28] The Nicaragua case involved provisions of the UN Charter where the ICJ is the highest interpretive body. For the *Case concerning Oil Platforms (Islamic Republic of Iran v. United States of*

One may contest that the real issue is whether or not states comply with IC rulings, and the ICJ was in fact ignored in the Nicaragua case. Compliance with IC decisions and international law could certainly bear improvement, though it is not clear that compliance with international rulings is much worse than compliance with federal rules or domestic supreme court rulings.[29] But the real effectiveness test for ICs is not compliance but the counter-factual of what the outcome would have been absent the IC. Those concerned with *effectiveness* should ask whether the IC contributed to moving a state in a more law-complying direction. Those interested in IC *influence* are concerned with whether an IC contributed to changing a state's behavior in ways that would not otherwise have occurred. In these unusually contentious cases, the rulings influenced politics and policy, and they arguably influenced states in the direction of greater law adherence. The WTO ruling led to a change in US and Argentinean use of safeguards in the cases at hand. Moreover, any Doha Round negotiations regarding the Safeguard Agreement will take place with the understanding that current WTO law requires that states show that damages were 'unforeseen.' For the ICJ case, the Nicaragua team was trying to undermine the legitimacy of Reagan's policy by turning against the US the same arguments it had used in its 1980 ICJ case against Iran (*Case concerning United States Diplomatic and Consular Staff in Tehran (U.S. v. Iran)*, Judgment, 1980 ICJ Reports 3 (May 24) (Reichler 2001: 23–4). Their efforts worked, and even the ICJ's critics acknowledge that the ruling had costs. Robert Bork argues: 'Even before the Court's decision, Carlos Arguello, Nicaragua's ambassador to the Netherlands...announced that a decision against the United States would be a serious political and moral blow to them. And so it was' (Bork 1989/90: 7). More concretely, Congress was deeply divided on Contra-Aid, and supporters of the suit hoped an ICJ ruling would shift the votes of a few key politicians. The strategy arguably worked; fifteen days after the ICJ's first ruling against US efforts to summarily dismiss the suit, Congress for the first time voted against Contra-aid (Reichler, 2001: 34).

America) ICJ decision of 6 November 2003, the ICJ based its jurisdiction claim on a friendship, commerce, and navigation treaty that existed between the Shah's Iran and the US (Bekker 2003).

[29] Compliance with IC rulings are actually quite high especially when one considers that it is often the hardest of cases that end up in front of an IC (the easier cases having settling out of court): 65 to 75% of ICJ decisions (Paulson 2004), 62% of GATT rulings (Busch and Reinhardt 2000a: 471), and 88% of WTO rulings (up until 2000) have led to full or partial compliance (Posner and Yoo 2004: 41). Compliance rates with European law violations pursued by the Commission and with decisions of the European Court of Human Rights appear to be even higher (Börzel 2001; Zorn and Van Winkle 2001). Compliance rates with the Inter-American Court of Human Rights are far less impressive (Posner and Yoo 2004: 41), but it is also true that the Inter-American court has very few cases—a fact which may be related to the low compliance levels. We do not actually know whether compliance rates for ICs are vastly worse than compliance rates for national supreme court decisions. The one study that has compared compliance across three levels (the national, the EU, and the WTO) found that national compliance was no better, and in some respects worse, at the national compared to the supranational and international levels (Zurn and Joerges 2005).

My focus on hard cases led me to select cases where ICs decided against powerful states. But the point is not that ICs upset powerful states. The US wins many of its cases brought to international courts. Indeed during the same time period as the ICJ's Nicaragua ruling, the Reagan administration asked for and embraced an ICJ ruling in the Gulf of Maine demarcation case because letting the ICJ decide the boundary dispute allowed the US and Canadian federal governments to distance themselves from a decision that was bound to make fishermen working in the border area unhappy.[30] Despite acrimonious ICJ cases which Iran and the United States protested (and largely ignored), Iran and the United States cooperated with a specially created claims tribunal that resolved disputes over the frozen Iranian assets. These other cases highlight how powerful and weak actors alike appeal to ICs to enhance the credibility of a decision, even if they do not always follow international legal decisions. The reality that ICs do remain useful, even if they sometimes make unwanted rulings, undermines the appeal of any 'nuclear' recontracting option, to the point that this option is 'off the table'.

There are also many less difficult cases, where states would not have agreed in advance to expansions of international legal authority over certain domains of law, yet they were not bitterly opposed to the international judicial rulings that were made.[31] Arguably the ECJ's *Kriel* ruling (and the ECHR's *Smith and Grady*)[32] decision fits this category in that there was already a growing support for expanding the role of women in the Germany military (and for relaxing the ban on homosexuals in the military).

In the hard and less hard cases discussed here, legal rulings were part of a larger strategy where judges in essence worked with sympathetic actors within states to help promote political change (Harlow and Rawlings 1992). Often governments were not particularly unhappy with slippage—indeed in some cases judicial decision-making facilitated a desired change as in the *Kriel* case discussed above. Where political actors were unhappy, they sought to impugn the authority of the court rather than to impose sanctions, as in the WTO's and ICJ's cases discussed above.

This discussion has admittedly covered only a handful of cases. Hard cases can show the limitations of an explanation (in this case that sanctioning concerns drive IC decision-making), but they cannot show it in a general way nor can they establish the merits of an alternative explanation. There are a few larger N studies that have sought to test how appointment and power politics affect IC decision-making (Kilroy 1995, 1999; Posner 2004; Posner and De Figueiredo

---

[30] *Delimitation of the Maritime Boundary in the Gulf of Maine Area* (Can./U.S.), 1984 ICJ Reports 246 (12 October).

[31] Judicial politics literature focusing on the European context is replete with such examples: see Chapters 7, 8, and 9; Cichowski (2004); Conant (2002); Green Cowles et al. (2001); Stone Sweet (2004); Tallberg (2003). Within the area of human rights, there is also extensive literature on how non-governmental actors use international law (including sometimes international courts) as vehicles of political change: Risse, Ropp, and Sikkink (1999); Sikkink (2005); Sikkink and Lutz (2001).

[32] See note 304.

2004; Voeten 2008).[33] These studies fail to show that sanctioning concerns influence judicial decision-making[34] though Erik Voeten does find modest support for the argument that appointing judges for shorter terms can moderate judicial activism (Voeten 2007). While limited in their generalizability, cases studies can show how ICs interact with powerful actors. ICs rely on legal techniques to provide authority for their rulings, and know that anger in one case will not lead to sustained political boycotts (which is not to say there are no costs to angering powerful states). Even where ICs lack sufficient authority to induce respect for their rulings, they influence the political process by providing a focal tool to organize political coalitions within and across states, and a legitimacy boost to actors trying to challenge arguably illegal state policy. A conclusion suggested by these cases is that any quantitative study of international judicial decision-making must equally test for how concerns other than sanctions—like rhetorical, legitimacy and legal concerns, legal background, party affiliation, and socialization contexts—shape IC decision-making.

V. Conclusion: Moving Beyond P–A Presumptions

The main disagreement with P–A theory is over its assumption that states have a special hierarchical power by virtue of their unique contracting power. This assumption puts the focus of state–IC relations on recontracting powers—appointment mechanisms and sanctioning tools—to the exclusion of other sources of power and of actors other than states and ICs. The analysis offered here suggests that being a member of the Principal confers relatively little power of its own in delegation to Trustees because Trustees have been given discretionary authority, because Trustees care more about their reputation than Principal sanctioning, and because both states and ICs are seeking to convince a larger beneficiary (domestic publics) of the legitimacy of their actions. In challenging the epistemology of P–A theory, and providing a theoretical explanation for Trustee independence, this article challenges rational expectations arguments that seek to first require one to show ICs are acting independent of state wishes before any claim of IC influence can stick.

To reject P–A analysis is not to say that politics does not matter in international judicial decision-making. Merely by enforcing the law ICs serve as the handmaiden of the political interests behind international law—powerful states.

---

[33] Kilroy's study focuses on the ECJ. It is discussed in Conant (2007).

[34] Bernadette Kilroy actually finds that non-compliance concerns matter more than the power of the states in the case. Eric Posner and Michael De Figueiredo find judicial bias, but not due to sanctioning concerns of judges. Erik Voeten explores a variety of factors that may shape the decisions of individual judges on the ECHR. He finds very little support that sanctioning concerns (such as not reappointing a judge) shape individual judicial behavior, and more support that policy concerns shape ECHR judges' behavior (2007, 2008).

States as litigants influence which questions are raised in court. And political factors such as domestic politics within a country, legal muscle in the case, and compliance concerns surely influence which actors tend to win in court, which cases are settled out of court, how judges exercise their judicial discretion, and what happens to legal rulings after they are issued. To question the utility of P–A theory is simply to say that a different sort of politics is at play, a politics where states' monopoly power to recontract matters little, where internationally negotiated compromises can be unseated through legal interpretation, where states can come to find themselves constrained by principles they never agreed to, and where non-state actors have influence and can effectively use international law against states.

The thrust of this argument is that the presumption should be in favor of IC independence rather than Principal control. Giving up the idea that states are the hidden puppet-masters of ICs allows us to instead focus on how international politics is being transformed by the existence of an alternative venue of international politics—namely international legal arenas. The possibility of IC review of state policy may make states more willing to negotiate and settle out of court so as to avoid providing international legal bodies with an opportunity to establish legal precedents.[35] Rulings and interpretations backed by international judges may help shape international rhetorical politics, and differences in a litigant's ability to muster skilled legal teams may be an alternative means through which power comes to shape international political and legal outcomes.[36]

This analysis also helps explain the current legitimacy politics surrounding ICs and international law. The more unhappy powerful states are about IC independence and influence, the more we will hear about the illegitimacy of international legal bodies. Within the United States, conservative writers are vociferously questioning the legitimacy, utility, impartiality, effectiveness, and authority of ICs (Barfield 2001; Bork 2003; Posner 2004; Posner and De Figueiredo 2004; Rabkin 2005), while more multilaterally oriented scholars are seeking to bolster the legitimacy, authority, and democratic accountability of international courts (Helfer and Slaughter 1997, 2005; Schulte 2004; Terris, Romano, and Swiggart 2008). This debate suggests that ICs do have both autonomy and influence, otherwise why should US-based conservatives bother to impugn international courts and their judges? Social science analyses should help cut through ideology, so long as we study the politics that ensue *because* states do not control ICs, and *because* international court rulings influence the political process.

---

[35] Early work on this topic includes: Davis (2006); Reinhardt (2000); Tallberg and Jönsson (1998).

[36] Early work on this topic includes: Davis and Blodgett (forthcoming); Guzman and Simmons (2004).

12

Private Litigants and the New International Courts (2006)

There has been a revolution in the creation and use of international courts (ICs). Nineteen ICs were created since 1990, so that today there are 26 international legal bodies that meet the *Project on International Courts and Tribunal's* definition of an IC.[1] Not only are there more ICs, but most of these ICs are also 'new-style international courts' with compulsory jurisdiction (in which no consent to litigation is required) combined with enforcement jurisdiction and access for private (i.e. non-state) litigants. IC usage is increasing too; roughly 70 per cent of the total international judicial activity and rulings have come in the past 14 years alone.[2]

The edited special volume of *Comparative Political Studies* in which this article first appeared builds on an extensive scholarship showing that private access has helped transform European courts into constitutional legal bodies, facilitating private and group litigation strategies to pressure national and supranational policy change. Drawing from the European experience, scholars have developed general theories of how ICs with private litigant access have a greater ability to influence state behavior (Alter 2001; Helfer and Slaughter 1997; Slaughter, Keohane, and Moravcsik 2000). If private access transforms the nature of international judicial politics, why would sovereignty-jealous states ever agree to let private actors into ICs? I posit a functional explanation of the design trend: As international governance has expanded, the roles ICs are designed to play have expanded to replicate at the international level the types of legal checks on public authority that one finds at the domestic level. The expansion in roles drives design decisions because if an IC is to play an administrative review, constitutional review, or enforcement role, it must have compulsory jurisdiction, and if an IC is to play a war crimes role or administrative review role, private actors must have

---

[1] According to Project on International Courts and Tribunes (PICT), ICs are permanent institutions composed of independent judges that adjudicate disputes between two or more entities, one of which is a state or international organization. They work on the basis of predetermined rules of procedure and render decisions that are binding. See PICT's synoptic chart. Since it was last updated, the Caribbean Court has come into existence and a criminal tribunal for Sierre Leone was created <http://www.pict-pcti.org/matrix/matrixintro.html>.

[2] 70% (19,568 of 27,904) of the admissible cases are since 1990, and 69% (15,396 of 22,206) completed rulings, opinions, or orders are since 1990.

standing in front of the court. But because private access is limited to specific judicial roles, expanded private access does not per se presage the rise of ICs on the European model in which private actors use international legal mechanisms to influence domestic policy.

Section I explains why scholars expect ICs with private access to facilitate private-actor participation in law-making and rights claiming, leading to ICs that are more politically influential. Section II provides evidence of the trend toward creating ICs with compulsory jurisdiction combined with enforcement authority and access for non-state actors—what I am referring to as the 'new' ICs. Section III develops the functional argument and examines 20 ICs identifying which roles they were created to serve and the design of these courts by role. Section IV analyzes data on IC usage to consider whether the trend toward 'new style' ICs presages a rise of ICs on the European model. Section V concludes by asking what kind of democracy private access to ICs helps generate.

I. How Are ICs with Compulsory Jurisdiction and Private-Actor Access Different from ICs without Compulsory Jurisdiction and Private-Actor Access?

In international law, 'compulsory jurisdiction' means that the defendant does not need to first give consent for the legal case to proceed. Most scholars believe that compulsory jurisdiction and access for private litigants contributes to IC independence (Helfer and Slaughter 1997, 2005; Posner and Yoo 2005), and most also associate IC independence with greater IC effectiveness, believing that judicial independence enhances the legitimacy and authority of courts (Gordon et al. 1989; Schneider 1998: 627–9; Walker 1988).[3] In addition, scholars see private access as fundamentally changing the nature of an IC, making it a transnational instead of an interstate institution (Keohane, Moravcsik, and Slaughter 2000). Private access is important because private actors are more numerous and would appear especially likely to pursue cases that are either too politically 'hot' or a low priority for international commissions or states with limited resources and conflicting priorities. Private-actor cases also tend to have domestic enforcement components, bringing international law into the domestic realm, thereby harnessing domestic actors to help enforce international rules (Hathaway 2005; Helfer and Slaughter 1997, 2005; Keohane et al. 2000; Slaughter 2000, 2004; Slaughter and Bosco 2000). Even without the domestic component, more cases create more opportunities for courts to intervene in policy debates and facilitate incremental decision-making, which can be used to build political support for legal doctrine with time (Alter 2001: 188–9; Helfer and Slaughter 1997: 314–18; Slaughter et al. 2000: 482).

---

[3] For a dissenting view, see Posner and Yoo (2005).

Much of the literature linking private access and compulsory jurisdiction to IC effectiveness is based on European examples and has as an implicit assumption that private actors are the plaintiffs, instigating international litigation to assert their rights or influence national policy. But private access simply means that private actors have standing in front of ICs. War crimes courts allow private actors to assert their rights and put before the court all relevant arguments, but private actors will be the defendants in war crimes courts. And many private-access cases are challenging international organizational behaviors, not national policy. Still, the above logic holds—private actors are more numerous and motivated by personal incentives; thus, ICs with private access are likely to hear more rights claims and be better able to develop their jurisprudence, legitimacy, and authority. Although authors are careful to note that private-litigant access is no guarantee of rights protection or IC influence,[4] the logic of the arguments point only in one direction. ICs with private access and compulsory jurisdiction should be better able to induce state respect for international law compared to ICs lacking these design features.

II. The New ICs

'Old-style' ICs—the Permanent Court of Justice, the Permanent Court of Arbitration, and the International Court of Justice—were primarily dispute resolution bodies. Although these courts may have had enforcement authority on paper, without compulsory jurisdiction ICs could only really be used for interpretive disputes in cases where both parties agreed to abide by the interpretation of the law given by the IC. This limitation was intentional, with states refusing compulsory jurisdiction provisions to allow them to avoid IC authority (Levi 1976: 70–1). What I am calling the 'new-style ICs' are the now very large number of ICs that (a) have compulsory jurisdiction and are thus genuinely designed at least in part to hold states accountable to their international obligations (as evidenced by compulsory jurisdiction combined with an explicit or implicit jurisdiction to hear cases involving state non-compliance) and (b) allow private actors access. There is a clear trend toward the 'newer' style ICs, as revealed in Table 12.1 that includes 20 ICs meeting the *Project on*

---

[4] Private litigants may choose not to use international legal mechanism, and litigation strategies not backed up by a post ruling politics tend to be less influential: Chapter 8; Conant (2002); Harlow and Rawlings (1992); Helfer (2002). Stone Sweet notes that political actors can block or stop the process of judicializing politics (Stone Sweet 1999), and Helfer and Slaughter note that factors such as the nature of violations, the extent to which a rule of law ethos prevails within the domestic system, and the relative cultural or political homogeneity of states within a supranational legal system may influence whether or not international litigation is effective (Helfer and Slaughter 1997). Also, as Posner, Yoo and Hathaway note, states can choose to ignore ICs and their rulings (Hathaway 2005; Posner and Yoo 2005).

Table 12.1. Old-style and new-style international courts, by date established

International Courts	Date Established/Created[a]	Compulsory Jurisdiction	Jurisdiction for Non-compliance Suits	Private-Actor Access	Total Cases (last year included in figures)[a]
Old-style courts					
International Court of Justice (ICJ)	1945/1946	Optional protocol			104 contentions cases filed, 80 judgments, 23 advisory opinions (2003)
Judicial Tribunal for the Organization of Arab Petroleum Exporting Countries (OAPEC)	1980/1980	So qualified as to be meaningless[b]		X By optional state consent	2 cases (1999)
International Tribunal for the Law of the Seas (ITLOS)	1982/1996	Optional protocol (exception, seabed authority, and seizing of vessels)		Seabed authority and seizing of vessels only	13 judgments (2004)
New-style courts					
European Court of Justice (ECJ)	1952/1952	X	X	X	2,497 infringement cases by Commission, 5,293 cases referred by national courts, 7,528 direct actions (2004)
European Court of Human Rights (ECHR)	1950/1959	X	X	X (as of 1998)	8,810 cases deemed admissible, 4,145 judgments (2003)
Benelux Court (BCJ)	1965/1974	X	X	Indirect[c]	No data
Inter-American Court of Justice (IACHR)	1969/1979	Optional protocol	X	Commission is a gatekeeper	104 judgments, 18 advisory opinions, 148 orders for provisional measures (2003)
Court of Justice of the Andean Community (ATJ)	1979/1984	X	X	X	31 nullifications, 108 infringement cases, 711 preliminary rulings (2004)

			ECJ hears these cases		
European Community Court of First Instance (CFI)	1988/1988	X	X	X	2,083 decisions from 3,003 cases filed (figures exclude staff cases; 2004)
Central American Court of Justice (CACJ)	1991/1992	X (some exceptions)[d]	X	X	65 cases, 21 advisory opinions, 30 rulings, 7 cases dismissed for lack of competence, 7 cases in progress (2004)
European Free Trade Area Court (EFTAC)	1992/1995	X	X	(Via national courts, advisory opinions only)	59 opinions (2003)
Economic Court of the Commonwealth of Independent States (ECCIS)	1992/1993	X	X	X	47 cases, not clear if they are ruled on yet (2000)
Court of Justice for the Common Market of Eastern and Southern Africa (COMESA)	1993/1998	X	X	X	3 judgments, 1 order (2003)
Common Court of Justice and Arbitration for the Organization for the Harmonization of Corporate Law in Africa (OHADA)	1993/1997	X	X	X	4 opinions, 27 rulings (2002)
International Criminal Tribunal for the Former Yugoslavia (ICTFY)	1993/1993	X	X	X (defendant only)	75 public indictments, 18 completed cases, 11 judgments (2003)
General Agreement on Tariffs and Trade (GATT)[e]	1953 to 1993				229 cases, 98 rulings
World Trade Organization (WTO) Appellate Body[f]	1994	X	X	X	304 disputes formally initiated, 59 appellate rulings, 115 panel reports (2003)
International Criminal Tribunal for Rwanda (ICTR)	1994/1995	X	X	X (defendant only)	58 cases in progress, 17 completed cases (2003)

Continued

Table 12.1. (Continued)

International Courts	Date Established/Created[a]	Compulsory Jurisdiction	Jurisdiction for Non-compliance Suits	Private-Actor Access	Total Cases (last year included in figures)[a]
International Criminal Court (ICC)	1998/2002	X	X	X (defendant only)	3 situations under investigation but no rulings to date
Caribbean Court of Justice (CCJ)	2001/2005	X	X	X	Began operation April 2005
International Criminal Tribunal for Sierra Leone (ICTSL)	2002/2002	X	X	X (defendant only)	11 indictments proceeding, 2 withdrawn because of death (2003)
Total international judicial activity					29,261 admissible cases filed or under investigation

Note: Data compiled by author, based on the best information available on the Project on International Courts and Tribunes website, updated by visiting the websites of the international courts and consulting scholarship where available. The data on the number of cases is updated in Chapter 2. I have excluded a number of African courts for lack of information about them. ECCIS data are from Dragneva (2004). I have excluded from consideration private access when it only includes suits brought by employees of the international organization.

[a] Because I am interested in the decision to delegate authority to ICs, I focus on the year on the year of treaty establishment. But ICs are only created after a sufficient number of states have actually deposited their ratification of the treaty. There can be significant lags between when ICs are established in treaties compared to when they are actually created, which can account in part, but only in part, for variation in the number of rulings and the judicial activity of ICs.

[b] Judicial Tribunal for Organization of Arab Petroleum-Exporting Countries court has an implicit compulsory jurisdiction, but only as long as the disputes do not infringe on the sovereignty of any of the countries concerned. Also, for cases involving firms, jurisdiction must be consented to by the state.

[c] Indirect means that cases with private litigants would come through national courts' references to the international court.

[d] As a general rule, consent to the Central American Court of Justice's contentious jurisdiction is implicit in the ratification of the Protocol of Tegucigalpa. However, consent must be explicitly given in the case of (a) territorial disputes (in which case consent to jurisdiction has to be given by both states party to the dispute), (b) disputes between states member of the Central American Integration System and states that are not members, and (c) cases in which the court sits as arbitral tribunal.

[e] General Agreement on Tariffs and Trade does not meet Project on International Courts and Tribune's definition because there was no permanent court. This is the reason that NAFTA is not included on the table as well.

[f] World Trade Organization Appellate Body replaced General Agreement on Tariffs and Trade and has a permanent appellate body.

International Court and Tribunal's definition of an *international court.*[5] At this point, we can fairly say that most ICs fit this new-style model, and nearly every IC created since 1990 fits this new style. The final column supports the notion that ICs with compulsory jurisdiction and private access hear more cases, but it also shows that not all new-style ICs are equally active. The table generally includes data up until 2003 or 2004. Table 2.1 in Chapter 2 updates the usage data through 2006.

There is no explanation for this turn to enforcement through ICs, and it is not my goal to offer one. Rather, I am interested in explaining the design trend toward creating new-style ICs as opposed to old-style ICs. Scholars have generated lists of reasons to delegate to ICs—transaction cost-reducing reasons (to have courts fill in incomplete contracts, to create decentralized systems to monitor compliance), enforcement reasons, strategic reasons, and credibility reasons (Alter 2003a; Elster 2000; Garrett and Weingast 1993; Hathaway 2005; Majone 2001, 2003; Scott and Stephan 2006; Simmons 2002)—but providing reasons why delegation may be attractive does not explain why delegation is more common or is taking a different form today compared to the past. Those who focus on the timing of the trend offer observations that are surely correct: the end of the Cold War likely facilitated the creation of many of the new ICs, and the proliferation of regional trade agreements has contributed to a proliferation of ICs operating within specific regions (Brown 2002; Romano 1999). Such explanations do not really explain why we have more delegation to ICs or account for the change in IC design. We come closer to an explanation of the design trend in the work of James McCall Smith and Alan Sykes. McCall Smith seeks to explain delegation to more legalized dispute resolution mechanisms. His cases are all trade agreements, but he finds that delegating enforcement to more legalized third-party dispute resolution bodies (with compulsory jurisdiction, private access, binding rulings, and permanent legal bodies) is associated with deeper trade agreements with more specified obligations and a greater desire by parties to have compliance with the agreement (McCall Smith 2000). Sykes identifies political economy incentives to allow private judicial access to enforce bilateral investment treaties compared to trade treaties—treaties that may or may not be enforced through ICs. Sykes provides a potential explanation of states' preferences for private access (to domestic or international courts), but he is focused exclusively on investor agreements (Sykes 2005).

---

[5] Excluded due to lack of information are the African Court of Human Rights (not yet established), the Southern African Development Community Tribunal (not yet established), the Court of the African Union (2003), three different courts of the Economic Community of West African States (established 1996 to 2001), and the East African Court of Justice (2001). A decision was made to merge the African Court of Human Rights into the African Union; hence, my report of 26 ICs meeting PICT's definition. In this analysis I counted the Tribunal of First Instance separately from the ECJ. In subsequent analyses I count the ECJ and TFI together.

III. A Functional Explanation of the Design Trend in Delegation to ICs

This article posits a functional explanation whereby IC design decisions follow from the functional jurisdictional task assigned to courts. The jurisdictional categorization comes from the way a number of domestic legal systems organize themselves—by creating separate administrative courts to hear complaints against the actions of public administrators, civil courts to resolve disputes among private actors, criminal courts to enforce state law, and constitutional courts to review the compatibility of national law with constitutional provisions.[6] Courts with different designated jurisdictions often have appointment procedures and designs that differ. For example, administrative courts hear suits raised by private actors, and the courts themselves can be part of the administrative agencies they review or draw judges from the ranks of administrators. Criminal courts, by contrast, have prosecutors who bring cases against private or public actors who violate the law. Civil law judges can have different training procedures and qualifications compared to administrative court judges. Meanwhile, constitutional courts tend to be separate entities with judges that have lifetime appointments, or non-renewable appointments, to reinforce their independence from the political branches they oversee.

The following discussion separates the four roles courts play. The original article was my first attempt to articulate these four roles. I have updated the language a little, for clarity. This article appeared as part of a special edition that focused on rights claiming in front of international courts. For this reason I focused on how the types of rights claimed can vary by judicial role. The roles are described as Weberian 'ideal types,' meaning synthetic intellectual constructs with a conceptual purity that often cannot be found in reality (Gerth and Mills 1958: 59–60). My discussion of 'role morphing' considers how these ideal types are artificial.

This functional metric differs from other scholars' arguments about the role of courts in the political process. Martin Shapiro sees all courts as government tools to maintain social control over the population (Shapiro 1981). Rational choice scholars see courts as efficiency devices that fill in incomplete contracts, generate information useful to parties, and facilitate monitoring of compliance (Garrett and Weingast 1993; Milgrom, North, and Weingast 1990; Posner and Yoo 2005; Raustiala 2004; Tallberg 2003). Liberal scholars see international legal systems as pre-commitment devices to reassure the weak that the powerful will follow similar rules (Elster 2000; Ikenberry 2001; Moravcsik 1997). The argument here does not contradict these alternative perspectives, but we may well find that courts in

---

[6] American and common law legal systems are not organized this way. French and German civil law legal systems, however, separate judicial roles these ways. These systems are replicated in many countries of the world.

certain roles fit these different arguments differently, meaning that the constitutional courts may be pre-commitment devices and that administrative, civil, and criminal courts may be more focused on social control and so forth.

The four judicial roles defined

Dispute adjudication

Dispute adjudication in its ideal-typical form is private law adjudication. Two private parties subject to the law bring a dispute to a judge, who renders an interpretation of the law that binds both parties. These disputes are usually conceptualized as arising from contractual disagreements—differences in opinions regarding duties and obligations owed to each other—though the 'contracts' which give rise to the duties and obligations are often informal and implicit. Shapiro identifies this judicial role as participating in social control.[7] In delegating to judges the authority to interpret the law, state actors are seizing the desires of the parties to have a judicial resolution of a dispute as an opportunity to bring their laws into the private realm, into neighborly disputes, private business interactions, and even family decisions. In choosing the legal outcome, judges are choosing the state's desired resolution—that custody of a child goes first to blood relatives, that firms be accountable for their actions, etc.

Dispute adjudication is the only judicial role lacking a minimum design requirement; dispute resolution mechanisms can work even if the process is not compulsory, the parties pick the judges, the decision is only declaratory, and the ruling is not at all based on pre-existing rules. Indeed, arbitration, mediation, 'good offices', and judicial proceedings are all different forms of dispute resolution, effective as long as the two parties are convinced that the dispute resolution mechanism is fair.

Although there is no minimum functional design requirement, design choices influence how a court plays its dispute adjudication role. The old-style courts were all dispute adjudication courts. Although some of these courts were also nominally given the mandate to help enforce the law, absent compulsory jurisdiction, these ICs could only really be used to resolve disagreements about the law (because recalcitrant states would simply block a case from proceeding). Where an international dispute adjudication mechanism is coupled with compulsory jurisdiction, disputes can still be settled outside of court or through arbitration, but negotiation is more likely to take place 'in the shadow of the law' because there is a credible background threat of litigation that can shape the bargaining positions of negotiators (Mnookin and Kornhauser 1979; Tallberg 2002; Tallberg and Jonsson 1998)—and thus, dispute adjudication can be used by litigants to enforce international law. Because dispute adjudication is for contract

---

[7] Shapiro, *Courts: A Comparative Political Analysis*, pp. 17–20.

disagreements, access is usually limited to those who sign the contract. For inter-state treaties, access is often limited to states only. Because states can sign contracts with private actors, a number of ICs allow access (usually by mutual consent) for private contract holders to raise 'breech of contract' charges against foreign governments or international organizations. Sometimes, however, dispute adjudication is extended beyond the contract signatories to any affected individual. Once access extends beyond the signatories of the agreement, the contract starts to resemble a statute rather than a mutually binding agreement, and more rights are created. A reason to extend wide access is to harness private actors as monitors and co-enforcers of the contract (Raustiala 2004).

Criminal enforcement and infringement proceedings

Although it is commonly said that courts enforce the law, it is always governments with a monopoly on the legitimate use of force that enforce the law. States can enforce the rules on their own—using their extensive coercive power to punish those who violate their rules. In a rule of law system, however, the task of overseeing the legitimate use of coercive power is delegated to judges. In this 'enforcement' role, the judge essentially monitors the state's use of its coercive power, and thereby s/he helps convince the public that the state is not abusing its power.

How do we know an enforcement role when we see it? Criminal law enforcement is the easiest to recognize. A court is given jurisdiction over a body of law that defines crimes regarding persons and/or property, and cases are raised by a public prosecutor who charges a defendant with violating the law. If the prosecutor manages to convince the judge that the defendant violated the law, the judge will authorize the state to do what would otherwise be illegal and illegitimate—to deny a person his or her liberty, to seize his or her property, or to violate the law in retaliation. Since guilty parties are unlikely to submit themselves to judicial proceedings about their behavior, enforcement roles require that courts have compulsory jurisdiction.

War crimes tribunals mirror their domestic criminal counterpart—public prosecutors raise cases and the defendant is an individual—thus, war crimes courts have private access. Infringement cases are usually raised by *commissions* (a less harsh term than *prosecutor* though their role is largely the same) with governments or public actors as defendants in the cases. The international level adapts the traditional enforcement model by allowing states to raise infringement suits against other states, and sometimes even allowing private actors to initiate infringement suits. In these cases, there is not a dispute about the meaning of the law but, rather, the defendant is charged with having violated international rules.

Criminal enforcement is not really intended to be a tool to enhance private participation or rights claiming. Prosecutors are arguably serving a public role in promoting victims' rights, but the victim is usually in the background of the case. The legal process also arguably helps protect the rights of the accused—their right to a fair trial and not to be arbitrarily harmed by the state—but the prosecutors are usually not private actors, the defendants did not choose the terrain of the case, and the defendants often lack sufficient command of the legal rules to assert their rights, which is why defendants often do not view the criminal legal process as aimed at enhancing their participation or rights-claiming abilities. An exception to this rule is the two international legal systems that authorize private actors to raise infringement suits (the Andean and Central American systems)—though this possibility has not been exploited much at all by private actors (see Part III).

Administrative review (public law litigation)

The functional role of administrative review is to hold public officials (as opposed to legislative bodies) accountable by providing a means for the subjects of administrative actions to challenge public decisions (Edley 1990). ICs with jurisdiction to hear cases regarding the legality of a public action, policy, or regulation, actions to annul, or 'failure to act' charges regarding decisions or non-decisions of executive bodies have administrative review powers. For administrative review to exist in any meaningful way, the actors subject to government decision-making must have standing to bring suits challenging arguably illegal government behavior, and the public decision-maker defendant must be compelled to participate. Thus, the minimum administrative review design criteria include compulsory jurisdiction and access rules that allow actors affected by administrative decision-making to challenge arbitrary decisions.

The substance of the administrative law combined with how the court's administrative review jurisdiction is defined will largely define the suits the court hears. When the law itself requires public comment periods before administrative rules are adopted, the weighing of competing public interests and adequate explanations for administrative decisions, administrative courts can provide private litigants with a powerful procedural tool to assert rights and challenge administrative policies (Bignami 2005; Edley 1990). When administrative rules grant broad discretion to administrators and the jurisdiction of administrative courts only allows for cases where administrative decisions are arbitrary or capricious, litigants may be barred from pursuing procedural irregularities and unable to challenge the policies themselves. Whether administrative review generates broad or narrow rights-claiming possibilities, there is an intended distinction between holding public officials accountable to legislative intent (administrative review) and holding legislative bodies accountable to the constitution (constitutional review), which is why administrative review tends to be less politically controversial compared to constitutional review.

Constitutional review

For many people, administrative review is sufficient to ensure that there is a rule of law in which public and private actors are equally required to follow the law. But some political systems have opted to create absolute limits on what legislative bodies can do, entrusting constitutional review bodies with the authority to review the validity of the law itself. Constitutional review bodies have jurisdiction to assess the validity of laws and acts of legislative bodies, ensuring that procedural rules for law-making are followed, the policy or law coheres with the constitution or treaty, and the legislative action is not *ultra vires* (exceeding the legislator's authority). In a federal context, constitutional courts also police the constitutionally defined border of federal and state authority, ensuring that neither legislative body encroaches on the power of the other. Because sovereigns usually do not like to be checked by courts, constitutional review only exists if a court's constitutional jurisdiction is compulsory. Access rules for constitutional review will shape the extent to which constitutional review is about rights claiming. Sometimes, judicial constitutional review can only be triggered by members of the legislative body (e.g. a state or a group of legislators), in which case the respect for the constitution is primarily ensured through legislative self-policing and constitutional review is primarily about minority legislative actors challenging decisions made by the majority (Stone 1992). Other constitutional systems allow private actors to access legal bodies either directly or via ordinary national courts, turning constitutional review into a means for private actors to participate in the legislative process (Stone Sweet 2000).

Role morphing: Relaxing the ideal types

The ideal-type constructs imply that courts and cases are easily classified into a single role. In reality, a single case can involve questions that span roles. Judicial role morphing occurs when the judge embraces an opportunity presented in a case to expand beyond their designated role. Because judges tend to apply precedent, and because legal rulings are themselves a source of law (Hathaway 2001), rulings that morph roles can become a source of judicial authority and thus courts created for one role can end up serving more than their designated role (as happened in the EU). Some contexts and roles are more subject to morphing compared to others. For example, dispute resolution mechanisms may morph into a sort of decentralized enforcement when paired with compulsory jurisdiction because the plaintiff can get the legal system to enforce the law against the defendant. This morphing may well be intentional, providing a way for agreements to be enforced without devoting state resources for a prosecutor and thus avoiding the possibility that the prosecutor may be more zealous than some may like. Dispute resolution and criminal enforcement may morph into constitutional review because the subjects of international law are usually sovereign states, and thus, implicitly, the ICs may be ruling on the compatibility of state policy with international rules. Indeed, the distinction between enforcing international human rights agreements and constitutional review may in practice become meaningless. To the extent a judge moves from investigating the application of a law to investigating the law itself, the distinction between administrative review and constitutional review can become meaningless.

Although roles can morph, they don't always morph. Moreover it is still ana-
lytically useful to keep the four roles distinct. The starting roles provide insight
into the reason ICs were created in the first place. They shape the initial design of
the legal institution and suggest certain logic of appropriateness for international
judges as they carry out their charge.

The functional argument about the design of ICs

The claim of the functional argument is that the jurisdictional role combined
with how states want the IC to play its role drives the design of the IC. At the
international level, treaty drafters break down the types of legal issues ICs can
adjudicate into separate treaty articles, with different access and compulsory jurisdiction rules for each article. The judicial role is defined by the types of questions the court has authority to hear, and it is usually quite clear where consent
to jurisdiction is required and where private actors are allowed to raise suits (and
on what basis). Table 12.2 indicates which ICs have which roles and the design
of the IC for the role.[8] Some ICs have explicit authority to hear only one type of
legal suit, and others have jurisdiction to hear a variety of types of legal questions;
thus, some ICs appear under multiple roles.

The evidence in support of the functional argument comes via correlation. If
function were not related to design, we would expect the rules for access and compulsory jurisdiction to be randomly distributed (as opposed to clustered by role),
and we would expect design choices to be constant within a single IC. Instead,
in every case except the Inter-American Court of Human Rights (IACHR; signified in dark gray), the design of the IC matches or exceeds (denoted in light
gray) the minimum-design criteria for the functional role, and we find that individual courts vary in design depending on the judicial role. That a number of
ICs have designs that exceed the minimum design criteria does not vitiate the
functional argument. Rather, mismatch between the minimal design and what
we find allows us to identify which court designs call for further explanation.
Investigating which courts have which roles and which courts exceed the minimum-design criteria enhances the credibility of the functional argument in that
the design variation itself becomes less surprising. The rest of this section investigates this variation.

The most prevalent role one finds for ICs is that of a dispute adjudication
mechanism (13 of the 20 ICs). Given that old-style ICs pretty much only played
a dispute adjudication role, should we ask why even some ICs were not given a
dispute adjudication role? One finds no dispute adjudication role where it would

---

[8] I do not consider whether an IC can play a role via an advisory opinion because such opinions
are not binding; nor do I consider IC roles with respect to employees of the international organization. For space reasons, I have removed a discussion on the relationship between remedies and
roles. Each role also has corresponding minimum-design remedy that could be added as a dimension of Table 12.2.

Table 12.2. Design of international court by Role

Judicial Role	Expected Minimum Functional Design Requirements	ICs with role	Compulsory Jurisdiction	Private Access
Dispute Adjudication Jurisdiction to "interpret the meaning of the law" or to "ensure that the law is respected," jurisdiction to resolve disputes.	**No minimum requirements** but according to PICT's definition of an IC, it must be possible for one litigant to be a state or government entity.	ICJ	see note A	see note A
		ITLOS		
		WTO	X	
		EFTAC	X	see note B
		ECJ	X	
		OAPEC		
		CCJ	X	see note D
		ECCIS	X	
		CACJ	X	X
		OHADA	X	X see note D
		COMESA	X	X see note E
		BCJ	X	
		ACJ	X	
Criminal Enforcement Jurisdiction regarding an enumerated list of crimes or jurisdiction to hear infringement suits against states.	**Compulsory Jurisdiction** **Access rules**-Public plaintiff, public or private defendants.	ICC	X	As Defendant
		ICTY	X	As Defendant
		ICTR	X	As Defendant
		ICTSL	X	As Defendant
		EFTAC	X	
		ECJ	X	
		ACJ	X	X see note F
		COMESA	X	
		CACJ	X	X see note G

	IACHR	see note H	X (post 1998)
	ECHR	X	X
Administrative Review Jurisdiction in cases concerning the "legality of any action, regulation, directive, or decision" of a public actor, or the public actor's "failure to act."			
Compulsory Jurisdiction Defendant will be a public actor. If administrative review is to have any meaning, the public defendant must be required to participate in proceedings.	ITLOS-Seabed Authority	X	X
	ECJ & CFI	X	X
	EFTAC	X	X
Access rules- Actors subject to the decisions of administrative agencies must have access to court to challenge administrative decisions affecting them.	ACJ	X	X
	COMESA	X	X
	BCJ	X	X
	CACJ	X	X
Constitutional Review Jurisdiction to review the legality of any legislative act, regulation, directive, of an IO.	COMESA	X	X
Compulsory Jurisdiction	ECJ	X	X
Access rules: Can be limited to states, or allow private access too.	ACJ	X	X
	CACJ	X	X
	Post 1998 ECHR?	X	X
	CCJ?	X	X

Bold indicates that the design exceeds the minimum criteria. If the functional argument is correct, only bolded design choices call for further explanation. A) *ITLOS*- compulsory jurisdiction & private access exists only in cases involving the seizing of vessels, and the plaintiff's government must consent to the case being raised. B) *EFTAC* can review preliminary ruling requests, but its opinions are not binding. C) *CCJ* is authorized to decide on a case by case basis if the needs of "justice" require allowing private access for the case. This design reflects that the CCJ has replaced the Caribbean Privy Council. D) *OHADA*- Private actors can directly appeal national court rulings to OHADA court. E) *COMESA*- private actor access is limited to contracts between private actors and COMESA institutions. F) *ECHR*- Pre- 1998 only a Commission could raise cases. In 1998 the Commission was eliminated and direct access for private actors was allowed (Protocol 11), substantially altering the role the ECHR de facto plays. G) *CACJ*-Has general authority to hear infringement suits brought by any actor with standing, including states, private actors, and community institutions but no designated supra-national prosecutor. H) IACHR does not meet the minimum design criteria.

either create redundancy (e.g., the European Court of Justice [ECJ] handles the dispute resolution cases instead of the Court of First Instance [CFI]) or where the legal system is primarily about criminal enforcement (the four criminal courts, the two human rights courts).

A lot of ICs exceed the minimum design for dispute resolution; these courts fit the arguments of McCall Smith and Sykes. McCall Smith tested the notion that there is a trade-off between allowing state discretion and increasing treaty compliance. Analyzing a wide sample of trade agreements, including bilateral agreements that do not create ICs, McCall Smith found that a choice for more legalized dispute resolution (permanent legal bodies, compulsory jurisdiction, with sanctioning remedies) was associated with deeper trade agreements in which the aspiration was to create a common market (McCall Smith 2000). This finding supports the argument that states may give compulsory jurisdiction to dispute resolution bodies to encourage morphing into an enforcement role, and it could explain why the designs of the European Free Trade Area Court, Caribbean Court of Justice (CCJ), Central American Court of Justice (CACJ), Court of Justice of the Andean Community (ATJ), Economic Court of the Commonwealth of Independent States, and Benelux Court include compulsory jurisdiction; because they are embedded within common market systems. It also explains the World Trade Organization Appellate Body in which compulsory jurisdiction was added precisely to enhance enforcement, with states recognizing that there would be sovereignty costs (Jackson 1997). Alan Sykes, who investigated the argument that private access helps reassure private investors that domestic investment rules will be respected, helps us understand why the ICs in international organizations aimed at promoting foreign direct investment, such as the Common Court of Justice and Arbitration for the Organization for the Harmonization of Corporate Law in Africa (OHADA), include compulsory jurisdiction and private access via appeals of national court rulings (Sykes 2004). The Court of Justice for the Common Market of Eastern and Southern Africa (COMESA), International Tribunal for the Law of the Seas (ITLOS), CCJ, and CACJ remain unexplained by either argument. For the COMESA and ITLOS courts, private access is primarily limited to contract disputes between private parties and COMESA and ITLOS institutions. ITLOS, however, also allows for private access and compulsory jurisdiction for disputes regarding vessels that are seized in fishing or territorial disagreements.[9] For the CCJ, private access via appeals of national court rulings (Article XXV) exists because the CCJ is replacing the Privy Council that, as part of the commonwealth system, had served as an appellate body for rulings of Caribbean courts (Pollard 2003). I do not know the origins of CACJ design decisions.

---

[9] The boat's flag state must first agree to adjudication, but thereafter, fishermen can sue to have their boat released (Noyes 1998: 138).

Criminal enforcement is the next largest role (12 ICs). Only four of these ICs exceed the minimum design by allowing private access (the four criminal enforcement mechanisms are for use against private individuals; thus, private access is functionally required). The European Court of Human Rights (ECHR) and the ATJ did not originally allow private access for their infringement process, suggesting that private access, because it was not required for the functional role, was excluded. The ECHR created an optional protocol in the 1990s that allowed members to opt for direct access for their citizens (agreeing to private access became a requirement for accession to the European Convention on Human Rights in 1998). For the ATJ, private access was added in the *Protocolo de Cochabamba* in 1996 (Arteaga 2004) with a goal of increasing transparency and popular participation in the Andean community (this provision appears to be a dead letter).[10] The CACJ remains a design exception. The CACJ court has jurisdiction for infringement suits, but the institution lacks a prosecutor and instead allows pretty much any actor to raise an infringement case (O'Keefe 2001). As Section IV notes, there have been 26 admissible infringement suits raised by private actors, though in some of these, the private actor was a member of a CACJ institution acting in a private capacity.

Administrative review authority has been given to seven ICs if one counts the ECJ and CFI together (these two courts split the administrative review tasks for the EU between them). In each case where an IC was given administrative review power, there is also a supranational administrator. This correlation suggests that administrative review was created in large part to replicate the types of administrative checks one finds at the domestic level. Although all six administrative review courts can conduct administrative review vis-à-vis supranational bodies, only four of them can also hear appeals against national administrative decisions (ECJ, ATJ, COMESA, CACJ).[11] In the EU, private appeals were allowed (via the preliminary ruling mechanism) because domestic administrators were often the primary actors implementing European rules. The ATJ replicated the ECJ design intentionally (Keener 1987). The reality that domestic actors would be implementing international rules may also explain why the COMESA and CCJ courts have administrative review roles as well, though I do not know enough to say. The CACJ simply lists a series of court competences (Article 22 of the Court's

---

[10] Articles 25 and 31 authorizing private actors to use national legal mechanisms to enforce Andean rules were part of the Protocol of Cochabamba (10 March 1996). Based on an interview with a drafter of Decision 472, a.k.a the Protocol of Cochabamba, Quito Ecuador, 18 March 2005.

[11] Common Court of Justice and Arbitration for the organization for the Harmonization of Corporate Law in Africa and Economic Court of the Commonwealth of Independent States bodies do not meet my classificatory criteria in that they do not have nullification powers; nor are they explicitly granted a right to rule on the legality of any action, regulation, directive, or decision of a public actor. Their cases will inherently involve appeals of national legal decisions, which means that they will be reviewing decisions of public actors, but they do not meet the definition of administrative review bodies.

statute), allowing administrative challenges to come from private actors, states, and members of the Central American institutions.

Only four of the international legal systems were explicitly created with constitutional review authority, meaning the explicit authority to review the validity of the law itself—the EU, ATJ, CACJ, and COMESA courts. These four regional integration systems have multiple institutions and what are essentially supranational legislative bodies that can create binding rules that are directly applicable in the national realm; thus, it appears that the granting of constitutional review authority followed from the decision to grant supranational legislative authority. The CCJ's role in the common market is yet to be defined; thus, it is potentially a fifth IC with constitutional review authority (Pollard 2003). One may also question whether the design of the ECHR has changed so much with time that it is at this point more of a constitutional court than a criminal enforcement court.

If we think that compulsory jurisdiction and private access provides courts with cases states may not have wanted raised, and with opportunities for ICs to pronounce on many issues, the trend in empowering ICs makes little sense. Yet if we think that compulsory jurisdiction and private access was accorded to allow ICs to play certain desired functional roles—to allow for the administrative review of the actions of supranational administrators, to create constitutional level checks on supranational legislative bodies, and because private access is inherent to war crimes trials, the expansion of private access makes more sense. When we understand that the compulsory jurisdiction in dispute resolution transforms dispute resolution into an enforcement mechanism, we can see why a higher than minimum design can be attractive. When we understand, however, that compulsory jurisdiction contributes to morphing of roles we can also see why it may be eschewed even though it is functionally necessary as in the IACHR case. Thus, the functional argument helps us better understand the variation in IC design we observe. In identifying design variations within a single role, the functional argument gives us a first cut way to understand why courts with similar jurisdictional roles (such as the ECHR and IACHR, the World Trade Organization Appellate Body, and the International Court of Justice) can vary in how they play their role.

IV. More European Courts?

A number of institutions outside of Europe (e.g. the ATJ, CACJ, CCJ, and African economic systems) have tried to mimic the European model; they have created supranational administrative and legislative bodies and ICs with administrative and constitutional roles to check the behavior of these supranational actors. These systems are designed to promote rights claiming and democracy within supranational polities and to create checks on the exercise of supranational authority. A separate question is whether private access will lead to a replication of the independence and effectiveness of European ICs vis-à-vis states. The scholarship discussed in Section I posits that compulsory jurisdiction and private access will help ICs influence state behavior (Helfer and Slaughter 1997), and it has been criticized for drawing general conclusions from the somewhat unique European context (Alvarez 2003; Posner and Yoo 2005).

By examining the usage of ICs with private access, we can get a sense of whether and how private access leads to a replication of the European model. Table 12.1 identified 14 ICs with private access in which ICs could issue binding rulings. Four of these courts are war crimes courts where private actors are the defendants in the case, not the plaintiff using litigation to promote their rights. Excluding war crimes courts—the recently created CCJ and the largely unused Benelux Court[12]—one finds nine ICs where private actors could be using international legal mechanisms to enforce international rules vis-à-vis member states—three European courts and six non-European courts. Table 12.3 identifies private-litigant-inspired cases that have been raised in these ICs.

The real bone of contention is whether ICs with private access will allow rights claiming vis-à-vis states. Most of the data reported by ICs are highly aggregated, making it unclear whether or not private access is leading to law enforcement vis-à-vis supranational actors or national governments. For ECHR cases, one can say that most if not all of the cases are raised by private actors targeting national policies and behaviors. For the ECJ and CFI, direct action cases by definition target EU authorities, not national governments. Although many people assume that ECJ preliminary ruling cases involve private-actor challenges to national rules, these cases may also challenge the rules and policies of supranational actors. Indeed the best evidence we have is that most preliminary ruling cases are actually challenges to EU rules and Commission decisions, not questions about the compatibility of national rules and European law.[13] The Andean data is through 2003. In the Andean system, as of 2003 there were 714 preliminary ruling cases, and most of these challenge national implementation of Andean rules with respect to intellectual property (96 per cent) (data updated in Helfer, Alter, and Guerzovich 2009). In addition, there have been three direct action cases in which the target of challenge was a national policy. The ITLOS court has heard no challenges to decisions of the Seabed authority, and most of the cases involve state-to-state dispute. As of 2003, there have been seven private ITLOS cases raised by the owners of vessels. The CACJ has heard 34 private-actor cases, 26 of which targeted a national policy. (I have no information about the 90 rulings by

---

[12] Since publication I have found statistics on the usage of the Benelux Court. It has heard 137 cases referred by national courts, and thus initiated by private actors. See Table 2.1. Since the Benelux Court is European, this additional data mainly adds the general finding here.

[13] Jurgen Schwartz reviewed German references from 1960 to 1986 and found that roughly 40% of the national references in his sample were about the compatibility of European Court law with national law (Schwartz 1988). Chalmers reviewed UK references and found a similar result (Chalmers 2000), suggesting that more than half of national references do not involve questions about national policies or rules.

Table 12.3. Cases in ICs Raised by Private Litigants

International Court	Total Docket	Private actor cases (last year of data)	Private actor cases targeting state practices
European Courts (minus EFTAC & Benelux)			
European Court of Justice (ECJ)	2497 infringement cases by Commission, 5293 cases referred by national courts, 7528 direct actions (2004)	5293 cases referred by national courts, 7528 direct actions (2004)[1]	An unknown percentage of the 5239 preliminary ruling cases (see note 11)
European Court of Human Rights (ECHR)	8810 cases deemed admissible, 4145 judgments (2003)	8810 cases deemed admissible, 4145 judgments (2003)	8810 cases deemed admissible, 4145 judgments (2003)
European Court of First Instance (CFI)	2083 decisions from 3003 cases filed (figures exclude staff cases) (2004)	3003 direct action cases (2004).	
Potential Private Actor Cases from "European" courts			*21695 admissible cases (96% total potential private cases)*
Non-European Courts			
International Tribunal for the Law of the Seas (ITLOS)	13 judgments (2003)	7 "prompt release of vessels" rulings	7 "prompt release of vessels" rulings
Court of Justice of the Cartagena Agreement (Andean Pact) (ACJ)	31 nullifications, 108 infringement cases, 711 preliminary rulings raised by private actors in national courts (2004)	711 preliminary rulings raised by private actors in national courts, 10 nullification challenges, 3 private infringement suits[2] (2004)	711 preliminary rulings raised by private actors in national courts, 10 nullification challenges, 3 private infringement suits[2] (2004)
Central American Court of Justice (CACJ)	65 Cases, 21 Advisory Opinions, 30 rulings, 7 dismissed, 7 pending (2004)	34 cases raised by private actors (2004)[3]	26 admissible private actor v. state actor cases

Economic Court of the Common-Wealth of Independent States (ECCIS)	47 cases, not clear if they are ruled on yet (2000)	47 cases, presumably all private actor cases. It is not clear if they have been ruled on yet (2000)	Presumably all 47 cases involve private appeals of national court rulings.
Court of Justice for the Common Market of Eastern and Southern Africa (COMESA)	3 judgments, 1 order (2003)	3 judgments, 1 order presumably all of which are private litigant cases (2003)	Presumably all 4 cases involve private appeals of national court rulings.
Common Court of Justice and Arbitration for the Organization for the Harmonization of Corporate Law in Africa (OHADA)	4 opinions, 27 rulings (2002)	4 opinions, 27 rulings presumably all of which are private litigant cases (2002)	Presumably all 31 cases involve private appeals of national court rulings.
Potential Private Actor Cases from non-European Courts			*847 opinions and rulings (724 are Andean Tribunal rulings)*

[1] Figures from ECJ's annual report: http://curia.eu.intr/en/plan/index.htm. I have excluded appeals cases. Direct action cases include anything brought directly to the ECJ, including cases brought by national administrative actors and labor disputes raised by the employees of European level institutions. Preliminary ruling cases are raised by private actors and could include challenges to national policies and decisions and challenges to EU policies and decisions.

[2] Data complied by author is based on material available from <http://www.communidadandina.org/normativa.asp>. Private litigants lacked standing to raise infringement suits until 1996. Thus, in 1987, a private litigant's case was dismissed for lack of competence. These have been only three private actor cases since the change in access rules; one of these was dismissed and one was abandoned.

[3] Data complied by author from material from <http://www.ccj.org.nl/>.

the Economic Court of the Commonwealth of Independent States, COMESA, and OHADA, but I assume that all of these cases involve appeals of national court rulings applying international legal rules.)

These data suggest that with the exception of the ECHR, private access may be focused as much on rights claiming vis-à-vis international institutions as it is on rights claiming vis-à-vis national governments. It also suggests that private enforcement through international legal mechanisms remains largely a European phenomenon. Ninety-six per cent of the total IC judicial decisions potentially involving private actors have been issued by European courts, 3.2 per cent from the Andean Tribunal, leaving less than 1 per cent of all possible private-litigant-inspired rulings in other courts. Let me underscore that this sample only represents cases raised by private actors that reach the rulings stage. Many cases raised by commissions and states are on behalf of private actors, many cases settle before the ruling stage, and private actors also use domestic courts to enforce international rules—thus, there are ways other than direct access for private-actor suits to be pursued and for private participation to occur. The comparison is unfair in that European courts have been around a lot longer than the other six courts have. Although one could control for the per annum usage of courts, a larger difference would still remain—the other six institutions do not have as dense a web of legal rules actors may call on to enforce. Although multiple factors could account for why European courts hear so many more cases, the overall statistics suggest that it is far from clear whether European courts are the model or the exception.

V. Democracy and Access to Justice in the New ICs

This article asks the following question: Why the proliferation of ICs with compulsory jurisdiction and private-litigant access? Scholars expect private access to be associated with more effective ICs, by which they mean ICs more capable of inducing state compliance with international rules. The obvious question the scholarship raises is why sovereignty-jealous states would ever agree to private access if it is likely to lead to more challenges to their behavior.

The previous section developed a functional argument whereby judicial roles require specific minimum designs for a court to actually fulfill its given role. It argued that compulsory jurisdiction is functionally required for constitutional review, administrative review, and criminal enforcement roles—and one finds compulsory jurisdiction empirically associated with all ICs playing these roles, with the exception of the IACHR. Access for subjects of administrative rulings is functionally required for administrative review, and one finds that all ICs with administrative review powers allow private access for these roles. We also find private access for international war crimes courts because the defendant in the case is inevitably an individual. The creation of war crimes courts and ICs with administrative and constitutional roles explains in large part the trend toward new-style ICs. Indeed, although only some of the dispute resolution ICs included compulsory jurisdiction and even fewer allowed private access, all administrative and constitutional ICs had private access and compulsory jurisdiction.

This correlation of compulsory jurisdiction and private access with certain judicial roles suggests an explanation for why, with time, one finds an increasing number of ICs with compulsory jurisdiction and private access. Increasingly, states are creating international institutions with legislative and administrative authority. If international judicial roles were not expanded, these international governance bodies would actually have fewer checks than their domestic counterparts do. The checks have to be international; judicial review of international actors is outside of the authority of domestic courts, and creating multiple national checks on international actors would be a recipe for chaos. Although I have not proven that the change in IC design follows from the change in international governance and the types of tasks delegated to international organizations, this functional argument makes empirical sense. States display little desire to generally increase the effectiveness of international law vis-à-vis states; nor do they universally allow compulsory jurisdiction and private access. The correlation between compulsory jurisdiction and private access on one hand and certain judicial roles on the other is strong. The fact that the same court has different access rules for different roles suggests that functional considerations are shaping access-rule decisions.

The functional argument gives us a good starting point to understand the variation in design we observe, and it identifies questions for further analysis—such as why do some courts have design features below or above the minimum-design criteria, and why are some courts given some roles whereas others are given other roles? The previous section suggested a logic to giving certain powers to one court and not another, providing further support for the functional argument. But a handful of design decisions could not be explained by functional arguments. Even when design choices are functionally required, we must remember to avoid the functionalist fallacy (Hall 1986); we cannot prove intent based on the function a court serves, and functional arguments will never tell us about how ICs actually fulfill their functional roles or if they stay within the functional boxes created in the founding treaties.

This article appeared as part of a special edition of *Comparative Political Studies* that focused on rights claiming in international courts. It is clear that private access to ICs to challenge supranational actors can help facilitate rights claiming, international organizations' accountability, and the rule of law within supranational governance systems. But I find that these tools have not taken a deep hold outside of Europe. Perhaps the problem is that it is too early to say. In many cases where we find new-style ICs, either the court or the larger institution in which it is embedded is fairly new. Until these institutions develop governance rules that affect people's lives, we should not expect much international litigation. Once there are meaningful rules, the Andean experience suggests that existing institutions can spring to life.[14]

Notwithstanding the fact that the vast majority of ICs now have compulsory jurisdiction and allow at least partial private access, it is still the case that most ICs provide fairly limited resources for private citizens to use. ICs provide private litigants with new tools to challenge the administrative and legislative actions of supranational bodies, and sometimes private actors can use these tools to challenge national implementation of supranational rules. Usage of these tools, however, is primarily limited to Europe and to intellectual property law in the Andean community. This is not to say that the new-style ICs are not creating qualitative changes in international politics. Many of the newer style ICs are able to help enforce international rules against states—though not per se in suits raised by private actors—and this change remains meaningful. Also, as international institutions engage in more administrative regulation, administrative review of their actions will also be meaningful. It is just less clear from this analysis that outside Europe private access is an important key to the story of how ICs are transforming international relations or state behavior. At a minimum, this study suggests caution in generalizing across ICs based purely on design features. The study also suggests that greater attention be given to the content of the cases litigated, breaking down aggregated statistics by the role the IC is playing so that we can have a better sense of what ICs are actually doing. Only then can we really understand how ICs facilitate rights claiming by states and private actors alike

[14] The Andean Tribunal is the third most active IC in existence. I have three co-authored articles appearing on this topic. See Helfer, Alter, and Guerzovich (2009); Helfer and Alter (2009); Alter and Helfer (2009).

13

Law and Politics in Europe
and Beyond (2009)

There is a wide interest in identifying the factors that gave rise to the European Court's political power, in part because the ECJ is seen as having positively contributed to European integration, but also because we are in a moment in time where a new history of international courts is being written. We are trying to figure out whether having an International Criminal Court dampens the forces that lead to war crimes. We are exploring whether European integration can successfully be spread to newer European member states, which are different in so many ways from states that joined the European Community in the 1960s, 1970s, and 1980s. And we are in a new period of regionalism, with regional international courts being created to facilitate economic cooperation, shore up new investment and property rules, and promote greater respect for human rights in the region. It is in this context that the history of the ECJ is being re-examined, by myself and others, so as to perhaps understand what may be coming in international politics. This conclusion aims to identify what we might study with respect to the ECJ and other international courts, in order to gain insight into how these legal experiments underway may develop.

This book, a retrospective focused on the political power of the European Court of Justice, reveals that the ECJ is both a fairly typical and an exceptional international court. Typical elements include that the ECJ's role ended up broader than states had imagined, and that the ECJ has been willing to render rulings which powerful states and powerful actors dislike. Also typical is the ability of ECJ rulings, including its controversial rulings, to redirect policy and politics. European law's influence, and the ECJ's influence, reaches beyond the cases that are litigated. At the same time, clearly there are issues and geographical areas where the ECJ is either sidelined and/or unable to bring states into compliance and areas where European rules remain ineffective in shaping state behavior. This was the case for much of the history of the Coal and Steel Community (see Chapter 3); it has been the case for EU member states that have a challenge enforcing their own laws, let alone European laws (Börzel 2001); and it is increasingly likely to be the case in newer member states where the rule of law is far from established. The reality of order without law, where laws and judicial institutions are ignored even if bringing law in could benefit certain actors, exists for all legal systems (Ellickson 1991). Indeed it does not appear that the European Union's laws on the books are any more or less respected than are domestic laws in large federal states (Börzel 2001; Zürn and Joerges 2005).

Also increasingly typical is that the European Court was created to be more than simply an international dispute resolution body. The ECJ was created to play the roles of enforcer of European law, and to be the administrative and constitutional review authority on European Community legal issues. Because member states intended the ECJ to play these other roles, they gave the ECJ compulsory jurisdiction, and allowed the Commission and private actors to raise cases. Because they anticipated that national courts would be the primary actors hearing disputes regarding national application of European rules, they allowed the ECJ to hear references from national courts (Pescatore 1981). Chapter 2 showed that today most other ICs have compulsory jurisdiction and access for non-state actors to initiate disputes. Chapter 12 showed that most ICs are 'new style' courts with compulsory jurisdiction and private access and argued that IC design follows the role delegated to the court (dispute adjudication, enforcement, constitutional review, and administrative review). Chapter 12 identified a number of ICs with enforcement, administrative, and constitutional review roles. In fact over half of operating ICs have been delegated an enforcement role (11 out of 20), 40 per cent (eight out of 20) have been delegated an administrative review role, and at least four, possibly six, international courts have been delegated explicit constitutional review roles (Alter 2008: 62).[1]

There are, however, many exceptional elements that set Europe's supranational courts apart from the rest. In terms of activity, Europe's supranational courts are in a league of their own, as a comparison of the top five most active ICs reveals (see Table 13.1). Judicial activity is a poor proxy for a court's influence, since not all legal rulings are of equal political significance. But at some level judicial activity suggests that ICs are useful for litigants, worth the cost and effort of bringing an IC into a dispute. The far greater level of ECJ and ECHR activity suggest that these courts are simply more useful for promoting issues litigants care about and thus more politically relevant.

The constitutionalization of the European legal system, discussed in Chapters 3 to 6, was by all accounts key in expanding the power and influence of the ECJ, and thus in generating its high level of activity. The ECJ was an important creator of this change, showing a level of legal activism and political success that is unique for an international court.[2] This transformation in itself makes the ECJ more similar to national constitutional courts than to international courts.

---

[1] The special issue of *Comparative Political Studies* in which Chapter 12 first appears has other chapters which suggest that the ECJ experience is more general (though most of the other chapters focus on European cases). See Cichowski (2006).

[2] The ECHR has, to be sure, been totally transformed into a sort of constitutional legal body. But the most important reforms giving rise to this change occurred through decisions by the European Commission for Human Rights and via institutional reforms adopted by states. See Helfer (2008).

Table 13.1. Legal activity of the five most active international courts

International Courts	Date Established/ Created	Cases raised since founding up to 2006
European Court of Justice (ECJ) (including its Tribunal of First Instance)	1952/1952	17,697 rulings including preliminary rulings, direct actions, appeals, and infringement suits
European Court of Human Rights (ECHR)	1950/1959	7,528 judgments from 12,310 cases deemed admissible
Court of Justice of the Cartagena Agreement (Andean Community) (ATJ)	1979/1984	1,267 rulings including preliminary rulings, infringements, and nullifications
World Trade Organization (WTO)	1994/1994	271 panel reports and appellate body rulings
International Court of Justice	1945/1949	100 judgments and advisory opinions from 111 cases filed

Data from Alter (2008: 58–60). WTO data includes panel reports through 2005.

These unusual aspects of the ECJ call for explanation. The introduction to this volume focused on general take away insights that the European experience reveals about law and politics, domestic and international. This conclusion considers lessons one can draw from the ECJ's extraordinary history for what the future of international courts may hold. Section I examines factors that the ECJ's experience suggests are neither necessary nor sufficient for an IC to become politically powerful, and it hazards an explanation of why the ECJ has been so exceptional. The explanation I offer is basically an educated hunch that needs further research to substantiate. Section II identifies the type of scholarship that might reveal the validity of this hunch. While we probably know more about the European Court's legal history than any other international court, there are still many black holes in our knowledge because we have not really investigated how the ECJ's development was influenced by transformations within national systems. The gist of this section is that as we examine EU enlargement, and the political power of other ICs, we should not replicate the format of early European legal studies. Rather, we should start from the current position of European legal integration studies, exploring how supranational and international law evolves in interaction with changes in national and international contexts. Section III goes out on a limb, daring a big picture answer to what the exceptional experience of the ECJ suggests for international law more generally.

I. Lessons from the ECJ Experience

Using the ECJ's exceptional history as a laboratory to understand international or supranational law can allow one to make the negative case—if it is not true in the ECJ context, it probably is not true more generally. But it is harder to make the positive case—that something is true for the ECJ does not mean it is true more generally. In terms of the negative case, the ECJ experience suggests that legal traditions may be an excuse for inertia, but they are not per se a barrier to the expansion and penetration of international rules into domestic legal orders. The ECJ experience also suggests that there is an undue scholarly focus on the design of international courts as potentially explaining the politics that ICs evoke. In terms of the positive case, my focus here is what perhaps explains why the EC experience has been so exceptional.

The negative case: What the ECJ experience tells is probably not true

Civil law/common law, monism/dualism: Legal traditions as a hindrance to international law

Since I am an American, and a political scientist, usually judges and lawyers presume that I do not understand civil law systems. I am told that the civil law tradition differs from the common law tradition,[3] creating barriers on judge-made legal innovation. To the extent there is variation in how civil law court systems are responding, judges and lawyers tend to assume the difference comes from variation in national constitutions, especially variation regarding whether a national legal system is monist (recognizing the supremacy of international law) or dualist (requiring international legal rules to be transcribed into national law before they become effective).[4] Basically, judges are saying that they do their job

---

[3] In common law systems precedent is a source of law. In civil law systems, legal precedents are not considered a source of law. This difference is more formal than real. Even civil law systems rely on precedent, otherwise legal interpretation would constantly shift. The main difference is that in common law systems, judges will cite precedent as a basis for their rulings. Civil law judges are more likely to replicate the legal reasoning so as to suggest that the legal analysis applies only to the case at hand. In both systems, judges rely on precedent as a guide in decision-making, and legal interpretation develops in a largely path dependent way. For more on this distinction see Merryman and Pérez-Perdomo (2007).

[4] Monist legal systems conceive of international law and national law as part of a single system. Monist legal systems usually contain constitutional or legislative provisions that give international rules legal validity within a national legal order. By contrast, dualist legal systems see international law as separate from domestic law. As a formal legal matter, in dualist systems international rules only gain legal effect through domestic incorporation. In practice, however, conflicts between national and international rules create the same sorts of political problems regardless of whether the national legal system is monist or dualist.

as they understand it, which hinders efforts to incorporate international legal practices into domestic legal systems.

It used to be common for European lawyers to explain variations in national court willingness to embrace European law by claiming that dualist and monist legal systems, or civil and common law legal systems, respond differently when faced with international legal obligations. The ECJ's history, however, suggests that such differences are not all that important, or at least that their significance is dwarfed by other factors. The early European Economic Community contained both dualist and monist member states. It had member states with long histories of courts being denied the power of judicial review, and countries that responded to the atrocities of World War II by creating constitutional courts and insisting that judges assert their power to review the legality of legislative laws and governmental policies. The enlarged Europe of the 1970s had both common law and civil law countries. None of these differences—save possibly the existence of powerful national constitutional courts—has been shown in any reasonable way to create significant let alone insurmountable limits on the penetration of European law into national legal and political systems. Nor do such variations account for empirical trends in the way European legal integration has proceeded within and across member states or in the timing in which key European legal doctrines were incorporated into national legal systems (Carrubba and Murrah 2005; Mattli and Slaughter 1998).

My educated hunch based on the European experience leads me to expect that the fact that a country has a civil law or dualist legal tradition will not be a significant hindrance to compliance with or national judicial enforcement of international laws. Let me be clear about my argument here. Legal traditions may well influence national judicial behavior; the real question is which aspects of this culture matter, and how do cultural variables matter. We may find that civil law courts refer repeat cases to international courts, or repeat legal arguments within their rulings, where common law courts use the shorthand of applying precedents, thereby generating variation in the number of explicit references to international courts or international laws. We might also find that courts in dualist countries prefer an official instruction to apply international rules where courts in monist countries will on their own apply the rules. These variations may generate statistically significant correlations when we measure international law related judicial activity, but still not be meaningful in that they do not in themselves signify variation in respect for international rules.[5] Moreover, there may be other factors related to national legal institutions that are far more important

---

[5] For example, Carrabba and Murrah do find that numerically speaking, courts in countries with dualist legal systems tend to make more references to the ECJ compared to their counterparts in monist countries. But for them, other factors are more significant. Meanwhile studies that look at Commission infringement actions suggest that countries where national courts refer more cases are not necessary less compliant, nor is there any evidence to suggest that dualist or civil law countries as a class are less likely to comply with European law (Börzel 2001).

in shaping judicial behavior—such as the training process of lawyers, the way in which judges are selected and get promoted within the national system, and how the mandate and authority of courts is distributed within the national legal system. And legal institutional factors may themselves matter less than factors such as public opinion or the position of the government on the issue.

To the extent that legal culture simply means inertia, the culture itself may be explaining very little since inertia is the normal state of affairs. Blaming legal tradition is convenient; it suggests that judges continue to be disinteresed servants of the law. It is just that they are doing the old job of being a judge and perhaps not the new one. Clearly, adding the enforcement of international rules to a judge's list of responsibilities brings an element of disruption. Most lawyers have a very limited training in international law, which makes the idea of interpreting and enforcing international rules daunting. There needs to be a reason for judges to take on this new and daunting task.

The European experience suggests that neighborhood effects—the effects generated by the behaviors of important actors within the larger neighborhood of states that are bound to the same set of international rules—may be more important than local cultural factors in shaping how national courts interact with international courts and international law. In Europe, the fact that other countries were accepting European Court authority mattered, as did the reality that by staying out of the Euro-law game (refusing to make references or speak to European legal issues), national judges were more likely to cede any influence they might have over the development of ECJ jurisprudence (see Chapter 5). In the Andean context, the Secretariat overcame the reticence of Ecuadorian and Peruvian courts to refer cases to the ATJ by raising an infringement suit, and by pointing out the practices of these courts' Colombian counterparts (Helfer and Alter 2009). Legal tradition provides a comfortable home to stay in. But where your governments, your citizens, or your neighbors are all changing, it becomes clear that it is time to leave your comfortable home. As Chapter 4 explained, the European Commission also put significant resources into training a generation of lawyers to understand and be comfortable with European law. Deep change probably does require such an investment, which means it may also require generations to achieve.

It is somewhat ironic that foreign judges expect the fact that I am American to mean that I probably do not appreciate the legal limitations judges face in other contexts. United States Supreme Court judges are famous for their legally creative, politically influential rulings. But they are also famous for often ignoring international legal obligations.[6] Both the American and European experiences suggest to me that powerful constitutional courts are going to be less willing to cede to other actors the final authority to interpret how international law impacts

---

[6] The most recent case is *Medellin v. Texas* Case No. 06–984, 552 U.S. ___ (2008) (25 March 2008).

a national polity—a reality that has nothing to do with legal tradition. I would expect the existence of a strong constitutional court, and federalism, to be barriers to the reach of international law and international courts into national legal systems, because I expect actors whose power reigns supreme within their domain to chafe at ceding supreme interpretive authority to another actor. Both in the case of legal inertia and when constitutional courts generate limitations, hindrances can be surmounted where a political will exists. Absent such a will, however, bureaucratic politics and inertia will serve as drags, though not an inherent limitation, on efforts to promote greater respect for international rules.

International court design as it contributes to international court politics

Scholarship that emphasizes the design of international courts also makes general claims about how design shapes court independence, behavior, and effectiveness. Scholars have expected courts with private access (what Keohane et al. call transnational courts, and Helfer and Slaughter call supranational courts) to be busier and more effective than courts without private access (what Keohane et al. call interstate courts) because

a steady flow of cases...allows a court to become an actor on the legal and political stage, raising its profile in the elementary sense that other litigants become aware of its existence and in the deeper sense that interpretation and application of a particular legal rule must be reckoned with as a part of what the law means in practice. Litigants who are likely to benefit from interpretation will have an incentive to bring additional cases to clarify and enforce it. Further, the interpretation or application is itself likely to raise additional questions that can only be answered through subsequent cases. Finally, a court gains political capital from a growing caseload by demonstrably performing a needed function...(2000: 482)

Scholars have expected judges to be less activist in legal systems where legal rules are easier to change, and where appointments for judges are shorter in length (Tsbelis and Garrett 2001; Stephan 2002). Scholars have expected judges to be either more or less independent and effective depending on whether the legal systems has compulsory jurisdiction and private access (Posner and Yoo 2005; Helfer and Slaughter 2005). And scholars (and most lay people) often expect courts to be more effective where sanctions can be attached to adverse legal decisions (Downs 1998).

The ECJ's experience raises questions about how important institutional design actually is. The European Coal and Steel Community's (ECSC) ECJ was not significantly different in design compared to the Economic Community Court—it had compulsory jurisdiction, access for private actors, a High Authority with the power to enforce ECSC rules, and implicit sanctioning power (the ECSC could fine states and firms, and withhold transfer payments). Yet, as Chapter 3 (*The Theory and Reality of the European Coal and Steel Community*) shows, the ECJ and High Authority were largely unable to induce respect for ECSC rules— across nearly the entire 50-year history of the ECSC! Chapter 4 (*Jurist Advocacy*

Movements in Europe) compares the ECJ to its clone the Andean Tribunal of Justice, a comparison that also belies the simplistic equation that has a court's design shape the influence, independence, activism, or effectiveness of an IC. Chapter 11 shows that differently designed ICs can still act as Trustees that shift the political context. Chapter 12 (*Private Litigants and the New International Courts*) makes this case more generally, showing how the ECJ's design is not unique, yet the experience of Europe's supranational courts is exceptional.

These findings suggest that international relations approaches which focus on how variations inherent to the contract between state-principals and international agents shape the political behavior of both, will not be helpful in explaining variation in IC activism. The influence of the ECJ, which for most of its history has lacked formal sanctioning tools, compared to the influence of the WTO's Appellate Body and the ATJ which do have formal sanctioning abilities, suggests that contrary to the expectations of many, the ability of a legal system to attach punitive sanctions to adverse legal rulings may not be a key determinant shaping whether or not international legal systems are seized in the first place, let alone whether they are able to help induce respect for international rules. The reason is that most people like to see themselves as law-abiding (Tyler 2006). Usually it is enough for a court to brand a behavior as 'illegal' or 'inconsistent with the rule of law' to bring most actors into compliance with the law. For those actors who will only respond to sanctions, the legal sanctions international courts have at their disposal are quite often insufficient to induce a change in behavior—which may be why compliance with the WTO is most likely to occur before a case reaches the ruling stage of the WTO process (Busch and Reinhardt 2001b).

How does IC design matter then? In the introduction I argued that whether an international court has compulsory jurisdiction seems to be the most important design factor that influences whether or not an IC is likely to render politically inconvenient decisions. This argument was based on the finding that in all three cases of ICs ruling against powerful countries discussed in Chapter 11, the ICs had compulsory jurisdiction. Meanwhile, neither the ICJ nor the WTO has private access, yet they have still been influential. And few of the ICs with private access analyzed in Chapter 12 have been known to disappoint powerful actors. While hardly conclusive, this finding makes sense. Without compulsory jurisdiction, the only cases that reach a court are those where both parties are happy to let a court decide. The selection effect of cases in itself influences the likelihood of compliance. Clearly compulsory jurisdiction leads to court cases where compliance with the ruling becomes more problematic (Busch and Reinhardt 2000b). But compliance is not the same things as effectiveness (Raustiala 2000: 388). It is not clear that courts with compulsory jurisdiction are any less effective than courts without compulsory jurisdiction (Helfer and Slaughter 2005)—though there is much to suggest that courts with compulsory jurisdiction are more likely to introduce the shadow of an adverse legal ruling into in-court and out-of-court negotiations (Tallberg and Jönsson 1998).

The design of a court is not irrelevant. A lack of compulsory jurisdiction creates fundamental limitations on what and when an IC will be able to influence legal interpretation. Moreover, if those actors who might want to bring a legal suit cannot do so, a force for political change will be blocked. Because design features co-vary with roles a court comes to play (administrative review, constitutional review, dispute adjudication, and enforcement), we may also find correlations supporting the notion that certain designs create certain politics. The analysis of Chapter 12 supports the notion that ICs with private access to initiate disputes are more active than ICs without private access, but it also argues that designs follow from the roles delegated to ICs. I think that what is really going on is that administrative review roles require private access, and international courts with administrative review authority tend to be the most active international courts. I expect politics to vary significantly by the role a court plays. I expect constitutional review roles to be more controversial than administrative review roles, for example. If the role is driving court design and the politics that ensue, then it is the role and not the design that matters. Also, studying the ECJ reveals how factors exogenous to the IC—activation by others, and the presence of societal actors who share the IC's interests—shape the role a court ends up playing in a political system. For all of these reasons too much emphasis on IC design is probably misplaced.

The larger question the ECJ case alone cannot answer is: when do international laws and international courts become embedded into national politics? When do international legal institutions penetrate the surface of the state to interact with government decision-makers and private actors so as to influence domestic and international politics (Hathaway 2005; Helfer 2008: 131)? At the end of the day, the ECJ's extraordinary political power seems to stem from a few factors specific to its context. National courts will apply ECJ rulings, thus governments know that even if they do ignore an ECJ ruling, eventually they are likely to be called to account for violations of European law. European populations expect their governments to adhere to the rule of law, and thus it is politically costly to be seen as flouting legal authority. Moreover, ultimately European governments want the European Union to succeed, and thus they accept that compromise will be part of EU membership. The question remains, however, how did we get to this reality from where European countries were in the 1950s and 1960s?

The positive case: Why has the ECJ's history been so exceptional?

What is so unique about Europe that its supranational courts have come to have such significant political roles? The ECJ had a number of factors in its favor. Europe's legal fields were more developed than legal fields in many other countries, which is to say that there is greater political prestige accorded to legal actors

in Europe, and well developed traditions and customs surrounding legal practices in Europe which could be fairly easily adapted to the cause of European legal
integration. The European integration project was also not simply a collection of
economic or functionally beneficial agreements. Rather, a fervent set of actors
saw European integration as part of a larger political endeavor of building peace
in Europe, united under a rule of law so as to limit any return to authoritarian
practices. These factors, discussed in Chapter 4, were important in the history of
Europe, though they are not per se unique. (And they did not translate in the 1960s
into a constitutionalization of the Council of Europe's human rights system.)

These factors at best provide part of the story. The Euro-law movement was
committed and active, but small. How were the vast majority of actors not committed to the European integration as a social or economic project brought along
in support of the ECJ's constitutionalization project? My 2001 book, partly summarized in Chapters 4 and 5, focused on how national judges became co-opted
into the ECJ's project, explaining how support for the ECJ's supremacy doctrine
spread within the French and German judiciaries eventually co-opting national
governments into accepting a fundamental political transformation that ceded
important elements of national sovereignty in ways they did not intend, want,
or ever really endorse (Alter 2001). But the story is incomplete in that it focuses
mainly on explaining the acceptance of European law supremacy by national
judiciaries. It cannot answer the larger question of how we got to the political
reality described above, where populations and government officials expect political actors to adhere to the rule of law.

I am increasingly coming to believe that the ECJ's story is part of a larger institutional and political evolution wherein courts in Europe have become the political actors of today, capable of ending Italian practices of dividing power among
Christian Democratic and Socialist parties so as to exclude the Communist Party
from power, capable of stripping Augusto Pinochet's immunity, thus contributing to an international human rights justice cascade that has reverberated around
the world (Sikkink and Lutz 2001). Europe's particular history of wanting to
overcome the legacy of World War II, including the deadly war among neighbors,
the judicial collaboration with authoritarian regimes, and the egregious tramp-
ling of individual rights, was key in facilitating national transformations, and the
ECJ's success. Europe's World War II history mattered in a few ways.

First, Europe's history helped to build the networks behind pro-European
jurist advocacy movements. In the late 1940s, European countries were ruled
politically by former members of the anti-fascist resistance. Many of these initial political leaders continued in politics, although quite a number ended up
with powerful positions but not as political leaders themselves. Those actors who
did not themselves stay in government became representatives in international
legal negotiations, and they later used their political offices to aid the European
integration project (Madsen and Vauchez 2005). It is not unique for opposition

politics to create a networked class of actors who become central in building a new polity. It is, however, unusual for law and constitutional development to be so central to the agenda of such actors, and for international law to figure so highly as part of their reformist agenda.

Europe's history also emboldened jurists—lawyers, judges, and legal scholars—as a group. In the 1950s and 1960s European states were expanding their role in national economies.[7] Political liberals and national judges responded by creating checks on political bodies as they expanded their role, though for different reasons. Liberals wanted to limit as much as possible government involvement in the economy. They were a constant constituency to challenge state authority, but they did not always or even mostly succeed in their legal efforts. Jurists as a group mainly wanted to ensure that governments' expanded role adhered to the rule of law. Originally, many jurists' conception of what constituted the rule of law was rather limited. It did not include courts conducting constitutional review of national law, and the legal rights protected by courts tended to be more procedural than fundamental in that there were few courts, in even fewer countries, assessing whether constitutional guarantees were adequately respected by the political branches of government. Over time, basic rights became politically important. It is increasingly common for jurists today to frame their discourse and agenda around a 'rights'-based politics, and thus to be part of a vanguard demanding democratic constitutional reforms (Halliday, Karpik, and Feeley 2007: Introduction), but this is a more recent transformation both in Europe and in the larger international context.

Somewhat distinct is that in Europe, jurists were joined in their more narrowly conceived endeavor of promoting the rule of law by civil servants. Under authoritarian rule (and during parts of Europe's history), ideology and political loyalty were key criteria shaping appointment and promotion in civil service positions. European bureaucracies became professionalized in the 1950s and 1960s, meaning that expertise and competence rather than political connections emerged as the basis for appointment and promotion within national administrations.[8] Civil servants with expertise and competence chafe at political manipulations of rules, and thus they became a constituency in support of judges rejecting politically inspired interpretations of legal rules. Thus lawyers had actors within the state they could appeal to and work with to help realize their objective of having governments respect the rule of law.

Finally, Europe's experience with World War II fundamentally changed popular attitudes in Europe. European citizens mobilized time and again to demand their government adhere to the democratic objectives they expected. This synergy between the ECJ's objective of building supranational legal checks on

---

[7] Mauro Cappelletti discusses how the expansion of the European welfare state contributed to the expansion of European judicial authority. See Cappelletti (1989: 15–23)

[8] I am indebted to Antoine Vauchez for this insight.

supranational political authority and the larger agenda within European states and societies of creating legal checks on political power created a willingness for national judges to work with the ECJ by referring cases involving European law (the interpretation of which was outside of the competence of national judges). Because of European citizens' commitments to many of the ideals embedded into European Community law, because national judges agreed to enforce European laws, and because civil servants were committed to adhering to legal rulings, bringing the ECJ into specific policy debates could be a potent political tool.

II. Going Forward: Research Questions for the Study of Transnational Legal Politics in Europe and Beyond

The argument above is more of a call for further research than a well developed argument. What would we need to know to substantiate my speculations? For the European story we would need to know more about the development of post-war national legal institutions, and how legal developments influenced and were influenced by European legal integration. Mauro Cappelletti (1989: ch. 2) offers a persuasive narrative about how the expansion of European welfare states contributed to an enlarged role for judges, but his account is also mainly an intuition. We would also need to know more about how synergies develop. Why do international law-domestic law synergies not develop in other contexts? Why are technical rules sometimes better for promoting international legal integration while in other contexts constitutional norms, like basic rights laws, connect better to domestic agendas? Why, for example, did a synergy develop around enforcing fairly technical European Community rules (an administrative law dynamic) rather than the more far-reaching and politically central tenets of the European Convention on Human Rights (a constitutional law dynamic)? These questions are far from academic since many practioners and scholars are trying to unlock the factors contributing to the creation of a stable and independent domestic rules of law.[9]

In terms of the study of Europe, the empirical and theoretical agenda this argument suggests would be to investigate the development of powerful national legal institutions, which I believe is one of the defining features of post-World War II European politics. The judiciary was one of the many political institutions that had been discredited through collaboration during World War II. Lawyers and politicians realized that significantly different legal structures needed to be created, but they had to work with the stock of lawyers, professors, and judges that existed. It took new generations of lawyers, professors, and judges entering the legal apparatus, and rising into positions of authority for change to occur. Also newly established legal structures—constitutional courts and new

---

[9] For example, see Hammergren (2007); Maravall and Przeworski (2003); O'Donnell (2004).

administrative systems—needed to build their authority, to create a new reality that scholars could study and explicate, and that legal actors within national legal systems could respond to and emulate. Given how long these changes took, it is not surprising that political scientists who focused on European politics in the 1950s, 1960s, 1970s, and even the early 1980s missed what was happening. Legal evolutions became impossible to ignore in the 1990s because judges started successfully challenging the practices of powerful political elites. Now that we now know the end of the story—in the 1990s administrative and legal actors became key contributors to large-scale political changes, and judicial review has emerged as an important force of policy-making and institutional change—we need to go back in time to add courts back into our earlier understandings. There is strong scholarship on the rise of constitutional courts in Europe (see for example Stone Sweet 2000), but less scholarship on larger social and political changes within national bars, judiciaries, and educational systems. We need to investigate why and how Europe's legal institutions changed in the post-World War II era.

Beyond legal institutional changes, we need to investigate how these changes contributed to legal and political developments in Europe. We need to connect, as Francesca Bignami, Rachel Cichowski, and Peter Lindseth are doing, European level changes to national evolutions (Bignami 2005; Cichowski 2007; Lindseth 2003, 2005). And we need to connect legal changes to larger political changes within and across states. We should be able to locate the construction of a legal and administrative European state into the construction of the economy, and into the construction of constitutional democracy, to see how economic and political conditions shaped these developments. Concretely, we should be able to link European legal developments to our understandings about how 'modern capitalism' was built in Europe in the 1950s and 1960s (Shonfield 1969). We should also be able to identify how legal institutions were part of the 'embedded liberal' meta compromise shaping international and European economic systems in the 1960s, 1970s, and early 1980s (Ruggie 1983; Cappelletti 1989). We should be able to see how legal institutions were part of Alan Milward's explanation regarding how European integration helped European countries deliver this embedded liberal compromise, and thus how European integration helped resuscitate the political *raison d'être* of the postwar European state (Milward 1992). We should be better able to link the histories of European Community integration and the growing authority of the European Convention on Human Rights. And we should be better able to understand how institutional developments benefited from the external threat of the cold war, and the unprecedented economic growth and stability in post-war Europe. When we understand these relationships, we will better understand the pushmi-pullyu relationship[10] between law and politics.

---

[10] The pushmi-pullyu was the name of the two-headed creature connected at the waist in Hugh Lofting's tales of Dr Doolittle. The pushmi-pullyu had heads pointed in opposite directions. In order for the pushmi-pullyu to walk, the two heads had to work together—one had to walk backwards, so the other could go forwards. For law to work it must induce political actors to voluntarily

Such understandings are relevant beyond Europe. It has long been recognized that political institutions facilitate economic development. More recently it has been suggested that legal institutions are important for political stability and economic prosperity (Halliday, Karpik, and Feeley 2007; Maravall and Przeworski 2003). But it is far from clear how we get to legal institutions that can facilitate economic and political development, and how variation in legal institutions is related to variations we find in cross-national and cross-temporal economic and political development. Post-World War II Europe is a good place to investigate these questions.

Equally important is that we move forward intellectually rather than replicate the past. European legal integration provides a model in that it represents a case of successful penetration of international rules and international court authority into domestic realms. It is also a model in the heterogeneity of scholarly approaches that have been used to study European legal integration. Among those who know the European case well, we have made advances on understanding the limits of legal formalism, and in investigating how political factors enter into judicial decision-making and legal interpretation (see Chapters 1 and 2 for more). One can hope that the study of the many new domestic and international legal institutions can skip some of these steps that the study of European legal integration has gone through, and thus that we can learn from Europe in another way as well. At the end of the introduction I identified five scholarly eddies in particular that I hope we can move beyond.

There are many old questions to investigate in the European context, since we know so little about the legal changes in the post-war period. But there are also many new questions to address. In Europe, the end of the Cold War opened the floodgates for EU membership. There is of course a burgeoning literature focusing on how European Union membership affects Central European countries' policy and politics (Jacoby 2004; Kelley 2004; Schimmelfennig 2003; Vachudová 2005). EU enlargement also offers a cornucopia of ways to investigate how domestic legal institutions reform, how external forces influence domestic reform efforts, and how legal authority gets built (or not built). The current generation of scholars has a chance to document how legal institutions are evolving independently from and in relationship to national political reforms, and to investigate if the EU or other external legal obligations (e.g. the Council of Europe, WTO membership) accelerate or are undermined by domestic institutional evolution.

The question of how enlargement affects institutional development in new member states is especially interesting because the latest set of entrants are both emerging from authoritarian rule and seeking to industrialize in ways that can integrate these countries into the global economy. Newer EU members are thus

yield, and if they are to yield, the legal process must take into account deeply felt political concerns even if it leads to outcomes that are poorly reasoned from a legal perspective. This analogy comes from Alter (2002: 120).

more comparable to domestic polities in other regions of the world. One would expect the European Union to again present a case that is located on the far side of a continuum in terms of international factors being likely to shape domestic development. The former Soviet satellite countries have a number of extremely compelling reasons to truly embrace democratic forms of governance and the rule of law—including membership in the EU. Indeed the EU serves as an anchor with common sets of rules and a model of how these rules are meant to be implemented, and nowhere in the world is there an institution as willing or invested in helping domestic reformers as the European Union. Of course there are many counter-forces at work, and while incentives are strong they may not be strong enough. I do not assume the European Union will be highly success-ful in inducing desired changes in former Soviet satellites, nor is it likely that all or even most changes that occur will be because of EU efforts. Rather, once again we should expect that if the Europeans cannot influence their neighbors, then the EU and other international efforts may be even less likely to influence legal and political development in other regions of the world.

III. Generalizing from the European Case

The introduction and the previous sections have suggested how we can learn from the European case. To the extent the ECJ experience is an exceptional case of international judicial success, we can build negative insights. In other words, that certain factors were not important to success in Europe suggests that they may well not be necessary or sufficient for international legal success in other contexts. The introduction identified many factors which have generated vari-ation in the influence of the ECJ; these same factors may generate variation in the influence of courts in other contexts. To the extent that we can explain why the ECJ was so successful in becoming embedded within national political sys-tems, we can learn the factors that shape how international legal institutions (law, international organizations, and international courts) become embedded into national political systems. And we can start studying new questions by build-ing on the sociology of knowledge developed in Europe, where legal positivist types of explanations as well as simple narratives of how political actors influence international courts have been debunked.

In terms of the big picture lessons, the ECJ experience suggests that there are two routes to greater respect of international law. Powerful governments may see having international law as in their interests, and thus they may choose to help political and judicial actors build an international rule of law. Or, sub-state actors who believe in the rule of law can lend their support to the international legal endeavor. European legal integration followed both routes, but during the 1960s and 1970s the greatest steps towards building an integrated federal legal order came through judicial rather than political evolution.

Different dynamics animate each of the routes, which is to say that the dynamics shaping governmental interests differ from the dynamics shaping the interests and behavior of sub-state actors. The political role of ICs will be largest where there is both government support for international rule and sub-state actor involvement. This might mean that for international courts to play a larger role, domestic legal institutions may need to be powerful on their own in addition to being supportive of international court authority.

The sub-state route will be harder to pursue in authoritarian regimes, especially if the government opposes a larger role for international actors. Thus we may find it harder for international law to become embedded in national legal order where there are few liberal democracies in the neighborhood of states. Meanwhile, if legal actors lack legitimacy and independence, ICs and domestic courts are likely to enforce very clear law, but they are more likely to be legal formalists sticking to the letter of the law and hesitating to fill in legal lacunae (Ginsburg and Moustafa 2008). Chapter 10 suggested that even the ECJ retreats in such an environment, avoiding creating rulings that might exacerbate already existing divisions within the larger polity. Thus in contexts of weak legal authority and regime complexity, we may find ICs playing a more limited role out of a fear that their ruling may be unseated by other politically authoritative institutions and because such environments tend to be politically hazardous making it hard to identify broad and stable pockets of social support for existing rules.

This argument is somewhat unsatisfying in that it says that chickens hatch where there are fertile eggs. Of course the larger question is—where are there fertile eggs? I have suggested that Europe remains a place where we can study this question, by examining how European legal systems have worked to overcome their authoritarian pasts. It is also clearly true that there are fertile eggs in a wider variety of issue areas and political contexts. I have suggested that fertile eggs exist where administrations are professionalized and where domestic courts have political power of their own.

We are seeing independent legal actors emerging in a broader number of contexts, including in the context of authoritarian regimes that are undergoing significant economic reform efforts, such as China. We are also witnessing a proliferation of international courts, and a rise in international litigation (Romano 1999). Thus there are more opportunities for international law and international courts to grow in their political roles by linking synergistically to the agendas of legal and political actors on the ground, and thus to embed international legal institutions into national political development.

But there are also more opportunities for political contestation regarding what these rules mean, and regarding the extent to which domestic actors want to be constrained by legal rules that their government did not have a significant hand in drafting or shaping. Indeed one can find evidence of forces that favor an enhanced role for international law. And one can observe counter-forces that emphasize the foreign, democracy-undermining, sovereignty-compromising nature of international law (indeed the very success of the forces favoring insti-tutionalizing international law are likely leading to the mobilization of counter-forces). While we cannot know which forces will win in the end, we can study how contestation around international law occurs and shapes legal and political evolutions.

The ECJ has traditionally been a case where these questions are investigated, and in light of European enlargement the ECJ remains a particularly relevant laboratory of investigation. But increasingly there are other active ICs where one can also investigate these issues. It is my hope that by elucidating some of the many elements that have shaped the political role of the ECJ, I may spark others to join me in this project of investigating how delegating authority to international courts is transformative of international politics.

APPENDIX

Related Essays Not Included in This Volume

Articles on the ECJ

'The Making of a Supranational Rule of Law: The Battle for Supremacy'. In *Europe Today*, Ronald Tiersky (ed.) (Boulder: Rowman and Littlefield, 1st edn, 1999; 2nd edn, 2004).

'Explaining National Court Acceptance of European Court Jurisprudence: A Critical Evaluation of Theories of Legal Integration'. In *The European Courts and National Courts;* Anne-Marie Slaughter, Alec Stone-Sweet, and Joseph Weiler (eds) (Oxford: Hart Publishing, 1998) 225–50.

'Law, Political Science and EU Legal Studies' (2002) 3(1) *European Union Politics* 113–36.

Articles on other international courts

Articles on the Andean Tribunal of Justice:

'Islands of Effective International Adjudication: Constructing an Intellectual Property Rule of Law in the Andean Community' With Laurence Helfer and Maria Florencia Guerzovich. (Forthcoming 2009) 103 *American Journal of International Law.*

'Building Judicial Supranationalism in the Andes: Understanding the Preliminary Reference Patterns in the Andean Community' With Laurence Helfer. (Forthcoming 2009) 42 *Journal of International Law and Politics.*

'Nature or Nurture: Judicial Lawmaking in the European Court of Justice and the Andean Tribunal of Justice' With Laurence Helfer. Manuscript in progress.

Articles on the World Trade Organization's dispute settlement system:

'Resolving or Exacerbating Disputes? The WTO's New Dispute Resolution System' (2003) 79(4) *International Affairs* 783–800.

Articles on delegation to international courts

'Delegating to International Courts: Self-Binding vs. Other-Binding Delegation' (2008) 71(1) *Law and Contemporary Problems* 37–76.

'Designing International Legal Mechanisms to Help Enforce Trade Agreements' in Kazuya Hirobe (ed.), *Institutional Approaches to Regionalism* (2008) (in Japanese).

'Delegation to International Courts and the Limits of Recontracting Political Power' in Darren Hawkins, Daniel Neilson, Michael J. Tierney, and David A. Lake, *Delegation under Anarchy* (Cambridge: Cambridge University Press, 2006).

'Do International Courts Enhance Compliance with International Law?' (2003) 25 *Review of Asian and Pacific Studies* 51–78.

Bibliography

1973. Conflicts between Treaties and Subsequently Enacted Statutes in Belgium: État Belge v. S.A. 'Fromagerie Franco-Suisse Le Ski' 72(1) *Michigan Law Review* 118–128.

Abbott, K. and D. Snidal. 'Why States Act through Formal International Organizations' (1998) 42(1) *Journal of Conflict Resolution* 3–32.

Abbott, K. and D. Snidal. 'Hard and Soft Law in International Governance' (2002) 54 (3) *International Organization* 421–456.

Abbott, K. and D. Snidal 'Pathways to International Cooperation'. In *The Impact of International Law on International Cooperation*, ed. E. Benvenisti and M. Hirsch (Cambridge: Cambridge University Press, 2003).

Abraham, R. *Droit international, droit communautaire et droit français, Le Politique, L'Economique, Le Social* (Paris: Hachette, 1989).

Aggarwal, V. K. *Institutional Designs for a Complex World: Bargaining, Linkages and Nesting* (Ithaca: Cornell University Press, 1998).

Alemanno, A. 'European Court rejects damages claim from innocent bystanders in the EU-US "Banana War" 12 ASIL Insight 21: October 22, 2008 (<http://www.asil.org/insights081022.cfm>).

Alter, K. J. 'Explaining National Court Acceptance of European Court Jurisprudence: A Critical Evaluation of Theories of Legal Integration'. In *The European Courts and National Courts*, ed. A.-M. Slaughter, A. Stone-Sweet and J. Weiler (Oxford: Hart Publishing, 1998).

Alter, K. J. *Establishing the Supremacy of European Law: The Making of an International Rule of Law in Europe* (Oxford: Oxford University Press, 2001).

Alter, K. J. 'Law, Political Science and EU Legal Studies' (2002) 3(1) *European Union Politics* 113–136.

Alter, K. J. 'Do International Courts Enhance Compliance with International Law?' (2003a) 25 *Review of Asian and Pacific Studies* 51–78.

Alter, K. J. 'Resolving or Exacerbating Disputes? The WTO's New Dispute Resolution System' (2003b) 79(4) *International Affairs* 783–800.

Alter, K. J. 'Delegation to International Courts and the Limits of Recontracting Power'. In *Delegation and Agency in International Organizations*, ed. D. Hawkins, D. A. Lake, D. Nielson and M. J. Tierney (Cambridge: Cambridge University Press, 2006).

Alter, K. J. 'Delegating to International Courts: Self-binding vs. Other-binding Delegation' (2008) 71 *Law and Contemporary Problems* 37–76.

Alter, K. J. Book manuscript in progress. *The New Terrain of International Law: International Courts in International Politics*.

Alter, K. J. and L. Helfer. 'Nature or Nurture: Judicial Lawmaking in the European Court of Justice and the Andean Tribunal of Justice'. Forthcoming 2009.

Alter, K. J. and S. Meunier. Forthcoming 2009. 'The Politics of International Regime Complexity' *Perspectives on Politics*.

Alvarez, J. 'The New Dispute Settlers: (Half) Truths and Consequences' (2003) 38 *Texas International Law Journal* 405–444.

Arteaga, W. K. 'La Necesidad de la Integración y el Orden y ordenamiento Jurídico Comunitario'. In *Testimonio Comunitario* (Quito: Tribunal de Justicia de la Comunidad Andina, 2004).

Avery, W. P. and J. D. Cochrane. 'Innovation in Latin American Regionalism: The Andean Common Market' (1973) 27(2) *International Organization* 181–223.

Ball, C. 'The Making of a Transnational Capitalist Society: The Court of Justice, Social Policy, and Individual Rights Under the European Community's Legal Order' (1996) 37(2) *Harvard International Law Journal* 307–388.

Baquero-Herrera, M. 'The Andean Community: Finding her feet within changing and challenging multidemensional conditions' (2004) 10 (Summer) *Law and Business Review of the Americas* 577–612.

Barents, R. 'New developments in measures having equivalent effects' (1981) 18(3) *Common Market Law Review* 271–308.

Barfield, C. *Free Trade, Sovereignty, Democracy* (Washington D.C.: American Enterprise Institute, 2001).

Barfield, C. 'WTO Dispute Settlement System in Need of Change' (2002) 37(3) *Intereconomics* 131.

Barnard, C. 'A European Litigation Strategy: The Case of the Equal Opportunities Commission'. In *New Legal Dynamics of European Union*, ed J. Shaw and G. More (Oxford: Clarendon Press, 1995).

Barnett, D. F. and R. W. Crandall. *Up from the Ashes: The Rise of Steel Minimill in the United States* (Washington D.C.: Brookings Institution, 1986).

Barnett, D. F. and R. W. Crandall. 'Steel: Decline and Renewal'. In *Industry Studies*, ed. L. L. Deutsch (New York: M.E. Sharpe Inc., 2002).

Barnett, M. N. and M. Finnemore. *Rules for the world: international organizations in global politics* (Ithaca, N.Y.; London: Cornell University Press, 2004).

Bassett, P. 'Penalties Rising for Bias at Work' *The Times,* 15 May 1996.

Beach, D. *Between law and politics: the relationship between the European Court of Justice and EU member states* (1st edn) (Copenhagen: DJØF Publ., 2001).

Bebr, G. 'The Rambling Ghost of "Cohn-Bendit": *Acte Clair* and the Court of Justice' (1983) 20 *Common Market Law Review* 439–472.

Bekker, P. 'The World Court Finds that US Attacks on Iranian Oil Platforms in 1987–1988 Were Not Justifiable as Self-Defense, but the United States Did Not Violate the Applicable Treaty with Iran' (2003) *ASIL Insight* <http://www.asil.org/insights/insigh119.htm>.

Benvenisti, E. 'Reclaiming Democracy: The Strategic Uses of Foreign and International Law by National Courts' (2008) 102(2) *American Journal of International Law* 241–276.

Bermann, G., R. Goebel, W. Davey, and E. Fox. *Cases and Materials on European Community Law, American Casebook Series* (St. Paul: West Publishing Co., 1993).

Bessko, Z. 'Going Bananas over EEC Preferences? A Look at the Banana Trade War and the WTO's Understanding on Rules and Procedures Governing the Settlement of Disputes' (1996) 28 *Case Western Reserve Journal of International Law* 265.

Bignami, F. 'Creating European Rights: National Values and Supranational Interests' (2005) 11 *Columbia Journal of European Law* 241–352.

Blom, J., B. Fitzpatrick, J. Gregory, R. Knegt, and U. O'Hare. 'The Utilisation of Sex Equality Litigation Procedures in the Member States of the European Community, a comparative study' (1995) Commission of the European Union, DG V.

Boltho, A. *The European Economy: Growth and Crisis* (Oxford: Oxford University Press, 1982).

Bork, R. 'The Limits of "International Law"' (1989/90) (Winter) *The National Interest*: 3–10.

Bork, R. H. *Coercing virtue: the worldwide rule of judges*. (American ed.) (Washington, D.C.: AEI Press, 2003).

Börzel, T. 'Non-compliance in the European Union: pathology or statistical artifact' (2001) 8(5) *Journal of European Public Policy* 803–824.

Börzel, T. 'Participation Through Law Enforcement: The Case of the European Union'. (2006) 39(1) *Comparative Political Studies* 128–152.

Bourdieu, P. 'Force of Law: Toward a Sociology of the Juridical Field' (1987) 38 (July) *Hastings Law Journal* 805–853.

Bourdieu, P. and L. J. D. Wacquant. *An invitation to reflexive sociology* (Chicago: University of Chicago Press, 1992).

Bourgeois, J. H. J. 'The European Court and the WTO: Problems and Challenges'. In *The EU, the WTO and the NAFTA: Towards a Common Law of Trade*, ed. J. H. H. Weiler (Oxford: Oxford University Press, 2000).

Bourn, C. and J. Whitmore. *Anti-discrimination law in Britain* (3rd edn) (London: Sweet and Maxwell, 1997).

Bribosia, H. 'Report on Belgium'. In *The European Courts and National Courts*, ed. A.-M. Slaughter, A. Stone-Sweet and J. Weiler (Cambridge: Hart Publishing, 1998).

Brinkmann, H.-V. Rechtsfragen der Europäischen Integration. 1965 (Heft 24) *Neue juristische Wochenschrift* 1120–1121.

Brown, C. 'The Proliferation of International Courts and Tribunals: Finding your way through the Maze' (2002) 3 *Melbourne Journal of International Law* 453–475.

Brown, K. 'Government to demand curb on European Court' *Financial Times*, 2 February 1995, 9.

Brown, L. N. *The Court of Justice of the European Communities* (4th edn) (London: Sweet and Maxwell, 1994).

Brusoni, S., and L. Orsenigo. 'State-Owned Enterprises and Managerial Structure: The Italian Experience in Steel and Oil'. In *Innovation Systems and European Integration (ISE)*, edited by C. Edquist. Linkoeping University Sweden: European Commission Report Sub Project 3.2.4 Corporate Governance and Innovation Performance.

Buffet-Tchakaloff, M.-F. *La France devant la cour de justice des communautés européennes* (Aix-en-Provence: Presses Universitaires d'Aix-Marseille, 1984).

Burley, A.-M. 'International Law and International Relations Theory: A Dual Agenda' (1993) 87 *The American Journal of International Law* 205–239.

Burley, A.-M. and W. Mattli. 'Europe Before the Court' (1993) 47(1) *International Organization* 41–76.

Busch, M. and E. Reinhardt. 'Testing International Trade Law: Empirical Studies of GATT/WTO Dispute Settlement'. In *The Political Economy of International Trade*

Law: Essays in Honor of Robert Hudec, ed. D. L. M. Kennedy and J. D. Southwick (Cambridge: Cambridge University Press, 2000a).

Busch, M. and Reinhardt, E. 'Bargaining in the Shadow of the Law: Early Settlement in GATT/WTO Disputes' (2000b) 24 (November–December) *Fordham International Law Journal* 148–172.

Caldeira, G. and J. Gibson. 'The Legitimacy of the Court of Justice in the European Union: Models of Institutional Support' (1995) 89(2) *American Political Science Review* 356–376.

Capelli, F. 'Les Malentendus provoqués par l'arrêt sur le *Cassis de Dijon*' [1981] *Revue du Marché Commun* 421–435.

Caporaso, J. and J. Jupille. 'Transforming Europe: Europeanization and Domestic Change'. In *Europeanization and Domestic Structural Change*, ed. M. Green Cowles, J. Caporaso and T. Risse (Ithaca: Cornell University Press, 2001).

Caporaso, J. and J. Keeler. 'The European Union and Regional Integration Theory'. In *The State of the European Union*, ed. C. Rhodes and S. Mazey (Boulder: Lynne Rienner/Longmann, 1995).

Cappelletti, M. *The Judicial Process in Comparative Perspective* (Oxford: Clarendon Press, 1989).

Carpenter, D. *The Forging of Bureaucratic Autonomy* (Princeton: Princeton University Press, 2001).

Carrubba, C. J. and L. Murrah. 'Legal Integration and Use of the Preliminary Ruling Process in the European Union' (2005) 59(2) *International Organization* 399–418.

Carter, A. *The politics of women's rights* (London: Longman Group, 1988).

Cassia, P. and E. Saulnier. 'L'Imbroglio de la Banane' (1997) (411) *Revue du Marché commun et de l'Union européenne* 527–544.

Chalmers, D. 'Judicial Preferences and the Community Legal Order' (1997) 60 (2, March) *Modern Law Review* 164–199.

Chalmers, D. 'A Statistical Analysis of Reported Decisions of the United Kingdom Invoking EU Laws 1973–1998' (2000) *Jean Monnet Paper, Harvard Law School* 1/2000.

Chalmers, D. 'The Dynamics of Judicial Authority and the Constitutional Treaty' (2004a) *Jean Monnet Working Paper, Harvard Law School* 5/04.

Chalmers, D. 'The Satisfaction of Constitutional Rhetoric by the European Judiciary' (2004b) Paper read at Alteneuland: The Constitution of Europe in an American Perspective' April 28–30, 2004, at New York <http://www.jeanmonnetprogram.org/conference_JMC_Princeton/program.html>.

Cichowski, R. 'Women's Rights, the European Court and Supranational Constitutionalism' (2004) 38 *Law and Society Review* 489–512.

Cichowski, R. 'Introduction: Courts, Democracy, and Governance' (2006) 39(1) *Comparative Political Studies* 3–21.

Cichowski, R. *The European Court and Civil Society: Litigation, Mobilization and Governance* (Cambridge: Cambridge University Press, 2007).

Claes, M. and B. de Witte. 'Report on the Netherlands'. In *The European Courts and National Courts*, ed. A.-M. Slaughter, A. Stone Sweet and J. Weiler (Cambridge: Hart Publishing, 1998).

Clever, P. 'EuGH-Rechtsprechung im Sozialbereich- Kritik, aber auch hoffnungsvolle Zuversicht' (1995) 34(1) *Zeitschrift für Sozialhilfe und Sozialgesetzbuch* 1–14.

Cohen, A. 'Constitutionalism Without Constitution: Transnational Elites Between Political Mobilization and Legal Expertise in the Making of a Constitution for Europe (1940s–1960s)' (2007) 32(1) *Law and Social Inquiry* 109–136.

Cohen, A. and M. R. Madsen. 'Cold War Law: Legal Entreprenuers and the Emergence of a European Legal Field (1946–1965)'. In *European Ways of Law*, ed. V. Gessner and D. Nelken (Oxford: Hart, 2007).

Cohen-Jonathan, G. 'Observations. Cour constitutionnelle allemande et règlements communautaires' (1975) *Cahiers de droit Européen* 173–206.

Collins, D. *The European communities: the social policy of the first phase*. 2 vols (London: M. Robertson, 1975).

Conant, L. 'Europeanization and the Courts: Variable Patterns of Adaption among National Judiciaries'. In *Transforming Europe: Europeanization and Domestic Change*, ed. J. Caporaso, M. Green Cowles and T. Risse-Kappen (Ithaca: Cornell University Press, 2001).

Conant, L. *Justice contained: law and politics in the European Union* (Ithaca: Cornell University Press, 2002).

Conant, L. 'Individuals, Courts, and the Development of European Social Rights' (2006) 39(1) *Comparative Political Studies* 76–100.

Conant, L. 'Review Article: The Politics of Legal Integration' (2007) 45: Annual Review *Journal of Common Market Studies* 45–66.

Craig, P. 'Report on the United Kingdom'. In *The European Courts and National Courts*, ed. A.-M. Slaughter, A. Stone-Sweet and J. Weiler (Oxford: Hart Publishing, 1998).

Curtin, D. and K. Morelmans. 'Application and Enforcement of Community Law by Member States: Actors in Search of a Third Generation Script'. In *Institutional Dynamics of European Integration*, ed. D. Curtin and T. Heukels (Dordrecht: Martinus Nijoff Publishers, 1994).

D'Amato, A. 'Trashing Customary International Law' (1987) 81 *American Journal of International Law* 101–106.

Daley, A. *Steel, State, and Labor: Mobilization and Adjustment in France* (Pittsburg: University of Pittsburgh Press, 1996).

Dashwood, A. and A. Arnull. 'English Courts and Article 177 of the EEC Treaty' (1984) *Yearbook of European Law* 255–302.

Davies, W. 'The Constitutionalisation of the European Community: West Germany between Legal Sovereignty and European Integration 1958–1975', Dissertation, German, Kings College, London, 2007.

Davis, C. 'Does the WTO Create a Level Playing Field for Developing Countries? Lessons From Peru and Vietnam'. In John Odell (ed.) *Negotiating Trade: Developing Countries in the WTO and NAFTA* (Cambridge: Cambridge University Press, 2006), pp. 219–256.

Davis, C. and Bermeo Blodgett, S. 'Who Files? Developing Country Participation in WTO Adjudication' (Forthcoming 2009) *Journal of Politics*.

Dehaussy, J. 'La supériorité des normes internationales sur les normes internes: à propos de l'arrêt du Conseil d'État du 20 October 1989, Nicolo' (1990) 117 *Journal du Droit International* 5–33.

Dehousse, R. *The European Court of Justice: The Politics of Judicial Integration* (New York: St. Martin's Press, 1998).

Denning, L. Introduction to article 'The European Court of Justice: Judges or Policy Makers?' The Bruge Group Publication, Suite 102 Whitehall Court, Westminster, London SWIA 2EL, 1990.

Dezalay, Y. and B. G. Garth. *The internationalization of palace wars : lawyers, economists, and the contest to transform Latin American states* (Chicago: University of Chicago Press, 2002).

Dezalay, Y. and B. G. Garth. 'From the Cold War to Kosovo: The Renewal of the Field of International Human Rights' (2006) 2 *Annual Review of Law and Social Science* 231–255.

Diebold, W. *The Schuman Plan: A Study in Economic Cooperation 1950–1959*, ed. C. o. F. Relations (New York: Praeger, 1959).

Dinan, D. *Europe Recast: A History of the European Union* (Boulder: Lynn Rienner, 2004).

Donner, A. *The Role of the Lawyer in the European Communities, The Rosenthal Lectures* (Evanston: Northwestern University Press, 1968).

Downs, G. 'Enforcement and the Evolution of Cooperation' (1998) 19 (Winter) *Michigan Journal of International Law* 319–344.

Dragneva, R. 'Legal Institutions for Economic Integration in the Commonwealth of Independent States' Paper read at Annual Meeting of the Comparative Law and Economics Forum, 25–26 June 2004, at Zurich.

Druesne, G. 'La primauté du droit communautaire sur le droit interne – L'Arrêt de la Cour de Cassation du 24 Mai 1975' (1975) *Revue du Marché Commun* 378 –390.

Duchêne, F. *Jean Monnet: the first statesman of interdependence* (1st edn) (New York: Norton, 1994).

Dudley, G. and J. Richardson. 'Competing advocacy coalitions and the process of "frame reflection": a longitudinal analysis of EU steel policy' (1999) 6(2) *Journal of European Public Policy* 225–248.

Edley, C. *Administrative Law: Rethinking Judicial Control of Bureaucracy* (New Haven: Yale University Press, 1990).

Ehlermann, C. 'Primauté du droit communautaire mise en danger par la Cour Constitutionnelle Fédérale Allemande' (1975) (181) *Revue du Marché Commun* 10–19.

Ellickson, R. C. *Order without law: how neighbors settle disputes* (Cambridge, Mass.: Harvard University Press, 1991).

Ellis, E. *European community sex discrimination law* (Oxford: Clarendon, 1991).

Elster, J. *Ulysses unbound: studies in rationality, precommitment, and constraints* (Cambridge; New York: Cambridge University Press, 2000).

Epstein, L. and J. Knight. *The choices justices make* (Washington, D.C.: CQ Press, 1998).

Esser, J. and W. Fach. 'Crisis Management "Made in Germany": The Steel Industry'. In *Industry and Politics in West Germany: Toward the Third Reich*, ed. P. Katzenstein (Ithaca: Cornell University Press, 1989).

Everling, U. 'Sprachliche Mißverständnisse beim Urteil des Gerichtshofes der Europäischen Gemeinschaften zur Umsatzausgleichsteuer' (197) 5 (15 May) *Außenwirtschaftsdiensts des Betriebs-Beraters* 182–184.

Everling, U. 'Will Europe Slip on Bananas? The Bananas Judgment of the European Court of Justice and National Courts' (1996) 33 *Common Market Law Review* 401–437.

Fitzpatrick, B., J. Gregory, and E. Szyszczak. 'Sex Equality Litigation in the Member States of the European Community, A Comparative Study: Commission of the European Union DG V, 1993.

Folsom, R. *European Union Law in a Nutshell* (2nd edn) (St. Paul: West Publishing, 1995). Foster, P. 'Director Wins £140,000' *The Times of London*, 26 April 1996.

Franck, T. 'Some Observations on the ICJ's procedural and Substantive Innovations' (1987) 81 *American Journal of International Law* 116–121.

Friedrich, C. J. 'Introduction: The Background of These Studies and the Development of the Draft Constitution'. In *Studies in Federalism*, ed. R. Bowie and C. Friedrich (Boston: Little Brown, 1954).

Garrett, G. 'The European Community's Internal Market' (1992) 46(2) *International Organization* 533–560.

Garrett, G. 'The Politics of Legal Integration in the European Union' (1995) 49(1) *International Organization* 171–181.

Garrett, G., D. Kelemen, and H. Schulz. 'The European Court of Justice, National Governments and Legal Integration in the European Union' (1998) 52(1) *International Organization* 149–176.

Garrett, G. and B. Weingast. 'Ideas, Interests and Institutions: Constructing the EC's Internal Market'. In *Ideas and Foreign Policy*, ed. J. Goldstein and R. Keohane (Ithaca: Cornell University Press, 1993).

Gaudet, M. 'Introductory Message' (1963) 1(1) *Common Market Law Review* 1–2.

Gerth, H. and C. W. Mills. *From Max Weber: Essays in Sociology* (New York: Galaxy Books, 1958).

Gillingham, J. *Coal, steel, and the rebirth of Europe, 1945–1955: the Germans and French from Ruhr conflict to Economic Community* (Cambridge, UK; New York, NY, USA: Cambridge University Press, 1991).

Ginsburg, T. and T. Moustafa. *Rule by law: the politics of courts in authoritarian regimes.* (Cambridge UK; New York: Cambridge University Press, 2008).

Glendon, M. A., M. W. Gordon, and C. Osakwe. *Comparative Legal Traditions, American Casebook Series* (St. Paul: West Publishing Co, 1985).

Goldstein, J., M. Kahler, R. Keohane, and A.-M. Slaughter. *Legalization in World Politics* (Cambridge: MIT, 2001).

Goldstein, L. F. *Constituting Federal Sovereignty: The European Union in Comparative Context.* (Maryland: Johns Hopkins Press, 2001) <http://www.press.jhu.edu/books/title_pages/1363.html>.

Golub, J. 'Using the Judiciary to Preserve Sovereignty'. DPhil, Oxford University, 1994.

Golub, J. 'Rethinking the Role of National Courts in European Integration: A Political Study of British Judicial Discretion', ed. E. U. Institute. EUI Working Paper Law/12, 1995.

Golub, J. 'The Politics of Judicial Discretion: Rethinking the Interaction between National Courts and the European Court of Justice' (1996) 19(2) *West European Politics* 360–385.

Gordon, E., S. J. Burton, R. Falk, T. M. Franck, and C. Nezis. 'The Independence and Impartiality of International Judges' (1989) 83 *American Society of International Law Proceedings* 508–529.

Gordon, P. H. and S. Meunier. *The French challenge: adapting to globalization* (Washington, D.C.: Brookings Institution Press, 2001).

Gormley, L. W. 'Cassis de Dijon and the communication from the Commission' (1981) 6 *European Law Review* 454.

Gormley, L. 'The application of community law in the United Kingdom, 1976–1985' (1986) 23 *Common Market Law Review* 287–323.

Gormley, L. W. 'Actually or potentially, directly or indirectly? Obstacles to the free movement of goods' (1989) 9 *Yearbook of European Law* 197–208.

Gourevitch, P. 'The Second Image Reversed: the International Sources of Domestic Politics' (1978) 32(4) *International Organization* 881–911.

Green Cowles, M., J. A. Caporaso, and T. Risse-Kappen. *Transforming Europe: Europeanization and domestic change, Cornell studies in political economy* (Ithaca, NY: Cornell University Press, 2001).

Greene, J. 'A Losing Streak at the WTO' (2001) *Legal Times* 1.

Gregory, J. *Sex, race and the law: Legislating for equality* (London: Sage, 1987).

Groenendijk, N. and H. Gert. 'A Requiem for the European Coal and Steel Community' (2002) 150(5) *The Economist* 601–612.

Grunert, T. 'Decision-Making Processes in the Steel Crisis Policy of the EEC: Neocorporatist or Integrationist Tendencies?' In *The Politics of Steel: Western Europe and the Steel Industry in the Crisis Years (1974–1984)*, ed. Y. Meny and V. Wright (Berlin: Walter de Gruyter, 1987).

Guzman, A. T. and B. Simmons. 'Power Plays and Capacity Constraints: The Selection of Defendants in WTO Disputes' (2004) 34 *Journal of Legal Studies* 557–598.

Haas, E. *The Uniting of Europe* (Palo Alto: Stanford University Press, 1958).

Haas, E. *Beyond the Nation-State: Functionalism and International Organization* (Stanford, CA: Stanford University Press, 1964).

Haas, E. *The Obsolescence of Regional Integration Theory* (Berkeley: University of California Press, 1975).

Haas, P. M. 'Introduction: Epistemic Communities and International Policy Coordination' (1992) 46(1) *International Organization* 1–36.

Hagan, J. and R. Levi. 'Crimes of War and the Force of Law' (2005) 83(4) *Social Forces* 1499–1534.

Hall, P. A. *Governing the economy: the politics of state intervention in Britain and France, Europe and the international order* (New York: Oxford University Press, 1986).

Hall, P. A. *The Political power of economic ideas: Keynesianism across nations* (Princeton, NJ: Princeton University Press, 1989).

Halliday, T. C., L. Karpik and M. Feeley. *Fighting for political freedom: comparative studies of the legal complex and political liberalism, Oñati international series in law and society* (Oxford; Portland, Ore.: Hart, 2007).

Hammergren, L. A. *Envisioning reform: improving judicial performance in Latin America* (University Park: Pennsylvania State University Press, 2007).

Hanrahan, C. The US-European Union Banana Dispute. CRS Report RS20130, 1999.

Harding, C. 'Who Goes to Court in Europe: An Analysis of Litigation against the European Community' (1992) 71(2) *European Law Review* 104–125.

Harlow, C. 'A Community of Interests? Making the Most of European Law' (1992a) 55 (May) *Modern Law Review* 331–351.

Harlow, C. 'Towards a Theory of Access of the European Court of Justice' (1992b) 12 *Yearbook of European Law* 213–248.

Harlow, C. and R. Rawlings. *Pressure Through Law* (London: Routledge, 1992).

Harries-Jenkins, G. 'Women in Extended Roles in the Military: Legal Issues' (2002) 50(5) *Current Sociology* 745–769.

Hartley, T. *The Foundations of European Community Law* (4th edn) (Oxford: Clarendon Press, 1994).

Hathaway, O. 'Path Dependence in the Law: The Course and Pattern of Legal Change in a Common Law System' (2001) 86 *Iowa Law Review* 606–661.

Hathaway, O. 'Between Power and Principle: A Political Theory of International Law' (2005) 71(2) *University of Chicago Law Review* 469–536.

Hawkins, D. and W. Jacoby 'How Agents Matter'. In *Delegation and Agency in International Organizations*, ed. D. Hawkins, D. A. Lake, D. Nielson and M. J. Tierney (Cambridge: Cambridge University Press, 2006).

Hawkins, D., D. Lake, D. Nielson and M. Tierney 'Delegation under Anarchy: States, International Organizations and Principal–agent Theory'. In *Delegation and Agency in International Organizations* (Cambridge: Cambridge University Press, 2006).

Helfer, L. 'Regime Shifting: The TRIPS Agreement and New Dynamics of International Intellectual Property Making' (2004) 29(1) *Yale Journal of International Law* 1–81.

Helfer, L. and K. Alter. 'Building Judicial Supranationalism in the Andes: Understanding the Preliminary Reference Patterns in the Andean Community'. Forthcoming 2009. 42 *Journal of International Law and Politics*.

Helfer, L., K. Alter, and M. F. Guerzovich. 'Islands of Effective International Adjudication: Constructing an Intellectual Property Rule of Law in the Andean Community'. Forthcoming 2009. 103 *American Journal of International Law*.

Helfer, L. and A.-M. Slaughter. 'Toward a Theory of Effective Supranational Adjudication' (1997) 107(2) *Yale Law Journal* 273–391.

Helfer, L. and A.-M. Slaughter. 'Why States Create International Tribunals: A Response to Professors Posner and Yoo' (2005) 93 (May) *California Law Review* 899–956.

Helfer, L. R. 'Overlegalizing Human Rights: International Relations Theory and the Commonwealth Caribbean Backlash Against Human Rights Regimes' (2002) 102(7) *Columbia Law Review* 1832–1911.

Helfer, L. R. 'Redesigning the European Court of Human Rights: Embeddedness as a Deep Structural Principle of the European Human Rights Regime' (2008) 19(1) *European Journal of International Law* 125–159.

Highet, K. 'Evidence, The Court and the Nicaragua Case' (1987) 81 *American Journal of International Law* 1–56.

Hinarejos Parga, A. 'Bundesverfassungsgericht decision of 18 July 2005 (2 BvR 2236/04) on the German European Arrest Warrent Law' (2006) 43(2) *Common Market Law Review* 583–595.

Holland, D. *Women and equalities* (Memorandum 940252). Transport and General Workers Union, 1994.

Hooghe, L. and G. Marks *Multi-level governance and European integration, Governance in Europe* (Lanham, MD: Rowman and Littlefield Publishers, 2001).

Horowitz, D. *Courts and social policy* (Washington, DC: Brookings Institution, 1977).

Hoskins, K. *Integrating Gender: Women, Law and Politics in the European Union* (London: Verso, 1996).

Howell, T. R., W. A. Noellert, J. G. Kreier and A. W. Wolff. *Steel and the State: Government Intervention and Steel's Structural Crisis* (Boulder: Westview Press, 1988).

Ikenberry, G. J. *After victory: institutions, strategic restraint, and the rebuilding of order after major wars* (Princeton: Princeton University Press, 2001).

Ipsen, H. P. 'Haager Kongress für Europarecht und Bericht über die aktuelle Entwicklung des Gemeinschaftsrechts' (1964) *Neue juristische Wochenschrift* (Heft 8) 339–343.

Ipsen, H. P. 'Europäishe Gemeinschaftsrecht'. Tubigen: Mohr J.C.B. and P. Steibeck (eds). (1972) Conference paper on file with author.

Ipsen, H. P. 'Europarecht—25 Jahrgänge 1966–1990' (1990) 25(4) *Europarecht* 323–339.

Isaac, G. 'A propos de l'"amendement Aurillac": Vers une obligation pour les juges d'appliquer les lois contraires aux traités?' (1980) *Gazette du Palais II*: Doctrine: 583–585.

Jackson, J. H. 'The Great 1994 Sovereignty Debate: United States Acceptance and Implementation of the Uraguay Round Results' (1997) 36 *Columbia Journal of Transnational Law* 157–188.

Jacoby, W. *The enlargement of the European Union and NATO : ordering from the menu in Central Europe* (Cambridge; New York: Cambridge University Press, 2004).

Jacot-Guillarmod, O. *Creating a European economic space: Legal aspects of EC-EFTA relations* (Dublin: Irish Center for European Law, Trinity College, 1989).

Johnston, A. I. 'Treating International Institutions as Social Environments' (2001) 45(4) *International Studies Quarterly* 487–515.

Jones, K. A. 'Forgetfulness of Things Past: Europe and the Steel Cartel' (1979) 2(1) *The World Economy* 139–154.

Josling, T. E. 'Bananas and the WTO: Testing the New Dispute Settlement Process'. In *Banana wars the anatomy of a trade dispute*, ed. T. E. Josling and T. G. Taylor (California: Institute for International Studies Stanford University, 2003).

Jung, Y. and E. J. Kang. 'Toward an Ideal WTO Safeguards Regime—Lessons from US Steel' (2004) 38 (Winter) *International Lawyer* 919–944.

Kagan, R. 'Power and Weakness' (2002) *Policy Review* No. 113.

Kahn, P. 'Unequal Opportunities: Women, Employment and the Law'. In *Gender, Sex and Law*, ed. S. Edwards (London: Croom Helm, 1985).

Kari, J. *The Role of Preliminary Rulings in the European Community, Dissertations Humanarum Litterarum 16* (Helsinki: Suomalainen Tiedeakatemia, 1979).

Katzenstein, P. J. *Policy and politics in West Germany: the growth of a semisovereign state, Policy and politics in industrial states* (Philadelphia: Temple University Press, 1987).

Keck, M. E. and K. Sikkink. *Activists beyond borders: advocacy networks in international politics* (Ithaca, NY: Cornell University Press, 1998).

Keeling, D. 'The free movement of goods in EEC law: Basic principles and recent developments in the case law of the Court of Justice of the European Communities' (1992) 26 *The International Lawyer*.

Keener, E. B. 'The Andean Common Market Court of Justice: Its Purpose, Structure, and Future' (1987) 2(1) *Emory Journal of International Dispute Resolution* 37–72.

Kellermann, A. E., W. M. Levelt-Overmars and F. H. M. Posser. 'Primus Inter Pares: The European Court and National Courts: The Follow-up by National Courts of

Preliminary Ruling ex. Art. 177 of the Treaty of Rome' A Report on the Situation in the Netherlands: European University Institute Working Paper. Law No 90/6, 1990.

Kelley, J. G. *Ethnic politics in Europe: the power of norms and incentives* (Princeton, NJ: Princeton University Press, 2004).

Kenney, S. J. *For Whose Protection?: Reproductive Hazards and Exclusionary Policies in the United States and Britain* (Ann Arbor: University of Michigan Press, 1992).

Keohane, R., A. Moravcsik and A.-M. Slaughter. 'Legalized Dispute Resolution: Interstate and Transnational' (2000) 54(3) *International Organization* 457–488.

Kilpatrick, C. 'Effective utilisation of equality rights'. In *Sex Equality Policy in Western Europe*, ed. F. Gardiner (New York: Routledge, 1992).

Kilroy, B. 'Member State Control or Judicial Independence: The Integrative Role of the Court of Justice'. Paper read at American Political Science Association Conference, 31 August–3 September 1995, at Chicago.

Kilroy, B. 'Integration through Law: ECJ and Governments in the EU'. Dissertation in Political Science, Department of Political Science, UCLA, Los Angeles, 1999.

Kipping, M. 'Inter-Firm Relations and Industrial Policy: The French and German Steel Producers and Users in the Twentieth Century' (1996) 38(1) *Business History* 1–25.

Kipping, M., R. Ruggero and J. Dankers. 'The Emergence of New Competitor Nations in the European Steel Industry: Italy and the Netherlands' (2001) 43(1) *Business History* 69–96.

Kokott, J. 'Report on Germany'. In *The European Courts and National Courts*, ed. A.-M. Slaughter, A. Stone Sweet and J. Weiler (Cambridge: Hart Publishing, 1998), 77–131.

Kuemmel, G. 'Changing State Institutions: The German Military and the Integration of Women'. Paper read at European Consortium for Political Research, 18–21 September 2003, at Marburg.

Lachaume, J.-F. 'Une victoire de l'ordre juridique communautaire: l'arrêt Nicolo consacrant la supériorité des traités sur les lois postérieures' (1990) *Revue du Marché Commun* 384–394.

Lagrange, M. Note. (1968) 15 *Recueil Dalloz Sirey* 286–289.

Lauwaars, R. H. 'The "model directive" on technical harmonization'. In R. Bieber et al. (eds) *1992: One European market? A critical analysis of the Commission's internal market strategy* (Baden-Baden: Nomos Verlagsgesellschaft, 1988), 151–173.

Lecourt, R. 'Le Rôle du droit dans l'unification européenne' (1964) *Gazette du Palais* 49–54.

Lecourt, R. 'La Dynamique judiciaire dans l'édification de l'Europe' (1965) 64 Mai *France Forum* 20–22.

Lecourt, R. *L'Europe des Juges* (Brussels: Établissements Émile Bruylant, 1976).

Lecourt, R. 'Quel eût été le droit des communautés sans les arrêts de 1963 et 1964?' In *Mélanges en Hommage à Jean Boulouis: L'Europe et le Droit* (Paris: Editions Dalloz, 1991).

Lenaerts K. 'Two hundred years of US Constitution and thirty years of EEC treaty-Outlook for a comparison'. In ed. K. Lenaerts (1988) *Two hundred years of U.S. Constitution and thirty years of EEC treaty* (The Netherlands: Kluwer Law and Taxation Publications, 1988), 7–24.

Leonard, A. M. *Judging inequality* (London: Cobden Trust, 1987).

Lester Q.C., A. 'Discrimination: What can lawyers learn from history' (1994) (Summer) *Public Law* 224–237.

Levi, W. *Law and Politics in the International Society* (Beverly Hills: Sage Publications, 1976).

Liebert, U. 'Europeanizing the Military: The ECJ and the Transformation of the Bundeswehr'. *Jean Monnet Center for European Studies* Working Paper 2002/7.

Lindseth, P. 'History and Institutions: The Postwar Constitutional Settlement and European Integration'. Dissertation (History Dept, Colombia University, New York, 2002).

Lindseth, P. 'The Contradictions of Supranationalism: Administrative Governance and Constitutionalization in European Integration Since the 1950s' (2003) 37(2) *Loyola of Los Angeles Law Review* 363–406.

Lindseth, P. 'Always Embedded Administration: The Historical Evolution of Administrative Justice as an Aspect of Modern Governance in The Economy as Polity'. In *The Economy as Polity* eds B. S. Christian Joerges and P. Wagner (London: UCL Press (Routledge-Cavendish), 2005).

Lister, L. *Europe's Coal and Steel Community* (New York: Twentieth Century Fund, 1960).

Louis, J.-V. *The Community Legal Order, The European Perspectives Series* (Brussels: Commission of the European Community, 1990).

Lovenduski, J. *Women and European politics: Contemporary feminism and public policy.* (Sussex: Harvester, 1986).

Lovenduski, J. and V. Randall. *Contemporary feminist politics: Women and power in Britain* (Oxford: Oxford University Press, 1993).

Lutz, E. and K. Sikkink. 'International Human Rights Law and Practice in Latin America' (2000) 54(3) *International Organization* 633–659.

Lyons, R. 'European Union Banana Controversy' (1994) 9 *Florida Journal of International Law* 165–188.

Macrae, D. 'Institution and Decision-Making Changes'. In *Legal Issues of the Maastricht Treaty*, eds D. O'Keefe and P. Twomey (London: Chancery Law Publishing, 1994).

Madsen, M. R. 'From Cold War Instrument to Supreme European Court: The European Court of Human Rights at the Crossroads of International and National Law and Politics' (2007) 32(1) *Law and Social Inquiry* 137–159.

Madsen, M. R. and A. Vauchez 'European Constitutionalism at the Cradle. Law and Lawyers in the Construction of a European Political Order (1920–1960)'. In *In Lawyers' Circles. Lawyers and European Legal Integration*, eds A. Jettinghoff and H. Schepel (The Hague: Elsevier Reed, 2005).

Maduro, M. P. *We the court: the European Court of Justice and the European Economic Constitution: a critical reading of Article 30 of the EC Treaty* (Oxford: Hart Publishing, 1998).

Maier, C. S. *In search of stability: explorations in historical political economy, Cambridge studies in modern political economies* (Cambridge, UK; New York: Cambridge University Press, 1987).

Majone, G. 'Two Logics of Delegation: Agency and Fiduciary Relations in EU Governance' (2001) 2(1) *European Union Politics* 103–122.

Majone, G. 'Information, Commitment, and the Transformation of European Governance'. Paper read at Conference on 'Transformations of Statehood from a European Perspective', at Vienna, 23–25 January 2003.

Mancini, F. 'The Making of a Constitution for Europe' (1989) XXIV *Common Market Law Review* 595–614.

Mancini, F. and D. Keeling. 'From CILFIT to ERTA: The Constitutional Challenge Facing the European Court' (1992) 11 *Yearbook of European Law* 1–13.

Mancini, F. and D. Keeling. 'Democracy and the European Court of Justice' (1994) 57(2) *Modern Law Review* 175–190.

Mancini, F. and D. Keeling. 'Language, Culture and Politics in the Life of the European Court of Justice' (1995) 1(2) *Columbia Journal of European Law* 397–413.

Mann, C. *The Function of Judicial Decision in European Economic Integration* (The Hague: Martinus Nijhoff Press, 1972).

Mantilla, G. P. *Derecho Andino* (Quito: Tribunal de Justicia del Acuerdo de Cartagena, 1992).

Maravall, J. M. and A. Przeworski. *Democracy and the Rule of Law* (Cambridge: Cambridge University Press, 2003).

Marks, B. A. 'A Model of Judicial Influence on Congressional Policy Making: Grove City College v. Bell (1984)'. In *Working Papers in Political Science*, ed. S. University. (Stanford: Hoover Institution, 1988).

Masclet, J.-C. 'Les articles 30, 36, et 100 du traité CEE à la lumière de l'arrêt *Cassis de Dijon*' (1980) *Revue de Droit Européen* 611–634.

Mathieu, G. 'Dans l'histoire de la CECA, du rose et du gris' *Le Monde*, 9 May 1970, 6.

Mattera, A. 'L'Arrêt *"Cassis de Dijon"*: une nouvelle approche pour la réalisation et le bon fonctionnement du marché intérieur' (1980) *Revue du Marché Commun* 505–513.

Mattli, W. 'Ernst Haas' evolving thinking on comparative regional integration: of virtues and infelicities' (2005) 12(2) *Journal of European Public Policy* 327–348.

Mattli, W. and A.-M. Slaughter. 'Revisiting the European Court of Justice' (1998) 52(1) *International Organization* 177–209.

Mazey, S. 'The Development of EU Equality Policies: Bureaucratic Expansion on Behalf of Women?' (1995) 73 (Winter) *Public Administration* 591–609.

Mazey, S. 'The European Union and women's rights: from the Europeanization of national agendas to the nationalization of a European agenda?' (1998) 5(1) *Journal of European Public Policy* 131–152.

McAdams, R. H. 'The Expressive Power of Adjudication' (2005) (5) *University of Illinois Law Review* 1045–1122.

McCall Smith, J. 'The Politics of Dispute Settlement Design' (2000) 54(1) *International Organization* 137–180.

McCall Smith, J. 'Compliance Bargaining in the WTO: Ecuador and the Bananas Dispute'. In *Negotiating Trade: Developing Countries in the TWO and NAFTA*, ed. J. Odell (Cambridge: Cambridge University Press, 2006).

McCall Smith, J. and J. Tallberg. 'Bargaining in the Shadow of the Law: Interstate and Supranational Dispute Settlement'. Unpublished manuscript on file with the author (forthcoming 2009).

McCann, M. *Rights at Work: Pay Equity Reform and the Politics of Legal Mobilization* (Chicago: Univeristy of Chicago Press, 1994).

McClenahan, W. 'The Growth of Voluntary Export Restraints and American Foreign Economic Policy 1956–1969' (1991) 20 *Business and Economic History* 180–190.

McCrudden, C. 'Women, employment and European equality law: Some tentative con-clusions and issues for the future'. In *Women, employment and European equality law,* ed. C. McCrudden (London: Eclipse, 1987), 178–187.

McCubbins, M. and T. Schwartz. 'Congressional Oversight Overlooked: Police Patrols Versus Fire Alarms'. In *Congress: Structure and Policy,* eds M. McCubbins and T. Sullivan (Cambridge: Cambridge University Press, 1987).

McIlroy, J. *The permanent revolution? Conservative law and the trade unions* (Nottingham: Spokesman, 1991).

Meehan, E. and Collins, E. 'Women, the European Union and Britain' (1996) 49(1) *Parliamentary Affairs* 221–234.

Meehan, E. M. *Women's rights at work: Campaigns and policy in Britain and the United States* (New York: St. Martin's, 1985).

Meier, G. 'Aktuelle Fragen zur Umsatzausgleichsteuer' (1967a) Heft 3 *Außenwirtschaftsdienst des Betriebs-Beraters* 97–101.

Meier, G. 'Zur Aussetzung der Einsprüche gegen Umsatzausgleichsteuerbescheide' (1967b) Heft 2 *Außenwirtschaftsdienst des Betriebs-Beraters* 75–77.

Meier, G. 'Rechtsprobleme einer EG-Alkoholmarktordnung' (1977) Heft 7 *Recht der Internationalen Wirtschaft* 415.

Meier, G. 'Vorgeschichte'. In *Die Cassis-Rechtsprechung des Gerichtshofs der Europäischen Gemeinschaften.* Loseblattssammlung, 4. Auflage (Hamburg: Behr's Verlag, 1991).

Meier, G. 'Der Streit um die Umsatzausgleichsteuer aus integrationspolitischer Sicht' (1994) 40(2) *Recht der Internationalen Wirtschaft* 149–151.

Mény, Y. and V. Wright. *The Politics of Steel: Western Europe and the Steel Industry in the Crisis Years (1974–1984)* (Berlin: Walter de Gruyter, 1987).

Meron, T. 'Judicial Independence and Impartiality in International Criminal Tribunals' (2005) 99 *American Journal of International Law* 359–369.

Merryman, J. H. and R. Pérez-Perdomo. *The Civil Law Tradition* (Stanford: Stanford University Press, 2007).

Meunier, S. 'Trade Policy and Political Legitimacy in the European Union' (2003) 1 *Comparative European Politics* 67–90.

Meunier, S. and K. Nicolaidis. 'Who Speaks for Europe? The Delegation of Trade Authority in the European Union' (1999) 37(3) *Journal of Common Market Studies* 477–501.

Milgrom, P., D. North and B. Weingast. 'The Role of Institutions in the Revival of Trade: The Law Merchant, Private Judges, and the Champagne Fairs' (1990) 2 *Economics and Politics* 1–23.

Milward, A. *The Reconstruction of Western Europe 1945–1951* (London: Methuen and Co Ltd, 1984).

Milward, A. *The European Rescue of the Nation-State* (London: Routledge, 1992).

Mnookin, R. and L. Kornhauser. 'Bargaining in the Shadow of the Law: The Case of Divorce' (1979) 88 *Yale Law Journal* 950–997.

Moe, T. M. 'The Politics of Structural Choice: Towards a Theory of Public Bureaucracy'. In *Organizational Theory: From Chester Barnard to the Present and Beyond,* ed. O. E. Williamson (Oxford: Oxford University Press, 1990).

Moore, J. N. 'The *Nicaragua* Case and the Deterioration of World Order' (1987) 81 *American Journal of International Law* 151–159.

Moravcsik, A. 'Negotiating the Single European Act: national interests and conventional statecraft in the European Community' (1991) 45(1) *International Organization* 19.

Moravcsik, A. 'Liberal Intergovernmentalism and Integration: A Rejoinder' (1995) 33(4) *Journal of Common Market Studies* 611–628.

Moravcsik, A. 'Explaining International Human Rights Regimes: Liberal Theory and Western Europe' (1997) 1(2) *European Journal of International Relations* 157–189.

Moravcsik, A. *The Choice for Europe* (Ithaca: Cornell University Press, 1998).

Moravcsik, A. The European Constitutional Compromise and the Neo-functionalist Legacy (2005) 12(2) *Journal of European Public Policy* 349–389.

Morris, P. E. and P. W. David. 'Directives, Direct Effect and the European Court: The Triumph of Pragmatism' (1987) (April and May) *Business Law Review* 85–88 and 116–118, 135–136.

Morris, A. E. and Nott, S. M. *Working women and the law: Equality and discrimination in theory and practice* (London: Routledge/Sweet & Maxwell, 1991).

Murphy, W. *Elements of Judicial Strategy* (Chicago: Chicago University Press, 1964).

Nicolaïdis, K. 'Mutual recognition among nations: the European Community and trade in services', Ph.D. dissertation, Harvard, Cambridge, MA, 1993.[1]

Noyes, J. E. 'The International Tribunal for the Law of the Seas' (1998) 32(1) *Cornell International Law Journal* 109–182.

Nyikos, S. 'The European Court of Justice and National Courts: Strategic Interaction within the EU Judicial Process'. Dissertation in Political Science, Department of Political Science, The University of Virginia, 2000.

O'Donnell, G. 'Polyarchies and the (UN) Rule of Law in Latin America'. Working paper/ Helen Kellogg Institute for International Studies, University of Notre Dame; no. 254: (Notre Dame, IN: The Institute, 1998).

O'Donnell, G. 'The Quality of Democracy: Why the Rule of Law Matters' (2004) 15(4) *Journal of Democracy* 32–46.

O'Donovan, K. and Szyszczak, E. *Equality and sex discrimination law* (Oxford: Basil Blackwell, 1988).

O'Keefe, T. A. 'How the Andean Pact Transformed Itself into a Friend of Foreign Enterprise' (1996) 30 (Winter) *International Lawyer* 811–824.

O'Keefe, T. A. 'The Central American Integration System (S.I.C.A.) at the Dawn of a New Century: Will the Central Americna Isthmus Finally be able to Achieve Economic and Political Unity?' (2001) 13(3) *Florida Journal of International Law* 243–261.

Olson, M. *The Logic of Collective Action* (Cambridge: Harvard University, 1965).

Olson, S. M. 'The political evolution of interest group litigation'. In *Governing through courts*, ed. R.A.L. Gambitta, M. L. May, and J. C. Foster (Beverly Hills, CA: Sage, 1981), 225–258.

Ophüls, C. F. 'Quellen und Aufbau des Europäischen Gemeinschaftsrechts' (1963) Heft 38 *Neue juristische Wochenschrift* 1697–1701.

Painter, A. A. '*Cassis de Dijon* digested' (1991) 2(1) *Business Law Review* 199–200.

Pannick, D. *Sex discrimination law* (Oxford: Clarendon Press, 1985).

Paulson, C. 'Compliance with Final Judgments from the International Court of Justice since 1987' (2004) 98 (June) *American Journal of International Law* 434–457.

---

[1] For her more recent work see Nicolaïdis, K. 'Trusting the Poles? Constructing Europe through mutual recognition', (2007) 14(5) *Journal of European Public Policy* 682–698.

Pellet, A. 'Le Conseil constitutionnel, la souveraineté et les traités – A propos de la décision du Conseil constitutionnel du 31 décembre 1997 (traité d'Amsterdam)' *Les Cahiers du Conseil constitutionnel*, n° 4, 1998, pp. 113–122.

Pescatore, P. 'Les Travaux du "Groupe Juridique" dans la négociation des Traités de Rome' (1981) XXXIV (1–4) *Studia Diplomatica (Chronique de Politique Etrangère)* 159–178.

Pescatore, P. 'La clarence du législateur communautaire et le devoir du juge'. In *Gedächtnisschrift für L.-J. Constantinesco* (Cologne: Carl Heymanns Verlag, 1983).

Pierson, P. 'The Path to European Integration: A Historical Institutionalist Perspective' (1996) 29(2) *Comparative Political Studies* 123–163.

Pierson, P. *Politics in Time: History, Institutions and Social Analysis* (Princeton: Princeton University Press, 2004).

Pierson, P. and S. Leibfried. 'Semi-Sovereign Welfare States: Social Policy in a Multi-Tiered Europe'. In *European Social Policy: Between Fragmentation and Integration*, eds P. Pierson and S. Leibfried (Washington DC: Brookings Institution, 1995).

Plötner, J. 'Report on France'. In *The European Courts and National Courts*, eds A.-M. Slaughter, A. Stone Sweet and J. Weiler (Oxford: Hart Publishing, 1998), 41–75.

Pollack, M. 'Delegation, Agency and Agenda Setting in the EC' (1997) 51(1) *International Organization* 99–134.

Pollack, M. *The Engines of Integration: Delegation, Agency, and Agency Setting in the European Union* (Oxford: Oxford University Press, 2003).

Pollard, D. E. E. 'The Original Jurisdiction of the Caribbean Court of Justice'. Paper read at Legislative Drafting Facility: The Thirtieth Course of International Law, at Rio de Janeiro Brasil, 2003 <http://www.caricom.org/ccj-index>.

Posner, E. A. 'The Decline of the International Court of Justice'. John M. Olin Law and Economics Working Paper (No. 233), 2004.

Posner, E. A. and M. De Figueiredo. 'Is the International Court of Justice Biased?' University of Chicago Law and Economics Paper (No. 234), 2004.

Posner, E. A. and J. C. Yoo. 'A Theory of International Adjudication'. Paper read at John. M. Olin Law and Economics Working Paper No. 206, 2004.

Posner, E. A. and J. C. Yoo. 'A Theory of International Adjudication' (2005) 93(1) *California Law Review* 1–72.

Prescal, S. and N. Burrows *Gender discrimination law in the European community* (Aldershot: Dartmouth, 1990).

Putnam, R. 'Diplomacy and Domestic Politics: the Logic of Two Level Games' (1988) 42(3) *International Organization* 427–460.

Rabkin, J. A. *Law without nations?: why constitutional government requires sovereign states* (Princeton, NJ: Princeton University Press, 2005).

Rasmussen, H. *On Law and Policy in the European Court of Justice.* (Dordrecht: Martinus Nijhoff Publishers, 1986).

Raustiala, K. 'Compliance and Effectiveness in International Regulatory Cooperation' (2000) 32 *Case Western Reserve Journal of International Law* 387–440.

Raustiala, K. 'Police Patrols and Fire Alarms in the NAAEC' (2004) 3 (Spring) *Loyola of Los Angeles International and Comparative Law Review* 389–413.

Raustiala, K. and D. Victor. 'The Regime Complex for Plant Genetic Resources' (2004) 58(2) *International Organization* 277–309.

Reich, N. 'Judge-Made "Europe a la carte": Some Remarks on Recent Conflicts between European and German Constitutional Law Provoked by the Banana Litigation' (1996) 7 *European Journal of International Law* 103–111.

Reichler, P. 'Holding America to Its Own Best Standards: Abe Chayes and Nicaragua in the World Court' (2001) 42 *Harvard International Law Journal* 15–46.

Reinhardt, E. 'To GATT or Not to GATT: Which Trade Disputes Does the US Litigate, 1975–1999'. Paper read at American Political Science Association Conference, at Boston, MA, 2000.

Rice, R., J. Harding and D. Hargreaves 'EU States Ordered to Pay for Breaches of European Law' *Financial Times,* 6 March 1996, p. 12.

Richardt, N. 'Transforming Europe's Welfare Regimes—Policy Innovation through European Gender Equality Laws in the United Kingdom and in Germany'. Dissertation in Political Science, Northwestern University, Evanston, 2006.

Risse, T., S. Ropp and K. Sikkink. *The Power of Human Rights: International Norms and Domestic Change* (Cambridge: Cambridge University Press, 1999).

Robertson, A. H. *European Institutions—Cooperation: Integration: Unification.* (2nd edn). (New York: Frederick A. Praeger, 1966).

Rodden, J. 'German Banana Republic?' (2001) 38(2) *Culture and Society* 68–74.

Rodriguez Lemmo, M. A. 'Study of Selected International Dispute Resolution Regimes, with an Analysis of the Decisions of the Court of the Andean Community' (2002) 19 *Arizona Journal of International and Comparative Law* 863–929.

Romano, C. 'The Proliferation of International Judicial Bodies: The Pieces of the Puzzle' (1999) 31 *New York University Journal of International Law and Politics* 709–751.

Rosenberg, G. *The Hollow Hope* (Chicago: University of Chicago Press, 1991).

Rubenfeld, J. 'The Two World Orders' (2003) XXVII (4) *Wilson Quarterly* 22–36.

Rubenstein, M. 'Beyond the whinge' (1991) 11(2) *Oxford Journal of Legal Studies* 254–263.

Rudolf, B. 'European Union: Compulsory Military Service' (2005) 3(5) *International Journal of Constitutional Law* 673–679.

Ruggie, J. 'International Regimes, Transactions and Change: Embedded Liberalism in the Postwar Economic Order'. In *International Regimes,* ed. S. Krasner (Ithaca: Cornell University Press, 1983).

Rupp, H. H. 'Die Grundrechte und das Europäische Gemeinschaftsrecht' (1970) 9 *Neue juristische Wochenschrift* 353–359.

Sabourin, P. 'Le jardin à la française du Conseil d'État' (1990) *Recueil Dalloz Sirey* 136–141.

Sacriste, G. and A. Vauchez. 'The Force of International Law: Lawyer's Diplomacy on the International Scene in the 1920s' (2007) 32(1) *Law and Social Inquiry* 83–107.

Sacks, V. 'The equal opportunities commission—ten years on' (1986) 49 *Modern Law Review* 560–592.

Salas, M. and J. H. Jackson. 'Procedural Overview of the WTO EC-Banana Dispute' (2000) 3(1) *Journal of International Economic Law* 145–166.

Saldias, O. *Supranational Courts as Engines of Disintegration* Berlin Working Paper on European Integratoin No. 5 Frei Universität Berlin, 2007 <http://www.fu-berlin.de/polsoz/polwiss/europa/arbeitspapiere/2007-5_Saldias.pdf>.

Sandholtz, W. and J. Zysman. 'Recasting the European Bargain' (1989) 42(1) *World Politics* 95–128.

Sarat, A. and S. A. Scheingold. *Cause lawyering and the state in a global era*, *Oxford socio-legal studies* (Oxford; New York: Oxford University Press, 2001).

Scharpf, F. 'The Joint-Decision Trap: Lessons from German Federalism and European Integration' (1988) 6 (Autumn) *Public Administration* 239–278.

Scheingold, S. *The Rule of Law in European Integration* (New Haven: Yale University Press, 1965).

Scheingold, S. 'The Law in Political Integration: The Evolution and Integrative Implications of Regional Legal Processes in the European Community'. Harvard University Center for International Affairs, Cambridge Massachusetts, 1971.

Schepel, H. and R. Wesseling. 'The Legal Community: Judges, Lawyers, Officials and Clerks in the Writing of Europe' (1997) 3(2) *European Law Journal* 165–188.

Schimmelfennig, F. *The EU, NATO and the Integration of Europe* (Cambridge: Cambridge University Press, 2003).

Schmidt, S. 'Only an Agenda Setter? The European Commission's Power over the Council of Ministers' (2000) 1(1) *European Union Politics* 37–61.

Schneider, A. K. 'Democracy and Dispute Resolution: Individual Rights in International Trade Organizations' (1998) 19 (Summer) *University of Pennsylvania Journal of International Economic Law* 587–638.

Schulte, C. *Compliance with Decisions of the International Court of Justice* (Oxford: Oxford University Press, 2004).

Schwartz, H. *The Struggle for Constitutional Justice in Post-Communist Europe* (Chicago: University of Chicago Press, 2000).

Schwartz, J. *Die Befolgung von Vorabentscheidungen des Europäischen Gerichtshofs durch deutsche Gerichte* (Baden-Baden: Nomos Verlangsgesellschaft, 1988).

Scott, R. E. and P. B. Stephan. *The Hardening of International Law: Contract Theory and International Law Enforcement* (Cambridge: Cambridge University Press, 2006).

Seidl-Hohenveldern, I. 'Review of Bodo Borner's Studien zum deutschen und europäischen Wirtshaftsrecht' (1984) 78(1) *American Journal of International Law* 282–284.

Shanks, C., H. K. Jacobson and J. H. Kaplan. 'Inertia and Change in the Constellation of International Governmental Organizations, 1981–1992' (1996) 50(4) *International Organization* 593–627.

Shapiro, M. 'Comparative Law and Comparative Politics' (1980) 53 *Southern California Law Review* 537–542.

Shapiro, M. *Courts: A comparative political analysis* (Chicago: University of Chicago Press, 1981).

Shonfield, A. *Modern Capitalism* (Oxford: Oxford University Press, 1969).

Sieder, R., L. Schjolden and A. Angell. *The Judicialization of Politics in Latin America*, *Studies of the Americas* (New York; Basingstoke: Palgrave Macmillan, 2005).

Sikkink, K. 'International Law and Social Movements: Towards Transformation. A Typology of Relations between Social Movements and International Institutions' (2003) 97 *American Society of International Legal Procedings* 301–305.

Sikkink, K. 'The Transnational Dimension of the Judicialization of Politics in Latin America'. In *The Judicialization of Politics in Latin America*, eds R. Sieder, L. Schjolden and A. Angell (New York: Palgrave MacMillan, 2005).

Sikkink, K. and E. Lutz. 'The Justice Cascade: The Evolution and Impact of Foreign Human Rights Trials in Latin America' (2001) 2 *Chicago Journal of International Law* 133.

Sikkink, K. and C. B. Walling. 'Errors about Trials: The Emergence and Impact of the Justice Cascade' Paper read at Princeton International Relations Faculty Colloquium, 27 March 2006, at Princeton NJ.

Simmons, B. 'Compliance with International Agreements' (1998) 1 *Annual Review of Political Science* 75–93.

Simmons, B. 'Why Commit? Explaining State Acceptance of International Human Rights Obligations'. Paper read at Delegation to International Organizations, at Park City Utah, 2002.

Slaughter, A.-M. 'International Law in a World of Liberal States' (1995) 6 *European Journal of International Law* 503–538.

Slaughter, A.-M. 'Judicial Globalization' (2000) 40 (Summer) *Virginia Journal of International Law Association* 1103–1124.

Slaughter, A.-M. *A New World Order* (Princeton: Princeton University Press, 2004).

Slaughter, A.-M. and D. Bosco. 'Plaintiff's Diplomacy' (2000) 79(5) *Foreign Affairs* 102–116.

Slaughter, A.-M., R. Keohane and A. Moravcsik. 'Legalized Dispute Resolution, Interstate and Transnational' (2000) 54(3) *International Organization* 457–488.

Smith, G. *The European Court of Justice: Judges or Policy Makers?* The Bruge Group Publication, Suite 102 Whitehall Court, Westminster, London SWIA 2EL (1990).

Stein, E. 'Lawyers, Judges and the Making of a Transnational Constitution' (1981) 75(1) *American Journal of International Law* 1–27.

Stein, N. 'Yes, We have no Profits' (2001) 144(11) *Fortune* 182–196.

Steinberg, R. H. 'Judicial Lawmaking at the WTO: Discursive, Constitutional and Political Constraints' (2004) 98(2) *American Journal of International Law* 247–275.

Stelzenmüller, C. 'Bürgerin in Uniform' (2000) *Die Zeit*, 5 January 2000.

Stephan, P. B. 'Courts, Tribunals and Legal Unification—The Agency Problem' (2002) 3 *Chicago Journal of International Law* 333–352.

Stöcker, H. A. 'Einzelklagebefugnis und EWG-Kommissionsentscheidung: Alternative oder kumulierter Rechtsschutz in Umsatzausgleichsteuersachen' (1967) 40 *Der Betrieb* 1690–1692.

Stone, A. 'The Birth and Development of Abstract Review: Constitutional Courts and Policymaking in Western Europe' (1990) 19(1) *Policy Studies Journal* 81–95.

Stone, A. *The Birth of Judicial Politics in France: The Constitutional Council in Comparative Perspective* (New York: Oxford University Press, 1992a).

Stone, A. 'Where Judicial Politics are Legislative Politics: The French Constitutional Council' (1992b) 15 *Western European Politics* 29–49.

Stone, A. 'Judging Socialist Reform—The Politics of Coordinate Construction in France and Germany' (1994) 26(4) *Comparative Political Studies* 443–469.

Stone, A. and M. Shapiro. 'The New Constitutional Politics of Europe' (1994) 26(4) *Comparative Political Studies* 397–420.

Stone Sweet, A. 'Judicialization and the Construction of Governance' (1999) 32(2) *Comparative Political Studies* 147–184.

Stone Sweet, A. *Governing with Judges* (Oxford: Oxford University Press, 2000).

Stone Sweet, A. *The Judicial Construction of Europe* (Oxford: Oxford University Press, 2004).

Stone Sweet, A. and T. Brunell. 'Constructing a Supranational Constitution: Dispute Resolution and Governance in the European Community' (1998a) 92(1) *American Political Science Review* 63–80.

Stone Sweet, A. and T. Brunell 'The European Court and the National Courts: A Statistical Analysis of Preliminary References, 1961–95' (1998b) 5(1) *Journal of Public European Policy* 66–97.

Stovall, J. G. and D. E. Hathaway. 'US interests in the Banana Trade Controversy'. In *Banana Wars: The Anatomy of a Trade Dispute*, eds T. E. Josling and T. G. Taylor (California: Institute for International Studies Stanford University, 2003).

Streeck, W. 'From Market Making to State Building? Reflections of the Political Economy of European Social Policy'. In *European Social Policy: Between Fragmentation and Integration*, eds P. Pierson and S. Leibfried (Washington DC: Brookings, 1995).

Sunstein, C. R. 'Social Norms and Social Roles' (1996) 96 (May) *Columbia Law Review* 903–968.

Sutton, P. 'The Banana Regime of the European Union, the Caribbean, and Latin America' (1997) 39(2) *Journal of Inter-American Studies and World Affairs* 5–36.

Sykes, A. 'Public v. Private Enforcement of International Economic Law: Of Standing and Remedy', U Chicago Law & Economics, Olin Working Paper No. 235, 2004 <http://papers.ssrn.com/sol3/papers.cfm?abstract_id=671801>.

Szyszczak, E. 'Remedies in sex discrimination cases'. In *Remedies for breach of EC law*, eds J. Lonberg amd A. Biondi (Chichester: Wiley, 1997), 105–115.

Tallberg, J. 'Delegation to Supranational Institutions: Why, How, and with What Consequences?' (2002a) 25(1) *West European Politics* 23–46.

Tallberg, J. 'Paths to Compliance: Enforcement, Management and the European Union' (2002b) 56(3) *International Organization* 609–643.

Tallberg, J. *European Governance and Supranational Institutions: Making States Comply* (London: Routledge, 2003).

Tallberg, J. and C. Jönsson. 'Compliance and Post-Agreement Bargaining' (1998) 4(4) *European Journal of International Relations* 371–408.

Tamanaha, B. Z. *On the Rule of Law: History, Politics, Theory* (Cambridge: Cambridge University Press, 2004).

Tangermann, S. 'The European Common Banana Policy'. In *Banana Wars: The Anatomy of a Trade Dispute*, eds T. E. Josling and T. G. Taylor (California: Institute for International Studies Stanford University, 2003).

Taylor, R. 'Forced Birth of a Flexible Employer' *Financial Times*, 1 June 1996, p. 7.

Taylor, T. G. 'Evolution of Banana Multinationals'. In *Banana Wars: The Anatomy of a Trade Dispute*, eds T. E. Josling and T. G. Taylor (California: Institute for International Studies Stanford University, 2003).

Terris, D., C. Romano and L. Swiggart (forthcoming) *The International Judge: An Introduction to the Men and Women to Decide the World's Cases.*

Thelen, K. *How Institutions Evolve: The Political Economy of Skills in Comparative-Historical Perspective* (New York: Cambridge University Press, 2004).

Trades Union Congress 'Using European equality legislation'. Paper presented at the European Equality Legislation Seminar, Congress House, London, 1991.

Tremolada, E. 'Application of the Andean Community Law in Bolivia, Ecuador, Peru, and Venezuela in Comparison with the European Union Experience' (2006) 6(3) *Jean Monnet/Robert Schuman Paper Series*.

Tsebelis, G. *Nested Games: Rational Choice in Comparative Politics* (Berkeley: University of California Press, 1990).

Tsebelis, G. and G. Garrett. 'The Institutional Foundations of Intergovernmentalism and Supranationalism in the European Union' (2001) 55(2) *International Organization* 357–390.

Tsoukalis, L. and R. Strauss. 'Crisis and Adjustment in European Steel: Beyond Laissez-Faire' (1985) 23(3) *Journal of Common Market Studies* 207–228.

Turner, J. I. 'Transnational Networks and International Criminal Justice' (2005) 105 *Michigan Law Review* 985–1032.

Tyler, T. *Why People Obey the Law* (Princeton: Princeton University Press, 2006).

Vachudová, M. A. *Europe undivided: democracy, leverage, and integration after communism* (Oxford; New York: Oxford University Press, 2005).

Vargas, J. 'Shifting the Balance of Power Between Domestic Groups: The European Court and British Equal Treatment Policy'. Honor's Thesis for a Bachelor of Arts degree, Harvard University, 1995.

Vargas-Hidalgo, R. 'The Crisis of the Andean Pact: Lessons for Integration Among Developing Countries' (1979) 27(3) *Journal of Common Market Studies* 213–226.

Vaubel, R. 'Principal–agent problems in international organizations' (2006) 1 *Review of International Organizations* 125–138.

Vauchez, A. 'Europe's first Trustees: Lawyers' politics at the outset of the European Communities (1950–1970)' (2007a) <http://papers.ssrn.com/sol3/papers.cfm?abstract_id=1028694>.

Vauchez, A. 'Une élite d'intermédiaires. Genèse d'un capital juridique européen (1950–1970)' (2007b) 166–167 *Actes de la recherche en sciences sociales* 54–66.

Vauchez, A. 'Integration through law: Socio-History of EU Political Common Sense'. In European University Institute (EUI), Robert Schuman Centre of Advanced Studies Working Paper. Fiesole, 2008.

Villa, P. *The Structuring of Labor Markets: A Comparative Analysis of the Steel and Construction Industries in Italy* (Oxford: Clarendon Press, 1986).

Voeten, E. 'The Politics of International Judicial Appointments: Evidence from the European Court of Human Rights' (2007) 61(4) *International Organization* 669–701.

Voeten, E. 'The Impartiality of International Judges: Evidence From The European Court of Human Rights' (forthcoming 2009) 102 *American Political Science Review* 4.

Vogel, D. 'Protective regulation and protectionism in the European Community: The creation of a common market for food and beverages'. Paper presented at the meeting of the European Community Studies Association, 1991. [See Vogel, D. *Barriers or Benefits?* (Washington D C: Brookings, 1997).]

Vogel-Polsky, E. 'L'article 119 du traité de Rome peut-il être considéré comme *self-executing?*' *Journal des Tribunaux* 82e année' (4570 15 April 1967) 283–287.

Vogel-Polsky, E. 'National institutional and non-institutional machinery established in the Council of Europe Member States to promote equality between women and men' (Strasbourg: Council of Europe, Committee for Equality between Men and Women, 1985) <http://www.amazon.co.uk/National-institutional-non-institutional-machinery-established/dp/B0007B4LPW>.

Volcansek, M. *Judicial Politics in Europe* (New York: Peter Lang Publishers, 1986).

Volcansek, M. 'Judges, Courts and Policy-Making in Western Europe' (1992) 15 (July) *Western European Politics* 1–8.

Voss, R. 'Federal Republic of Germany National Report'. In *Article 177 Experience and Problems*, eds H. Schermers, C. Timmermans, A. Kellermann and J. S. Watson (Amsterdam: Elsevier Science Publishing Company, 1987).

Walker, G. d. Q. *The Rule of Law* (Melbourne: Melbourne University Press, 1988).

Warner, I. *Steel and sovereignty: the deconcentration of the West German steel industry, 1949–54* (Mainz: P. von Zabern, 1996).

Warren, C. 'Legislative and Judicial Attacks on the Supreme Court of the United States—A History of the Twenty-Fifth Section of the Judiciary Act' (1913) 47 *American Law Review* 161. Cited in Hart and Wechsler *Federal Courts and the Federal System* (3rd edn). (University Casebook Series, New York: The Foundation Press, 1988), 516.

Warren, K. *World steel: an economic geography* (New York: David and Charles Newton Abbot, Crane, Russak, 1975).

Weatherhill, S. 'Reflections on EC Law's "Implementation Imbalance" in Light of the Ruling in Heley Lomas'. In *Law and Diffuse Interests in the European Legal Order*, eds L. Kramer, H.-W. Micklitz and K. Tonner (Baden-Baden: Nomos, 1997).

Webber, D. and O. Cadot. 'Banana Splits: Policy Process, Particularistic Interests, Political Capture, and Money in Transatlantic Trade Politics' (2002) 4(1) *Business and Politics* 109.

Weiler, J. 'The Community System: The Dual Character of Supranationalism' (1981) 1 *Yearbook of European Law* 257–306.

Weiler, J. 'The Transformation of Europe' (1991) 100 *Yale Law Journal* 2403–2483.

Weiler, J. 'A Quiet Revolution—The European Court of Justice and its Interlocutors' (1994) 26(4) *Comparative Political Studies* 510–534.

Wendt, P. 'Kein Rechtsschutz im Umsatzausgleichsteuer-Sachen?' (1967a) 48 *Der Betrieb* 2047–2048.

Wendt, P. 'Ungeklärte Fragen im Streit um die Unmsatzausgleichsteuer' (1967b) Heft 9 (September) *Außenwirtschaftsdienst des Betriebs-Beraters* 348–354.

White, E. 'In search of the limits to Article 30 of the EEC Treaty' (1989) 26 *Common Market Law Review* 235–280.

Williamson, J. 'What Washington Means by Policy Reform'. In *Latin American Adjustment: How Much Has Happened*, ed. J. Williamson (Washington, DC: Institute for International Economics, 1990).

Wils, G. *Prejudiciële vragen van Belgische rechters en hun gevolgen, Pradvies* (Belgium: Tjeenk Willink, 1993).

Wolff, A. W. 'Assuring America's Continuing Support for the WTO: Solving the Problems of the WTO Dispute Settlement System' (2000).

Zoller, E. *Droit des relations extérieures* (Paris: Presses Universitaires de Paris, 1992).

Zorn, C. and S. Van Winkle. 'Government Responses to the European Court of Human Rights'. Paper read at International Conference on the Effects of and Responses to Globalization, 31 May–1 June 2001, at Bogazici University, Istanbul, Turkey.

Zuleeg, M. 'Bundesfinanzhof und Gemeinschaftsrecht'. In *75 Jahre Reichsfinanzhof-Bundesfinanzhof*, ed. P. d. Bundesfinanzhofs (Bonn: Stollfuß Verlag, 1993).

Zurn, M. and C. Joerges. *Governance and Law in Postnational Constellations: Compliance in Europe and Beyond* (Cambridge: Cambridge University Press, 2005).

Zysman, J. *Governments, markets, and growth: financial systems and the politics of industrial change, Cornell studies in political economy* (Ithaca: Cornell University Press, 1983).

Index